VIRGINIA HISTORICAL SOCIETY

DOCUMENTS

Volume 9

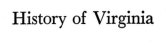

History of Virginia

Edmund Randolph (1753–1813)

A copy by F. J. Fisher from an original now lost, this portrait hangs in the
Virginia State Capitol at Richmond. Owned by the Virginia State Library

Edmund Randolph

History of Virginia

Edited with an Introduction by
Arthur H. Shaffer

Published for
The Virginia Historical Society

The University Press of Virginia
Charlottesville

Published with the assistance of the
Old Dominion Foundation

Foreword

Although as much of the original form of the manuscript as possible has been retained, some changes have been made. As an aid to the reader, the manuscript has been divided into chapters, and the spelling, punctuation, and capitalization of the entire text, including quotations and paraphrases, have been modernized. A confusing numbering system, references to documents which were to be included in an appendix, marginal dates, and various marginal notations made by later readers on the manuscript have been omitted. Much of the early part of the work consists of passages taken more or less verbatim from William Stith's *History of Virginia*. These sections have been identified with special brackets (⌐ ⌐) in the text. The editor has also added those portions of John Marshall's *Life of Washington* and David Hume's *History of England* that Randolph clearly intended to include. The passages from Marshall's work have also been indicated with special brackets in the text.

I am much indebted to Mr. John Melville Jennings, director of the Virginia Historical Society, for preparing that part of the Introduction dealing with provenance of the manuscript of Randolph's *History*. The editor would like to thank the staff of the Virginia Historical Society for their kind assistance. My research was expedited by the financial assistance of the University of Missouri, Saint Louis. For his cogent criticisms and helpful suggestions about the form and content of the Introduction, I am especially grateful to Professor Lyle W. Dorsett of the University of Missouri, Saint Louis. I also want to thank Mrs. Peggy Braden, Mrs. Janet Dunlap, and Mrs. Janis Shine for excellent work in typing a difficult manuscript. I am deeply indebted to Mr. William M. E. Rachal, editor of publications for the Virginia Historical Society, for his patience, encouragement, and wise counsel. And I am especially indebted to Professor Keith B. Berwick of the University of California, Los Angeles, for his continuous inspiration and guidance. It is to Professor Berwick that this work owes its inception, though not its errors, for which I alone am responsible.

Arthur H. Shaffer

Saint Louis, Missouri
June 1, 1969

Contents

Introduction

Vita

By all odds Edmund Randolph (1753–1813) should have achieved an important place in American history. He was descended from a family long prominent in one of history's most successful ruling classes. Since the 1680's, when his great-grandfather William Randolph purchased Turkey Island on the James River, his forebears had played a pre-eminent role in Virginia's affairs. His grandfather Sir John Randolph, the only native Virginian ever knighted, his father, John, and his uncle, Peyton Randolph, had all been king's attorneys and members of the House of Burgesses. As a boy, Edmund had the good fortune to meet at his father's table the colony's most distinguished men. As a student at the College of William and Mary, he had an excellent chance to observe the operations of government at first hand, and like other students with important connections, he had the fortunate opportunity to bring himself to the attention of the colony's rulers.[1] As a young college graduate reading law in his father's office, he was following family tradition; the law, after all, had opened the door of opportunity for the Randolphs and made them one of Virginia's leading families.[2]

Not only was Edmund Randolph born to the charmed circle; he was born in 1753 and, therefore, came to manhood during the Revolution, a time of crisis when reputations and careers could be made on a stage even larger than that which Virginia offered. And he reached maturity when Virginia's ruling gentry dominated the national political scene. Even the Loyalism of his father, who followed Lord Dunmore, the royal governor, into exile in England, did not prevent Edmund from assuming a high place in the inner circle of patriots. Whatever distrust may have been sown by his father's actions was quickly uprooted by Peyton Randolph's trust in his nephew. Peyton had taken him into his family and designated him, after his father, his heir. When Randolph decided to enter the army, General Washington welcomed him as an aide-de-camp. When the sudden death of his uncle forced him to return home, he was immediately elected mayor of Williamsburg and

1. Charles S. Sydnor, *Gentlemen Freeholders: Political Practices in Washington's Virginia* (Chapel Hill, N.C., 1952), p. 3.

2. Hamilton J. Eckenrode, *The Randolphs: The Story of a Virginia Family* (New York, 1946), p. 77. The only full-length biography of Edmund Randolph is Moncure D. Conway, *Omitted Chapters of History Disclosed in the Life and Papers of Edmund Randolph* (New York, 1888).

the representative of the College of William and Mary to the Virginia Convention of 1776. And when he married that same year it was to Elizabeth Nicholas, a daughter of Robert Carter Nicholas, the state treasurer.

At twenty-three Randolph was the youngest delegate to the Convention, but he was chosen to serve with such men as Patrick Henry, Robert Carter Nicholas, Richard Bland, and George Mason on the committee to draft a declaration of rights and "a plan of government." Though his role was minimal, he did valuable service in presenting the views of the absent Thomas Jefferson on several key issues. Both Jefferson and Randolph questioned the right of the Convention to create a permanent constitution. As Randolph wrote, "Mr. Jefferson, who was in Congress, urged a youthful friend in the Convention to oppose a *permanent* constitution until the people should elect deputies for the special purpose. He denied the power of the body elected . . . to exceed some temporary regimen. . . . The attempt to postpone the formation of a constitution until a commission of greater latitude and one more specific should be given by the people was a task too hardy for an inexperienced young man." [3]

Despite Randolph's evaluation of himself as "an inexperienced young man," he must have made a good impression. At the close of the Convention he was selected as the state's first attorney general, a post he held for the next ten years. During those years, he continued to build a highly successful law practice, interrupted only by two terms in the Continental Congress (1779, 1780–81). And then in 1786, at the still youthful age of thirty-three, he was elected governor of Virginia. Thus, in a few short years Edmund Randolph achieved the state's highest public office. Young, intelligent, attractive, ambitious, and wellborn, he seemed to be on the threshold of a brilliant political career.

As the governor of the largest and most populous state, Randolph was in a position to shape events. A leading advocate of a new federal Constitution, he was instrumental in persuading George Washington to attend the Philadelphia Convention in 1787. It was Governor Randolph who "opened the main business of the Convention" with a lengthy speech denouncing the defects of the Articles of Confederation and the existing state constitutions. "We see that the confederation is incompetent to any one object for which it was instituted." The essential weakness and "our chief danger," he said, "arises from the demo-

3. See below, pp. 251–52.

cratic parts of our constitutions. It is a maxim which I hold incontrovertible, that the powers of government exercised by the people swallows up the other branches. None of the constitutions have provided sufficient checks against the democracy." [4] Yet despite his early advocacy, Randolph refused to sign the completed document because he thought it insufficiently republican. He was especially strenuous in his opposition to "a unity in the executive" as "a foetus of monarchy," [5] and he even went so far as to publish a *Letter . . . on the Federal Constitution* (1787) in criticism of the document.

By the time the battle for ratification began in Virginia, Randolph had reversed himself once again and stood with James Madison and Edmund Pendleton in favor of ratification. But not until after the Convention began its daily sessions did the young governor openly declare his final position on the Constitution. Only then did the public learn the direction of his allegiance. Charged by many with behavior of the rankest inconsistency, Randolph insisted always that his policy had been constant. His objections to the Constitution, so he declared, were as strong on June 4, 1788, as they had been in September 1787. But he had come to believe, by the time of the Convention, that if Virginia did not accept the Constitution the Union would be disrupted, perhaps dismembered. "The accession of eight states," he declared to the Convention, has "reduced our deliberations to the single question of Union or no Union." [6] Thus persuaded, he said, he could not do otherwise than vote with the Federalists.

Randolph's candid opinion of the Constitution and the reasons for his long indecision may never be uncovered. Anxious for a political career, still young, and with bright prospects for service in government, perhaps he hesitated to burn his bridges behind him. Open approval of the Constitution would ill serve him should Virginia refuse to accept its terms and to join the Union. Yet, in like token, opposition to the proposed Constitution might blight a career in the new government if the states approved it. Too cautious, too attentive to the individual desires of the people he had represented in the Federal Convention, Randolph enmeshed himself in a network of hesitancy and irresolution. Gradually he came to see that Virginia could be reconciled to

4. Forrest McDonald, *E Pluribus Unum: The Formation of the American Republic, 1776–1790* (Boston, 1965), p. 166; Max Farrand, ed., *The Records of the Federal Convention of 1787* (New Haven, 1937), I, 26–27.

5. Farrand, *Records of Federal Convention*, I, 166.

6. Jonathan Elliot, ed., *Debates in the Several State Conventions on the Adoption of the Federal Constitution* (Philadelphia, 1861), III, 652.

the new government. He realized that chances of adopting a constitution to please all the people were slim indeed, and that prolonged discussion of the nature of the Union would lead only to more acrimonious and dangerous controversy and rivalry. Firmly decided at last upon the right—or the expediency—of the Federalists' cause, he joined their ranks and helped lead them to victory.[7]

With the formation of the new government, Randolph was appointed attorney general by Washington. The office was one of considerable difficulty, not even possessing the status of a department. The attorney general was regarded rather as the legal adviser of the President, the department heads, and the Congress. The Judiciary Act closely limited the duties of the attorney general: he was simply upon request of the President or the heads of departments to give opinions on matters of law, and nothing more.[8] The government was merely one of his clients, paying an annual retainer of $1,500, one half the salary of cabinet officers. Randolph was expected to earn a living by pursuing his private legal work.[9] The problem of earning a living was compounded by Randolph's chronic indebtedness. Though he had inherited Peyton Randolph's estate, it had been bankrupted by the war. He was impoverished by a large family, his wife's long illness, and the disruption of his law practice while he was governor of Virginia.[10] In a letter written in 1790 Randolph complained of the frustrations of his situation: "I am a sort of mongrel between the State and the United States; called an officer of some rank under the latter, and yet thrust out to get a livelihood in the former. . . . I cannot say much on this head without pain, which, could I have foreseen it, would have kept me at home to encounter my pecuniary difficulties there, rather than add to them here." [11]

Despite serious handicaps, Randolph did remarkably well as attorney general and even succeeded in expanding the responsibilities of the office.[12] But his most serious problem was the growing conflict over Hamilton's financial policies and particularly the battle between Hamilton and Jefferson within the cabinet. Holding to the tradition that a public man should take a stand on specific issues but never

7. Keith B. Berwick, "Moderates in Crisis: The Trials of Leadership in Revolutionary Virginia" (Ph.D. dissertation, University of Chicago, 1959) , pp. 120–22.

8. Leonard D. White, *The Federalists: A Study in Administrative History, 1789–1801* (New York, 1948), p. 166.

9. *Ibid.*, p. 164.   10. *Ibid.*, pp. 169–70.   11. Conway, *Randolph*, p. 135.

12. See White, *Federalists*, pp. 166–69.

tie himself permanently to any faction proved extremely difficult for him. Caught in a cross fire between warring elements in Washington's cabinet, he steadfastly clung to a position of nonpartisanship despite the increasing growth of party spirit. His friend Jefferson felt that Randolph should always support him in the cabinet, and on a number of important issues such as the unconstitutionality of the national bank and the continued validity of the Treaty of 1778 with France, he did side with Jefferson. When Hamilton attacked Jefferson publicly for having Philip Freneau, the editor of the strongly Republican *National Gazette,* on the payroll of the State Department, Randolph wrote a series of articles vindicating the Secretary of State.[13] However, he did not hesitate to differ from his friend whenever the occasion seemed to justify it. In frustration Jefferson characterized Randolph as "the poorest cameleon I ever saw, having no colour of his own, and reflecting that nearest him." [14]

When Jefferson resigned from the cabinet in mid-1793, Washington, after hesitating for several months, appointed Randolph secretary of state. The job would have been a difficult one under any circumstance. As a new and relatively weak nation, the United States was caught in the conflict between the two great superpowers, Great Britain and France, and the people of the United States were divided in their opinions and affection between the two. Randolph was able to rid the country of Edmond Charles Genêt, the offensive French minister, but did protect him from arrest at the request of the French government. He approved of the recall of Gouverneur Morris as minister to France and the appointment of James Monroe as his successor. Faced with such thorny problems any secretary of state ran the serious risk of ruin—Jefferson had withdrawn, Timothy Pickering was dismissed, and two foreign ministers of distinction had to be recalled. But with the rest of the cabinet now aligned with Hamilton, and with Randolph determined to play the role of nonpartisan, disaster was assured.[15]

The ultimate blow came as a result of Randolph's opposition to Jay's Treaty. He had advised the President against acceptance of the treaty, while Secretary of War Timothy Pickering and Secretary of the Treasury Oliver Wolcott urged acceptance. Naturally the British government was anxious to discredit Randolph, and when the English

13. John C. Miller, *The Federalist Era, 1789–1801* (New York, 1960), pp. 91–92.

14. Quoted in Dice Robins Anderson, "Edmund Randolph," *The American Secretaries of State and Their Diplomacy* (New York, 1927–29), II, 100.

15. *Ibid.,* 102–3.

intercepted a letter written by the French minister Joseph Fauchet to his government, the British minister George Hammond delivered it in July 1795 to Secretary Wolcott. Since the dispatch (No. 10) had been written nearly a year before (October 31, 1794), its contents were hardly relevant to the current dispute, but the paragraphs mentioning the secretary of state held promise of ending his inconvenient opposition to final ratification of Jay's Treaty. Fauchet had written a rambling account in which he seemed to imply that Randolph had made improper revelations to him and had indicated that French money would be welcome. When Randolph was called in and questioned by Washington and the cabinet under humiliating circumstances, he angrily resigned. That same year, he wrote an elaborate *Vindication* that did little to clear his name but was notable for its intemperate attack upon Washington. Although there can be little doubt that Randolph was innocent of any wrongdoing, it is clear that both the British and the partisans of Hamilton in the cabinet were after his scalp and successfully tricked Washington into wielding the knife.[16] Though conscience often made Edmund Randolph a vacillator, his conscience also demanded that he remain nonpartisan in the face of the white-hot political partisanship of the 1790's. It was James Madison who most accurately summarized Randolph's political obituary: "His greatest enemies will not easily persuade themselves that he was under a corrupt influence of France, and his best friends can't save him from the self-condemnation of his political career." [17]

In 1795 Randolph was still a relatively young man, but even though he lived for another eighteen years he never again took part in public affairs. He spent his years of retirement in Richmond pursuing a highly successful private law practice, and with the exception of his role as senior defense counsel in the famous Aaron Burr conspiracy trial, he remained absent from public view. But these were not happy years. The malevolence of his political enemies followed him even into retirement. Pickering and Wolcott had gone over his accounts as secretary of state after he had resigned from office and produced a shortage of $49,154.89 in diplomatic and consular funds. It was easy enough to find a shortage since the law made the secretary of state responsible for all such funds. With the records in the hands of his enemies Randolph was helpless. Eventually he turned over all his property to his brother-in-law, Wilson Cary Nicholas, who gave bonds to the

16. See Irving Brant, "Edmund Randolph, Not Guilty!," *William and Mary Quarterly*, 3d ser., VII (1950), 180–98.   17. *Ibid.*, 197.

government for the total claim and paid it off in twenty years, with interest. However, some zealous Treasury Department official computed compound interest on the whole amount for the period when it was being discharged and entered a new claim for $61,355.50, which stood for the next sixty-five years.[18] Finally, Edmund Randolph succumbed to the family disease of paralysis and died on September 12, 1813.

"The Virginia Character"

No doubt the circumstances of his involuntary retirement and the malevolence of his enemies occupied much of Randolph's thoughts during these last years. But he must have also felt a desire not only to justify his behavior as secretary of state but to relate the pattern of his entire public career to the shape of Virginia and national politics. As his vehicle he turned once again to a project he had begun some years earlier, a history of Virginia.[19] Randolph's unique quality as a historian was his ability to generalize from his own personal political experience, with its cycle of early success and subsequent disaster, to a broader understanding of the political and social institutions of Virginia, which shaped both him and his generation of remarkably able leaders reared in the Old Dominion. And while this angle of vision colored his perspective it also led to important insights. The whole pattern of the *History*—its organization, the choice of events, even its omissions—testify to a concerted effort to arrive at an understanding of what Randolph regarded as the genius of Virginia's political system. He firmly believed that the Virginia experience could serve as the model for a truly virtuous republic; the ideals and practices of Virginia politics had, after all, infused and informed the whole movement for independence in the Revolution. It occurred to him that the lamentable partisanship of contemporary American politics, of which he had been a casualty, could be reduced to order if practical rules for political conduct could be established. Randolph sought those

18. *Ibid.,* 180–81.

19. Randolph was gathering material for a history as early as 1785 or 1786. In a letter to William Waller Hening dated April 15, 1815, Thomas Jefferson wrote that "Mr. Randolph contemplating writing a history on Virginia, borrowed all the Mss. from my library while I was in France."

rules where men of learning in his age were accustomed to seek: in examples of times past. Thus, Edmund Randolph's *History of Virginia* offers important insights into the pattern of Randolph's career, his personal philosophy, and the practice of politics in revolutionary Virginia.

As formal history the *History of Virginia* has a number of serious shortcomings: there are wide gaps in the narrative, it is often poorly organized, and at times the style is almost incoherent, perhaps because the extant copy is only a later transcription of the original. But Randolph's *History* would more properly be called a historical essay. The author never intended to write a definitive history. What we do have is an impressionistic essay by a man whose understanding of Virginia society had few rivals. His original plan was to divide the *History* into three separate but interrelated essays, each with a distinct style dictated by the nature of the material. The first section was to deal with the origins of Virginia society to the time of the First Continental Congress. The second, Randolph's personal account of the Revolution, was to include the period from 1774 to the ratification of the Federal Constitution. (Unfortunately, the existing manuscript runs only to 1782.) And the third section, either never completed or lost, was to have been what would today be described as a social and cultural analysis of Virginia society.

The opening section was not intended merely to meet an obligation to introduce the main business of the *History*. It stands as an integral part of the whole without which Randolph's interpretation of Virginia history in general, and the Revolution in particular, cannot be fully understood. Randolph selected specific episodes from the Virginia past—the founding of Virginia, the dissolution of the Virginia Company, the struggle against the Commonwealth, Bacon's Rebellion, the Glorious Revolution, the Pistole Fee controversy, and the Stamp Act crisis—with the intention of analyzing the circumstances that led to the development of a spirit of freedom and independence and what he referred to as the "Virginia character."

Pausing at the point of the dissolution of the Virginia Company, Randolph reflected that "whatever may be the defects of the foregoing narrative, an estimate may be made of the faculties or qualities which the colony actually possessed in the year 1624." He was particularly impressed by the fact that the dissolution of the Company "caused an agitation so little serious." Even though there was ample ground for insurrection, he found it "a lesson not unworthy of adoption in seasons

even the most enlightened to count the cost of popular tumult before
it is excited and clearly to see the effect of the war before it is waged."
The soil of Virginia had nurtured a people who had found the happy
balance between overcivilization and barbarism, a people "equally
aloof from the frenzy of reform and the abjectness of vassalage." [20]

These passages are indicative of Randolph's conception of Virginia's
political development during the colonial period. Virginians had
somehow avoided pollution by those frenzies so characteristic of English politics. "It is the happiness of the Virginia character," he wrote,
"hardly ever to push to extremity any theory which by practical
relations may not be accommodated." [21] Thus, the colony was able to
survive uncontaminated by "the fanaticism and hypocrisy of Cromwell"
or by "the poison of the licentiousness of the second Charles." [22] Again,
in the controversy over the pistole fee (1752–55), Virginia's leaders
"were as bold as the time would permit." They wisely eschewed an
appeal to arms: "Their opposition would have been folly had a resort
to force constituted a part of it." For "to know when to complain with
truth and how to complain with dignity was characteristic of watchful
patriots and ample for the only end which could then be projected." [23]
Randolph's *History* is persistent and unremitting in its elaboration of
the ideals of a society uninfected by party spirit and dedicated to the
maximum of liberty consistent with order and stability. "The preceding history," he concluded, "contains repeated instances of loyalty
debased by no servile compliance and of a patriotic watchfulness never
degenerating into the mere petulance of complaint." [24]

It was when Randolph proceeded to a discussion of the Revolution
that the connection between those events in the colonial past and the
revolutionary era becomes apparent. The stage had been set by detail-
ing the evolution of the "Virginia character"; those traits were now to
be tested in a new and more serious crisis. The actions of the British
government were only a backdrop; the crux of the matter was the
quality of the Virginia character under stress. Randolph's contribution
to American historiography is in his examination of the dynamic relationship between the external events of the revolutionary controversy
and the Virginia character he delineated. Unlike other American
historians of his day, Randolph centered his narrative and analysis on
events in Virginia. In his opinion, the conflict did not become an
American phenomenon until the formation of the First Continental

20. See below, p. 147.   21. P. 157.   22. P. 153.   23. P. 163.   24. Pp. 160–61.

Congress in 1774; he viewed the events between 1765 and 1774 in the context of past reactions to English abuses of Virginia liberties. Even Randolph's mode of organization underscored this point; although the *History* is divided into topic headings throughout, when the narrative reaches the year 1765 there is no pause. The first break comes in 1774 under the title "Introduction to That Part of the History Embracing the Revolution." Even more revealing (if we can believe the copyist who produced the extant copy of the manuscript), the pagination changes and reverts back to page one not at 1765 but at 1774. In short, Randolph treated the period from the Stamp Act crisis to the First Continental Congress as a unit directly related to Virginia's past history and the emergence of the Virginia character. Thus, Randolph affirmed his belief in the evolutionary pattern of Virginia's history.

This pattern had been one of devotion to constitutional principles and a repugnance for sudden, especially violent, change. For Randolph, as with other Virginians of his generation, "constitution" was the most hallowed term in his vocabulary. The constitution was guarantor of basic rights and liberties, and no violation of rights by arbitrary and illegal procedures, regardless of the circumstances, can admit to justification, though he reluctantly conceded that the hazardous circumstances of early Virginia may have demanded unusual measures. Each new charter, each new governmental reorganization, each change of government, is discussed in detail, especially with an eye to future consequences. Randolph denounced Sir Thomas Dale for resorting to martial law and for allegedly promulgating the *Lawes Divine, Morall, and Martiall.* Though he admired Dale as a governor he felt that even such an admirable man was bound to be corrupted by so much power.[25] And it was with this same perspective that he chose to identify the major issues in the Virginia Company's struggle for survival against the crown. He reduced the warring factions within the Company to two clear-cut positions: a liberal republican group led by Sir Edwin Sandys and a self-seeking royalist faction represented by the earl of Warwick and Sir Thomas Smith. Randolph paid little attention to conditions within the colony as a major cause of the Company's dissolution, and he was unwilling to admit that in the long run Virginia may have benefited from becoming a royal colony.[26]

This same belief in the constitutional bias of the "Virginia character" is evident in Randolph's treatment of the Revolution. The traits of character Virginians exhibited in the contest with Great Britain were

25. Pp. 58, 82.   26. See Chapter III below.

the same distinctive qualities they had displayed throughout their
history. As in every other challenge to traditional rights and privileges,
the Virginians responded with appropriate forcefulness and unmis-
takable dignity, with reason and moderation, and with arguments
based upon sound constitutional principles. Opposition to the Stamp
Act and other revenue measures was less the result of "hasty feeling"
than of "theoretic reasoning." Even the "specific doctrine which condemned taxation without representation had been often quoted as a
fundamental one of colonial freedom, and every generation of lawyers
imbibed it in their studies." [27]

Naturally, in dealing with the Revolution, Randolph found it difficult to stick to a narrow definition of legality; the Revolution, after
all, represented a severing of legal bonds. But the actions of Great
Britain are cast in terms of illegality; it is they who are violating
English constitutional liberties, and it is Virginia that is defending
legality, albeit by extralegal means. In order to delineate the legal
character of the Revolution more sharply Randolph contrasted it with
Bacon's Rebellion. He decried the fact that the rebellion "has lately
received a historical gloss, the object of which is to metamorphose
it into one of those daring efforts which gross misrule sometimes suggests, if it may not strictly vindicate." Randolph counseled the reader
to be cautious of justifying any rebellion with the warning that "in the
descent to revolutions, the path is easy," but "in the attempt to rise
again lies the difficulty." Just because "the whole force of precedent,"
he wrote, "having been already obtained in the successful resistance
of the American colonies to Great Britain, we ought not to sanction a
new case in which tyranny is less palpable or less clearly mediated.
Let the transaction therefore be seen in its real character." [28]

When Randolph referred to the genius of the Virginia political
system he also meant its ability to act responsibly and imaginatively
in the face of challenges from without and stresses from within—its
ability, that is, to moderate any tensions that threaten the proper
aspirations of a free people. His most important point was that Virginia not only "produced public agents suitable to every crisis and
service" but was able to adjust its conception of leadership as the
situation dictated.[29] And by "agents suitable to every crisis" Randolph meant, of course, Virginia's leading citizens, those members of
the gentry who occupied positions of power in the House of Burgesses.
Naturally the revolutionary crisis demanded somewhat different qual-

27. P. 166.   28. Pp. 153, 156.   29. P. 178.

ities of leadership than the relatively placid times that had preceded it: "As soon as the favor of the British court generated a suspicion inconsistent with the purity of Virginian patriotism, and more particularly, when it was foreseen that if battles were to be fought, they were to be fought by men who had no other stake or hope than their own country, the old standard of distinction was abolished and a new one substituted on the single foundation of fitness for the rising exigency." [30]

Although Randolph's approach would seem to indicate an aristocratic bias, it was neither aristocratic nor democratic: it rested, instead, upon a highly realistic appraisal of the dimensions of life and thought in his "native country." Randolph's Virginia was what Walter Bagehot called "a deferential society," operating from a body of ideas that were essentially elitist. This view begins with the assumption that government should be entrusted to men of merit who are obliged to use their talents for the benefit of the public, and while elected representatives are chosen by the public at large, they are not the tools of the people but their political superiors. Both the people and their leaders had clearly defined political roles. The people of Virginia demonstrated early "the awe which the character of a truly great and patriotic man . . . will have upon the sturdy sons of labor and of courage"; [31] in short, the ability to recognize and follow talented leadership.

The function of the gentry was to ascertain the best interests and feelings of their constituents, a function rendered more practicable because the channels of communication were left open. "Even if the fancied division into something like ranks, not actually coalescing with each other, had been really formed, the opinions of every denomination or cast would have diffused themselves on every side by means of the professions of priest, lawyer, and physician, who visited the houses of the ostentatious as well as the cottages of the planters." [32] Since the ruling gentry were able to mold public feelings by public example, the people gained a greater confidence in the motives and propriety of the struggle against Great Britain. Their leaders "had at stake fortunes which were affluent or competent and families which were dear to them; neither of these blessings would they have jeopardized upon a political speculation in which their souls were not deeply engaged." [33] In this sense, Randolph properly discerned that Virginia society had achieved something at once different from and superior to either aristocracy or democracy—a politics which held in

30. P. 177.   31. P. 147.   32. P. 194.   33. Pp. 208–9.

balance the ingredients of responsibility and responsiveness to the popular will, a politics of consensus in which the strength of the political structure was tested repeatedly by tensions within a framework of consent.

Randolph did not succeed in resolving the questions posed by this remarkably adaptive political and social structure, but he did provide vital clues. He recognized that the great Virginians of the revolutionary epoch—Washington and Henry, Mason and Jefferson, Pendleton and the Lees—were less the product of individual genius than of a mature and sophisticated political system. To underscore this point, Randolph included a series of biographical sketches of the men who dominated Virginia during the revolutionary crisis. Although differences in personality and ability are never completely submerged, the purpose of these sketches was to delineate those qualities of character and mind common to Virginia's revolutionary leadership. In varying degrees the fourteen men included in Randolph's pantheon of heroes possessed certain virtues in common: formal learning and oratorical skills, republican manners and force of character. These were the qualities that Randolph considered indispensable to the ideal republican leader.

Most of those cited were singled out as men of learning, an impressive accomplishment "with such scanty means as existed in a colony whose chief ambition looked to the general system of education in England." [34] Of Thomas Jefferson he wrote: "In mathematics and experimental philosophy, he was a proficient. . . . He panted after the fine arts and discovered a taste in them. . . . The theories of human rights he had drawn from Locke, Harrington, Sidney, English history, and Montesquieu, [which] he had maturely investigated in all their aspects, and [he] was versed in the republican doctrines and effusions which conducted the first Charles to the scaffold." [35] John Blair "was adept in classical learning, mathematics, divinity, various branches of natural philosophy, belles lettres, and the law." [36] While Randolph celebrated the varied accomplishments of Jefferson and Blair, he also placed a high value on the more specific ability of Richard Bland "as an antiquary in colonial learning." With this knowledge, Bland was able to enlighten "the people" with "a pamphlet overflowing with historical facts, which reinforced the opposition to the ministry." [37] Even George Washington, who as a "youth had developed no flattering symptoms of what the world calls genius," still "possessed a fund of qualities" of mind—"he had been conspicuous for firmness, for a judg-

34. P. 181.   35. Pp. 181–182.   36 P. 191.   37. P 190.

ment which discriminated the materials gathered by others of a quicker
and more fertile invention, and for a prudence which no frivolousness
had ever checkered"—which had "no specific direction to any particular
calling but were instruments for any crisis."[38]

Randolph also placed great emphasis on the ruling gentry's oratorical skills. Richard Henry Lee had nurtured "a species of oratory rare
among a people backward in refinement. He had attuned his voice
with so much care that one unmusical cadence could scarcely be pardoned by his ear. . . . His speech was diffusive, without hackneyed
formulas, and he charmed wheresoever he opened his lips. In political
reading he was conversant, and on the popular topics dispersed through
the debates of Parliament, his recollection was rapid and correct."[39]
Even Thomas Ludwell Lee, too timid to speak in the House of
Burgesses, was an orator "when the formality of a public did not
agitate him."[40] For Randolph, learning and oratory were essential
equipment for a leadership bound by a political code that would not
tolerate large doses of demagoguery or rash action but required the
more difficult techniques of persuading the electorate through logic,
reason, and good sense.

As high a premium as Randolph placed on learning and oratory,
the qualities of leadership he admired most were those traits of character that enabled a man to influence others through example and
admiration. "In official rank and ostensible importance," Peyton Randolph "stood foremost in the bands of patriots" largely because he
enjoyed a reputation as a man of decorum and moderation.[41] The
"frankness" of Benjamin Harrison, "though sometimes tinctured with
bitterness, was the source of considerable attachment."[42] "The propriety and purity" of Robert Carter Nicholas's "life were often quoted,
to stimulate the old and to invite the young to emulation, and in an
avocation thickly beset with seductions [Nicholas was then treasurer
of Virginia], he knew them only as he repelled them with the quickness of instinct."[43] George Wythe's "character, rather than his actions,
rendered him a valuable resource to the infant Revolution."[44] In each
of these cases it was force of character which provided the best resource
for leadership.

Finally, in Randolph's view, Virginia society before the revolutionary crisis tended to celebrate an aristocratic style of life; but the new
circumstances of the Anglo-American controversy called for men of

38. P. 187.   39. P. 184.   40. P. 192.   41. P. 183.   42. P. 190.   43. P. 184.
44. P. 191.

more republican habits. George Mason had "an indifference for distinction, . . . a disposition not averse from hospitality," and a "hatred
for pomp" despite being endowed "with ability to mount in any line"
and "a fortune competent to any expense." These attitudes, according
to Randolph, were a direct product of "that philosophical spirit which
despised the adulterated means of cultivating happiness." [45] Edmund
Pendleton he characterized as a man who "lived at home with the
unadulterated simplicity of a republican; from abroad he imported
into his family no fondness for show." [46] Randolph's high regard for
republican manners, however, was not a suggestion that deference
should be abandoned as the guiding principle of Virginia society; he
was merely suggesting a type of informality between classes possible
only in a stable social order in which everyone knows his place. Thus,
Pendleton's "amiableness bordered on familiarity without detracting
from personal dignity." [47]

The rhetorical enthusiasm of these sketches does not mean that
Randolph necessarily subscribed to the filiopietistic school of biography
popularized in the early nineteenth century by Mason Locke Weems
and William Wirt. Indeed, several of these men—Washington, Patrick
Henry, Richard Henry Lee—had at one time or another been bitter
political enemies of Randolph. He was not praising the accomplishments of individuals as much as he was celebrating a system of which
these men were the best product. Randolph exaggerated their virtues
to show that the system required men ambitious for political distinction
to conform to the system's code. This last point is the most revealing
lesson to be found in Randolph's portrayal of Patrick Henry.

Of the fourteen men selected as the best representatives of Virginia's
revolutionary leadership, Patrick Henry understandably emerges as the
most dramatic but oddly enough as the most representative as well. It
was Henry, according to Randolph, who at the outset of the conflict
with Great Britain took command of the newly emerging leadership
in the House of Burgesses: "They wanted a leader," and "at this
critical moment, Patrick Henry appeared as a member from the county
of Louisa." Randolph was quick to concede Henry's shortcomings; as
a scholar he had little training and was more orator than thinker; "in
black-letter precedents he was never profound." "Nor was he absolutely
exempt from an irregularity in his language, a certain homespun pro-
nounciation, and a degree of awkwardness in the cold commencement
of his gesture." The important point, however, was that Henry

45. P. 192.   46. P. 186.   47. *Ibid.*

abounded in those qualities which were particularly suited to the present crisis. "For grand impressions in the defense of liberty, the Western world has not yet been able to exhibit a rival. . . . In this embryo state of the Revolution, deep research into the ancient treasure of political learning might well be dispensed with. It was enough to feel, to remember some general maxims coeval with the colony and inculcated frequently afterwards." Since he was "identified with the people, they clothed him with the confidence of a favorite son." [48]

Considering Henry's reputation as a firebrand it seems odd that Randolph should cast him as the prototype of a ruling group celebrated for its decorum, moderation, and learning. But Randolph had grasped an important point; despite Henry's flamboyant behavior and seemingly radical tone he was an establishment man who played by the rules of the game of Virginia politics. "From education he derived those manners which belonged to the real Virginia planter and which were his ornament, in no less disdaining an abridgment of personal independence than in observing every decorum interwoven with the comfort of society." Even his vehement and often sarcastic tone was softened "by a demeanor inoffensive, conciliating, and abounding in good humor." [49] In short, Henry differed from his fellows only in his individual capabilities and personality, not in basic assumptions about the rules of the game and the social order.

Responsibility versus Responsiveness

Randolph's conception of the evolutionary nature of Virginia society and his commitment to constitutionalism and to a political system in which government was the responsibility of extraordinary men do much to explain his behavior as a public figure and his criticism of contemporary American politics. Whatever the personal motives behind his vacillation over the Federal Constitution, his arguments were based on a fixed set of constitutional principles. His devotion to a political system in which men of power were expected to be responsive but not necessarily responsible to the will of their constituents made him virtually an anachronism by the time of his dismissal in 1795 as secretary of state. Not that his conception of political ethics was unique;

48. Pp. 167, 168, 179, 181, 178.   49. Pp. 178, 179.

the same principles were, in fact, an accepted part of the conventional wisdom of the period. It was his insistence on rigidly applying them to his every public act that made Randolph unsuitable for high national office in the partisan atmosphere of the 1790's.

Given his conception of government and a rapidly changing set of political dynamics on the federal stage, Randolph was miscast in his role as a cabinet official. His long experience as a lawyer and as attorney general of Virginia better suited him for a seat on the Supreme Court. Ironically, only three weeks before British Minister Hammond produced the letter that ruined Randolph, Attorney General William Bradford and others told him that they wished to advise the President to name him to the Court. Realizing some of them wanted to get him out of the way of Jay's Treaty, Randolph wrote to the President that he would not accept a seat on the Court because "I do not think it right in itself, and . . . the world would not think it so." [50]

As a casualty of a rapidly changing set of political dynamics Randolph could not help contrasting what he regarded as Virginia's political system with the style of politics that had led to his destruction. Generalizing from his own experience Randolph forecast the downfall of the Virginia dynasty. His enthusiastic tribute to Washington—"I rejoice that I have lived to do justice to . . . Washington" [51]—can only be taken as an ironic tribute. The Washington he was celebrating was the prepresidential Washington yet to be infected by the spirit of faction. Randolph was not merely implying that Washington had succumbed to the temptations of political power through faction. He also was conveying his belief that the very qualities of leadership that in Virginia had served to neutralize partisan politics in favor of a broad evolutionary development within the context of a tradition of political responsibility were being undermined. He had discerned that the great Virginians of the revolutionary era were less the product of their individual genius than of a unique political system. And despite their varied political persuasions, as the products of that system they had a great deal in common. The characteristics of Virginia's ruling gentry that he celebrated in his biographical sketches were the very characteristics that were being compromised at the federal level.

Eventually, the Virginians' commitment to practical politics came into calamitous conflict with their political ideals. Indeed, one can view their tenure on the federal stage as a systematic if unwitting abandonment of those ideals in practice but not in principle. Increas-

50. Brant, "Edmund Randolph, Not Guilty!," p. 198.   51. See below, p. 5.

ingly, their concern for a viable federal republic cut them off from their roots in the local community. Increasingly, the demands of professional political organization made untenable their commitment to amateur politics. The addition of new political processes served to elevate the "representative" style of politics over the "responsible" style. And ultimately, the very qualities of statesmanship which had hitherto been the prerequisite for high political office became a disqualification. "Availability" became the order of the day, but that far the Virginians were unable to go.[52]

To have discerned this much is an achievement which alone would commend Randolph's *History* to students of revolutionary politics. Randolph saw the necessity for tracing the wellsprings of power to their sources in the structure and quality of Virginia society. In particular, Randolph saw Virginia politics as the touchstone of the colony's moral fiber. It stood as the bulwark of virtue and liberty, and the test of its efficacy was its ability to act responsibly and imaginatively in the face of challenges from without and stresses from within—its ability, that is, to moderate any tensions that threaten the proper aspirations of a free people. In this sense, Randolph properly discerned that Virginia society had achieved something at once different from and superior to either aristocracy or democracy—a politics which held in balance the ingredients of responsibility and responsiveness to the popular will. If he failed to explore fully the implications of his discovery, he nonetheless identified the basic task of students of the Revolution in Virginia.

The *History of Virginia* as History

Edmund Randolph's *History of Virginia* stands as a synthesis of the dual qualities of eighteenth-century American historical writing: the influence of European intellectual thought and the special exigencies of the American experience. Like his European predecessors—Voltaire, David Hume, and William Robertson, with whose works he was familiar—Randolph was concerned less with the facts of the past than with the lessons that could be drawn from those facts. In the tradition of

---

52. I am indebted here to a paper delivered at the Kansas City meeting of the Mississippi Valley Historical Association (April 23, 1965) by Keith Berwick entitled "The Virginia Dynasty: A Study in Political Mortality."

these earlier philosopher-historians, he regarded his subject, in J. B. Black's terms, as "an addendum to philosophy." Just as the eighteenth-century historian "turned to history to provide them with data, so they illumined their history by the aid of their philosophy and impressed upon it a meaning and a value which it never before possessed." [53]

Along with other American historians of the revolutionary era—including Jeremy Belknap, Samuel Williams, and David Ramsay—Randolph regarded didactic history as an important advance over earlier forms of historical writing. In common with others of his age he was not overly concerned with the past for its own sake, only for its usefulness to the present. He was therefore anxious to dissociate his function as historian from that of the mere chronicler of events. History was an important phase of philosophic inquiry. More specifically, Randolph rejected mere factual history as not only uninformative but dull. "Although the mass of colonial documents," he wrote, "contains some valuable information, it is crowded with matter which at this day carries with it no degree of interest. At the hazard, therefore, of the imputation that I have taken too great liberties in pruning them, I shall be chiefly attentive to such only as connect the various parts of the Virginia character and delineate the situation of Virginia at different stages most worthy of notice." This approach to the past Randolph referred to as emphasizing "the dignity of history." [54]

Randolph's use of the phrase "the dignity of history" is significant. What he meant was not merely that history should be written in a dignified manner but that it should be written about dignified events and characters. This amounts to a variation on the maxims laid down by Voltaire and Hume regarding the selection of data and the subject matter appropriate to historical writing.[55] By these maxims many facts were altogether too trivial to be noticed by the historian, who should properly concentrate upon those transactions which commanded attention because of their inherent interest or because of the instruction to be derived from them. A history that was truly dignified would therefore be truly useful as well, because it would serve as an inspiration to dignified thought and action. Randolph, who borrowed this idea from William Robertson,[56] refined its meaning to include a concern for beauty of construction; and although Randolph's prose leaves much

---

53. J. B. Black, *The Art of History: A Study of Four Great Historians of the Eighteenth Century* (New York, 1965), pp. 20–21.

54. See below, pp. 3, 4.   55. Black, *Art of History*, p. 131.   56. *Ibid.*

to be desired, it is due to the fact that the surviving manuscript is a carelessly constructed transcription of the original made some years after Randolph's death.

For the revolutionary generation of American historians a dignified history was one that came to grips with the sudden and unexpected appearance of a new and collective form of existence. With the birth of a new nation, Americans were forced to face the requirements of establishing a new historical identity. If the Revolution had given birth to a new society, it had also created a desire to discover its historical antecedents and to establish the role various individuals and states had played in the genesis of that society.[57] No concept was dearer to the revolutionary generation of historians than the conviction that there was a basic unity and purpose to American history. The Revolution may have marked a crucial turning point, but rather than a break with the past it was regarded as the culmination of a process that had begun with the colonization of English North America. "The discovery of America," wrote David Ramsay, "is the first link in a chain of causes, which bids fair to enlarge the happiness of mankind, by regenerating the principles of government in every quarter of the world." [58] It was generally agreed that the Revolution had demonstrated the characteristic features of the American people and society, and that those characteristics did not date just from the Declaration of Independence but back to the very origins of American society. The Revolution had served merely as a process of self-discovery in which Americans had fully come to realize and accept the republican character of their society. This conviction was dramatized by the remarkable fact that in 1776 thirteen colonies of widely divergent origins and background, without the cement of a political union, had acted as one. Thus, to discover how a community of "principles and feelings," to use the words of John Adams, had come into being would underscore the basic unity of the American experience.[59]

If the revolutionary generation of historians was committed to creat-

57. For the historiography of the revolutionary generation of historians, see David D. Van Tassel, *Recording America's Past: An Interpretation of the Development of Historical Studies in America, 1607–1884* (Chicago, 1960), pp. 31–86; and Arthur H. Shaffer, "The Development of a National Tradition: Historical Writing in America, 1783–1820" (Ph.D. dissertation, University of California, Los Angeles, 1966).

58. Robert L. Brunhouse, ed., "David Ramsay, 1749–1815: Selections from His Writings," American Philosophical Society, *Transactions*, new ser., LX, pt. 4 (1965), 191.

59. Wesley Frank Craven, *The Legend of the Founding Fathers* (New York, 1956), pp. 74–75.

ing a unified American history, their desire to define a past for the new nation also stimulated new rivalries. Before the Revolution the primary focus of interest was on each colony's distinct relationship to Great Britain and the English past. Since the Revolution and the creation of the United States gave them a common political identity, and by implication a common history, local historians were anxious to legitimatize their state's claim to a proper place in the nation's past. It was as if state historians were reflecting the schizophrenic character of nationality in the early days of the Republic. The Federal Constitution had provided for a system of dual sovereignty, a dual loyalty to state and to nation. Therefore, the historian could and did manifest a pride of statehood within a framework of a common national identity by characterizing his state as an embodiment of national ideals.

Randolph's *History* reflects this dualism in the revolutionary generation's search for a national historical identity: a local history that would fit the pattern of a unified national history. As a nationalist Randolph recognized, though never explicitly stated, that after 1789 there no longer existed an independent state history. This realization led him to the urgency of establishing Virginia's unique past. Therefore, in reading the *History* one should never forget that Randolph was writing as a Virginia patriot, poised to defend the unique qualities of his "native state" and the crucial role he felt Virginia had played in American history. As the "earliest among the British settlements in North America," Virginia was clearly regarded by Randolph as the progenitor of American republicanism. Of Pocahontas's dramatic intervention on behalf of Captain John Smith, a man he regarded as the colony's savior, Randolph wrote: "Let the Virginia patriot ascribe the preservation of Smith to that chain of grand events of which the settlement of Virginia was destined to be the foremost link, and which finally issued in the birth of our American Republic." [60]

Since American historians were bent on showing that the Revolution was not a chance event but, in the words of John Daly Burk, grew "out of the temper and habits of the people," [61] the origins of American society was a matter of no little importance. The fact that Randolph devoted over half the existing manuscript to the period from 1607 to 1624 illustrates his interest in and his recognition of the importance of the colonial origins of Virginia. He confessed that while this "portion

---

60. See below, pp. 24–25.
61. *An Oration Delivered on the Fourth of March 1803 . . . to Celebrate the Election of Thomas Jefferson, and the Triumph of Republicanism* (Petersburg, Va., 1803), p. 7.

of our history" was the "least capable of being rendered interesting" it could not be omitted "as it contains many of the elements of our political history and perhaps of our political ability." [62] Randolph was vague as to just how the "Virginia character" had developed, but he did provide some guidelines. He implied a causative relationship between the New World environment and the republican character of Virginia society. Fortunately "nature had withheld from the soil the precious metals but had bestowed richer treasures in its luxuriance and rapidity of vegetation." "The kindness of the climate to grains and plants imported from the Old World . . . numerous species of valuable timber, ores adapted to the calls of labor and genius opened prospects more truly splendid than those which dazzled, seduced, and corrupted the Spanish conquerors in the south." [63]

While Randolph made only a few such references to the effect of the physical environment on the development of the "Virginian character," it can be safely assumed that nature would have played a large role in the topical portion of the *History*.[64] American historians were particularly anxious to discuss the impact of nature on man in the New World as a counterweight against attacks by a number of European writers who had applied such derogatory adjectives as degenerate, unhealthy, nauseous, and monstrous to the American environment.[65] The most important statement of this thesis appeared in Buffon's *Histoire Naturelle* (1749–1804) and was incorporated into Diderot's *Encyclopédie* (1751–72). Buffon was impressed by what he believed to be striking differences between the animal and the plant life of North America and Europe. He concluded that the two continents were similar: the difference lay in their geological ages. Buffon theorized that since America was more recently formed geologically it was in a state of growth too early for the mature development of modern animals, men, and institutions. What made his approach so persuasive was that it interpreted deviations from nature as Europe knew it as evidence of the youth and, therefore, the inferiority of America to the rest of the world. The Abbé Corneille DePauw in his *Recherches philosophiques sur les Americains* (1768) contended that the American Indian lacked virility and was closely akin to the beasts. The Indian was neither vicious nor virtuous; "the timidity of his soul, the weakness of his intellect, the necessity of providing for his subsistence,

---

62. See below, p. 23 *n.*   63. P. 146.   64. P. 3.

65. For a discussion of this fascinating debate, see Ralph N. Miller, "American Nationalism as a Theory of Nature," *Wm. and Mary Qtly.*, 3d ser., XI (1955), 74–95.

the powers of superstition, the influences of climate lead him far wide of the possibility of improvement." [66] By implication if the environment had a degenerating effect on the Indian, then it followed that America's European inhabitants would likewise be affected.

There were many rejoinders to these accusations. Thomas Jefferson's *Notes on the State of Virginia* (1784) was the most widely read, and it formed a basis for a number of other works, such as Jedidiah Morse's *History of America in Two Books* (1787), James Challender's *Sketches of the History of America* (1795), and Randolph's *History of Virginia*. Randolph resented "these European naturalists who debase all the energies of the American world," and he even went so far in his defense of the American man and his environment as to repeat William Stith's characterization of the Chickahominy tribe as "a stout, daring, and free people . . . governed in a republican form by their elders. . . . Such a happy influence had liberty, and such visible incitement did firm property give to the industry of even that lazy and improvident people." [67] This defense of the Indian was an indirect way not only of defending nature in America but of proving that far from being a hindrance the environment of the New World had been a distinct advantage. "The proper nursery of genius, learning, industry, and the liberal arts," wrote Hugh Williamson in his *History of North Carolina* (1812), "is a temperate climate, in a country that is diversified by hills, enjoying a clear atmosphere. In no other country do these circumstances occur, in so extensive a degree as they do in America, at least in North America." [68]

But Randolph was not an environmental determinist. Clearly he regarded the material abundance of Virginia as an important factor in the development of the "Virginia character." Yet if the physical world had had any direct effect on the development of Virginia society, it was through the isolation which 3,000 miles of ocean had afforded to perfect the forms and institutions of society, and it was indeed fortunate that this opportunity lay in the hands of Englishmen. The Revolution had done little to undermine Randolph's admiration for England and especially English constitutional principles. "A people proud of English blood" had inherited the virtues of the "English character," but because of Virginia's isolation from the mother country they had avoided the worst of England's political vices. Virginia, for example, was "inoculated" by the Glorious Revolution "without the

66. *Ibid.,* 77.   67. See below, pp. 12, 64–65.
68. *The History of North Carolina* (Philadelphia, 1812), I, 174.

poison of those prejudices which still ran unmitigated in the bosom of England." [69]

The propelling force behind Virginia's constitutional and political evolution was the interaction of American Englishmen with the mother country. This interpretation is seen especially in Randolph's treatment of the rise and fall of the Virginia Company. His major source was William Stith's whiggish *History of the First Discovery and Settlement of Virginia* (1747). Although Randolph copied long passages verbatim, a practice common to historians of the period, he did not slavishly follow Stith's interpretation of events. He often paused to draw his own conclusions and frequently changed the meaning of events by omitting selected passages from Stith's narrative. For example, he was able to place even greater emphasis on the revocation of the Virginia Company's charter as an act of Stuart despotism by largely omitting those portions of Stith's account dealing with conditions in Virginia, thereby giving the distinct impression that the course of events was dictated almost entirely by domestic politics in England. But if Randolph's account is not a simple reproduction of Stith he did offer the same general interpretation of events. Stith's *History* is written in the style of what could be called the "whig interpretation of history." He interpreted the history of Virginia as a story of liberty, of repeated efforts to establish and defend the ancient constitutional rights of Englishmen against the tyrannical ambitions of the crown and some of Virginia's early governors.[70]

For Randolph it was this struggle between crown and Company and other similar contests throughout the colonial period that taught Virginians a proper respect for their rights as Englishmen and the proper means for upholding those rights. Other American historians of the period took pride in the colonists' overt resistance to incursions by the mother country. John Daly Burk, for example, in his *History of Virginia* (1804–5) doggedly set out to prove false the "universally received opinion . . . that Virginia was distinguished for her invariable loyalty, and her submissive and tractable temper, during the greater part of her colonial existence." [71] But Randolph took pride in Virginia's tractable, if not submissive, temper; the genius of the "Virginia character"

69. See below, pp. 147, 158.
70. For Stith, see Van Tassel, *Recording America's Past*, pp. 26–27.
71. *The History of Virginia, from Its First Settlement to the Commencement of the Revolution* (Petersburg, Va., 1822), II, 233.

was its ability to uphold a "loyalty debased by no servile compliance" and to retain "a patriotic watchfulness" that never degenerated "into the mere petulance of complaint." [72]

It was with this same emphasis on the Englishness of the "Virginia character" that Randolph treated the coming of the Revolution in Virginia. "This is an era illustrious indeed in the annals of Virginia. Without an immediate oppression, without a cause depending so much on hasty feeling as theoretic reasoning, . . . with fraternal attachment to the transatlantic members of the empire, . . . with a subserviency in cultivating their manners and their fashions, in a word with England as a model of all which was great and venerable—the House of Burgesses in the year 1765 gave utterance to principles which within ten years were to expand into a revolution." Randolph was, of course, taking full measure of the ironic fact that the Englishness of the "Virginia character" was a major cause of the Revolution. "We have seen that until the era of the Stamp Act almost every political sentiment, every fashion in Virginia appeared to be imperfect unless it bore a resemblance to some precedent in England." But that very bias made it inevitable that Virginia would take offense at violations of her liberties; "the spirit . . . which she had caught from the charters, the English laws, the English constitution, English theories . . . had diminished her almost idolatrous deference to the mother country and taught her to think for herself." [73]

Thus, Randolph echoed the predominant patriot interpretation of the Revolution. There is the same emphasis on constitutional issues as the "heart of the matter," the same emphasis on the remarkable lack of internal disorder during a crisis of such profound proportions, and the same contention that the rash and illegal behavior of the British government alone led to a progressive disintegration of the colonial American's sturdy loyalty to the Empire. The "remonstrances against the Stamp Act," he wrote, "breathed loyalty"; the years from 1765 to 1774 "resembled that season between two old friends when the language begins to be embittered and the heart is gnawed, a rupture is dreaded but the cause is not forgiven." However, by 1774 a transformation in public sentiment had been reached, and this "new state of things" transformed the conflict from a traditional defense of Virginia's liberties to an American Revolution. "Now indeed . . . a deeper tone broke forth. The public mind had been familiarized to

72. See below, pp. 160–61.   73. Pp. 166, 176.

an appeal to arms at first as only a possible event, which was sincerely deprecated, and afterwards, as a probable one, which might be imposed by necessity." [74]

Randolph defined the character of Virginia society in much the same terms as did those historians groping for a definition of national character—as an expression of the "political genius" of the Virginia people. Like other historians of the period, he interpreted the "Virginia character" (i.e., the national character) in almost exclusively political terms. American nationality had been a product of the Revolution, and since the Revolution had been a particularly political phenomenon it was only natural that the revolutionary generation of historians would impart a peculiarly political bias to the national character. For those who were working to emphasize national unity, to stress other than political characteristics could only serve to magnify the diversity rather than the unity of American society. Randolph had also offered a definition of the "Virginia character" that served a dual function. On the one hand, he explained the Anglo-American conflict and the society that emerged from the Revolution as a direct outgrowth of the colonial society that had preceded it. Yet he still maintained that the break with Great Britain had resulted from the actions of the English government, not from any desire for independence on the part of the colonists. Moreover, works such as Randolph's _History of Virginia_ offer important insights into the intellectual history of the early years of the Republic—the tension between local and national loyalties, the difficulties of a people unaccustomed to thinking in national terms who still felt a strong imperative to identify the basic elements of a national character and a desire to understand the Revolution not as a chance event but as the fruition of the national character.

74. Pp. 176, 175, 177.

The Manuscript

By John Melville Jennings

Randolph, four years prior to his death, unveiled the plan for his *History of Virginia* in the December 26, 1809, issue of the Richmond *Enquirer*. Inasmuch as the prospectus proved fundamental some sixty years later in identifying the unsigned manuscript copy of the work from which the present text was transcribed, it is reprinted here in its entirety:

A NEW HISTORY OF VIRGINIA.

A friend has put into the hands of the Editor, the subjoined plan of the work. It is understood to come from the pen of a native of Virginia; but the form and conditions of the publication are not yet fixed. The author has been personally conversant with most of the public transactions which he relates, from the beginning of the American revolution to the close of the History.

THE PLAN OF THE WORK.

The early history of Virginia must, from its novelty, have been very attractive The state, in which man was found here, was unknown in Europe, except from speculations, exercised on facts, too few and too imperfectly understood, to become the groundwork of philosophy. A soil, fresh from the hands of nature—animals, peculiar in kind, species and variety—vegetables, with qualities unexplored—minerals, exhibiting forms and combinations, not before observed; and a climate, coinciding with none of the calculations, fitted to that of the old world in the same latitudes—produced phœnomena, which went beyond the then existing theories.

But at this day, many of those subjects have been discussed with so much precision, as to exclude every hope of favor to an attempt, which should result in nothing more than a mere change of attitude. This work, therefore, will be divided into epochs; each presenting some prominent feature in the affairs of Virginia, and the whole of them comprehending our entire history. It will be detailed, however, only where it may excite a degree of interest.

The public archives, in their present condition, afford scarcely any light, until the revolution, which gave birth to independence, and even until the year 1782, until it was finally acknowledged. To the printed narratives, prior to those periods, and to some scattered documents, which have escaped the ravages of time and of war, the appeal must now be made.

Difficult as the task may be, to transplant into this history the events of the American Union, yet they will be incorporated in such a manner as not to incumber it with the recital of any, to which Virginia may not have borne a marked relation, or attached a particular feeling. It will be attempted by narrating the influential measures, and in describing the important actors, so as to correspond with the expectation of him, who reads in quest of useful information. It would, indeed, have been omitted altogether, after the appearance of General Washington's life by Chief Justice Marshal[1] were it not impossible to view Virginia in an insulated situation, from the assembling of the first Congress in September, 1774, to the close of the war. A naked abridgment would be a piracy on that work; while the pursuit of a plan equally extensive would be a repetition, not venial.

The first epoch commences with the charter of discovery, granted to Sir Humphrey Gilbert by Queen Elizabeth, of England, on the 11th day of June, 1578, and embracing the dissolution of the proprietary government in the year 1624.

The second, terminates with Bacon's rebellion, as it was called, in the year 1676.

The third, includes the opposition of the house of Burgesses to the exaction of Governor Dinwiddie, in the year 1752, of a pistole, as a fee on every new patent for land.

The fourth, reaches to the stamp act in the year 1765, with which will be connected the declaration of Independence, and the war which followed.

The fifth, ends with the adoption of the Constitution of the United States.

And the sixth, contains an illustration of the influence of that Constitution upon Virginia, and her general history from the time of its operation in the year 1789. Here too, the federal transactions of the United States may properly hold a place, upon the foregoing plan for recording their revolutionary ones.

Some topics, which a regard to chronology may not suffer to be interwoven at full length, upon the first mention of them, but which leave not their due impression, when occurring in fragments only, will be examined in separate essays—

The principal of these are:
1. Religion.
2. Literature, arts and sciences.
3. Government.
4. The Laws.
5. Natural History under many of its principal heads.

      6. Manufactures.

      7. Commerce, Coin, &c.

      8. Population.

      9. Military Force.

     10. Manners and National Character.

     11. The Aborigines, as far as facts will justify.

It is impossible to avoid a biographical sketch of many in legislative, executive and judicial departments, and in various professions. But this will be done with a temper superior to partiality or personal acrimony, and adapted to display examples for the observance of the Statesman, the Judge, the Lawyer, &c.

Important public papers will be collected in an appendix.

The original or holograph manuscript of the *History* passed upon Randolph's death in 1813 to his only son, Peyton, who, in the August 26, 1815, issue of the Richmond *Enquirer,* offered the publication rights for sale. The work was described at that time as follows:

TO PRINTERS.

The Subscriber is willing to dispose of the copy-right of a work intitled, "THE HISTORY OF VIRGINIA," by Edmund Randolph. This history comprehends all the important events which occurred in Virginia, from her first settlement down to the adoption of the Federal Constitution. In the progress of the work, the author seems to have had constantly in view the emancipation of that country from her colonial dependence, and to have marked the causes which gradually led to that event, and fitted her for it. Many characters, w[hi]ch deserving of renown, who are necessarily overlooked in a more general history of the United States, are here brought into view, and their actions rescued from oblivion, or the perishable memorial of tradition. Independently of Washington, whose life is interwoven with the history of his country, the author has paid a just tribute to men who acted in a more limited sphere, but whose influence was sensibly felt in the important measures which brought about the Revolution. Of Patrick Henry—of his zeal and his eloquence—a very copious notice is taken.— Thomas Jefferson is drawn, such as he appeared at that period, without borrowing one tint from the passions and prejudices of the present day. Richard Henry Lee occupies a high station among the worthies of the Revolution; besides a multitude of others, who at that time shone with no inconsiderable lustre, and to whom an appropriate station is assigned. For the satisfaction of those who may wish to purchase the copy-right of this work, I shall subjoin a few extracts.

The proceedings of the Convention, held in Richmond in the year 1775, one of the most interesting events of that day are particularly detailed.

A general sketch is also given of the course of the debates in the general Convention, which met in Philadelphia in 1787. This derives no small interest from being the narration of an eye-witness.

Of the execution of this work, it does not become me to speak. But no delicacy ought to restrain me from saying (what indeed is known to many others) that the composition of the work was the favourite object of the author's pursuit, for many years before his death—that he had access to every document necessary for his undertaking—that he was personally and intimately acquainted with the men and measures described, during the period of his political life—and that he possessed a dispassionate temper, superior to any prejudice.

I am unable to make any conjecture about the size of the work, when reduced to print. It consists of many manuscript volumes of different sizes.

Should any one wish to contract for the copy-right, a letter addressed to me in Richmond, Virginia, will be duly attended to.

PEYTON RANDOLPH.

Richmond, August 19.

Those passages in the text describing Patrick Henry and George Washington also were printed respectively in the August 26 and September 2, 1815, issues of the *Enquirer,* as samples of the narrative style and skill of the author.

Randolph's grandson, the younger Peter V. Daniel, was perhaps unknowingly alluding to the holograph text when he informed the Virginia Historical Society in 1878 that during his childhood—he was born in 1818—"a manuscript copy of such a work" had been in the custody of his mother, Lucy Nelson (Randolph) Daniel, the author's daughter.[75] A portion of that manuscript, Daniel explained, had been lost "whilst loaned, it was said, to William Wirt, Esq." But the loss occurred before Mrs. Daniel assumed custody of the manuscript, for Wirt, on page x of the preface to his *Sketches of the Life and Character of Patrick Henry,* published in 1817, does indeed acknowledge that he "availed himself of the kind permission of Mr. Peyton Randolph, to examine an extremely valuable manuscript history of Virginia, written by his father, the late Mr. Edmund Randolph; which embraces the whole period of Mr. Henry's public life."

The truncated manuscript that Wirt returned to the family was obviously placed in the custody of Lucy Daniel after her brother,

75. Virginia Historical Society, Executive Committee, Minutes, Liber A3, 1853-87, June 30, 1878.

Peyton Randolph, died in 1828. Peter V. Daniel further testified in 1878 that the manuscript was subsequently relinquished by the elder Mrs. Daniel to her brother's only son, Edmund Randolph, the name-sake and grandson of the author. It was accidentally destroyed by fire, Daniel continued, after it had been passed on to the younger Randolph. Hugh Blair Grigsby, the Society's president in 1878, was already aware of the fate of the manuscript, having noted in his diary in 1876 that "a part of it was certainly burned in New Orleans." [76] Grigsby's somewhat cryptic observation can be explained by the fact that the younger Edmund Randolph removed to New Orleans after graduating in law from the University of Virginia in 1837 and resided there until departing for California in 1849.[77]

The second known manuscript version of the work was accessioned by the Virginia Historical Society in 1860 as the gift of Nathaniel Francis Cabell of Nelson County. Cabell had acquired the volume from John Howard McCue of Staunton, "by whom it had been discovered in a lawyer's office in Staunton." [78] Cabell, in transmitting the manu-script to the Society's secretary, George W. Bagby, on July 30, 1860, stated:

The book contains 120 pages of MS. in as many large folio leaves beginning with page 11 and ending with 130. The alternate pages are blank, and on these are occasional addenda, with a "Memorandum for the reader" of two pages at the close, and many interlineations and corrections in the body of the book, all in a hand different from that in that hand of the transcriber, and which bears a strong resemblance to that of certain genuine letters of Gov: Randolph, which I had once in my possession.[79]

The fate of the Cabell-McCue copy was sealed in 1861, however, when, along with other manuscripts owned by the Society, it was deposited by Gustavus A. Myers, a member of the Society's Executive Committee, in the vault of a Richmond bank for safekeeping during the Civil War. The building and the contents of the vault were destroyed by fire when the city was evacuated on April 3, 1865.[80]

The present printed text of Randolph's *History* was transcribed from still another copy of the work, believed to be the only surviving version, that mysteriously came to light in the library of the Virginia Historical Society after the Civil War.[81] It was discovered in an as-

76. Hugh Blair Grigsby, Diary, 1876, in Virginia Historical Society library.
77. See P. O. Ray, "Edmund Randolph" in *Dictionary of American Biography*.
78. Virginia Historical Society, Executive Committee, Minutes.
79. *Ibid.*   80. *Ibid.*   81. *Ibid.*

semblage of several thousand printed books which the Society, for
want of a library building, had deposited in installments in 1867 and
1869 in the rooms of the Young Men's Christian Association of Richmond. The books, recalled in 1870, were inventoried by the Society's
officers who, during the course of their labors, uncovered and tenta-
tively identified the unsigned, untitled manuscript.[82] The identification
may have been made by the Society's newly appointed secretary, Robert
Alonzo Brock, or by Executive Committee member Charles G. Barney.
In announcing the discovery to President Grigsby on February 7, 1876,
William Wirt Henry, another member of the Executive Committee,
reported that "Dr. Barney took it away with him & after a disagreeable
correspondence with him we have at last recovered it & the internal
evidence is conclusive that it is by Ed. Randolph."[83] The manuscript
was shortly thereafter forwarded to Grigsby who, from March 9 to
April 3, 1876, carefully scrutinized its contents, concluding that it was
indeed "the work of E. Randolph."[84] But, alas, a thorough search
through the Society's surviving accession registers and minute books
failed to uncover any record of its provenance or receipt.

The possibility that the Cabell-McCue copy, given to the Society in
1860, might miraculously have escaped destruction on April 3, 1865,
occurred to the Society's officers. Nathaniel Francis Cabell and John
Howard McCue, who were still alive in 1876, examined the manuscript, however, and agreed that it was not the copy that had come
from them. Cabell, the more specific witness, pointed out that the
newly discovered copy was written on both sides of the folios, whereas
the copy that he and McCue had given in 1860 had carried text only
on the alternate pages.[85]

Peter V. Daniel was equally firm in denying that the newly discovered copy was the one that had formerly been in the possession of
his family. In 1878, Daniel, in no uncertain terms, declined an invitation by the Society to prepare the manuscript for publication, holding
that "it is neither authentic, correct or complete." Daniel, as a matter
of fact, informed his petitioners that "it would be an act unworthy of
your Society and a grievous injustice to the fame and memory of Edmund Randolph to publish the manuscript."[86] Inasmuch as he was

82. *Ibid.*, and William G. Stanard, "History of the Virginia Historical Society," *Virginia Magazine of History and Biography*, XXXIX (1931), 318–24.
83. Grigsby papers, in Virginia Historical Society Library.
84. Grigsby, Diary, 1876.
85. Virginia Historical Society, Executive Committee, Minutes.   86. *Ibid.*

Randolph's grandson, the Society reluctantly submitted to his judgment.

But the Society's officers—notably Grigsby, Henry, and Brock—were convinced that the manuscript was indeed a copy, albeit imperfect and incomplete, of Randolph's *History*. Brock, characteristically enough, transcribed portions of the text into his personal commonplace book, methodically setting forth his reasons for attributing the work to the statesman.[87] And Brock, two years after the death of the author's indignant grandson, Peter V. Daniel, announced in Volume X, page 208, of the Society's *Collections* (Richmond, 1891) that the manuscript had "been committed . . . to the well-known writer, Moncure D. Conway, for publication." Conway, who had already quoted extensively from the manuscript in his *Omitted Chapters of History Disclosed in the Life and Papers of Edmund Randolph* (1888), for unexplained reasons never fulfilled the assignment. The project was finally revived in 1935 when, under the auspices of "The Virginians of the City of New York," the Society published in the *Virginia Magazine of History and Biography* that portion of the manuscript treating "the Revolutionary History of Virginia." [88] The work is now being printed in its entirety for the first time.

The manuscript volume consists of 130 unnumbered folios, exclusive of two blanks of later vintage that were inserted between the two major sections of the work when the quires, seemingly in the 1870's, were bound in three-quarter calf. Folios [1–38] measure 12¾ by 7¾ inches in size; folios [39–46, 48–130] measure 12½ by 7¾ inches; and folio [47] measures 9¾ by 7¾ inches. The section of the work treating the period prior to the Revolution is paged 1 – [4] – [92a–92b] – [112]; the section headed "Introduction to that part of the history embracing the revolution," separated from the first section by the two aforementioned blank leaves, is consecutively paged 1 through 92.

The text is written in a clerkly but somewhat irregular hand, clearly not that of the author. Numerous blank spaces left in the transcription, moreover, are testimonials that the copyist, when confronted with an illegible or unfamiliar word or phrase in the source, did not have the advantage of consulting either the author or someone acquainted with the author's hand. Indeed, a comparison of the passages

87. Robert A. Brock, Commonplace Book, pp. 272–92, microfilm copy in Virginia Historical Society library.

88. XLIII (1935), 113–38, 209–32, and 294–315; XLIV (1936), 35–50, 105–15, 223–31, and 312–22; and XLV (1937), 46–47.

in the transcription relating to Patrick Henry and George Washington
with the same passages that were drawn from the holograph manuscript and published respectively in the August 26 and September 2,
1815, issues of the Richmond *Enquirer*, reveals various discrepancies,
supporting Daniel's complaint in 1878 that "there are omissions of
words, which he [the copyist] apparently could not decipher or understand, and in other parts, of whole sentences and pages, which it is
impossible to supply; whilst in other places, the author's words are
evidently changed to others, which are often even absurd or unmean-
ing." [89] In short, the transcription was not made under the supervision
of the author, who died in 1813, nor of his son, Peyton, who died in
1828. But the identity of the copyist and the circumstances under which
the transcription was made remain as mysterious as when the manuscript first came to light in the 1870's.

89. Virginia Historical Society, Executive Committee, Minutes.

History of Virginia

Preface

 My purpose is to write the history of my native country during the entire period of her existence, as a colony first, and as an independent state afterwards, until nearly the close of the eighteenth century.

In this time, Virginia will be seen rising from infancy and a wilderness, through various fortunes, into wealth, a character, and an influence which largely contributed to the establishment of American independence and to the formation of that most illustrious among civil acts, the Constitution of the United States of America.

In this view, her political worth and her other means of general happiness will be here blended, and the prospect of her future destinies traced with freedom and a fearless eye.

When certain topics cannot be fully interwoven in the body of the history with strict attention to chronology and unity, they will be subjoined under the proper heads such as, for example: 1. Religion, 2. Morals, 3. Manners, 4. Aborigines, 5. Slaves, 6. Natural History, 7. Arts and Sciences, 8. Literature, 9. Manufactures, 10. Commerce.[1]

Although the mass of colonial documents contains some valuable information, it is crowded with matter which at this day carries with it no degree of interest. At the hazard, therefore, of the imputation that I have taken too great liberties in pruning them, I shall be chiefly attentive to such only as connect the various parts of the Virginian character and delineate the situation of Virginia at different stages most worthy of notice. Hence I shall slightly touch the adventures, cruelties, perfidy, stratagems, and tales of the Virginian savage, in our early acquaintance with him. Indeed all the selections from our archives will be guided by the same criterion, of being interesting. For the impression which my history may make, I shall depend upon the nature of the facts recorded, their arrangement, a general simplicity of [desig]n and construction, trusting that I may convey that kind of

1. Apparently this part of the plan was among the lost portions of the manuscript.

knowledge of Virginia which would be required by natives or foreigners beginning to gather the elements of her history.

But to the former, I shall not make too profuse a sacrifice in the
shape of anecdote and little circumstances. Although having been bred
in daily familiarity with the whole of Virginian subjects, those might
tolerate them, and perhaps might be pleased with them, the latter
after the first transitory emotion would coolly condemn such a departure from the dignity of history.

I discover, however, that without much care I may imperceptibly
glide into mere commentaries and dissertations. The danger has met
me at almost every turn. But if I am not deficient in some cardinal
heads, and particularly in those associated with the events subsequent
to the year 1624, when Virginia seemed to be emerging from colonial
depression, I shall, in a great measure, fulfill what I expect from myself.

I shall then have explained the motives upon which the English
sovereigns and nation patronized and prosecuted "the adventure," as
the colony was called, the obstacles which frustrated the first efforts in
colonization, and the means employed in accomplishing it; and I shall
have collected the best information surviving to our times of the soil,
the kingdoms of nature, and the aborigines as they appeared to the
first English colonists.

But I do not mean by this to forego any observations or discoveries
which have been made by philosophers in later times upon any of those
subjects which may not be too strictly scholastic and may not anticipate
too far.

When I reach the Stamp Act and proceed to our Revolution, there is
scarcely anything which the most fastidious taste would wish to be
omitted or abridged. If it even admit not a latitude of descriptive
painting, it has a force of character which supersedes the necessity of
embellishment.

From various causes, our biography is surrounded with difficulties.
Many eminent men have sprung up on occasions so distant from their
birth as now to have no contemporary witnesses of early life at least—of
some truly distinguished, an unequivocal testimony can never be obtained, except where their acts have been rescued from simple tradition. These difficulties are increased to me by the circumstance that a
character frequently descends to posterity on the faith of some single
act of éclat, while all its disparagements are forgotten.[2] I confess too

2. See below, pp. 178–93.

that I sometimes fear lest I live too near the times of which I speak. But truth shall prevail.

From those who have preceded me in similar labors, I do not hesitate to quote without marks of quotation. Some of them wrote before the country could be said to have been explored in its political concerns with much accuracy, and almost all of them, who assume the title of historians, before the era of Virginian luster. I excuse the arrogance of treading over again the same old ground, by no profession of better lights, but by my anxiety to exhibit Virginia as she is—far from being perfect, but with faults which good sense and patriotism cannot fail to correct.

For transactions within my own knowledge, I appeal to my own veracity. If I err, multitudes of persons and records, of easy access, have me in their power. In the parallels between certain characters, if I should complete them, I shall stand upon no other basis than the comparative public utility of each. I rejoice that I have lived to do justice to that of Washington.

Chapter I   From the Discovery of America to the Departure of Captain John Smith from Virginia

 Almost every person, public or private, who manifested a zeal in measures tending to the discovery or settlement of Virginia has received from the pen of history or acts of public gratitude some tribute of praise.

With the glory of Columbus the world resounds.

Even Henry VII of England has been celebrated for the accident of having lost the opportunity of embracing the overture which that profound navigator had forwarded to him, of a participation in first labors in the New World. Roused by the splendors of their fame from his habits of aversion to untried and distant projects, he commissioned on November 5, 1495, Giovanni Caboto, called in the English language John Cabot,[1] a Venetian adventurer, and his three sons to sail under his flag and possess in his name countries toward the east, north, or west unoccupied by Christian people. Cabot coasted along what was afterwards distinguished as Virginia. But Henry was too deeply involved in a war with Scotland, had been too recently delivered from an insurrection of his subjects in the west, and paid too great a deference to the Pope and to Ferdinand of Aragon, with whose family he solicited for his son an alliance of marriage, to provoke them by a seizure of territory which Ferdinand claimed through a papal grant. The flattering report, therefore, of Cabot on his return was neglected by the English crown until the reign of Elizabeth.

It was an attribute of her genius and temper to improve fortunate incidents and to select able agents. In this instance her strength of mind was peculiar in despising the predictions that a new colony would be immediately impatient for independence. She comprehended and pre-

1. John Cabot (d. 1498) in March 1496 received a patent from Henry VII to discover and conquer for England unknown lands beyond the seas and sailed in 1497 to the North American coast, either to Newfoundland or Nova Scotia. Believing that he had found the outlying coast of Asia, he sailed again in 1498 to trade with China. The voyage was a disappointment, and he may have been lost during the voyage, after some considerable exploration had shown that this land was not Cathay (James A. Williamson, *The Cabot Voyages and Bristol Discovery under Henry VII* [Cambridge, 1962]).

ferred the pursuit of solid hopes in agriculture and commerce to the baneful precious metals, which were to be drawn from mines.

On June 11, 1578, she granted a charter of discovery to Sir Humphrey Gilbert.[2] He, notwithstanding his consummate naval skill and courage, perished on the Banks of Newfoundland, and the queen transferred the rights under that instrument to Walter Raleigh, since better known as Sir Walter Raleigh, the effective founder of Virginia.[3] He was endowed with the science demanded by the conjuncture.

Entertaining the most sanguine expectations from Raleigh, the queen gave him the aid of a patent for the exclusive vending of wines for a certain number of years, his private fortune having been shattered by his expenditures in the equipment of a fleet for her service.

Raleigh, being too much occupied at the court of his royal mistress to prosecute in person an expedition to America, fitted out in conjunction with Sir Richard Grenville and others two small barques under the command of Philip Amadas and Arthur Barlow.[4]

After taking the tedious and unhealthy circuit of the Canary Islands

2. Sir Humphrey Gilbert (1537?–83) twice set out with colonists to America. The first time his fleet was forced back by the Spaniards. Not only did his second venture in 1583 to set up a colony at St. John's Harbor, Newfoundland, prove unsuccessful, but Gilbert was lost with his ship in a storm on the homeward voyage (David B. Quinn, ed., *The Voyages and Colonizing Enterprises of Sir Humphrey Gilbert* [London, 1940], I, 62–64). Gilbert's charter was issued by Queen Elizabeth in June 1578, only a few months after England and the United Netherlands had signed a defensive alliance pledging mutual support against Spanish aggression. The charter was reprinted in William Stith, *History of the First Discovery and Settlement of Virginia* (Williamsburg, Va., 1747), pp. 4–6 (see also Mary Newton Stanard, *The Story of Virginia's First Century* [Philadelphia, 1928], p. 16).

3. Sir Walter Raleigh (1552–1618), the half brother of Sir Humphrey Gilbert, had been a soldier in France and Ireland and from 1581 had a steadily increasing influence in the English court. By 1584 he possessed many estates, sinecures, and monopolies, the rewards of royal favor, the income from which he generously expended on the American venture. The royal charter he secured in March 1584 was essentially a renewal of Gilbert's patent (David B. Quinn, *Raleigh and the British Empire* [London, 1947], pp. 35–49). For a copy of Raleigh's patent, see Quinn, ed., *The Roanoke Voyages* (London, 1955), I, 82–89.

4. In April 1584 Raleigh outfitted an expedition to explore the coast of North America and to choose a site for settlement. The expedition was led by Philip Amadas (1550–1618), a Plymouth man of whom little is known. Of Arthur Barlow we know little except that he had made a voyage for Sir Humphrey Gilbert in 1580 (Quinn, *Roanoke Voyages*, I, 78–79). Barlow wrote such a glowing report that Queen Elizabeth was delighted to accept the territory designated as Virginia in honor of her maiden state. The report was printed in Richard Hakluyt's *The Principall Navigations, Voyages and Discoveries of the English Nation* (1589), pp. 723–33 (collated with vol. III [1600], 246–51, and conveniently reprinted in Quinn, *Roanoke Voyages*, I, 91–115). Randolph's account conveys the mistaken impression that this exploratory expedition was the same one which sailed on April 9, 1585, to establish Roanoke Colony. The latter expedition was led by Sir Richard Grenville

and the West Indies by which the inexperience of those times conducted them, they came to the continent of Florida (as the northern
continent from Cape Florida was then called) and probably anchored
at the island of Ocracoke, between Cape Hatteras and Cape Fear.[5]

Many of the principles and habits of Virginia may be traced to their
rudiments in her remote history. They are scions from the parent stock.
In those very letters patent to which Raleigh succeeded, there are
germs of government, loose indeed and unguarded, but promising,
after some corrections, the fruits of peace and safety.

1. The laws against emigration were relaxed so as to permit a
laborer of the soil, an artist, a political or religious malcontent to find
an asylum in the colony.

2. It was constituted a country for a poor man, exempt from
feudal tyranny, abounding with resources from agriculture, not deprived of the chance of the fossil riches of the earth, and affording
encouragement to matrimony by the facility of supporting families.

3. The rights of emigrants were the same with those of native
English subjects, according to the laws and constitution of England.

4. Some of the powers of government were too harsh for seasons of
tranquillity and regularity. But they were delegated under the impulse
of dangers from a savage enemy and with some regard to the probable
tumults of faction.

5. Religious liberty, it is true, was fettered by the style in which the
Christian religion was covered by public patronage to a particular sect,
the Church of England, which was chosen for exclusive favor.[6] But
without discussing the merits of this mode of discipline and worship,
the Reformation, the hatred of popery in England, and the estate of
public opinion there swallowed up the recollection of any possible
variety in religious sentiment which might afterwards exist.

(*ca.* 1541–91), a west-country gentleman and adventurer who had projected an unsuccessful expedition to the South Seas as early as 1574 (Quinn, *Roanoke Voyages*, I, 17–23, and
A. L. Rowse, *Sir Richard Grenville* [London, 1937]).

5. In June 1585 the Grenville expedition anchored at Wocokon, an inlet at the southern
end of an island in the Banks of Wocokon between Portsmouth Island and Ocracoke
Island (Quinn, *Roanoke Voyages*, I, 189).

6. The best general treatment of Anglicanism in Virginia is George MacLaren Brydon,
Virginia's Mother Church and the Political Conditions under Which It Grew (Richmond
and Philadelphia, 1947–52). See also Edward L. Goodwin, *The Colonial Church in Virginia*
(Milwaukee, 1927); Spencer Ervin, "The Establishment, Government, and Functioning of
the Church in Colonial Virginia," *Historical Magazine of the Protestant Episcopal Church,*
XXVI (1957), 65–107; and William Stevens Perry, "The Foundations of Church and State
in Virginia," *ibid.,* pp. 34–64.

But let the defects of this system be what they may, the ancient colonization recognized no principles of human happiness like these.

Grenville, however, and his party of adventurers penetrated but a small distance into the mainland and continued on the spot for too short a time to acquire extensive or various information concerning the country. In the summer of the year, he returned to England, leaving behind him one hundred and eight persons under the government of Ralph Lane, assisted by Amadas and others of distinction.[7] His representations animated the queen to adopt the colony, by the name of Virginia, in reference to her maiden character.

This detachment of colonists, after Grenville's departure, chose the island of Roanoke at the mouth of Albemarle Sound for their first habitation and reconnoitered the surrounding lands for sixty miles. They also explored the nation of the Chesapeakes on Elizabeth River, in the neighborhood of the present town of Norfolk. Their site was supposed, for temperature of climate, fertility of soil, and convenience to the sea, not to be excelled by any in the world. The eye of mercantile sagacity, had it then ranged over the Chesapeake Bay ("the mother of waters" in the Indian tongue) and all its tributary streams, must have inferred the most copious exports and the most enlarged views of trade.

The colony next extended its researches to the rivers Meherrin and Nottoway. The powerful nation of the Weopomcocke, holding all the country from Albemarle Sound to the Chesapeake, came and acknowledged subjection to England. Even thus early it was the felicity of Virginia to have no reason to fear a foreign enemy while her strength was undivided by faction. The period of Grenville's visit was most auspicious for observing the primitive aspect and circumstances of the colony and the history and condition of the aborigines. But the facts recorded are few and very imperfect; the literature of the colony deserves not the name; anxious care and terror were hourly impending over them; a mathematical and philosophical apparatus were wanting; habits of patient thought had not been learned, so that in the scraps of

7. Sir Ralph Lane (1530–1603) was a soldier of over twenty years' service, an expert on fortifications who had been sent to Ireland in 1583 to plan the defense of the southwest coast against Spanish incursions. A man of strong convictions, he quarreled with Grenville over the detailed conduct of affairs and sent strongly critical reports about him back to England. When Grenville left for England, Lane showed admirable abilities as a leader, but he had little idea of how to build up the commercial and agricultural activities on which the permanence of the colony would depend. The "others of distinction" besides Amadas were Capt. Edward Stafford, a competent soldier and Lane's closest advisor, and Thomas Hariot, the scientific expert of the expedition (Quinn, *Sir Walter Raleigh,* pp. 72, 74–77).

history snatched at that time the virgin soil and the natives found have been transmitted to us rather in fables and conjectures than in the garb of genuine philosophy. To an antiquarian, however, the Latin volume composed by Thomas Hariot, reputed to be an expert mathematician, deserves notice.[8] The particles gleaned from this summary establish unusual fertility and vegetation. The latitude, the exposure to a broad surface of water, the annual accumulations of vegetable decays, the small elevation above the sea, the remoteness of lofty mountains bespeak a splendid luxuriance.

But as we reserve for a different place the general body of our observations on the three kingdoms of nature, we will encroach upon them now only so far as they may be said to have been a part of the original history, being in fact intermixed with it, without prematurely borrrowing the result of subsequent discoveries.

Objects permanent in their nature and productions constant in succession may therefore be noted as of that day, if their species can clearly be identified.

Among minerals, the existence of gold, silver, lead, pit coal, limestone, salt, medicinal waters belong to Virginia.

Among animals, many are now adjudged to have been within the claims of Virginia, notwithstanding some contrary pretensions in Europe.

Among vegetables, tobacco, maize, round potatoes, cymlings, and squashes were found by the English on their arrival.

But the most striking novelty was the American man. Inquiries were undoubtedly made as soon as they could be understood whence a being in human shape, with his fitness, his situation, and with his color, originated. The answer would probably have been that he sprang out of the earth. To be derived from nations separated for many thousand miles by large waters was above their conception; that a practicable

8. Thomas Hariot (1560–1621), an Oxford friend of Richard Hakluyt the younger (1552–1616), was retained for his navigational and scientific knowledge. In 1588 he published *A Briefe and True Report of the New Found Land of Virginia,* a publication that has become the most famous relic of Raleigh's first colony. The work received wide distribution through a 1590 edition issued by Theodore De Bry of Frankfort, in which were included reproductions of twenty-one original water colors by John White, another member of the expedition, depicting a number of subjects ranging from scenes of Indian manners and customs to botany and entymology (Wesley Frank Craven, *The Southern Colonies in the Seventeenth Century, 1607–1689* [Baton Rouge, La., 1949], pp. 51–52). For an edition containing the work of both men, see *Hariot's Narrative of the First Plantation of Virginia in 1585 Printed in 1588 and 1590, Reprinted from the Edition of 1590 with De Bry's Engravings* (London, 1893).

passage existed between America and Asia, nearer the pole, could have
excited no other sentiment than the laughter of unbelief. As from
tradition, so from the analogy of language, nothing could have been
called to dissipate the difficulties which for centuries have been themes
of debate. But skepticism may still be challenged to claim any accession
of force to the contradiction of the Scriptures, which assert the same
ultimate origin of all the children of men. Little confidence is to be
placed in the explanation given of the principles of the Indian religion, so easy it was for zealous Christian missionaries to misappre-
hend the sense of a savage conveyed in a barbarous phrase and to
distort to their own prejudices and prepossessions crude and equivocal
opinions. But the reports on this head augment the host of refutation
to the calumny of those European naturalists who debase all the
energies of the American world. The belief of the Indians was supposed
to be in one chief god, who has existed from all eternity; in his creation
of the world by subordinate instruments; in the immortality of the
soul, which after death would be carried up to the tabernacle of the
gods to eternal happiness or hurled into Popogosso, a great pit in
the farthest parts of the earth where the sun sets in perpetual fire and
torment.

In the arts, the Indians had made but small advance toward comfort
or convenience.[9]

Although the spirit of observation could not be very active, it must
be confessed that an opportunity for better uses was thrown away.
Justice and philanthropy might have erased cruelty and robbery from
the catalogue of expedients for establishing the dominion of England.
It might have been fixed on the stable foundation of affection in the
hearts of a people as yet almost without a crime. Then the parade of an
ardor to diffuse Christianity might have been, and ought to have been,
exchanged for some of its best dictates, mercy, peace, and good will.

But Grenville, while he remained in Virginia, possessed power uncontrolled, which is too often insensible to better motives than the
short and nervous system of terror. For a silver cup having been stolen
from him by an Indian, the theft was expiated only by the burning of
the towns and the destruction of the corn of the nation. This greatly

9. For the Indians of Virginia, see Ben C. McCary, *Indians in Seventeenth-Century Virginia* (Williamsburg, Va., 1957); Philip L. Barbour, *The Three Worlds of Captain John Smith* (Boston, 1964); and Nancy Oestreich Lurie, "Indian Cultural Adjustment to European Civilization," in James Morton Smith, ed., *Seventeenth-Century America: Essays on Colonial History* (Chapel Hill, N.C., 1959), pp. 33–60.

disproportionate revenge was speedily communicated throughout the Indian confederacies and effaced the first impressions of attachment to the colony by an unrelenting hatred to every Englishman. The supplies which the Indians had furnished in the most afflicting emergencies were withheld. Confusion and broils ensued among the colonists from being straitened in provisions, and Lane was obliged to canton them into small parties in quest of roots, oysters, and other accidental sustenance; and fearing extremities of the most dangerous kind, he resolved to transport to England his enfeebled remnant of men whenever he should have the means of doing so.

It happened that Sir Francis Drake was about this time returning with an English fleet under his command from his successes against the Spaniards in the West Indies and had been instructed by Queen Elizabeth to visit the colony and to afford them any necessary succor.[10] On an interview, he yielded to their importunity by equipping for them a ship of a hundred tons with four hundred men, provisions for four months, and preparations for a voyage to England. After various disasters to this ship and to another which he had substituted in its place, Drake took the whole colony on board of his fleet and in July landed them in England, thus rendering abortive this essay toward an establishment in Virginia.

The abrupt departure of Lane and his company was very unfortunate. For in a few days afterwards, a ship of one hundred tons, which had been fitted out by Raleigh, whose parental attention to the colony had never abated, arrived laden with stores. But after a diligent and fruitless inquiry for them, that ship also returned to England. Had Raleigh, as an erroneous translation of Hariot's treatise affirms, visited on this voyage his favorite desert, his versatile genius and indefatigable industry would probably have left an assurance of the fact, by some benefit or improvement generated by his presence and by some animating notices of the colony.[11] Probably, too, he could not have been torn himself from the fostering of his beloved project under his own eye.

To fill the measure of adverse fortune, Sir Richard Grenville, whose

10. Sir Francis Drake (1540?–96) was the central figure in the intermittent privateering war between Spain and England in the Caribbean from 1570 until the formal commencement of hostilities in 1585.

11. This reference is to a translation from Latin to English of Hariot's *Briefe and True Report* which gave the mistaken impression that Raleigh had actually accompanied the relief expedition led by Sir Richard Grenville (Stith, *Virginia*, p. 22).

return had been little expected, came with three ships well provided, and hearing nothing of Lane, disembarked fifty men at the island of Roanoke and sailed again to England.

In the following year, three other ships were dispatched under the command of Captain John White, with a meager sketch of a regular government, of which he was the chief, aided by a Council of twelve.[12] Raleigh, in his charter of incorporation, styles them the governor and assistants of the city of Raleigh in Virginia. They were commanded to seat themselves on the waters of the Chesapeake; but this luminous scheme for commercial grandeur [13] was discarded from that perverseness in which little minds delight, when they can vilify a scheme not their own by exclaiming against it as being too visionary or incompatible with some paltry advantage more immediate in its enjoyment.

The only intelligence of those fifty men proves that they were destroyed. The only vestiges of them were some human bones. The houses were overgrown with woods; the fort was defaced. Irritated by the persuasion that they had been murdered by the Indians, White began to re-act the bloody system of Grenville, and in a thoughtless mode of executing it, put to death an Indian who was one of the best friends of the English. On this occasion, the fidelity of Manteo, another Indian,

12. It is difficult to establish with any certainty whether this John White, governor of the 1587 colony, is the same John White who drew sketches of Virginia in 1585. The best evidence in favor of the governor and the artist being the same man is that Richard Hakluyt, the editor of White's work, careful editor that he was, would have almost certainly made the distinction clear if they were different men, as he did in other cases (see Quinn, *Roanoke Voyages*, I, 40–47; William Patterson Cumming, "The Identity of John White Governor of Virginia and John White the Artist," *North Carolina Historical Review*, XV [1938], 197–203).

13. These references to Roanoke Island, orders to "seat themselves on the waters of the Chesapeake," and "this luminous scheme for commercial grandeur" evidence the strong influence of Richard Hakluyt (1552?–1616) on early efforts at colonization. In a treatise known as the *Discourse of Western Planting* (1584), Hakluyt argued that Cabot's discoveries gave England a prior claim to North America and therefore Englishmen were obliged to assume the duty of civilizing and Christianizing its inhabitants. His major political argument was that a blow could be inflicted on Spanish power in America by providing bases for striking at Spanish treasure and fishing fleets. But even more important for their effect on Raleigh's enterprise were Hakluyt's economic arguments, buttressed as they were by a mass of detail. Two suggestions stand out: the first was to establish a maritime base for action against the Spanish, and the second to build up an economy that would supply all kinds of Mediterranean fruits and their products, wine, oil, foodstuffs, dyes, drugs, timber, and ship's stores. These objectives required the establishment of a colony at a good harbor as far south as possible without exposure to constant attacks from Spanish Florida. This ambitious scheme, which even included a list of the type of settlers needed, fired Raleigh's imagination (Quinn, *Sir Walter Raleigh*, pp. 59–62).

warm with affection toward the deceased, was put to a severe trial.[14]
He, however, forgave the murder of his countryman, either from im-
puting it to a mistake or from the charm in the honor of a title. He was
baptized, by the order of Raleigh, and designated Lord of Roanoke
and Dasemunkepeuc.

Raleigh, having expended £40,000 on Virginia and exhausted his
fortune, had submitted to the mortification of assigning his letters
patent to Sir Thomas Smith and others; but amidst his distress, he
gave £100 for planting the Christian religion in Virginia.[15]

The enthusiasm which had buoyed up Raleigh in his perplexities
were never felt by his assignees. For a whole year they were torpid. At
the end of it, White sailed for Virginia with three ships. On their arrival, the crews were so much discomforted by their vain searches for
the lost colonists that they would scarcely seek even for the sign which
had been stipulated in case of removal under circumstances of distress
or otherwise.

For distress, the word Croatoan without a cross was agreed upon.
The appearance of this sign and of some of the property of the colony
induced White immediately to steer for the Indian town Croatoan,
near Cape Lookout. But a violent storm became a pretext for diverting
his course to the West Indies, where lay a tempting harvest in the

14. Manteo, who had returned to England with the Amadas-Barlow expedition, was
installed at Roanoke as Raleigh's representative (*ibid.*, p. 109).

15. Sir Thomas Smith (1558–1625) was London's greatest merchant prince, the first
president of the East India Company, and an important member of the Levant Company. A key figure in the Virginia Company, he served as treasurer, the leading position
in the organization, until he was replaced by Sir Edwin Sandys in 1618 and after that,
along with Robert Rich, the second earl of Warwick, as leader of the group seeking to
remove Sandys and his followers from power (Wesley Frank Craven, *Dissolution of the
Virginia Company; The Failure of a Colonial Experiment* [New York, 1932]). The others
were a group of nineteen men, mainly London merchants, who sponsored the colony
and formed a sort of holding company for the settlers. Besides Smith, the group included
such men as Richard Hakluyt the younger, William Saunderson, Raleigh's friend and a
businessman, Richard Wright, Smith's chief assistant in running trading companies, and
Thomas Hood, the mathematical lecturer. Under a deed of March 7, 1589, Raleigh reserved to himself and his heirs one-fifth of the profits of gold and silver found in the
colony established by the new corporation, for which he promised to try to obtain a royal
charter (Quinn, *Sir Walter Raleigh*, pp. 120–21). Raleigh's gift of £100 for planting the
Christian religion among the Indians illustrates the close connection between religious
and commercial motives characteristic of these early colonizers (see Perry Miller, "The
Religious Impulse in the Founding of Virginia," *William and Mary Quarterly*, 3d ser.,
V [1948], 492–522, and VI [1949], 24–41; Louis B. Wright, *Religion and Empire: The
Alliance between Piety and Commerce in English Expansion, 1558–1625* [Chapel Hill,
N.C., 1943]).

plunder of the Spaniards. Some of the ships being driven to the Western Islands, the fate of the former colonists ceased to stir an enquiry, and they were never more heard of.

A deep wound still awaited Virginia. Grenville, on whom Raleigh depended for support in founding Virginia, lost his life in a naval action with the Spaniards. Raleigh's exertions for the recovery of the wretched colonists, whom the new proprietors of his patent had sacrificed by desertion, were unremitted.

But the dangers and accidents had been so numerous and grievous that the colonizing of Virginia, perhaps of America under English auspices, would have evaporated, or long slept, had not Bartholomew Gosnold,[16] who was captivated with his voyage to New England, met with a kindred soul in Captain John Smith.

They were indeed kindred souls in ardor, courage, love of enterprise to extravagance. They were, too, alike practiced in the naval art, and from study and the hints of the new voyagers to America a case of difficulty in theory was to them rare.

From the interchange of ideas between these two men, the spark, which had been more than half extinguished for many years from the assignment of Raleigh's patent, was kindled into a flame. Gosnold's voyage had enabled him to speak upon the authority of facts; Smith's talent of combination produced plans for the revival of the former project comprehensive, perspicuous, and overawing.[17]

But these highly gifted associates lived in times when personal prowess and personal qualities were not in themselves adequate advocates for so grand and extraordinary an object, when without the support of the rich and influential every part of it must dwindle, and finally expire.

They therefore engaged by vigorous representations many of the nobility, some of the literati, and considerable numbers of men of energy to unite with them in an application for two charters in different quarters, not interfering with each other. Thus in the very bud of our

16. Bartholomew Gosnold (d. 1607) came from an ancient Suffolk family which had risen to local prominence through advantageous marriages. Though he seemed destined for the clergy, he took to the sea as a privateer and in 1602 acquired some fame by his voyage to New England (Philip L. Barbour and Warner F. Gookin, *Bartholomew Gosnold, Discoverer and Planter* [Hamden, Conn., 1963]).

17. Randolph's contention that Capt. John Smith (1580?–1631) was Gosnold's equal as a collaborator in the Virginia venture is hardly likely. It was Gosnold who probably first interested Smith in the project, and it was Gosnold who was the guiding force behind the venture (Barbour, *Captain John Smith*, pp. 78–93).

existence, we perceive political fellowship between the northern and southern parts of our Union. For ages may it be preserved inviolate!

King James, a part of whose character it was to be liberal when the cost was small, did not hesitate to grant on April 10, 1606, to Sir Thomas Gates and others, among whom were in fact, though unnamed, Smith and Gosnold, two charters, one for a southern colony anywhere in Virginia between the 36th and 41st degrees of north latitude and another for a northern colony anywhere at the distance of at least one hundred miles from the other between the 38th and 45th degrees of north latitude.[18]

In these, as in the letters patent to Gilbert, may be observed concessions from the crown, which notwithstanding a degree of real harshness, were pregnant with the means of being wrought into a system of safety, tranquillity, and prosperity by some relaxations in the rulers and some acquiescences in the colonies. A deference to the mother country and royal authority and a consciousness of colonial weakness may have begotten carelessness and inattention in the grantees. Nay, the criticisms which the increasing lights of society would now lavish upon the first of these charters would probably have been classed at that day among the theories and apprehensions of overzealous politicians.

Its most prominent features in either aspect of indulgence or severity are the following:

1. The limits of Virginia, or the first colony, are from the plantation first made upon the coast for fifty miles along that coast toward the west and southwest and toward the east and northeast, with all the islands at the distance of one hundred miles.

In the progress of the Revolution, after the supremacy which Virginia had borne in the affection of the other colonies at its commencement had grown stale, it was contended with great asperity by Thomas Paine, the author of the pamphlet called *Common Sense,* that the lines would never close upon any principle, or that if they should close upon any principle they would comprise but a very scanty territory.[19] How-

---

18. Sir Thomas Gates (d. 1621), a Devonshire soldier knighted for valor at Cádiz in 1596, would later be governor of Virginia. The southern group was led by Sir Thomas Smith and included Gates, Edward Maria Wingfield, and Sir George Somers. The four patentees of the northern group were Sir Humphrey Gilbert's son, Raleigh Gilbert; Lord Chief Justice Popham's nephew, George Popham, and his son-in-law Thomas Hanham; and William Parker, a Plymouth merchant and ex-privateer.

19. Thomas Paine (1737–1809), famous as the author of *Common Sense* (1776) and *The Crisis* (1776–83), published on Dec. 30, 1780, a pamphlet under the title *Public*

ever this might have been, upon strict geometrical measurement, the question is now forever at rest, and it would be futile to revive it.

2. A Council of thirteen persons was to be appointed in Virginia to govern and order all matters and causes within it according to such laws, ordinances, and instructions as should be given them from time to time by the king and should be reasonable. A like Council was to be established in England for the "superior" management and direction of all matters respecting the government of the colony.

3. Of the mines of gold and silver the king was to receive a fifth, and of those of copper a fifteenth part.

4. The Council were at liberty to coin money.

5. The grantees were allowed to engage adventurers and emigrants from the English dominions.

6. They were also allowed to adopt all the means of self-defense, to forbid traffic to strangers within their precincts except on the payment of 5 per cent on the value and to English subjects except on the payment of half that rate.

7. For seven years, the exportations to Virginia from England or Ireland were to be free from custom or subsidy.

8. The inhabitants and their children were to enjoy within any other of the royal dominions the same liberties as native subjects.

9. The tenure of lands was to be in common socage and not *in capite*.

Besides this charter, the king issued on November 20, 1606, several instructions which were considered as laws. Of them the most important were:

1. That the true word and service of God be preached, planted, and used according to the rites and doctrine of the Church of England.

2. That persons withdrawing any of the people from their allegiance should be sent to England, if cause so required, there to receive condign punishment.

3. That tumult, rebellion, conspiracy, mutiny, sedition, murder, incest, rape, and adultery should be punished with death, upon sentence of the Council in Virginia, founded on conviction by a jury.

4. That the Council should punish all other wrongs, trespasses,

---

Good. Paine had been hired by the Indiana Company to prepare the pamphlet, an attack upon Virginia's trans-Allegheny land claims. The land companies were concerned about Virginia's refusal to cede her land claims unless Congress voided all land company purchases (Merrill Jensen, *The Articles of Confederation: An Interpretation of the Social-Constitutional History of the American Revolution, 1774–1781* [Madison, Wis., 1963], p. 233). The pamphlet is printed in Philip Foner, ed., *The Complete Writings of Thomas Paine* (New York, 1945), II, 303–33.

and misdemeanors by reasonable corporal punishment, damages, or other satisfaction; all manner of excess through drunkenness or otherwise; and all loitering or vagrant persons as they should think fit.

5. That for five years the colony should trade in one stock, or two or three stocks at the most, and should bring all the fruits of their labor into magazines or storehouses, for the management of which a cape merchant and other agents should be appointed.

6. That every person should take the oath of obedience to the king.

7. That the Council might make laws, not touching life or member, which were to continue in force until altered by the king.

8. That the king might from time to time make laws and give orders at his pleasure, provided they were consonant to the laws of England or the equity thereof.[20]

These provisions and the powers connected with them having been swept away by the American Revolution afford now not much ground for political comment; even as they are historical facts they would not repay the trouble of dilating on and discussing them. A ray of freedom shines here and there. A mass of despotism darkens the scene in many more places. We ought not, however, to forget that it is the office of truth to own that no body of practical oppression is known to have grown out of these extravagances. Individuals may have had reason to complain of some sufferings, though their enormity was seldom, if ever, sufficient to agitate or inflame the people at large.

Two ships and a smaller vessel were prepared by the Council in England for the conveying of such persons to Virginia as were tempted by these new arrangements to immigrate thither.[21] Copious advice and strong powers were added. But neither advice nor powers could prevent the most serious dissensions among the passengers during their voyage. Captain John Smith, who had been nominated a member of the Council in Virginia, was seized and committed to close custody on suspicion of a plan for usurping the government and creating himself the king of Virginia.[22] There is no difficulty in conceiving how a man like Smith, who possessed every energy which any situation could call forth, might

20. Although Randolph did not reprint the charter or the king's instructions in their entirety, the complete texts of both documents were available to him in Stith, *Virginia*. For a recent reprint of both documents, see Samuel M. Bemiss, ed., *The Three Charters of the Virginia Company of London with Seven Related Documents, 1606–1621* (Williamsburg, Va., 1957), pp. 1–22.

21. On Dec. 20, 1606, the *Susan Constant, Godspeed,* and *Discovery* sailed for Virginia under the command of Capt. Christopher Newport.

22. The president of the Council was Edward Maria Wingfield, and the other members were Bartholomew Gosnold, Christopher Newport, John Ratcliffe, John Martin, and George Kendall.

seem in the eye of prejudice to labor to eclipse for base purposes others whose souls were too narrow to sympathize with the great exertions prompted by great necessities in great minds.

This peril from discord having been surmounted, another more alarming presented itself. The ships had overrun their reckoning for three days without the discovery of land. The crews were so much depressed by the circumstance that they became impatient to relinquish the voyage. But a tempest drove them into port. The first land which they discovered was called Cape Henry in honor of the Prince of Wales, and the northern cape was named Charles after the second son of King James.

On the north side of the river Powhatan, since called James River, a peninsula about forty miles from the mouth was chosen by the president and his Council for a settlement, to which they gave the name of Jamestown, in like honor to the king.

Why Jamestown was preferred to the position recommended by Raleigh, with the strength of a command, to be made on the Chesapeake Bay, is not explained in the archives of the colony.[23] This pretermission of the Chesapeake deprived Virginia of the mighty advantages which the early conjunction of a splendid metropolis with an emporium of such capacities as the bay offered must unavoidably have conferred.

It was fortunate for the colony that the calamities which afterwards befell it, from sickness, unwholesome food, an exposure to the weather, and from the want of adequate shelter, brought them to a sense of Smith's importance, otherwise he might have fallen a victim to the malice of his enemies. Nor was it without some happy effects that the departure of Captain Newport from the colony, the death even of Gosnold, the disgrace of Wingfield and Kendall, and the imbecility of Ratcliffe and Martin devolved the government on Smith as the only remaining efficient member of the Council. He pressed forward the

---

23. A more suitable site than Jamestown had been located by members of the party, but Wingfield, who tended to place orders above on-the-spot observations, preferred a location which seemed to fulfill better the requirements of the expedition's instructions (Barbour, *Captain John Smith,* pp. 124–25). Although the peninsula was low-lying marshy land, this disadvantage was offset by a view for some distance both up and down the river, anchorage close inshore for seagoing vessels, and protection from attacks by the natives (Craven, *Southern Colonies,* p. 66). The choice of sites for both Jamestown and Roanoke Island was heavily influenced by Richard Hakluyt's strong suggestion that they be planted "upon an Ilande in the mouth of some notable river, upon the poynte of the lande entering into the river, if no such Iland be, were to greate ende" (*ibid.,* p. 34).

buildings at Jamestown and by exhortation and his own example quickly erected lodgings for the accommodation of all *but himself*.[24]

His next care was to ensure a stock of provisions from the savages. It was a degree of heroism to think even of attempting this. From his ignorance of their languages, he was almost destitute of the means of intercourse with them, and he was at the head of a very feeble force. His men had neither clothing nor other necessaries. But with only five or six of these, he went in a shallop down James River to Kiskiack in the neighborhood of the present town of Hampton,[25] with a determination to procure a supply of food at any risk. On his first application to the natives [26] for corn, he perceived that he was condemned as a famished dependent and that simple overtures of barter and courtesy would be discarded. Having therefore discharged his muskets among them, he pushed his boat on shore, upon which they fled into the woods. The panic was however merely momentary, for fifty or sixty of them returned armed with clubs, targets, bows, and arrows; and carrying before them their tutelary idol Okee, made of skins stuffed with moss, painted and decorated with chains and copper, they attacked the English. But a second volley of shot, which struck down their god,

24. Capt. Christopher Newport (1565?–1617), a privateer in the service of Sir Francis Drake, was chosen admiral of the little fleet because of his experience in West Indian waters, his demonstrated knowledge of navigation, and his known courage in the face of attack (K. R. Andrews, "Christopher Newport of Limehouse, Mariner," *Wm. and Mary Qtly.*, 3d ser., XI [1954], 28–41). Gosnold, who was ill for some months, died on August 22, 1607, to the consternation of the entire colony. President Edward Maria Wingfield (1586–1612), an ex-soldier of noble blood, was accused by the other councilors of favoritism in the distribution of food and expelled from the Council (Wesley Frank Craven, "Edward Maria Wingfield," *Dictionary of American Biography*). George Kendall (d. 1607), probably a relative of the Sandys family and a political spy in the service of Lord Salisbury, was also removed from the Council and later convicted of conspiracy and shot (Philip L. Barbour, "Captain George Kendall: Mutineer or Intelligencer?," *Virginia Magazine of History and Biography*, LXX [1962], 297–313). Of John Ratcliffe (d. 1610), who signed his name among the incorporators as Captain John Sicklemore alias Ratcliffe, almost nothing is known before and after his sojourn in Virginia. He was elected president in place of Wingfield. John Martin (d. 1632?), whose father was three times lord mayor of London, had given up his law studies to become a seaman. He commanded the ship *Benjamin* in Drake's expedition to the American coast in 1585–86 (James C. Southall, "Captain John Martin of Brandon on the James," *ibid.*, LIV [1946], 21–67; and Samuel M. Bemiss, "John Martin, Ancient Adventurer," *ibid.*, LXV [1957], 209–21).

25. Randolph mistakenly placed the lands of the Kiskiack (Chiskiack) Indians along the James River. They were part of the Algonquian nation and in 1608 lived along the York River, primarily in York County.

26. The name of Indians in Virginia is derived from the same source with that which the Spaniards in their first visit had given to the natives more to the southward. Columbus was long impressed with the opinion that his course would terminate in the western hemisphere in some connection with the ancient Indies—RANDOLPH'S NOTE.

alarmed them into proposals of peace, which was concluded on condition that Smith should restore to them their Okee and that the Indians should bring him venison, turkeys, wild fowl, and bread.[27]

During Smith's absence on his expedition to Kiskiack, the malcontents at Jamestown were eager in machinations for the desertion or abandonment of the colony. *His* object was single. The Spaniards were never more greedy of gold than he was eager for acquiring a plenty of provisions. He had nearly arrived at the head of Chickahominy River, which empties itself into James River a few miles above Jamestown, when he suddenly plunged up to his middle in a marsh and in that situation was compelled to surrender to a troop of Indian bowmen. After warming his limbs, which had been benumbed from the unusual coldness of that year, and learning that the companions of his journey had been slain, he assumed an air of supernatural power, pretending to explain many astronomical phenomena of the sun and the stars and the figure of the earth. At the same time, he gave to Opechancanough, a principal Indian chief, a round ivory compass.[28] The playing of the fly and the needle under the glass, which prevented them from being touched, astonished him, but convinced him of none of Smith's obstruse and sublimated reasoning; hence the stratagem was frustrated. In less than an hour, Smith, after having been tied to a tree, was conducted to Orapaks, a royal hunting seat of Powhatan and an Indian town, where the women and children stared with wonder at a human creature so dissimilar from any other whom they had before seen. The Indians then performed with exultation and frightful orgies and yelling their war dance to inspire him with fear.

From this apparatus and a promise of life, liberty, and women, the Indians felt an assurance that Smith would assist them in a projected assault on Jamestown.[29] But he knew not fear; and being superior to seduction, he was also endowed with the faculty of drawing profit from events which apparently pointed to adversity only. He therefore represented the extreme danger and difficulty of the movement, de-

27. Is not a sense of religion among untutored savages a manifestation, even, when checked or perverted by superstition and ignorance, a proof, that in man a religious tendency is natural?—RANDOLPH'S NOTE.

28. Opechancanough (d. 1644), the half brother of Powhatan, later rose to leadership of Powhatan's confederacy after his brother's death in 1618.

29. Here is one of the few notes of levity in a work devoid of humor. Life, liberty, property, and/or the pursuit of happiness come immediately to mind, but apparently the thinking behind the phrase life, liberty, and women is that for the Indians women represented both property and happiness (in that order?). It is unlikely that Smith's captors

scribed the great guns, the other warlike engines, and the springing of mines in such a manner as greatly to intimidate them. Under pretense of sending to Jamestown for toys, he persuaded one of them to go thither with a note from him. At the foot of it he instructed the people there how to behave toward the messenger and to send what he wrote for. Everything was delivered or happened as Smith foretold, who was now thought to be able to divine through a paper which spoke.

Although these demonstrations suppressed the attempt on Jamestown, Smith was led in triumph about the country to the rivers Pamunkey, Mattaponi, Piankatank, Nominy, and Potomac. After escaping numberless efforts to murder him, he was practiced upon with howlings and ceremonies of conjuration and carried to Werowocomoco, a seat of the Emperor Powhatan on the north side of York River in Gloucester County, opposite to the mouth of Queen's Creek.

[Powhatan,[30] who was himself there, was tall, well proportioned, of a sour aspect and a strong and hardy constitution.[31] His hereditary dominions, and those gained by conquest, were bound on the south by

---

were planning to attack Jamestown at this time. Smith himself suggested that a messenger be sent to Jamestown; the Indians agreed because it gave them an opportunity to spy on the settlement (Barbour, *Captain John Smith*, p. 161).

30. It must be confessed that the portion of our history which is least capable of being rendered interesting is that from the present moment to the dissolution of the Company. But it is impossible to omit it altogether, as it contains many of the elements of our political history and perhaps of our political ability. In parts it is susceptible of profitable abridgment, in the whole, of improvement on the style of Stith, their most authentic recorder from the archives of the colony as far as the year 1624. Still, too frequent an innovation in that style, which so fully corresponds with those archives, might often improperly disguise the evidence of colonial talent. Believing therefore, that my objects may be combined, I shall until that year generally preserve Stith's language, without any undue anxiety for its coincidence with the rules of modern elegance, or even modern criticism—RANDOLPH'S NOTE.

William Stith (d. 1755), the retired president of the College of William and Mary, was the pioneer in the writing of a comprehensive, scholarly history covering the period from Virginia's settlement to the dissolution of the Virginia Company in 1624. His *History of the First Discovery and Settlement of Virginia*, first published in 1747 at Williamsburg and at London in 1753, relied heavily on Capt. John Smith's version of the dissolution of the Company although he believed Smith to be somewhat bitter at the Company's failure to reward him for his services. Stith also used the records of the Virginia Company made available to him through the assistance of William Byrd. In addition, he cited Sir John Randolph's collection of "publick papers, and capital Records" as having "been of no little use to me." Edmund Randolph relied upon the 1747 Williamsburg edition. Those passages copied verbatim, those shortened by editing, or those in which the language has been only slightly altered while retaining Stith's original intent will be identified by special brackets in the text.

31. For Powhatan (d. 1618), his lands, and his reign, see James Mooney, "The Powhatan Confederacy Past and Present," *American Anthropologist,* new ser., IX (1907), 129–52;

James River and its branches from the mouth to the falls. They
stretched across the country over the Potomac River to that of Patuxent
in Maryland; and nations on the Eastern Shore, that is the isthmus
between the bays of Chesapeake and Delaware, owned subjection to
him. He lived in a barbaric state of magnificence and luxury, attended
by a large bodyguard, uncontrolled in any gratification of appetite,
worshiped by his subjects as a demigod, and generally unrelenting in
cruelty, even to torture. When Smith appeared before him, he was
about sixty years of age, somewhat hoary, and acted with a savage
grandeur and majesty. He was sitting before a fire upon a wooden
throne, clothed in a large robe of raccoon skins and wearing on his head
a coronet of feathers. On each side sat a young woman of sixteen or
eighteen years of age, and behind him were rows of men and women
painted and adorned in their best manner. The queen of Appomattox
was ordered to bear to Smith water for the washing of his hands and a
bunch of feathers by way of a towel. He was then feasted; and at the
end of a long consultation, two large stones were laid down by him, and
his head was placed upon them, that his brains might be beaten out
with clubs.⌐ [32] The next moment would have terminated the existence
of a man who was the prop and ornament, the soul of the Virginian
enterprise, had not some sudden impulse of love or compassion taken
possession of the heart of Pocahontas, who was Powhatan's favorite
daughter, then not fourteen years of age. All her entreaties to her
father for mercy to Smith being ineffectual, she caught his head in her
arms and covered it by resting her own upon it. Parental affection was
by this scene as rapidly moved as her feelings had been at first in Smith's
favor at the view of his prostration to be sacrificed. Her ascendancy in
her father's breast was demonstrated when the obdurate savage in one
instant counterfeited an excuse for saving Smith's life by assigning to
him the duty of making hatchets for royal use and bells, beads, and
copper for Pocahantas. Let the moralist and poet vie with each other in
the description of this extraordinary reverse in the fate of this most
extraordinary man. Let the Virginia patriot rather ascribe the preservation of Smith to that chain of grand events of which the settlement
of Virginia was destined to be the foremost link, and which finally

McCary, *Indians in Seventeenth-Century Virginia*, pp. 3–13; and Frank G. Speck, *Chapters
on the Ethnology of the Powhatan Tribes of Virginia*, Indian Notes and Monographs, I,
No. 5, Heye Foundation (New York, 1928).
    32. Stith, *Virginia*, pp. 53–55.

issued in the birth of our American Republic. Smith acquired in his captivity an extensive knowledge of the country of the Indian tribes and their languages. He returned under an escort to Jamestown, where he did not neglect the opportunity of increasing his influence with the Indians who accompanied him by further indications of the fatal force of gunpowder.[33]

Their confidence in him was such that they supplied him with provisions in great profusion and entrusted him with the sale of such as he did not want himself. Under his management a proper ratio would have been maintained between the baubles or ironmongery imported and the productions of the Indians but for an indiscreet license from Captain Newport (acting under authority from England) for a general trade between England and them.[34] Smith lost no time in exploring the bay of Chesapeake and its streams. But at Stingray Island on the Eastern Shore he narrowly avoided death from the sting of a poisonous fish. After examining every place on the bay and James River he perceived at Jamestown that confusions and disorders had prevailed there which he alone could quell. The old clamor against the want of supplies from England had subsided, partly from the provident care of Smith and partly from the awakened attention of the Council and Company in England. [But with the sensations which former habits of discontent had left behind, a hatred of Bancroft, the new archbishop of Canter-

33. Randolph's narrative of Smith's adventures with Powhatan and his daughter Pocahontas came either directly from Smith's *The Generall Historie of Virginia* (1624) or indirectly by way of Stith, who relied heavily on the captain's account. In Randolph's day Smith's *Historie* was accepted as accurate, but since the publication of Henry Adams's "Captain John Smith: Sometime Governour in Virginia, and Admirall of New England" in the *North American Review*, Jan. 1867, the captain's accounts of his rescue by Pocahontas and his exploits in the Mediterranean, Hungary, Turkey, and Russia have served to discredit him. However, recent scholarship, by carefully comparing Smith's accounts with newly discovered documentary evidence, has succeeded in clearing away much of the confusion surrounding his career (Laura P. Striker and Bradford Smith, "The Rehabilitation of Captain John Smith," *Journal of Southern History*, XXVIII [1962], 474–81). For a guide to the revisionist literature, see John Lankford, ed., *Captain John Smith's America* (New York, 1967). According to Richard Morton, this "incident is in keeping with Indian custom at that time and is the most reasonable explanation of Powhatan's treatment of Smith and later friendship for the English, which brought peace as long as Smith remained in Virginia" (*Colonial Virginia* [Chapel Hill, N.C., 1960], I, 13).

34. Randolph was probably referring to Captain Newport's dissipation of the colony's bartering power with the Indians in an effort to satisfy the Company's urgings to find gold. Unfortunately, this occurred during the winter of 1608 when the colony was in dire need of provisions, their own meager supplies having been destroyed by a fire (Barbour, *Captain John Smith*, p. 175).

bury, was now associated.[35] His notions were lofty in relation to the
government both of church and state, and he was therefore a strenuous
advocate for absolute power in the king and for a general conformity to
the Church of England. Many of the Puritans had been driven by his
ecclesiastical tyranny to resolve upon fleeing to Virginia. But being
disturbed at the numbers reported to be prepared to depart, the king,
on Bancroft's suggestion, prohibited them by proclamation.] [36] This
was the more readily done, as the soul of that prince never glowed with
one sentiment of religious liberty, and that sect was no less obnoxious
to him than to the prelate. No man can venture to pronounce how long
the ruin of the Stuart family might have been retarded, or even
whether it might not have been averted, had not these oppressed subjects then, and Cromwell and some of his partisans afterwards, been
confined by James to England, where their vehemence grew every day
more and more impetuous instead of being permitted to waste itself in
empty complaints at the distance of three thousand miles from home.

This was an era of prosperity to the colony, for Captain Smith by a
formal election of the Council and at the special instance of the colony
was elevated to the office of president. He had repeatedly been urged
to accept it; but with that modesty which almost always mixes with
intrinsic worth, he persisted in refusing it until he saw that it might be
rendered particularly subservient to the public good.[37] No sooner was
he inducted into the office than he discontinued the building of an
extravagant and ostentatious palace which his predecessor had begun,
[repaired the church, gave a new covering to the storehouse, finished
a magazine for receiving the importations from England, reduced the
irregular fort into form, renewed the watch, trained the troops, exercised the whole company in arms, and kept alive in the minds of the
Indians fear or respect for the colony which restrained their incursions.

[The collection of corn was the constant and primary object of his
solicitude, and no chance for any solid benefit eluded his vigilance and
activity. But Captain Newport, a frivolous, idle, interested man, timid
in difficulties and swollen with conceit, thwarted all his endeavors. He

35. Richard Bancroft (1544–1610), archbishop of Canterbury, 1604–10.
36. Stith, *Virginia*, p. 76.
37. Here is an example of Randolph departing from Stith to draw his own conclusions.
Stith simply states that "on the 10th of September [1608], . . . Captain Smith was invested
with the Government; which, till then, he would by no Means accept, tho' often importuned to it" (p. 76). Randolph interpreted Smith's refusals as evidence of exceptional
moral character. Clearly Randolph has placed Smith in a far better light than Stith
intended.

had been commanded by the Council and Company in England not to return without a lump of gold, or full intelligence of the South Sea in its supposed connection with Virginia through the country of the Monacan Indians above the falls of James River,[38] or one of the adventurers who had been sent out by Raleigh and of all of whom even conjecture was silent at any distance from Jamestown.

[Newport also brought with him for Powhatan a crown, a basin and ewer, a bed, bedstead, and other costly novelties, with orders for the ceremony of his coronation.

[Captain Smith, though vexed with the interruptions which Newport's whims gave to business of utility and absolute necessity, showed his superiority to the motive of envy by zealously cooperating with him in all the measures which had been adopted by the Council, almost under Newport's own dictating. Smith therefore undertook to deliver a message to Powhatan from Newport inviting him to Jamestown, there to receive the honors and presents allotted to him and to enter into concert for some grand revenge on the Monacans.][39]

A just sense of personal dignity is the natural growth of the soil of independence. Powhatan's reply was [that if Newport's king had sent him any presents, he also was a king and that was his land; that he would stay eight days to receive them; that Newport ought to come to him; that for him to go to the fort was too foolish a bait; that as to the Monacans, he could revenge his own wrongs; and that concerning salt water beyond the mountains, the stories of his people were unfounded. He then drew the figure of those regions upon the ground.][40]

The dilemma to which this coldness of Powhatan to the insignia of European monarchy reduced Newport was removed by the transportation of them by water to Werowocomoco, and on an appointed day, Powhatan attended for his coronation. But it was not easy to convince him that the presents would not hurt him. To a man with Smith's pursuit of substance in all things, the scruples of Powhatan argued the ridiculousness of the subject. The apparel, and particularly a scarlet cloak, were put upon Powhatan, not without a degree of force. Comprehending neither the meaning of a crown nor the bending of

38. The Monacan Indians, part of the Siouan tribes, were a confederacy living along the James River from the vicinity of the falls west to the Blue Ridge (James Mooney, "Siouan Tribes of the East," *Bureau of American Ethnology*, Bulletin 22 [1895]).

39. Stith, *Virginia*, pp. 76–78. The Monacans were traditional enemies of Powhatan. Smith suspected them of killing an Englishman.

40. *Ibid.*, p. 78.

the knee when it was to be placed on his head, he fatigued by resistance the persons who were the chief agents in the farce. At length, his shoulders being compressed by some of the English, he stooped a little; and three of them, who stood with the crown in their hands, placed it upon his head. This was announced to the crews of the boats by the firing of a pistol. In their turn they discharged volleys of musketry which at first startled the king, but he immediately recollected himself and testified his kindness for Newport by presenting to him his old shoes and mantle and a heap of ears of corn containing seven or eight bushels. This transaction forms no part of legitimate history, except as it was the opinion of the Stuart family that no occasion ought to be omitted for the diffusion of monarchical pomp.

Newport then with a hundred and twenty select men went to the country of the Monacans but discovered neither mines nor access to the South Sea. In the meantime the affairs of the colony had been deranged from Smith's absence, and particularly by the theft of their axes, hoes, powder, shot, and other necessaries. To save the colony from starving, he extorted a supply of corn from the Chickahominies.[41] These miscarriages in the expectation of the Company drew from them [a very angry letter to Smith, as president, complaining of the vain hopes with which they had been fed; of the very small fulfillment; and of the faction and silly project for dividing the country, concerning which the late president had written to the chief minister of state. They threatened that unless the charge of the whole of the present voyage to Virginia, amounting to £2,000, were defrayed by remittances in the ship sent, the colonists should be deserted and left as banished men. Smith more rationally dispatched the ship with samples of pitch, tar, glass, frankincense, and soap, and with wainscotting and clapboards, and two barrels of some kind of ore. To the letter his answer was plain and soldierlike. He enclosed a map of the bay and rivers, with the delineation of the countries upon their borders and of the nations who occupied them. This map ought to have confounded his enemies. It was executed with exactness and opened a great range of territory, over which he must have traveled with peril at every step.] [42]

It was not the smallest among Captain Smith's grievances that he

41. The Chickahominy tribe, part of the Algonquian nation, lived along the Chickahominy River in James City, Charles City, and New Kent counties.

42. *Ibid.*, pp. 82–83. The Virginia map is reproduced in Edward Arber and A. G. Bradley, eds., *Travels and Works of Captain John Smith* (Edinburgh, 1910), II, 384; and Ben C. McCary, *John Smith's Map of Virginia* (Williamsburg, Va., 1957).

was compelled by a scarcity of corn to stipulate with Powhatan as compensation for a shipload of it to build him a house, furnish him with a grindstone, a cock, and a hew, some copper and beads, and *fifty swords and muskets*. The power of imitating deadly weapons was not to be immediately apprehended, but the precedent of combining them with the consideration to be paid for the support of life must have been wrung from Smith by dire want. In truth the colony could never depend for peace or quiet on the warmest professions of Powhatan. His talent of insinuation illustrates his character. He once addressed Smith to this effect: ["I have some doubts about the reason of your coming hither; I am informed from many quarters that you come not to trade, but to invade my people and to possess my country. This makes me less ready to relieve you and frightens my people from bringing in their corn; and therefore to ease them of that fear, leave your arms aboard your vessels, since they are useless here where we are *all friends* and forever Powhatan's." He then with a vanity usual in persons who affect to be thought very old told Smith that he had himself seen the death of all his people thrice, and that not one of three generations was then living except himself; that he was now grown old and must die soon; that the succession to the crown would descend in order to his brothers and then to his sisters and their two daughters. He wished that their experience was equal to his, and that Smith's love to them might be no less than his to Smith. Powhatan next asked Smith why he should take that by force which he might have by love? Why he should destroy them who accommodated him with food? And what he could get by war, for they could hide their provisions and flee into the woods, and then he must perish from famine occasioned by wrongs to his friends. Powhatan desired to know the cause of his jealousy, since he saw *his* subjects unarmed and willing to supply his wants, if he would come in a friendly manner and not with swords and guns as if to invade an enemy; that he himself (Powhatan) was not so simple as not to know that it was better to eat good meat, lie well, and sleep quietly with his women and children, to laugh and be merry with the English, and being their friends to have copper, hatchets, and whatever else he wanted than to leave all, lie cold in the woods, feed upon acorns and roots and such trash, and be so hunted that he could not eat or sleep, that his tired men must watch, and if anything did but break, all would be crying out, here comes Captain Smith. In a miserable manner he was thus ending his miserable life, which might soon be Captain Smith's fate through his rashness and unadvisedness. He therefore earnestly exhorted Smith to peaceable counsels and above all insisted that the guns and swords, the grand cause of the jealousy and uneasiness of the Indians, should be removed and sent away.

[To this crafty language Captain Smith replied that it was the fashion of the English always to bear their arms, like their clothes, and that they would by no means part with them; that Powhatan's people came frequently to Jamestown and were entertained with their bows and arrows, without any exception; that if the English had intended him (Powhatan) any harm, they would long since have effected it, as was evident to him and all the world, especially considering the superiority of their arms; that although revenge was always in their power, yet from an inclination to mercy and friendship, they passed over the daily violation of the peace by Powhatan's people; and as to hiding his provisions and fleeing into the woods, that the colony should not starve, as he imagined, for they had a rule to find things hidden.

[Powhatan, perceiving that Smith was inflexible and would not dismiss his guard nor disarm them, addressed him with a sigh: "Captain Smith, I never used any werowance as kindly as yourself, yet from you I receive the least kindness of any. Captain Newport gave me swords, copper, clothes, or whatever else I desired, always accepting what I offered him, and would send away his guns when I requested him. No one refuses to sit at my feet or do what I demand, but you only. Of you I can have nothing but what you value not, and yet you will have what you please. Captain Newport you call father, and so you call me; but I see that in spite of both of us you will do what you will, and we must both study to humor and content you. If you intend as friendly as you say, send away your arms. For you see that my undesigning simplicity causes me thus nakedly to expose and to forget myself."] [43]

[Smith, knowing that Powhatan trifled only to deceive him, ordered men on shore to surprise him, but promised to appear without arms the next day. Powhatan endeavored to lull him by fallacious discourse with two or three of his women until he should secretly run off and direct the house to be surrounded with Indians. Upon which Smith rushed out with his pistol, sword, and target and made his way through them to his boat. Powhatan, from his anxiety to heal Smith's dissatisfaction with him, sent an ancient orator, with a great bracelet and

43. Stith, *Virginia*, pp. 86–88.

chain of pearl, apologizing for him upon the ground of his fears. Notwithstanding this Powhatan was meditating to massacre Smith in the night, he being detained by the ebbing of the tide.] [44] But Pocahontas, actuated by the same principle which had before rescued Smith from death, stole alone to him through the dark woods and warned him of his danger. Her magnanimity was conspicuous in refusing to receive those little presents with which she had been generally delighted. To her disinterestedness and frankness, the dissimulation and treachery of her father were a painful contrast. Upon Smith's return to Pamunkey [45] the same frauds were repeated upon him in similar snares by Opechancanough, the brother of Powhatan. Smith extricated himself from them with only sixteen men, dragged him by the hair from the presence and protection of three hundred Indians, and obtained everything of which he stood in need. Having tried his personal prowess in a contest with several Indian chiefs, Smith established a character too overawing to be insulted or to be deprecated in his wrath. He was therefore solicited to peace by the Indian tribes. Hence, Smith being delivered from all apprehension of hostility, as he had been from all convulsion by faction, the business of the colony was renewed with alacrity and success.

[Considerable quantities of tar, pitch, and soap ashes were made; houses were built; a well was sunk; blowing of glass was begun; nets and weirs for the taking of fish were constructed; blockhouses were erected to protect the colony from surprise by the Indians; domestic animals were multiplied; Hog Island was set apart for the raising of swine. The internal administration of the government displayed new vigor by the circumstance of Smith being in the possession of two voices in the Council and now alone in power, Martin the assistant being dead. The effect was immediately visible. The Indians every day brought into Jamestown wild meats of various sorts, and Powhatan was no longer backward in his exchanges of corn. Yet the defect in agriculture and the ignorance in preserving corn against rottenness and the rats (a species of vermin which had been lately imported from England) demanded the utmost care from Smith. But these flattering appearances were not permanent, for the malcontents at

44. *Ibid.*, p. 89.
45. The Pamunkey were a large tribe of the Algonquian nation living on the neck of land in King William County formed by the confluence of the Pamunkey and the Mattaponi rivers (Maurice A. Mook, "The Anthropological Position of Indians of Tidewater Virginia," *Wm. and Mary Qtly.*, 2d ser., XXIII [1943], 27–40).

Jamestown again interrupted the public tranquillity with conspiracies and risings, so as to require him to continue to be indefatigable and firm.] [46]

And yet Virginia may be said to have survived the earliest and most imminent of her dangers—the terrors of the Indians, the early factions at Jamestown for which even the humility in the objects of ambition afforded adequate food, the unhealthiness of the Virgin[ia] climate to European adventurers, and the abomination of idleness. Of reforms or improvements in these particulars Smith was the author, for the benefit of a new order of power, which he plainly foresaw to be approaching and which was shortly to wrest from him into other hands a command which a man of less patriotism and moderation than his own would sometimes shamefully purchase at any expense of principle. He labored sincerely and decisively for those who were to supersede his entire dominion.

Sufficient time had not elapsed for the experience of the operation of the charter of April 10, 1606, before King James was again importuned to grant a new one. Another was accordingly issued on May 23, 1609, with more ample powers and privileges. These were vast, as they lessened neither his purse nor his prerogative. The petitions of a conspicuous nobility, of a host of knights, and of other respectable individuals were therefore easily successful.[47] Judging from the numbers we may conclude that the Virginia Company had been able to silence the first adventurers, whose rage for the precious metals had alone prompted them into the "Action" (as the scheme of colonizing Virginia was then called), and to counteract the unfavorable representations of Captain Newport concerning the management of it.

In this second charter, the king recognizes as its basis and consideration the exertions of the emigrants who were the first settlers, so that Virginia might always oppose this admission to any other title derived from the crown; and the argument of a valuable consideration has been often urged with great weight in the disputes of the colony with

46. Stith, *Virginia*, p. 97. In August 1609 Gabriel Archer, John Ratcliffe, and John Martin, all hostile to Smith, returned to the colony.

47. Randolph was in error when he stated that the crown acquired "more ample powers and privileges" in the new charter. The royal Council of 1606 was abolished, and the entire control of the colony was placed in the hands of the Council of the Company and its head, the treasurer. Unlike the charter of 1606, that of 1609 created a joint-stock company. Besides 56 companies of the city of London there were also 659 individuals, including some knights but also a large number of professional men, merchants, artisans, and others (Morton, *Colonial Virginia*, I, 20). For a reprint of the charter, see Bemiss, *Three Charters of Virginia Company*, pp. 27–54.

the king, the governors of Virginia, and the Parliament of England.

It cannot be ascertained at present whether any individual of the grantees of this charter repaired to Virginia, as to an asylum for an opinion on government or religion which he could not enjoy without molestation at home. In fact avarice was generally the impulse, but it was fortunately capable of diversion from fictitious to real wealth, to agriculture, which can never mislead and steadily pursued will always aggrandize a people who are masters of a kind soil and climate.

The erection of the grantees into a body corporate was an important bulwark against encroachment, whether the facility of uniting counsels or speaking with emphasis and authority under oppression be considered.

It was a seed too of future importance, certainly of magnificence, to extend the territory for four hundred miles from the point of land called Cape or Point Comfort along the seacoast and with that breadth to the South Sea.[48] Without population, territory could not at once be power. But a fruitful and extensive dominion will necessarily attract cultivators who cannot be inactive in contriving comfort and happiness.

By imposing on the land the tenure of free and common socage instead of that *in capite,* a "slavery complicated and extensive was avoided. In England palliations had from time to time been applied by successive acts of Parliament which assuaged some temporary grievances of tenure, and James I had consented for a certain equivalent to abolish all the feudal severities, but the plan proceeded not into execution." [49] By this charter he anticipated the statute of Charles II, which destroyed at one blow military tenures and all their heavy appendages. This was a greater acquisition to the civil property of that

48. The geographical limits fixed by the new charter extended to an area along the coast two hundred miles northward from Point Comfort, an equal distance to the south, inland "from Sea to Sea, west and Northwest," and one hundred miles at sea on "both Seas."

49. These lines probably came from *Commentaries on the Laws of England* by Sir William Blackstone, professor of law at Oxford from 1758 to 1766. A four-volume work published between 1765 and 1769, it achieved wide distribution and influence in America. Randolph may well have used an edition by his fellow Virginian St. George Tucker under the title *Blackstone's Commentaries: With Notes of Reference, to the Constitution and Laws of the Federal Government of the United States and of the Commonwealth of Virginia* (Philadelphia, 1803). Like most historians of the revolutionary generation, Randolph attached great significance to the change from communal to private ownership of land. For example, Abiel Holmes observed that a "humiliating tenure, unworthy of freemen, was thus changed into that of common soccage, and with this advantageous alteration, freedom first rooted in colonial soil" (*American Annals* [Cambridge, Mass., 1805], I, 186).

kingdom than even Magna Carta itself, since that only pruned the luxuriance which had grown out of those tenures and nourished the principal stock. The liberality so obviously a part of the policy of an infant country, of unfettering the laws of alienage, was but faintly conceived by those who in this charter ought to have reflected what a clog upon the prosperity of Virginia the restraining of grants of lands to subjects of England natural born or denizens must prove.

Robertson supposes that two of the articles in this and the preceding charter were as unfavorable to the rights of the colony as others are to the interest of the parent state. "By placing the legislative and executive powers in a Council nominated by the crown and guided by its instructions, every person settling in America," according to him, "seems to be bereaved of the noble privilege of a freeman; by the unlimited permission of trade with foreigners, the parent state is deprived of the exclusive commerce which has been deemed the chief advantage resulting from the establishment of colonies." An apology for these oversights is from his own pen in these words:

But in the infancy of colonization and without the guidance of observation or experience, the ideas of men with respect to the mode of forming new settlements were not fully unfolded or properly arranged. At a period when they could not foresee the future grandeur and importance of the communities which they were about to call into existence, they were ill qualified to concert the best plan for governing them. Besides, the English of that age, accustomed to the high prerogative and arbitrary rule of their monarchs, were not animated with such liberal sentiments concerning either their own personal or political rights as have become familiar in the more mature and improved state of their constitution.[50]

To this it may be added that such of the first explorers of the wilderness as might have been the victims of any tyranny exercised by the Council in England were probably from their education unfitted to indulge in remote speculations and from the hardihood of their character indisposed to apprehend danger. Perhaps, too, they relied upon the birthright of English subjects. Had they or the grantees of the first charter refused to accept the letters patent and called for amendment in these respects, they would have been charged (as is the hackneyed practice in such cases) with entertaining unreasonable suspicions of men having no interest in usurpation and at the same time always within the power of the meetings of the great body of adventurers who were themselves under the protection of a gracious sovereign.

50. Robertson, *History of America*, p. 403.

Robertson in his character of statesman might have stigmatized a dread of evil to the commerce of the parent state as little less in those days than lese majesty, in supposing that no prerogative remained for correcting a disadvantageous intercourse with foreigners. It was real policy to see what might probably be done in the course of commerce before limits should be prescribed to it.

An exemption from taxes, except of 5 per cent on merchandise imported or exported for fifteen years, was a well-judged bounty to the industry of the colony.

All statutes, ordinances, and proceedings were required to be as near as conveniently might be to the laws, statutes, and policy of the realm of England, so that a colonist felt himself as secure, in words at least, as a native of England could be, and demanded no more.

The power to promulgate martial law was an engine of horror which was perhaps sheltered from animadversion and objection by keeping it within the pale of similar authority in England, though even there it was too gigantic and inexorable for a free government in time of peace.

Every construction and interpretation of the charter was directed to be the most ample and beneficial for the colony.

None were permitted to pass in any voyage to be made to Virginia but such as should have taken the oath of supremacy. This was an immediate exclusion of Roman Catholics; and although no other sect was then in view of the king's reprobation, yet it abolished the principal competition existing with the Church of England and thereby gave to her in Virginia the cornerstone of an establishment.

To this and the preceding charter, as we pass through the gradations of political character in Virginia, further observations may be appropriate.

A sense of rising dignity in the colony may be presumed from the superb offices which the Council in England instituted under this new charter. Lord De la Warr, formerly Sir Francis West, was appointed captain general of Virginia; Sir Thomas Gates, lieutenant general; Sir George Somers, admiral; Captain Newport, vice admiral; Sir Thomas Dale, high marshal; Sir Ferdinando Wainman, general of the horse.[51]

51. Lord De la Warr (1577–1618), a leading adventurer and member of the Company's Council, was appointed governor under the governmental reorganization authorized by the charter of 1609. The unfortunate experiment with joint command had caused so much grief that it was abandoned in favor of an absolute governor with authority to override his Council and remove any officer in the colony. There were few limitations on his power

These and other offices were ordained to be held for life. From the assumption of this pomp, the world would not have been disappointed if habit should have overflowed the colony with other titles equal in ostentation and equally destitute of utility with some of these, and even if tenure for life had been oftener repeated for the gratification of favorites in the erection of new offices. But the sequel has falsified a prospective view of this kind, and Virginia will be found in all her posts and employments to have been as simple as any colony or province the original auspices of which may have been of even less splendor.

Gates, Somers, and Newport sailed for Virginia with nine ships and five hundred emigrants. In that commanded by Somers were embarked those three personages and the essential part of the stores for the fleet; she was separated by a hurricane as far as to the island of Bermuda, where she foundered and perished. The rest, with the exception of a small vessel, arrived safely in Virginia with their passengers, of whom many were of high birth.[52] Among them were some who during the voyage infused such jealousies and prejudices against Captain Smith, then president, that a general hatred was implanted against him in the breast of those who were on board before they had seen him. But the affection of his soldiers and his integrity and prudence soon dissipated the malice of faction, which seemed to be a radical evil, and almost natural, since it sprang upon this first settlement of a wilderness.[53] But many of the Company were poor gentlemen, and

---

except that he must abide by his instructions, a provision understood to mean that the colonists were to enjoy, as guaranteed by both charters, "all Liberties, Franchizes, and Immunities" belonging to an English subject (Craven, *Southern Colonies*, p. 91). For De la Warr, see Isabel M. Calder, "Thomas West, Baron De La Warr," *DAB*. Sir George Somers (1554–1610) was a naval commander of considerable experience who had made a victorious voyage to the West Indies in 1596, had been knighted in 1603, and had held a seat in Parliament from 1604 to 1610 (Sidney Lee, "Sir George Somers," *DAB*). Sir Thomas Dale (d. 1610) had served first in the Netherlands in 1588 and then in 1595 proceeded to Scotland in the retinue of Prince Henry, remaining for some years before returning to the Netherlands about 1603. He continued to serve there off and on until 1611 when he entered the service of the Virginia Company (Darrett B. Rutman, "The Historian and the Marshal, a Note on the Background of Sir Thomas Dale," *Va. Mag. of Hist. and Biog.*, LXVIII [1960], pp. 284–94). Sir Ferdinando Wainman, also spelled Weynman, was the son of Jane West, an aunt of the third Lord De la Warr. He served in Virginia as master of the ordinance.

52. The fleet left England in May 1609 but ran into a hurricane in which 32 men were blown overboard, one ship was lost, and the *Sea Venture* wrecked on one of the Bermuda islands. The surviving seven ships finally landed at Jamestown in August.

53. Among the new arrivals were three former councilors, Captains Ratcliffe, Martin, and Archer, who, according to Smith, attempted to depose him from the presidency.

others of broken fortune were removed thither by their friends from the theater of their ancient licentiousness.

A censure like this, expressed with less reserve by Mr. Stith, a native historian of Virginia, conjoined with another hint from him of a like cast, probably misled the candid and philosophic mind of Dr. Adam Smith in the first edition of his theory of moral sentiments to trace the population of a very large district of America to progenitors who were convicted of criminal offenses. When that work was ushered into public, Dr. Arthur Lee, a Virginian who was in England for his education, is said to have personally convinced Dr. Smith of his mistake, and in the second edition, this national stain, it is believed, was expunged.[54] If there be any whose pride in remote ancestry will stimulate them to unravel a perplexed pedigree up to the persons whose names are enrolled in the charter, Stith has collected them. In the publication of that document in our appendix,[55] those names are omitted as a lumber which virtue and talents have long trampled underfoot by bringing the test of family honor nearer to the home and merit of the individual Virginia citizen.

I might probably have deduced Dr. Smith's error from the following passage in Stith: ⌜But besides these reputable people, to be transported at the Company's charge, the treasurer and Council received a letter from His Majesty commanding them forthwith to send away to Virginia a hundred dissolute persons, which Sir Edward Zouch, the knight marshal, would deliver to them in obedience to His Majesty's command.[56] The treasurer was told that the king's command was urgent and admitted no delay, and that fifty, at least, must with all speed be shipped off, notwithstanding his just representa-

54. Adam Smith (1723–90), famous as the author of the *Wealth of Nations* (1776), published his *Theory of Moral Sentiments* in 1759. Dr. Arthur Lee (1740–92), educated at Eton and the University of Edinburgh, where he received his M.D. degree in 1764, practiced medicine in Williamsburg from 1766 to 1768 and then returned to London to study law. In 1775 he was admitted to the bar. Deeply involved in English politics, he was a supporter of John Wilkes and the author of a number of political tracts, among them *Monitor's Letters* and *Junius Americanus*. In 1770 he was appointed London agent for the Massachusetts Bay Colony. During the Revolutionary War he represented the United States in France and Spain. In Virginia politics he and Randolph were usually in opposition.

55. The appendix was either never completed or lost with other portions of the original manuscript.

56. Sir Edward Zouch (1556–1625) was a member of the North Virginia Company and in 1620 became a member of the New England Council. His appointment as knight marshal of the King's household came in 1618.

tions how great inconveniency and expense would accrue to the
Company; that they could not well go in less than four ships, lest being
so many together they should mutiny and run away with the vessel;
that those four ships, to be got thus suddenly without taking advantage
of the vessels trading to America, would not stand the Company in
less than £4,000; and that, notwithstanding all, ships were not to be
procured so speedily at that time of the year (November). Yet nothing
which the treasurer could allege giving satisfaction, the Company were
obliged to appoint a committee of select merchants for obtaining shipping with all possible speed, and by good fortune for the additional
premium of £100, they procured a large ship to carry them off.

[Those who arc acquainted with British history and know how
severe a hand this king sometimes carried, even over his Parliaments,
will not be surprised to find him thus unmercifully insulting a private
company and loading them against all law with the maintenance and
extraordinary expense of transporting such persons as he thought
proper to banish, and that perhaps without any colorable pretext or
sufficient warrant of law at that time. I cannot, says Stith, but remark
how early that custom arose of transporting loose and dissolute persons
to Virginia, as a place of punishment and disgrace, which although
originally designed for the advancement and increase of the colony yet
has certainly proved a great prejudice and hindrance to its growth. For
it has laid one of the finest countries in British America under the unjust scandal of being a mere Hell upon earth, another Siberia, and only
fit for the reception of malefactors and the vilest of the people; so that
few people, at least few large bodies of men, have been induced
willingly to transport themselves to such a place; and our younger
sisters, the northern colonies, have accordingly profited thereby, for
this is one cause that they have outstripped us so much more in the
number of their inhabitants and in the goodness and frequency of their
cities and towns.] [57] There was no risk of contamination from a matri-
monial alliance of convicts with decent families. Their disabilities by
law degraded and excluded them from society, except as servants, and
from the rights of freemen, except in the protection of life and member. It cannot be denied, however, that from the extravagancies of
this motley multitude, some confusion and misery may have prevailed
in the colony.[58]

57. Stith, *Virginia*, pp. 167–68. This episode occurred in 1619, not in 1609. Randolph
returns to the events of 1609 on p. 42 below.
58. Convicts from the jails of Middlesex and other counties had been transported to

[The king had formerly issued his letters to the several bishops of the kingdom empowering them to collect money for erecting in Virginia a college in which infidel children might be educated in the true knowledge of God. Nearly £1,500 had been already paid toward it, and a larger sum was expected. Sir Edwin Sandys moved and obtained a vote of the Company that ten thousand acres of land should be laid off for the University of Henrico, a place formerly resolved on for that purpose. This was intended not only for the education of Indians but also for a seminary of learning for the English. In consequence of these resolves, Sir Edwin procured fifty men to be sent in the summer, and fifty men at the beginning of the next year, to be seated on these lands as tenants on halves. They were to have half the profits of their labor to themselves, and the other half was to go toward forwarding the building and the maintenance of the tutors and scholars; and as a man's labor was then computed at £10 sterling a year, it was expected that thereby would be established an annual revenue of £500 for this work. Mr. George Thorpe, a kinsman of Sir Thomas Dale, being a gentleman of His Majesty's privy chamber and one of the Council in England for Virginia, was sent over as the Company's deputy and superintendent of the college; and for his support, they granted three hundred acres of land, to be forever annexed to that place with ten tenants thereon.] [59] Much happy fruit from this institution at this time cannot be distinctly traced; its utility, however, was too obvious to be neglected.

[Sir Thomas Gates [60] was the first who by his wisdom and industry and valor in the midst of many difficulties had laid the foundation of

America as early as 1617. In 1619 fifty "Duty boys" were carried over in the ship *Duty* at the command of King James I (Susan Myra Kingsbury, ed., *Records of the Virginia Company of London* [Washington, D.C., 1906–35], I, 250, 270–71, 305–6, 424–77, 520; Charles M. Andrews, *The Colonial Period of American History* [New Haven, 1934–38], I, 135).

59. Stith, *Virginia*, pp. 162–63. In 1617 King James issued letters patent to help support the college. Three years later George Thorpe (1576–1622), a member of the king's Privy Council, was sent to Virginia to take charge of the projected institution's affairs. Whatever steps taken to erect buildings were halted by the massacre of 1622 in which seventeen persons living on the college lands, including Thorpe, perished. The Virginia Company still worked to keep the scheme alive, but the revocation of the Company's charter in 1624 ended any chance of reviving the project (Philip A. Bruce, *Institutional History of Virginia in the Seventeenth Century* [New York, 1910], I, 362–73; see also Robert Hunt Land, "Henrico and Its College," *Wm. and Mary Qtly.*, 2d ser., XVIII [1938], 453–98).

60. Sir Thomas Gates served as interim governor from the time of Lord De la Warr's appointment in May 1609 until his arrival in Virginia in Feb. 1610 and again from 1611 to 1614 (Isabel M. Calder, "Sir Thomas Gates," *DAB*).

prosperity in the colony; and building upon these foundations, he with great and constant severity had reclaimed, almost miraculously, the idle and dissolute persons in Virginia and reduced them to labor and orderly deportment of life. He had laid off public lands to yield them constant revenue, placed servants upon them and upon other public works for the Company's use, established an annual rent of corn from the farmers and of tribute from the barbarians, and had reared a great stock of cattle, goats, and other animals, and was the occasion of drawing many private planters into Virginia. But since the times of those men, all this public provision had been utterly wasted and destroyed; and instead of about a hundred persons, which were sent at the Company's charge within the two or three last years, on the arrival of Sir George Yeardley,[61] the governor, only three could be found remaining to the public.

[There had been remitted from Virginia twelve several commodities, sold openly to the great honor of the action and encouragement of adventurers. Since that exportation little had been returned except tobacco and sassafras, to which the people there applied themselves so entirely that they would have been reduced to starving in the last year had not the colonial magazine supplied them with corn and cattle from England. This had been the occasion of stopping and discouraging many hundreds of people who were providing for removal thither. Frequent letters had therefore been sent from the Council in England to the governor in Virginia to restrain that immoderate planting of tobacco and to cause the people to apply themselves to other and better commodities. A covenant too was drawn to be inserted in all future grants of land, that the patentees should not apply themselves wholly or chiefly to tobacco but to other commodities therein specified. Three thousand acres of land had been laid off for the governor, twelve thousand for the Company, and ten thousand, as we have seen, for the University of Henrico; and seventy-two persons had already

61. Sir George Yeardley (*ca.* 1587–1627) had been a soldier in the Netherlands and was a seasoned colonist, having come over with Gates in 1610 as captain of a company. He served as acting governor from Dale's departure in 1616 to Argall's arrival in 1617, and on Nov. 18, 1618, he was appointed governor for a one-year term. The Virginia Company wanted to draw upon the authority associated with high birth in English society, and since it was not always possible to recruit such men they used the expedient of securing a knighthood for Yeardley. In 1626 he was again appointed governor, this time by the crown, but died in office (Morton, *Colonial Virginia,* I, 54–55, 112; Nora Miller Turman, *George Yeardley, Governor of Virginia and Organizer of the General Assembly in 1619* [Richmond, 1959], pp. 95–105).

been placed on the Company's land, fifty-three on the governor's, and fifty on that of the college—a hundred and seventy-five in all. But not content with this, Sandys proposed that those tenants for the public should the next spring be increased to the number of three hundred, a hundred for the Company's land, a hundred for that of the college, and a hundred for that of the governor, who should be obliged at the expiration of his office to leave the same number to his successor; and thus the Company would be relieved from all further expense for his provision. He proposed also in the second place that a hundred boys and girls, of about twelve or thirteen years of age, should go as servants to the tenants and as apprentices. And because he understood that many people in Virginia, though residing there for some few years, were averse to continue there permanently and proposed after having earned some wealth to return to England, to the utter overthrow and dissolution of the plantations, Sandys advised and made it his third proposition that one hundred maids, young and uncorrupt, should be sent over as wives for the inhabitants, trusting that wives, children, and families would render them less movable and fix them and their posterity in that soil. Such of these maids as were already married to the public farmers were to be transported at the Company's expense; but of such as were afterward married to others, the husbands were to repay to the Company the charge of their transportation. In consequence of this proposition, ninety maids were accordingly sent the following spring.[62] Twenty heifers were also sent for every hundred tenants, threescore in the whole, which with their breed would soon raise a tolerable stock.

[Sandys, lastly, showed how much the Company were bound to give thanks to Almighty God for all his blessings in raising means to support and carry on this great work; and he particularly mentioned one unknown gentleman alone, who promised £500 on demand for the conversion and education of threescore Indian children, and that he had likewise in letters received assurance from sundry parts, and some of them very remote, that if the undertaking proceeded, money should not be wanted. Sandys then hoped, somewhat in the form of a

---

62. It seems that the transporting of young ladies to Virginia was one of the few profitable enterprises ever undertaken by the Virginia Company. The first group of 90 was sent in 1619. This year of 1619 was pregnant with circumstances for American development generally, not only for the transportation of wives, but for the arrival of the first African slaves and the convening of the first legislative assembly.

prediction, that by this and similar measures a foundation would be laid for a future great state. These propositions of Sandys were received with the applause which they well deserved. And with extreme care and diligence he saw them all afterwards put effectually into execution.] [63]

[The situation of the colony [64] was rendered more critical by the perfidy of a German who had escaped to the English from Powhatan, for he flattered himself that he might convert their distractions to his own private advantage, fled back again to that king with one of his concubines, and labored to gain him over to second some of the wicked schemes of the faction at Jamestown by assuring the Indians that when Lord De la Warr should arrive they might expect the most stupendous benefits. It is only from an extensive experience in the intrigues of civilized man that we should have looked for that testimony of sagacity which Powhatan's reply to him displayed. "They," said he, "who would betray Captain Smith, the *president,* to *him* (Powhatan) would certainly betray *him* (Powhatan) to the great Lord De la Warr to entitle them to pardon for their crimes." Powhatan confirmed his detestation of the German and of his female companion by ordering his attendants to beat out their brains on the spot.] [65]

With the traits of Smith's character the history of Virginia is decked in various parts. To no public agencies was he unequal, being neither alarmed at their magnitude nor confounded by their intricacy or number. In the suppression of faction he was rapid, undaunted, and peremptory. In doing right, he boldly exposed himself to the malice of his enemies, although they would so soon be in a condition of tampering with his successor to revise his presidential acts with malignity and would be confronted by himself, defenseless except in his own virtue. His stubborn integrity was crowned by his almost last act, in appointing Martin (who was inimical to him) as his successor from the expiration of his own presidential year until the arrival of Lord De la Warr.

---

63. Stith, *Virginia,* pp. 163–67. Sir Edwin Sandys (1561–1629), the son of the archbishop of York, a leader of the parliamentary cause, and for many years a prominent adventurer in both the Virginia and Bermuda companies, was elected treasurer of the Virginia Company in 1619. The above measures were inaugurated by Sandys in 1618 as part of his plan for reorganizing the Virginia Company. For an excellent discussion, consult Craven, *Dissolution of Virginia Company,* pp. 47–104. For a contemporary view, see *A Declaration of the State of the Colony and Affaires in Virginia* (London, 1620; reprinted in Kingsbury, *Records of Virginia Company,* III, 307–65).

64. At this point Randolph returns the sequence of events back to the year 1609.

65. Stith, *Virginia,* p. 103.

Martin on his part was so conscious of his own incompetency that he sealed his inferiority by paying to Smith the unusual homage of resigning the presidency to him. Smith, whose talent it was to combine many useful objects in the same general plan, immediately prepared to break the confederacy at Jamestown by detaching a Mr. West with one hundred and twenty men to make a settlement at the falls of James River and Martin with nearly the same force to Nansemond on the same river for a like purpose.[66] The latter expedition miscarried, and the former was on the point of proving abortive by the bad choice which West had made of a station liable to inundations and other inconveniences. He purchased from Powhatan a place at the falls a little below Rocketts adjoining the city of Richmond. The terms of sale were that the English should defend Powhatan against the Monacans, that he should relinquish to the English the fort, houses, and neighboring country for a quantity of copper and pay a tribute in corn and pucoons.[67] But West's company, considering the approaching change in the office of president as affording a season for tumult—and pampered with the opinion that the country of the Monacans abounded in gold and extended to the South Sea—rejected with insolence and contempt the interference of Smith and compelled him for safety to retire from the prosecution of the Monacan expedition, but not without a demonstration of energy in committing some of the mutineers to prison. To these outrages West's company added others on the Indians, who were subjects of Powhatan and who requested pardon of Smith, if they should thereafter defend themselves against the English, whom they charged as being worse enemies than the Monacans themselves. They offered even to follow Smith if he would lead them in suppression of the commotions which West's party had raised. But Smith understood too well the value of forbearance and the consequence of enlisting a foreign foe even against his refractory countrymen to accept their services. His wisdom and foresight

66. By the "confederacy at Jamestown," Randolph probably meant those members of the Council such as John Martin, Gabriel Archer, and John Ratcliffe who were contesting Smith's leadership. Francis West (1586–1614), the brother of Lord De la Warr, was also a strong opponent of Smith. He had been sent to the falls of the James River to forage for food but found nothing but acorns. Nansemond refers either to the river by that name or the tribe with extensive territory in the Isle of Wight, Nansemond, and Norfolk counties.

67. Smith purchased the site at the falls of the James River. The pucoons, a variety of plant used for making yellow or red dye, were tribute Powhatan agreed to pay King James.

were conspicuous in the event, for after he had sailed toward James-town about half a league, West's party were so severely attacked by the Indians that for the sake of his forgiveness, they surrendered them-selves to his discretion. His clemency excused all but six or seven of the ringleaders, whom he established at Powhatan.

Smith also ingratiated himself with the Indians by restitution and satisfaction where either might justly be demanded. What a brilliant assemblage was this of gentleness, firmness, and policy! What a noble element in a character who was to found an empire destined to pass through a variety of fortune and to be assailed by enemies of various descriptions.

But on his passage down the river, the powder in his bag caught fire and tore the flesh from his body and thigh for nine or ten inches in breadth. He quenched the fire in his clothes by leaping overboard and was with difficulty saved from drowning.

The confederates against his authority in Jamestown, observing his disability and torment, conspired to murder him in his bed. The heart of the assassin who was to have executed the deed failed. The rumor of his villainy drew Smith's old soldiers around him, and they entreated him only to approve, and they would bring the heads of the boldest of his enemies and lay them before him. But Smith was a genuine patriot, who to the spirit of revenge or personal fears would not sacrifice the welfare of his country. The *amor patria* was in him always active, always supported by courage, always guided by prudence. In a word, had it not been for his labors and prowess, Virginia must have been restored to the empire of Powhatan. There may be perhaps a limit beyond which a patriot cannot be required to forbear. But when he causes punishment to be inflicted, let it be done under the sanction of law and in the calmness of inquiry. Smith could procure no surgical relief for his wound, and from his agonies being declared to be beyond the hope of recovery in Virginia, he repaired to England in one of the ships then in the colony.

At his departure, he was solicited by several who called themselves presidents and councilors to resign to them his commission of presi-dent; but after giving them many stern repulses, he permitted it to be stolen from him, moved by a capricious fear, unworthy of himself, lest in his absence and before the coming of the new governor any derange-ment in the affairs of the government should be attributed to him. What shall be said of this momentary weakness except that Smith debilitated was not the former Smith.

On this conclusion of his career the sense of his public merit can be
most aptly shown by representing the condition in which he left his
beloved Virginia, and to this it would be most cordial to add a narrative of that course of life by which he was trained, hardened, and
prepared to plant and save the colony. Let Stith, to whose inspection
in the year 1746 every document in the archives of Virginia was submitted, be allowed to speak, rather than that fragments should be
gleaned from sources less complete. The facts cannot be rendered more
authentic. The happiness of his country is the standard by which every
retiring statesman is usually tried, and lessons from biography are
funds of instruction to foster patriotism. ⌜About Michaelmas 1609,
says Stith, Captain Smith left the country never again to see it. He
left behind him three ships and seven boats; commodities ready for
trade; the corn newly gathered; ten weeks' provision in the store; four
hundred and ninety odd persons; twenty-four pieces of ordinance;
three hundred muskets, with other arms and ammunition, more than
sufficient for the men; the Indians, their language, and habitations
well known to a hundred trained and expert soldiers; nets for fishing;
tools, of all sorts, with which to work; apparel to supply their wants;
six mares and a horse; five or six hundred hogs; as many hens and
chickens, with some goats and some sheep. For whatever had been
brought or bred here still remained. But this seditious and distracted
rabble (at Jamestown), regarding nothing but from hand to mouth,
riotously consumed, after Smith's wound from the powder, what there
were, and were studious only to color and make out some complaints
against Captain Smith. For this end, the ships were detained three
weeks at a great charge. But notwithstanding their perverse humors
and unreasonable clamors, Captain Smith was undoubtedly a person
of a very great and generous way of thinking and full of a high idea
of the public good and his country's honor. To his vigor, industry, and
undaunted spirit and resolution, the establishment and firm settlement
of this colony was certainly owing; and therefore it may not be unacceptable to the reader to have some further account of his person
and actions—and this we are enabled to do with the more authenticity,
as he has himself at the request of Sir Robert Cotton, the famous
antiquarian, left a brief relation of his principal travels and adventures.[68]

68. I should perhaps consider even this production of Smith's pen as deviating from
the unity of the history, were it not that every fact which tends to establish heroic virtue
has a natural affinity to the fame of him who, in whatever rank he may be held, enjoys

[He was born a gentleman, to a competent fortune, at Willoughby in Lincolnshire in the year 1579.[69] From his very childhood he had a roving and romantic fancy and was strangely set upon performing some brave and adventurous achievement. Accordingly, being about thirteen years of age at school, he sold his satchel and books and all he had to raise money in order to go secretly beyond sea. But his father dying just at that time, he was stopped for the present and fell into the hands of guardians more intent on improving his estates than him. However, at fifteen, in the year 1594 he was bound to a merchant at Lynn, the most considerable trader in those parts. But because he would not send him immediately to sea, he found means, in the train of Mr. Peregrine Bertie, second son to the Lord Willoughby, to pass into France. Here and in the Low Countries, he first learned the rudiments of war, to which profession he was led by a strong propensity of genius.[70] He was afterwards carried into Scotland with delusive hopes from a Scottish gentleman of being effectually recommended to King James.[71] But soon finding himself baffled in his expectations, he returned to Willoughby, his native place, where meeting with no company agreeable to his way of thinking, he retired into a wood, a good distance from any town, and there built himself a pavilion of boughs and was wholly employed in studying some treatises of the art of war and in the exercise of his horse and lance. But his friends, being concerned at such a whimsical turn of mind, prevailed with an Italian gentleman rider to the earl of Lincoln [72] to insinuate himself into his acquaintance; and as he was an expert horseman and his talent and studies lay the same way with Mr. Smith's, he drew him from his

---

the sublime one of being at least a father of a country whose great destinies, however promoted and approved by others, must ever be illuminated by the luster of Captain John Smith—RANDOLPH'S NOTE.

Sir Robert Bruce Cotton (1571–1631), "a truly extraordinary personage, a lingering spirit of the days of Elizabeth, delved into antiquities with the energy of a Camden or an Antonio Bosio. Once Smith came under his eye Sir Robert insisted that Smith prepare for him an autobiography which would explain Smith's somewhat incredible past" (Barbour, *Captain John Smith*, p. 381). In 1630 Smith published *The True Travels, Adventures, and Observations of Captaine John Smith*.

69. Smith was the son of a lower middle-class farmer.

70. Lord Willoughby de Eresby (1555–1601) was a nationally renowned military leader. Smith accompanied Peregrine Bertie to France in 1599. Smith probably went to the Low Countries in late 1596 or early 1597.

71. The Scottish nobleman was Lord Alexander Hume.

72. Henry Clinton, earl of Lincoln, was the master of Tattershall Castle. The Italian gentleman was Theodore Paleologue, a collateral descendant of Constantine XI, the last Greek emperor of the Eastern Roman Empire.

sylvan retirement to spend some time with him at Tattershall. But Smith's restless genius soon hurried him again into Flanders,[73] where lamenting to see such effusion of Christian blood, he resolved to try his fortune against the Turks. In order to do this he passed through France, with a variety of adventure and misfortune, in which he always showed a high and martial spirit. At Marseilles he embarked for Italy. But the ship meeting with much foul weather, a rabble of pilgrims on board hourly cursed him for a Huguenot, railed at Queen Elizabeth and his whole nation, and swore they would never have fair weather as long as he was in the ship. At last, the passions of these pious Christians rose so high that they threw him overboard, trusting, we may suppose, in the merit and supererogation of that holy pilgrimage to expiate the trifling offense and peccadillo of murder. However, Smith, by the divine assistance, got safe to a small uninhabited island against Nice in Savoy. From thence he was the next day taken off by a French rover, who treated him very kindly and with whom he therefore made the tour of the whole Mediterranean, both on the Mohammedan and the Christian coasts. At length after a desperate battle, having taken a very rich Venetian ship, the generous Frenchman set him ashore with his share of the prize, amounting to five hundred sequeem in specie and a box of rich commodities worth nearly as much more; and now out of curiosity ranging all the regions and principalities of Italy, he at last went to Vienna and entered himself a gentleman volunteer in Count Meldritch's regiment against the Turks.[74]

[He had not been long in the Christian army before he was distinguished for a man of great personal bravery; and in the sieges of Olumpagh and Alba Regalis,[75] he was the author of some stratagems which showed a happy talent for war and did signal service to the Christian cause. He was thereupon immediately advanced to the command of a troop of horse and was soon after made sergeant major of the regiment, a post at that time next to the lieutenant colonel. But Count Meldritch, a Transylvanian nobleman by birth, afterwards passed with his regiment out of the imperial service into that of his

73. Smith returned to the Low Countries in 1600.

74. Count Meldritch was probably Count Modrusch, whose family name was Frankopan. There were at least two Frankopans, George and Nicholas, who fit the story.

75. Olumpagh or Olimpach was the place known in Latin as Olimacum and in German as Limbach, today called "Lower" Limbach. Alba Regalis (or Alba Regia) is the Latin name for Székesfehérvár, known in German as Stuhlweissenburg, the seat of the Magyar kingdom.

natural prince Zsigmond Báthory, duke of Transylvania.[76] And here
endeavoring to recover some patrimonial lordship then in the possession of the Turks, he laid siege to a strong town chiefly inhabited
by renegadoes and banditti.[77] Whilst their works were advancing slowly
and with great difficulty, a Turkish officer issued forth out of the town
and challenged any Christian of the dignity of a captain to a single
combat; many were eager of the honor of humbling this haughty
Mussulman, but it was at last decided by lot in favor of Captain Smith.
Accordingly, the ramparts of the town being filled with fair dames
and men in arms and the Christian army drawn up in battalia, the
combatants entered the field, well mounted and richly armed, to the
sound of hautboys and trumpets, where at the encounter Smith bore
the Turk dead to the ground and went off triumphantly with his head;
but the infidel garrison being enraged at this, he afterwards engaged
two other officers, and being a great master of his arms and the management of his horse, he carried off their heads in the same manner. After
which, being attended with a guard of six thousand men, with the
three Turkish horses led before him, and before each a Turk's head
upon a spear, he was conducted to the general's pavilion, who received
him with open arms and presented him with a fine horse richly capar-
isoned and with a scimitar and belt worth three hundred ducats. Soon
after, the duke, coming himself to view his army, gave him his picture
set in gold, settled three hundred ducats upon him as a yearly pension,
and issued his letters patent of noblesse, giving him three Turks' heads
in a shield for his arms, which coat he ever afterwards bore and was
admitted and recorded in the herald's office in England by Sir William
Segar, garter principal king at arms.[78] But soon after, the duke of
Transylvania was deprived of his dominions by the emperor, and
Smith at the fatal battle of Roter Turm in the year 1602 was left
upon the field among the dreadful carnage of Christians as dead.[79]
But the pillagers, perceiving life in him and judging by the richness
of his habit and armor that his ransom might be considerable, took
great pains to recover him. After that, he was publicly sold among the
other prisoners and was bought by a bashaw, who sent him to Con-

76. Zsigmond Báthory had abdicated as ruler of Transylvania in 1599 but in 1602 was
conducting a military campaign to retrieve the throne.
77. This town most likely was Alba Iulia in Transylvania.
78. The patent was officially recorded in 1625 but was dated Dec. 9, 1603.
79. Roter Turm was the disastrous battle of Red Tower Pass.

stantinople as a present to his mistress, Charatza Trabigzanda, a beautiful young Tartarian lady.[80] Smith was then twenty-three years of age, in the bloom of life, and as it seems, of a very handsome person. For this young lady was so moved with compassion, or rather love, for him that she treated him with the utmost tenderness and regard. And to prevent his being ill used, or sold by her mother, she sent him into Tartary to her brother, who was Timor Bashaw of Nalbirts, on the Palris Moeotis.[81] Here she intended he should stay, to learn the language, together with the manners and religion of the Turks, till time should make her mistress of herself.

[But the bashaw, suspecting something of the matter from the affectionate expressions with which she recommended and pressed his good usage, only treated Smith with the greater cruety and inhumanity. Smith's high spirit, raised also by a consciousness of Trabigzanda's passion, could but ill brook this harsh treatment. At last, being one day threshing alone at a grange above a league from the house, the timor came and took occasion so to kick, spurn, and revile him that, forgetting all reason, Smith beat out his brains with his threshing bat. Then reflecting upon his desperate state, he hid the body under the straw, filled his knapsack with corn, put on the timor's clothes, and mounting his horse, fled into the deserts of Circassia. After two or three days' fearful wandering, he happened, providentially, on the Astrakhan, or great road that leads into Muscovy. Following this for sixteen days with infinite dread and fatigue, he at last arrived at a Muscovite garrison on the frontiers. Here he was kindly entertained and presented, as also at all the places through which he passed. Having traveled through Siberia, Muscovy, Transylvania, and the midst of Europe, he at length found his old friend and gracious patron the duke of Transylvania at Leipzig together with Count Meldritch, his colonel. Having spent some time with them, the duke at his departure gave him a pass intimating the services he had done and the honors he had received, presenting him at the same time with fifteen hundred ducats of gold to repair his losses. And although he was now intent on returning to his native country, yet being furnished with this money, he

---

80. He was purchased by one Bashaw Bogall. While Smith believed Charatza Trabigzanda (Tragabigzanda) to be her name, it was nothing but a description of who she was in Greek: a girl from Trebizond (Barbour, *Captain John Smith,* p. 58).

81. Charatza's brother was a petty official in charge of a timar, a sort of military fief, on the far side of the Black Sea.

spent some time in traveling through the principal cities and provinces
of Germany, France, and Spain. From the last, being led by the rumor
of wars, he passed over into Africa and visited the count of Morocco.
Having viewed many of the places and curiosities of Barbary, he at
last returned through France to England; and in his passage in a
French galley, they had a most desperate engagement for two or three
days together with two Spanish men-of-war. In England all things were
still and in the most profound peace, so that there was no room or
prospect for a person of his active and warlike genius, and therefore,
having spent some time in an idle and uneasy state, he willingly embarked himself with Captain Gosnold in the project of settling colonies
in America and came to Virginia.

[His conduct here has been sufficiently recited; and I shall finish
his character with the testimonies of some of his soldiers and fellow
adventurers. They own him to have made justice his first guide and
experience his second. That he was ever fruitful in expedients to provide for the people under his command, whom he would never suffer
to want anything he either had or could procure. That he rather chose
to lead than send his soldiers into danger, and upon all hazardous
or fatiguing expeditions always shared everything equally with his
company and never desired any of them to do or undergo anything
that he was not ready to do or undergo himself. That he hated baseness,
sloth, pride, and indignity more than any danger. That he would suffer
want rather than borrow and starve sooner than not pay. That he
loved action more than words and hated falsehood and covetousness
worse than death. And that his adventures gave life and subsistency
to the colony, and his loss was their ruin and destruction. They confessed that there were many captains in that age (as there are indeed
in all ages) who are no soldiers; but that Captain Smith was a soldier
of the true old English stamp, who fought not for gain or empty
praise but for his country's honor and the public good. That his wit,
courage, and success here were worthy of eternal memory; that by the
mere force of his virtue and courage, he awed the Indian kings and
made them submit and bring presents. That notwithstanding such a
stern and invincible resolution, there was seldom seen a milder and
more tender heart than his was. That he had nothing in him counter-
feit or sly, but was open, honest, and sincere, and that they never
knew a soldier before him so free from those military vices of wine,
tobacco, debts, dice, and oaths. From this account of Captain Smith
extracted from his own writings and the testimony of his contem-

poraries and acquaintances, it will be easily seen that he was a soldier of fortune, who had run through great variety of life and adventure. And indeed he was so famous for this in his own age that he lived to see himself brought upon the stage, and the chief dangers and most interesting passages of his life racked, as he complains, and misrepresented in low tragedies. I cannot therefore forbear transiently observing Oldmixon's mistake, who says that the company took him into their service because he was a noted seaman and famed for experience in wartime affairs. But to remark all the errors of our historians, but most especially of Oldmixon, the weakest, most idle, and erroneous of all others, would be an infinite work and too often interrupt and break the thread of my narration. I hope, therefore, the courteous reader will be satisfied with this short caution and animadversion once and for all; for to speak the truth ingeniously, I had rather find out and correct one mistake in my own than expose and ridicule twenty blunders in the histories of others. But to return to the affairs of Virginia.⏋ [82]

82. Stith, *Virginia*, pp. 107–13. John Oldmixon (1673–1742), an English writer, was the author of *The British Empire in America* (London, 1708). An imperialist, he argued that a more efficient administration would render the colonies more valuable to England. The work was filled with inaccuracies, and eighteenth-century Virginia writers, most notably Robert Beverley, in his *History and Present State of Virginia* (London, 1705; ed. Louis B. Wright, Chapel Hill, N.C., 1947), and Stith, exploited its shortcoming to discredit not only Oldmixon's *History* but also his imperial orientation (Van Tassel, *Recording America's Past*, p. 25).

Chapter II   From the "Starving Time" to the Death of
Powhatan

[The ship on which Gates, Somers, and New-
port had embarked and which, as has been
already mentioned, was separated from the
rest of the fleet by a storm was so much
racked by the sea and had become so shat-
tered and leaky that the water rose in the hold above two tiers of
hogsheads and the passengers were obliged to stand up to their middles
with kettles, buckets, and other vessels to bail it out; and thus they
bailed and pumped three days and nights without intermission, while
the water seemed rather to gain upon them than decrease.[1] At last, all
being spent with labor and seeing no hope in man's apprehension of
avoiding immediate sinking, they resolved to shut up the hatches and
to commit themselves to the mercy of the waves. In this dangerous and
desperate state, some who had good and comfortable waters brought
them and drank to one another, as taking their last leave till a more
happy and joyful meeting in the other world. But it pleased God in
his most gracious providence so to guide their ship to her best advantage that they were all finally preserved and came safe to shore.
For Sir George Somers had sat, all this time, upon the poop, scarce
allowing himself leisure either to eat or sleep, watching the ship and
keeping her upright, or she must otherwise long before have foundered. As he there sat, looking wishfully about, he most happily and
unexpectedly descried land. This welcome news, as if it had been a
voice from Heaven, hurried them all above the hatches to see what
they could with difficulty believe. Thus improvidently forsaking their
work, they gave such an advantage to the sea that they were nigh being
swallowed up. But none were now to be urged to do his best. Although
they knew it to be Bermuda, a place then dreaded and shunned by

1. This was the expedition that left England in May 1609. One ship was lost and another, the *Sea Venture*, was wrecked on the Bermuda Islands. The remaining seven ships
finally arrived at Jamestown in August 1609. The *Sea Venture* with Gates, Somers, and
Newport did not get to Virginia until May 1610.

all men, yet they spread all their sail and did everything else in their power to reach the land. It was not long before the ship struck upon a rock, but a surge cast her from thence and so from one rock to another till she was most luckily thrown up between two, as upright as if she had been on the stocks. And now the danger was lest the billows, overtaking her, should in an instant dash her to pieces; but on a sudden the wind lay and gave place to a calm, and the sea became so peaceable and still that with the greatest conveniency and ease they unshipped all their goods, victuals, and people and in their boats with extreme joy almost to amazement arrived in safety without the loss of a man, although the vessel struck more than a league from the shore.

⌈But the safe arrival of this company was not more strange and providential than their feeding and support were beyond all their expectations and hopes. For they found Bermuda one of the richest, pleasantest, and most healthful places they had seen. Being safe on shore, they disposed themselves some to search the island for food and water and others to secure what they could from the ship. Sir George Somers had not ranged far before he found such a fishery that in half an hour he took with a hook and line as many fish as sufficed the whole company; in some places they were so thick in the coves, and so big, that they were afraid to venture in amongst them; and Sir George Somers caught one that had before carried off two of his hooks and was so large that it would have pulled him into the sea, had not men got hold of him. Two of those rockfish would have loaded a man, nor could anywhere be found fatter or more excellent fish than they were. This caused them to live in such plenty, ease, and comfort that many forgot all other places and never desired to return from thence.

⌈In the meanwhile, the thoughts of the two knights were busily employed how to act in this embarrassed state of their affairs. At last it was resolved to fit out the long boat with the ship's hatches and to send Mr. Raven, a stout and able mariner, with eight more in her to Virginia for shipping, but they were never more heard of.[2] And such was the malice, envy, and ambition of some that notwithstanding Sir George Somers's eminent services, there arose great differences between the commanders, so that as if according to the observation of a Spanish author, the air of America was infectious and inclined men's minds to

2. This reference is to Masters Mate Henry Ravens, who set sail with the cape merchant Thomas Whittingham "in the long Boat, as a Barke of Aviso for Virginia with a commission for Capt. Peter Win as Lieut. Governor of Virginia" (Alexander Brown, *The Genesis of the United States* [Boston and New York, 1890], I, 416–17).

wrangling and contention.[3] They lived asunder, in the height of this their calamity, rather like mere strangers than distressed friends. But each of them resolved to build a vessel. During their stay at Bermuda for nine months, they built two cedar ships, which they rigged with what had been saved from the wreck of that which had been stranded, substituting for pitch and tar, lime and oil of turtles—Somers's was finished without any iron except a bolt in the keel.

[On their arrival in Virginia, they were astonished and shocked at the calamitous state of the colony. Captain Percy's indisposition had incapacitated him from exercising with vigor that authority without which the tumults of the people could not be subdued.[4] The expeditions of Martin to Nansemond and of West to the falls of James River had cost them their boats and almost half of their crews. The last supplies from England had been most lavishly consumed. Ratcliffe and thirty others, while trading with Powhatan upon a confidence in his professions of amity, had been slain. West had gone to England. Corn and contributions were withheld by the Indians. The hogs, sheep, goats, and other domestic animals were daily applied to the use of emigrants or destroyed by Indians. Indeed to such extremities was the colony reduced that for bread they exchanged with the natives swords, firelocks, and other deadly weapons, regardless of the fatal consequences of conferring on their enemies the means of abolishing that disparity in artificial which alone withstood the physical force of the Indians. The colonists even devoured with appetite starch, *skins* of horses, and dead bodies of the savages who had been buried; they abstained not from their own dead; and in one instance, a man killed his wife, salted her flesh, and had eaten a part of it before the fact was known. It wants nothing to fix the appellation of "the starving time" with justice to this.][5]

Human nature has scarcely a stock of credulity sufficient for it.

---

3. The identity of the Spanish author mentioned by Randolph remains a mystery, but a number of European writers regarded the air of the New World as harmful to Europeans. See above, pp. xxxiii–xxxiv.

4. George Percy (1580–1632) was the youngest brother of Henry Percy, ninth earl of Northumberland, and a direct descendant of the immortal Harry Hotspur of King Henry IV's reign. He kept a diary of his sojourn in Virginia which later found its way into the hands of Samuel Purchas and was published, in part, in *Hakluytus Posthumus, or Purchas His Pilgrimes* (London, 1625; repr. Glasgow, Scotland, 1905–7). In 1609 Percy was chosen by the Council in Virginia as governor upon the expiration of Smith's term of office (Barbour, *Captain John Smith*, pp. 110–11; John W. Shirley, "George Percy at Jamestown," *Va. Mag. of Hist. and Biog.*, LVII [1940], 227–43).

5. Stith, *Virginia*, pp. 113–17.

[Of five hundred persons living at the departure of Smith, not more than sixty men, women, and children survived six months, and even these subsisted for the most part on roots, herbs, acorns, walnuts, berries, and now and then on a little fish. It was impossible that their existence should have been prolonged for ten days under such severities.] [6]

[The happiest expedient which occurred to Gates and Somers, who were fatigued and stunned with mutual accusations and excuses from the people, was to transport the colony with the most practicable ease immediately to England. And in this fit of despondency, if Gates had not interposed, the houses and fort at Jamestown would have been destroyed, as a prelude to a general evacuation of Virginia.[7] Happily, between Hog Island and Mulberry Island the long boat of Lord De la Warr was seen by the fugitives. He was going up James River with three ships loaded with necessaries, and brought the colony back to Jamestown. On going ashore, devotion was his first duty, and energy his ruling principle. In a short speech to the company, he condemned them for their pride and sloth, and after a protestation of reluctance to unsheath the sword of punishment, he abolished every hope of impunity for a violation of the laws, while he avowed his readiness to shed his own blood in the cause and defense of good government; he then appointed officers. The effect was an instantaneous contest of subordination. The refractory now recommended order; and a general competition in industry ensued. The French who had been sent over to plant vines betook themselves to their employments. The English labored in the woods and in the grounds.] Lord De la Warr, not unmindful of his own fame, manifested his adherence to the impartiality which he professed from the beginning [by removing Martin from the Council for his weak, cruel, and disorderly behavior.] He showed that difficult as is the crisis when the mere rights of order combat with brutal force, to be timid or compromising was to tread on the confines of treason. Not fearing to look in the face of evil, [he investigated the situation of the colony as to provisions and found that there were enough for six months, when Sir George Somers, now above fourscore years of age and enjoying an estate in England suitable to his rank and desire, increased the catalogue of

6. *Ibid.*, p. 117.

7. Though this portion of the *History* is a close rendering of Stith, Randolph omitted the following remarks: "God, who did not intend, that this excellent country should be so abandoned, put it into the Heart of Sir Thomas Gates, to save the Town and Fortifications."

Virginian worthies by offering to undertake a voyage to Bermuda, where he had acquired a knowledge of that island's capacity to export to Virginia meat sufficient for her support for six months. After a long struggle with adverse winds, he reached Bermuda. But there nature was in him overpowered and on his deathbed he exhorted his men to be true and constant to the colony and without delay to return thither with what he had collected for their supplies. But the consternation and grief of his associates were soon buried in an obstinate disobedience to his dying injunctions. His heart and entrails being interred, they embalmed his body and sailed with it to England. Had not Captain Argall obtained in the meantime corn from the Indians on Potomac River, a second famine must have been the consequence of this dis-regard to honor and fellow feeling.] [8]

Lord De la Warr, from his imitation of the energetic example of Captain Smith having equally with him overawed the minds of the seditious, was able to detach a corps of laborers down James River in order to erect two forts, which might cover a pleasant plain in a whole-some climate, with plentiful springs and a large circuit of ground fit for wood, pasturage, corn, and garden fruits.[9] He intended to quarter in this place the new emigrants from England for a recovery from their confinement during their voyage. But he does not seem to have proposed Smith as a full model to himself, for in a town of a neighbor-ing tribe of Indians, he burned their houses, put their king and queen and their children to death, although acknowledged prisoners of war.[10] On the contrary Smith had not himself shed, nor permitted others to shed, one drop of Indian blood by way of punishment; he displaced cruelty by vigilance, prowess, and industry. No imitation had been experienced from the Indians when he revisited England from the

8. *Ibid.*, pp. 117–21. Sir Samuel Argall (1580?–1626) was a mariner of experience and ability. In 1609 he discovered a more direct route to Virginia, and in 1610 he made a voyage to New England surveying the coast from Cape Cod to Virginia. Argall, like John Smith, proved extremely able in dealing with the Indians, serving Lord De la Warr well in that capacity. He also served the Virginia Company by making some important geographic discoveries that included Delaware Bay. In May 1617 he replaced Sir George Yeardley as governor. Seymour Connor, "Sir Samuel Argall: A Biographical Sketch," *Va. Mag. of Hist. and Biog.*, LIX (1951), 162–75.

9. Two forts were built at Kecoughtan on a little river named Southampton by Lord De la Warr in honor of Shakespeare's friend and patron, but now shortened to Hampton. The forts were named for Princes Henry and Charles.

10. The action against the Indians at Kecoughtan was in reprisal for the deaths of several Englishmen ("Letter of the Governor and Council of Virginia to the Virginia Company of London [July 7, 1610]," Brown, *Genesis of the United States*, I, 402–13).

pressure of disease. The moment of Smith's return was critical, as the discontents of the Council there were boisterous. They panted for more rapid profit and were chagrined and murmured at the trifling remittances from Virginia. Their temper and views were mercenary, without one spark of liberality, and could not expand by the comprehension of slow and distant remuneration, although ultimately sure and contributing to the strength and aggrandizement of the parent state. [They therefore seriously deliberated whether it was better to replenish the funds of the Company or to annihilate the enterprise. They were urged to the latter idea from a suspicion of the integrity of the treasurer Sir Thomas Smith, and their payments were extorted only in a course of litigation. Sir Thomas Gates, whom Lord De la Warr had sent before him, was a powerful herald to that influence which he himself afterwards exercised. Gates had been adjured by the Company to deal plainly with them, and he with a solemn and sacred oath gave them a full account and state of things. He told them that all men knew that they lay at the mercy of politic princes and states, who for their own proper utility devised every method to grind their merchants and on any pretense to confiscate their goods and draw from them all manner of gain, whereas Virginia might in a few years furnish all their wants honorably and certainly.[11]

[Lord De la Warr too delivered an oration to the Council, which afforded general satisfaction. He declared his willingness to hazard his whole fortune upon the success of the colony, and to confirm it he offered to return immediately if the Council would second his endeavors.] [12] His representations were the more impressive as he had left behind him two hundred persons in sound health, witnesses of a good administration, and the natives to appearance tractable and friendly.

[In the character of high marshal of Virginia, Sir Thomas Dale had arrived with three ships, several hundred men and cattle, and provisions adequate to the consumption of a year.[13] The people were re-

---

11. Gates assured the members of the Company of the prospect of future returns in a variety of articles. His remarks were contained in a document entitled *A True Declaration of the Estate of the Colonie in Virginia, with a Confutation of Such Scandalous Reports as Have Tended to the Disgrace of So Worthy an Enterprise,* published in Nov. 1610 by the Council (reprinted in Peter Force, ed., *Tracts and Other Papers Relating Principally to the Colonies in North America* [Washington, D.C., 1836–46; repr. 1947], III, No. 1).

12. Stith, *Virginia,* pp. 121–22. De la Warr's testimony can be found in Brown, *Genesis of the United States,* I, 477–83.

13. Dale arrived on May 12, 1611, to assume his duties as governor.

lapsing into their former penury, from neglect in planting corn and their improvident reliance on the public stores, which in three months must be exhausted. At Jamestown, where riot and dissipation had banished every attention to duty, the houses were ready to fall. Having caused them to be repaired, he contemplated the building of a new town on the narrow part of Farrar's Island in James River upon high ground nearly surrounded with water.⌉ [14]

Dale's powers are not distinctly known but were the more alarming as being undefined and of a military nature. Sir Thomas Smith, the treasurer, without any sanction from the Council and Company in England, had armed him with articles and laws chiefly translated from the laws martial of the old countries, *severe and* bloody and abhorrent from the genius of a free people and the British constitution. This atrocity of imposing as an organ of legitimate communication with the officers of the colony such a system of terror stirred up no scrupulous inquiry in the breast of Dale, who was himself the despotic dispenser of it; and it is unfortunate for the cause of genuine freedom that any degree of usurpation, especially of that kind which affects the life of men, should ever be glossed by a supposed necessity.[15] For Dale clutched a conspiracy, which though deserving chastisement might have been quelled by the ordinary authority, proclaimed martial law, and executed it upon Abbott, Cole, Kitchins, and three others. ⌈Abbott had served long as a soldier in Ireland and the Netherlands and was a sergeant in the company of Captain Smith, who testified that he never knew in Virginia a more able soldier, less turbulent, of better wit, more hardy and industrious, or more forward to cut off those who en-

14. Stith, *Virginia*, p. 122. This new town, named Henrico in honor of Prince Henry, was located on the upper James ten or twelve miles below the falls. Envisioned as the colony's chief city, it never achieved its intended purpose.

15. Actually, Dale did not rule by undefined powers, and he was only partly responsible for the harsh steps taken to remedy the colony's disorders. In 1609 the governor had been given the authority to act as he saw fit to control the people. In the spring of 1610 Sir Thomas Gates issued certain laws and orders in accordance with this authority that were approved by Lord De la Warr upon his arrival. This authority was enlarged and exemplified by Dale on June 22, 1611, reduced to the form of a code by William Strachey (1572–1621), the colony's secretary, and was published after Strachey's return to England in 1612 by the Virginia Council as *Lawes Divine, Morall and Martiall* (reprinted in Force, *Tracts*, III, No. 2). It is inaccurate to assume that all Virginians were made subject to permanent martial law. They came under martial law only during those periods when they were engaged in military duties. Craven, *Southern Colonies*, pp. 105–6; Darrett B. Rutman, "The Virginia Company and Its Military Regime," in Darrett B. Rutman, ed., *The Old Dominion: Essays for Thomas Perkins Abernethy* (Charlottesville, Va., 1964). For Strachey, see S. G. Culliford, *William Strachey, 1572–1621* (Charlottesville, Va., 1965).

deavored to abandon the country or wrong the colony.] [16] In what this conspiracy consisted is not transmitted to us. It is called by Stith "a sudden and passionate deviation from his duty," and the penalty was immediate. The most meritorious character is no shield against the scythe of martial law, which never flags in performing the ebullitions of caprice and is never arrested by any tediousness in the forms of examination.

The others, it seems, were convicted of a plot to run away to the Spaniards.[17]

These proceedings, though sharp and summary, are reported by Stith to have been commended by all parties. This commendation is in such cases a real misfortune by being a precedent for the repetition of any enormity, springing perhaps from a hasty panic, mere suspicion, a conjecture unsupported or slightly canvassed.

[In August 1611, Sir Thomas Gates, being governor, superseded Dale as high marshal. He brought with him ships, men, cattle, hogs, and all needful munitions and provision; upon which Dale obtained from him a force to complete his town on Farrar's Island or Varina Neck, and having named it Henrico in honor of King James's son, Prince Henry, he there built a church, storehouses, and other convenient houses and protected it with a palisade. This was a great accession to the safety and accommodation of the colonists.] [18]

The former position of such a town is known to but few, although its ruins have been recently traced and distinguished on the lands of Thomas Mann Randolph.[19] If it were allowable to dream what super-

---

16. Stith, *Virginia*, p. 123.

17. The plot, as described by Smith, was to desert the colony and set a "course to Ocanahowan, five daies journey from us, where they report are Spaniards inhabiting." Smith admitted their guilt but claimed that the fault lay with Sir Thomas Dale's tyrannical practices (Lyon G. Tyler, ed., *Narratives of Early Virginia* [New York, 1907], pp. 303–4). Cole, Kitchins, and others had been acting as the guard to Don Diego de Molina, a Spanish spy, who persuaded them to attempt to reach the Spanish settlements in Florida (Alexander Brown, *The First Republic in America* [Boston and New York, 1898], pp. 158–211).

18. Stith, *Virginia*, pp. 123–24.

19. Probably Thomas Mann Randolph, Sr. (1741–93), a long-time representative for Goochland County in the House of Burgesses and a member of the Virginia Revolutionary Conventions of 1775 and 1776, lived at Tuckahoe in Goochland County but owned Varina tract in Henrico County. His son Thomas Mann Randolph, Jr. (1763–1828), the son-in-law of Thomas Jefferson and governor of Virginia from 1819 to 1822, had lived for a time on the Varina tract but his permanent home was a plantation at Edgehill, Albemarle County (William H. Gaines, Jr., *Thomas Mann Randolph, Jefferson's Son-in-Law* [Baton Rouge, La., 1966], esp. pp. 3–8. For Stith's description, see *Virginia*, p. 124).

stition might call to the imagination in the haunts of savages, converted
into civilized residence, and in the now derelict settlements of the first
emigrants, we ought to describe this town, which has been effaced by
the convenience of navigation at every man's door. But towns can
neither be created nor maintained by a fiat of simple authority, and
we have no classic ground, or gothic mythology, which belongs to the
Virginian history. The description therefore of this place, as given by
Stith in the year 1747, will be consigned to a note for the use of the
Virginia antiquarian, or of some recluse who may be fired by treading
on the subverted hopes of a sanguine and bold adventure.

Sir Thomas Dale nursed this town of Henrico with parental affection,
and for some injury to its inhabitants, assaulted and took the town of
the Appomattoc Indians, opposite to Mr. Charles Carter's residence at
Shirley on James River, and seated it under the name of New Bermudas. He also annexed to the freedom and corporation of Henrico
many miles of champaign and woodland, which he divided into hundreds, and on Rochdale Hundred many good houses were built, of
which no trace now appears.[20]

Virginia having assumed an importance and figure in the opinion
of the treasurer and Company, they were desirous of annexing to her
as an appendage the island of Bermuda, and therefore on March 12,
1611/12, they obtained a third charter, for all the islands in the ocean
within three hundred leagues of the coast betwixt the 41st and 30th
degrees of northern latitude. In this Bermuda was included.[21] It could
not be that mere extension of territory was coveted by the colony,
already holding by charter soil by a line four hundred miles on the
Atlantic and for the same breadth as far as the South Sea; nor could
there have existed at that time a very flattering prospect of advantage
from Bermuda as a position for an extensive commerce. The real object could have been no other than to secure that island as a granary

---

20. In 1611 Dale seized an extensive territory from the Appomattoc Indians near the
mouth of the Appomattox River. To create a hundred meant to set aside an area for
settlement by 100 families who were to form a judicial and military unit. The significance
of 100 families was soon lost and a hundred came to be purely territorial (Bruce, *Institutional History*, II, 287–94).

21. For a reprint of the charter, see Bemiss, *Three Charters of Virginia Company*, pp.
76–94. According to Wesley Frank Craven, this acquisition was designed "to infuse new
life into their American venture by capitalizing on a growing interest in the Bermudas."
Also the "central location in the western Atlantic promised a unique strategic advantage
with reference to possession of the mainland and of the West Indies and Newfoundland as
well" (*Southern Colonies*, pp. 109–10; see also Craven's *Introduction to the History of the
Bermudas* [Williamsburg, Va., 1938]).

and storehouse against famine, which its timely succors had more than once repelled from Virginia. It may not however be uncharitable to infer from the notorious selfishness of some of those who petitioned for this charter and were afterwards among the purchasers of it from the treasurer and Company that a sinister design was entertained throughout the entire transaction. The alienation was the more unpardonable and suspicious as the island was competent to its own supplies, and its defense was a burden of course to be thrown upon England as a branch of the protection to Virginia.

From the increasing character of Virginia in her relation to the mother country, several noblemen of high rank were eager to be enrolled in her second charter of 1609 as adventurers. The king also ceased to be inattentive to her when he devised a plan for enforcing redress against delinquent adventurers, released the disabilities of aliens and the prohibition on emigrants and an exportation thither, and permitted the institution of lotteries for the raising of money.

The spirit of gaming has been often lamented, and not always without cause, as breaking forth in Virginia in ways destructive of morals and estates. We do not stigmatize this permission as the direct parent of that evil; but it cannot be an excess of refinement to believe that the patronage of a sovereign supposed in his day to be friendly to religion must have protected from reprobation the germs of a vice which could not but insinuate itself into many other actions and beget a variety of evil habits. As this was the first instance in the English history of a public sanction to so pernicious a mode of levying money, the indulgence to an absurd and deceptive confidence of men in their own good fortune, it is to be regretted that the king, pressed by the remonstrance of the House of Commons, could not, when he recalled the license, exterminate the temper also to which it gave birth.[22]

Almost every occurrence in the life of Pocahontas is associated with some benefit to the colony.[23] Her original name Matoaka had been changed through some superstitious notion. For some reason or other she concealed herself on the banks of Potomac, to shun, as has been conjectured, the sight of those butcheries which, after the departure of Captain Smith, the English by their folly and rashness put it out of her

---

22. The Virginia Company had been licensed by the government in 1612 to conduct lotteries, which soon became its chief source of revenue. A royal proclamation of March 8, 1621, ended the Virginia lotteries, a loss which proved to be a major cause of the company's financial collapse (Robert C. Johnson, "The 'Running Lotteries' of the Virginia Company," *Va. Mag. of Hist. and Biog.*, LXVIII [1960], 156–65).

23. Barbour, *Captain John Smith*, esp. pp. 328–33.

power to avert. With what justice soever the character of an uncivilized Indian may have been drawn as cool, cruel, sullen, suspicious, and designing, a better class ought to be assigned to hers. Beautiful, engaging, and innocent, she had a compassionate and susceptible heart, looking however up to Smith as a second father, not as a companion for love. Her hiding place was within the knowledge of only a few friends, supposed to be trusty, and among others to Japazaws, king of Patawomeke, an ancient friend of the English from the first settlement of Virginia. ⌈Captain Argall, having received intelligence of the place to which she had retired, immediately employed it as the means of a peace with her father. He agreed to give Japazaws a copper kettle if he would bring her safe, till they could conclude such a peace. This savage would have done anything for the copper kettle; and therefore, having no decoy for her curiosity, because she had visited many ships, he made his wife pretend to be desirous to see one, and he affected to beat her for her importunity till she wept. But at last he told her that if Pocahontas would go with her, he was content; and thus taking the advantage of her good nature and obliging temper, they betrayed her aboard, where they were all kindly received and entertained in the cabin. The captain, when he saw his time, invited Pocahontas into the gun room, only to conceal from her that Japazaws was in any way guilty of her captivity. When he had received his reward, the captain sent for her again and told her she must go with him and be the instrument of peace between her country and the English; at this the traitor and his wife began to howl and cry, as much as Pocahontas, who by the captain's fair promises and persuasions pacified herself by degrees. They with their kettle and other baubles went joyfully ashore, and she to Jamestown, where although a frequent visitor before and often a kind preserver of the colony she had never been since Captain Smith left the country. A messenger was immediately dispatched to her father that he must ransom his daughter Pocahontas, whom he loved so dearly, with the men, guns, and tools of the English which he had stolen or surprised. This unwelcome news much troubled Powhatan because he loved both his daughter and those articles well, and it threw him into such perplexity that it was three months before he returned any answer. Then he sent back seven of the English and with each an unserviceable musket. He added an assurance that when they should deliver his daughter he would make full satisfaction for all injuries and give them five hundred bushels of corn, and would be the friend of the English forever. But they answered that his daughter should be well used, that they could not believe the rest of their arms were either lost or stolen from Powhatan, and that, therefore, they would keep his daughter till he sent them all back; but this answer displeased him so much that they heard no more from him for a long time. At last, in the beginning of the next year, Sir Thomas Dale took Pocahontas with him and went in Captain Argall's ship, with some other vessels belonging to the colony, up the river to the chief habitation of Powhatan at Werowocomoco, with a party of a hundred and fifty men, well appointed. Powhatan did not appear; and although the English announced that their business was to deliver up the emperor's daughter, upon restitution of the rest of their men and arms, yet were they received with many scornful bravadoes and threats. It was answered that if the English came to fight, they were welcome; but that as they loved their lives they ought to retire, or else they would be treated as Captain Ratcliffe had been. After some small skirmishes and considerable damage done to the Indians by burning their houses and spoiling all that the English could find, a peace was patched up. The messengers were immediately sent by the English to Powhatan, who told them that their men had run off for fear of being hanged, that Powhatan's men were dispatched to bring them back, and their swords and muskets should be brought the next day. But the English, perceiving that this was collusion only to protract the time till they could carry off their goods and provisions, told them that they should have a truce till the next day at noon; but that then if they had not a direct answer to their demands, or found them inclinable to fight, they should know when the English would begin by the sound of their drums and trumpets. Upon confidence in this truce, two of Powhatan's sons came on board the ship to see their sister. Finding her well, although they had heard the contrary, they greatly rejoiced and promised to persuade their father to redeem her and forever to be a friend with the English. Thereupon Mr. John Rolfe and Mr. Sparks went to Powhatan to acquaint him with the business. They were kindly received and entertained but not admitted into the presence of the emperor. They only spoke with Opechancanough, who promised to do his utmost with his brother to incline him to peace and friendship. But it now being April and time to prepare their ground and set their corn, they returned to Jamestown, without doing anything in the affair.

⌈Before this the same Mr. Rolfe, a worthy young gentleman, and of good behavior, had been enamored with Pocahontas, and she with him.[24] And now he imparted a knowledge of this to Sir Thomas Dale, through Mr. Ralph Hamor,[25] and wrote him a letter entreating his advice; and she likewise acquainted her brother with it. Sir Thomas Dale highly approved it. The report of an intended marriage between Rolfe and Pocahontas soon coming to the knowledge of Powhatan, it was found by his sudden consent to have been a thing long acceptable to him. For within ten days he sent Opitchapan, an old uncle of hers, and two of his sons to see the ceremony and to do what should be required from them for confirming it, as his deputies. It was therefore solemnized in the beginning of April 1613; and ever after there existed a friendly trade and commerce with Powhatan and all his subjects.

[The Chickahominies were a stout, daring, and free people. They had no werowance, or single ruler, but were governed in a republican form by their elders. These were their priests, and some of the wisest of their old men were assistants to them. In consequence of these principles of government, they took all opportunities of shaking off Powhatan's yoke, whom they looked upon and hated as a tyrant; and therefore, they had taken advantage of these latter times of hostility and danger, as well to the Indians as to the English, to assert their liberty. But seeing Powhatan so closely linked with the English both in affinity and friendship, they were in great concern and dread lest he should bring them again to subjection. To prevent which they sent an ambassador to Sir Thomas Dale, excusing all former injuries and promising ever after to be the faithful subjects of King James, to cancel the name of Chickahominies, and to be called Tassantessus, or Englishmen, and to be governed by Sir Thomas Dale, as the king's vicegerent. They only desired to be governed by their own laws, under their eight elders, as his substitutes. Sir Thomas Dale, hoping for some

24. John Rolfe (1585–1622) is best known as the husband of Pocahontas, but his fame also, and more importantly, derives from his introduction of tobacco as a staple crop. In 1611 Rolfe experimented with seed of the mild Spanish variety, and by June 1612 tobacco from the imported seeds were being cultivated at Jamestown. The success of Rolfe's experiment was evidenced by the exportation from Virginia of 20,000 pounds of tobacco in 1617 and twice that amount the following year (Melvin Herndon, *Tobacco in Colonial Virginia: "The Sovereign Remedy"* [Williamsburg, Va., 1957], pp. 2–3). Rolfe discussed his marriage to Pocahontas in a letter to Sir Thomas Dale, reprinted in Tyler, *Narratives of Virginia*, pp. 239–44.

25. Ralph Hamor (1589?–1626), the colony's secretary and the son of a prominent London merchant, had come to Virginia via the Gates-Somers shipwreck on Bermuda. He is best known for the publication in 1615 of *A True Discourse of the Present Estate of Virginia*. For a recent edition, see A. L. Rowse, ed., *A True Discourse* (Richmond, 1957).

benefit from this, willingly accepted their offer. On a day appointed he went with Captain Argall and fifty men to Chickahominy, where he found the people assembled, expecting his coming. They treated him kindly; and the next morning, having held a council, the peace was concluded on these conditions:

[1. That they should forever be called Englishmen and be true subjects to King James and his deputies.

[2. That they should neither kill nor detain any of the English or of their cattle, but should bring the cattle home.

[3. That they would be always ready to furnish the English with three hundred men against the Spaniards or any other enemy.

[4. That they would not enter any of the English towns before sending in word that they were now Englishmen.

[5. That every fighting man, at the gathering of corn, should bring two bushels of corn to the store as a tribute, for which he should receive as many hatchets.

[6. That the eight chief men should see all this performed or receive the punishment themselves; and for this diligence, they should have a red coat, a copper chain, and King James's picture, and be accounted his noblemen.[26]

[These articles were joyfully assented to and ratified by a great shout and acclamation; and one of the elders began an oration, addressing his speech first to the old men, then to the young, and then to the women and children, to make them understand how strictly they were to observe these conditions, and that the English would defend them from the fury of Powhatan or any other enemy whatsoever. And thus was their liberty once more protected, which indeed had its usual good effects even among these wild and savage nations. For although Chickahominy is far from being famous for good land, yet we are told that they had the largest fields and most plentiful crops of corn, and the greatest abundance of all other provisions and necessaries of any people then in the country. Such a happy influence had liberty, and such visible incitement did firm property give to the industry of even that lazy and improvident people.] [27]

Until this year a community of labor and soil and product had been observed in the colony, not from any religious principle, but from the

---

26. See Tyler, *Narratives of Virginia*, p. 311.

27. Stith, *Virginia*, pp. 123–31. For a description of the Chickahominy Indians, see Theodore Stein, "Chickahominy: The Changing Culture of Virginia Indian Community," *American Philosophical Society, Proceedings*, XCVI (1952), 157–225.

natural and intimate confederacy which binds men together in forests infested by wild beasts and savages more hostile. It was seen by this time that in real, unenthusiastic life such a state of things was impracticable—fed out of a common store, there was no motive of interest to any individual to labor honestly, to execute skillfully, or to augment the crop by any unusual exertion. The positive amount of labor in a week fell short of the proportion which might be reasonably required for a day. The term of five years which had been ordained by the king for the continuance of this community had expired. But it might have been too precipitate at once to cut off the accustomed resort to the general storehouse. Sir Thomas Dale intermingled the establishment of the rights of separate property with the contributions to the social store.[28]

Vanity in public men is not always harmless. It has often a kind of pride. That of Dale sought its reward in the grant of higher immunities to his new favorite, the establishment at Bermuda Hundred.

Notwithstanding some commotions, the satisfaction with Dale was general, as there was no longer cause to apprehend want. He was zealous in his patronage of the colony. It was debated in England whether it should be prosecuted or deserted. [In a letter to the treasurer,[29] Dale affirms that the dereliction of Virginia would not be less in mischief to England than the loss of France had been and entreats the Company not to be gulled and deceived by the clamorous reports of base people but to believe Caleb and Joshua; and if the glory of God and the conversion of poor infidels had not influence on the rich Mammons of the earth, yet he advises them to follow the dictates of their own avarice and to consult their proper interest and advantage. For he protests on the faith of an honest man, that the more he ranged and saw the country, the more he admired it; and that having seen the best parts of Europe, he declares with a solemn asseveration that put them all together he thought this country, if it were once well cultivated and settled with industrious people, would be equivalent to them.] [30]

These fluctuations in the order of those who were principally in-

28. In 1614 Dale was given permission to rent to each settler, as his indenture expired, three acres of cleared land. The result was that by 1617 most of the settlers had become farmers and the company's own lands were nearly deserted (Morton, *Colonial Virginia*, I, 41–42; see also Sigmund Diamond, "From Organization to Society: Virginia in the Seventeenth Century," *American Journal of Sociology*, LXIII [1957–58], 457–75).

29. This letter may have been the one entitled "From Jamestown in Virginia the 18th of June 1614," reprinted in Stanard, *First Century*, p. 122.

30. Stith, *Virginia*, p. 132.

terested in Virginia diversified only the objects of the appetite for American enterprise but did not diminish it. [For early in this year Sir Thomas Gates returned to England and left the government again to Sir Thomas Dale. Understanding that there was a colony of French in the northern part of Virginia about the latitude of 45°, he sent Captain Argall thither, to Port Royal and St. Croix, two towns lying on each side of the Bay of Fundy in Acadia.[31] Finding the French dispersed abroad in the woods, he surprised their ship and bark lately arrived from France. In them was much good apparel with other furniture and provision, which he brought to Jamestown. The pretense for this depredation on the French was founded on the English right of first discovery; and therefore in imitation of the Spaniards, they laid claim to the whole continent, although they really possessed and had sealed so small a part of it. But it is certain that we were, at that time, in profound peace not only with France, but the whole world. In his return Captain Argall likewise visited the Dutch settlement on Hudson's River; and he alleged that Captain Hudson,[32] the first discoverer, under whose sail the Dutch claimed that country, being an Englishman and licensed to discover those northern parts by the king of England, could not alienate that which was a part of Virginia from the English crown; he therefore demanded the possession, and the Dutch governor, being unable to resist, peaceably submitted himself and his colony to the king of England and to the governor of Virginia under him. Soon afterwards a new governor arrived from Amsterdam better provided. Under color of the purchase by the Dutch, and because the country lay void and unoccupied and consequently open to the first possession, he not only refused to pay tribute and acknowledgment, which had been agreed upon, but also began to fortify and put himself into a posture of defense. The claim of the English being either wholly waived at present or but faintly pursued, the Dutch in this same year made a firm settlement, which soon became very flourishing and populous. But upon a complaint some years after to King Charles I and by him represented to the states of Holland, they declared by a public instrument that they were no ways concerned in it,

---

31. Capt. Samuel Argall set sail in May 1613 in a well-armed warship, the *Treasurer.* He broke up the colony at Mount Desert and brought back 15 of its settlers, including two Jesuit priests. Later that year, under order from Gates, he returned to the New England coast and destroyed the buildings and fortifications of Mount Desert, Saint Croix, and Port Royal (Andrews, *Colonial Period*, I, 148–49).

32. Henry Hudson (d. 1611) had in 1609 claimed the Hudson River, as it was to be called, for his employers, the Dutch East India Company.

but that it was a private undertaking of the West India Company of Amsterdam, and so referred it wholly to His Majesty's pleasure.⌉ ³³ So true it is that a spirit of conquest, once entering into the character of an infant nation, sometimes becomes too buoyant for prudence and agriculture.

In Dale himself there was no unsteadiness. He persisted in the conviction of the excellence of Captain Smith's policy, in conciliating the affection of the Indians where it was compatible with the safety of the colony. ⌈By a messenger he solicited Powhatan for his other daughter in marriage for one of the English settlers. Powhatan inquired whether his daughter Pocahontas was contented with her situation; and being told that she would not on any account return and live with him, he laughed heartily and was greatly pleased to hear it.⌉ ³⁴ This strong excitement of his risibility, so much unlike the usual demeanor of the American Indian, was probably a compound of affection for his child and a persuasion that beyond the pale of savage life happiness did not exist.

⌈Powhatan betrayed many symptoms of uneasiness while Hamor, the English messenger, was expatiating upon the reciprocal emolument of an extended alliance between the English and Indians. He replied, "I gladly accept my brother's salute of love and peace, which whilst I live, I will punctually and exactly keep. I likewise receive his presents as pledges, with no less thankfulness. But as to my daughter, I sold her a few days since to a great werowance for two bushels of roanoke." ³⁵ Mr. Hamor told him that the roanoke was but a trifle to so great a prince, and by returning it, he might recall her and gratify his brother; and he further assured him that besides strengthening the strict band of peace and friendship between them he should have three times the worth of the roanoke for her in beads, copper, and other commodities. This extorted the truth from him, and he ingenuously confessed that the reason of his refusal was the love he bore to his daughter. Although he had many children, yet he delighted in none, he said, so much as her and could not possibly live without often seeing her, which he

33. Stith, *Virginia*, pp. 132–33. The English acquired New Netherlands, renamed New York, by conquest in 1664 during the second Anglo-Dutch War.

34. *Ibid.*, p. 134. Here Randolph seems to be picking up where he left off on p. 64 above.

35. Roanoke were black and white shells with holes which the Indians wore on strings about their arms and neck and used as a form of money (Hugh Jones, *The Present State of Virginia* [London, 1724; ed. Richard L. Morton, Chapel Hill, N.C., 1956], pp. 54, 163–64).

could not do if she lived among the English; for he had determined upon no terms to put himself into their hands or come among them. He therefore desired Hamor to urge him no further upon the subject but to return to his brother this answer: That he held it not a brotherly part to endeavor to bereave him of his two darling children at once. That for his part he desired no further assurance of English friendship than the promise which the governor had given, and that for himself Sir Thomas already had a pledge in one of his daughters, which as long as she lived would be sufficient; but if she should happen to die, he promised to give another. "And further," says he, "tell him, although he had no pledge at all, yet need he not distrust any injury from me or my people. There has been enough of blood and war. Too many have been slain already on both sides; and by any occasion arising from myself there shall never be more. I who have power to perform it, have said it. I am now grown old and would gladly end my days in peace and quietness; and although I should have just cause of resentment, yet my country is large enough, and I can go from you. And this answer I hope will satisfy my brother."⌉ [36]

Besides the internal domestic enemies of the colony, irritated as they were by not finding gold mines, it was now apparent that the Spanish nation were exploring the state of the colony with an eager eye to conquest, and thus pointed to a new quarter of hostility. ⌈A Spanish ship was seen to beat to and fro off Point Comfort; and at last, having sent a boat ashore for a pilot, Captain Davies, the governor of the fort, readily permitted Mr. John Clarke to go on board. He was no sooner there than the ship hoisted sail and carried him off to Spain. He was there strongly solicited to become an instrument and pilot to betray the colony. But he bravely and honorably resisted all their temptations and was therefore obliged to undergo a long captivity. At last, after four years' imprisonment, he with much difficulty returned to England. But the Spanish ship by some accident had left three of her own men behind, who were immediately seized and strictly examined. They said that having lost their admiral, they were forced into these ports, and that two of them were captains and in chief authority in the fleet. But some time after, one was discovered to be an Englishman who had been a pilot in the Spanish Armada, on the grand expedition against England in the year 1588, and not content with perfidy and baseness to his country, he began here to plot and persuade some malcontents to join

36. Stith, *Virginia*, pp. 135–36.

him in running away with a small bark. But they were apprehended, and some of them executed; and he, now lying at mercy, readily owned that there were two or three Spanish ships at sea equipped purposely to discover the state of the colony. But he said that their commission was not to be opened till they arrived in the bay of Chesapeake and that of anything further he was utterly ignorant. One of the Spaniards died here, and the other was sent to England. But this renegado was hanged at sea by Sir Thomas Dale on his voyage homeward.⌐ [37]

Sir Thomas Dale now attained the peculiar felicity of a man retiring with public gratitude from an office which had been arduous and critical. After an honorable service of five years, he embarked for England, accompanied by Pocahontas, her husband, Mr. Rolfe, and several young Indians of both sexes.[38]

⌐The prospects of the colony permitted all excessive grants to emigrants to be reduced. Hence instead of the ancient charter importation right or head right of one hundred acres of land to every person who should migrate, fifty acres, with a right to a further quantity when the first should be peopled and saved, that is *improved,* were given. Lands might be acquired also by purchase, upon the payment of £12 10s. for every hundred acres, not exceeding in the whole two thousand acres. This was denominated the adventure of the purse, and the sum was enormous, when the then value of money in the colony is calculated.[39]

⌐The colony had been under the necessity of buying corn from the Indians under taunts of bitter scorn and distressing difficulties. But the prudent management of Dale had opened a market and exchange for

37. *Ibid.,* p. 138. Capt. James Davis (d. 1624) was the commander of Fort Algernon at Point Comfort. John Clark (1576?–1623?) was a pilot sent aboard the Spanish ship to bring her into port. After several years of captivity he returned to England and later piloted the *Mayflower* to Plymouth. The three Spaniards imprisoned were Don Diego de Molina, sent to England by order of King James and then returned to Spain; Ensign Marco Antonio Perez, who died in Virginia; and Francis Lymbre, an English pilot who had lived in Spain for some years. Dale took Lymbre on his ship to England, but within sight of the English coast had him hanged on shipboard. Both Stith and Randolph mistakenly placed this episode in 1615. It actually occurred in 1611 (Stanard, *First Century,* pp. 107–8).

38. They arrived in England on May 13, 1616.

39. This change in land policy was initiated in 1616 by an announcement in a printed notice entitled *A Briefe Declaration of the Present State of Things in Virginia, and of a Division to Be Now made, of Some Part of Those Lands in Our Actuall Possession,* reprinted in Brown, *Genesis of the United States,* II, 774–79 (see also Craven, *Southern Colonies,* pp. 116–17; and W. Stitt Robinson, Jr., *Mother Earth: Land Grants in Virginia, 1607–1699* [Williamsburg, Va., 1957], pp. 16–17).

that article which the Indians would purchase with their clothing of skins or borrow upon a mortgage of their whole country.[40] Dale had seen how completely the cultivation of tobacco would encroach upon the labor necessary in that of corn and commanded that no tobacco should be planted until a certain proportion of corn ground sufficient for the master and each servant should be prepared and planted.[41] But no sooner had he departed than his law and his example were forgotten. Tobacco was pursued, the raising of bread neglected; neither the governor nor the people could withstand present gain, even in competition with the calls of life.⌉ [42]

This infatuation had it been momentary might perhaps have been pardonable, but it will be seen to have riveted two evils in the heart of Virginia, the declension of that agriculture which is the most safe and most honorable, and the encouragement of slavery, the most base of human conditions.

To analyze the cause of that extraordinary taste which has infested the world belongs not to this place. Most devoutly is it to be wished that the treatise which James I condescended to write against it, under the title of *A Counterblast to Tobacco,* had gratified by its success the vanity of its author.[43]

The usual consequence of the cultivation of tobacco was exemplified during this year in the scarcity of corn, which was aggravated by an additional number of emigrants to Virginia. ⌈This compelled Mr. Yeardley, the president, to demand from the neighboring tribes of the Chickahominies the tribute due to the colony in grain.[44] As they could draw forth for battle between two and three hundred men, they gave an affrontive answer to the requisition. Yeardley thereupon with one hundred able men repaired to their towns, where he received a contemptuous denial. He was told that he was only the servant of Sir Thomas Dale, that they had not withheld the tribute from his master according to agreement; but that as for him (Yeardley) they had no

40. Even though Powhatan remained hostile, Captain Argall was still able to open a profitable trade with the natives of the Potomac in copper trinkets, white beads, hoes, knives, bells, scissors, and hatchets for meat, corn, deerskins, and furs.

41. Dale required every tobacco planter to cultivate two acres of corn for himself and each manservant.

42. Stith, *Virginia,* pp. 139–40.

43. The tract was published anonymously in 1604.

44. When Dale left Virginia in April 1616 he appointed Sir George Yeardley as acting governor, a post Yeardley held until Argall returned from England in 1617.

orders to obey him or to give him any corn. This stoutness of heart was of short duration; for they could not obtain peace until they had fulfilled their former stipulations.⌉ [45]

Undoubtedly Opechancanough did on this occasion confirm in a glaring degree his reputation for craft. ⌈Neither his brother nor he could ever bring the obstinate Chickahominies firmly to their obedience. Being, therefore, as attentive to enslave them, as they were watchful and tenacious of their liberty, Opechancanough caught this opportunity and agreed with Mr. Yeardley to come to no terms with them without his advice and consent. And as the English passed down the river with their prisoners, he met them and pretended to the Indians that he had with great pains and solicitation procured them peace. To requite which service the Chickahominies cheerfully proclaimed him king of their nation and flocked from all parts with presents of beads, copper, and such other trifles as were in value and esteem among them. And he was glad to be content with this precarious acknowledgment from a free and resolute tribe. But the seasonable and vigorous chastisement of the Chickahominies from Yeardley and especially the friendship with Opechancanough and the whole imperial family kept the rest of the Indians in such awe and dependence that the English followed their labors with the utmost quietness and security. Many also of the savages daily brought them such provisions as they could get and would be their guides in hunting and sometimes hunt for them themselves. By such an intercourse and familiarity, the English and they lived together during the remaining term of Yeardley's government as if they had been one people. And Captain Smith tells us that Mr. Yeardley had some trained to kill him fowl with guns, as had likewise several other gentlemen in the country, and that these soon became as dexterous and expert as any of the English. But the captain's authority is rendered very suspicious in this by the records of our General Court, for long after, the governor and Council having received some queries from England, the fourth whereof was "What was the cause of the massacre, and who first taught the Indians the use of firearms?" in a court held November 1, 1624, Robert Poole and Edward Grindon, ancient planters and inhabitants of the country, appeared and declared upon oath their knowledge of the matter. Their depositions entirely clear Mr. Yeardley and show him to have been very cautious and careful in that point, and throw the whole blame

45. *Ibid.*, pp. 140–41.

upon Captain Smith himself, Sir Thomas Dale, and some other inferior officers and private persons.[46]

[Pocahontas, who had arrived in England, was well received and continued to foster and cement a friendly intercourse between the English and the nations subject to her father. Her name was changed into that of Lady Rebecca, and she was instructed with great care and attention in Christianity, spoke intelligible English, and was very civil and ceremonious after the English fashion. She was likewise delivered of a son, of whom she was extremely fond. And the treasurer and Company gave order for the handsome maintenance of both her and her child. Her company was courted, and she was treated with attention by many persons of the highest rank and quality; there has been indeed a constant tradition that the king was highly offended at Mr. Rolfe for marrying a princess. That anointed pedant, it seems, had so morbid a sense of the *ius divinum* and indefeasible right of Powhatan that he held it to be a great crime in any private man to connect himself in marriage with imperial progeny. He might likewise think consistently with his own principle that the rights to the dominion of Virginia would thereby be vested in Rolfe's posterity. However, it passed off without any further bad consequence than a little displeasure and murmuring.

[At the time of Pocahontas's arrival in England, Captain Smith was preparing for a voyage to New England. He was much concerned that the suddenness of his departure put it out of his power to render for her the service which he desired and she deserved at his hands. Being well acquainted at court and particularly favored and countenanced by Prince Charles, he drew up and presented to the queen, before she had reached London, a representation of her case and desert. In this he expresses the warmest gratitude to her and set forth her great affection and many services to himself and the whole English nation, adding that by her their quarrels had often been accommodated, their wants supplied, and dangers averted; that she, under God, had been the chief instrument of preserving the colony and confirming the settlement; that being taken prisoner, she had been the instrument of a firm peace and alliance with her father; that she was now married to an English gentleman who was not of ability to prepare her for attendance on Her Majesty; that she was the first Christian that ever was of her nation and the first Virginian that ever spoke English or had become

46. This reference is to the Indian uprising of 1622 (see Kingsbury, *Records of Virginia Company*, IV, 510–17).

an English subject; that being well received and honored by the great queen, beyond what her simple thought could conceive, she might be the cause of annexing another kingdom to His Majesty's dominions, but by bad usage her present love to the English and Christianity might be turned to scorn and fury, and all the good she had or might do, diverted to the worst evil; and therefore, he humbly recommended her to Her Majesty as a proper object of her favor and regard, on account of her birth, virtue, simplicity, and forlorn condition in a strange country.

⌈But before Captain Smith's departure, Pocahontas came up to London. Being offended by the smoke of the town, she was immediately removed to Brentford, whither Smith, with several of his friends, went to visit her. After a cold and modest salutation, she turned from him in a passionate manner, hid her face, and could not be brought to speak a word for two or three hours. But at last, she began to talk and reminded him of her many benefits to him and of the strict friendship between him and her father. "You," says she, "promised him that what was yours should be his and that you and he would be all one. Being a stranger in our country, you called Powhatan father, and I for the same reason will now call you so." Smith, knowing the jealous humor of the court, durst not allow that title, as she was a king's daughter, and therefore, he endeavored to excuse himself from it. But she, with a stern and steady countenance, said, "You were not afraid to come into my father's country and strike a fear into everybody but myself, and are you here afraid to let me call you father? I tell you then I will call call you father, and you shall call me child, and so I shall forever be of your kindred and country. They always told us that you were dead, and I knew no otherwise, till I came to Plymouth. But Powhatan commanded Tomocomo to seek you out and know the truth, because your countrymen are much given to lying."

⌈This Tomocomo (or Uttamatomakkin), as Smith calls him, was the husband of Matachanna, one of Powhatan's daughters, one of the chief of his council and of the priests, and was esteemed among the Indians wise. He was therefore sent upon this voyage by Powhatan to take the number of the people in England and to bring him a full and exact account of their strength and condition, and accordingly at Plymouth he procured a long stick, intending to cut a notch for every one he saw.[47] But he was soon tired with such an endless work, threw away

47. For details of Tomocomo's trip to England, see Barbour, *Captain John Smith*, pp. 331–32.

his stick, and being asked by the king after his return how many people were in England, he is said to have replied, "Count the stars in the sky, the leaves on the trees, and the sand upon the seashores, for such is the number of the people of England." But Sir Thomas Dale told Mr. Purchas that he believed him to be sent by Opechancanough, then king and governor in Powhatan's absence and retreat, not so much to number the people as to estimate their corn and trees.[48] For Namontack and such others as had been sent to England formerly, being ignorant and silly and having seen little else besides London, reported large numbers of men and houses and spoke of the corn and trees as few. It was therefore a general opinion among these barbarians that the English came into their country to get a supply of these deficient articles, which might perhaps be confirmed by their sending large quantities of cedar, clapboard, and wainscot to England and by their continual solicitude for corn. But Tomocomo, landing in the west and traveling thence to London, was soon undeceived and saw great cause to admire the English plenty. However, he pursued his estimate until his arithmetic failed him. Meeting with Captain Smith accidentally in London, they soon renewed their old acquaintance. He told the captain that Powhatan had commanded him to find him out and to urge him to show to him the English god, the English king, and queen, and prince, of whom he had told Powhatan so much. As to God, Captain Smith excused himself, explaining the matter in the best way he could; and as to the king, Smith told him he had already seen *him* and should see the rest of the royal family whenever he pleased. But Tomocomo denied that he had seen the king till by circumstances he was convinced of the fact. Then with a melancholy countenance he said: "You gave Powhatan a white dog, which he fed as himself, but your king has given me nothing, and yet I am better than your white dog." Such an acute insight had this barbarian into the penurious character of the king. Pocahontas was in great request and courteously entertained everywhere. Many courtiers and others of his acquaintance daily flocked to Captain Smith to be introduced to her. They generally acknowledged that the hand of God did visibly appear in her conversion and that they had seen many English ladies "worse favored," of less exact proportion, and less genteel carriage than she was. The Lady De la Warr carried

---

48. Samuel Purchas (1574–1626) is best known for his *Hakluytus Posthumus, or Purchas His Pilgrimes,* which first appeared in 1625. Namontack was a trusted servant of Powhatan who had traveled to England with Captain Newport (Barbour, *Captain John Smith,* p. 184).

her to court, attended by the lord, her husband, and many other persons of fashion and distinction. The whole court were charmed and surprised at the decency and grace of her deportment, and the king himself and the queen received her with honor and esteem. The Lady De la Warr and those other persons of quality also waited on her to masks, balls, plays, and other public entertainments with which she was wonderfully delighted.⌉ [49]

Virginia was, however, doomed to be harassed by every engine of faction. ⌈The Lord Rich, one of the Company in England, was great and powerful but most interested and artful.[50] Not content with that lawful and regular advantage which might be justly expected in a due course of time from the enterprise, but aiming at a sudden and extraordinary profit, although it should be by the spoil of the public and the oppression of private planters, and being prompted and assisted by some corrupt and avaricious persons, he threw himself at the head of a faction in the Company and drew over to his party as many dependents as he could. By their means and support, he hoped and endeavored to acquire such a sway both in Virginia and the Somer's Islands Company that the management of all things at home and the placing of all governors abroad should be entirely in his power and at his will. Although he was counteracted in his designs by many great and worthy members and a vast majority of the whole companies, yet he did at this time carry a very important point. Captain Argall, a friend and relation of Sir Thomas Smith, the treasurer, was one of Lord Rich's most fast friends and favorites. His lordship therefore, having concerted matters with him and entered into a partnership, procured him to be elected deputy governor of Virginia. Martial law was then the common law of the country; yet the better to invest him with the exercise of so despotic an authority, he obtained for him the place of admiral of the country and the seas adjoining.

⌈With these views and powers had Captain Argall been arrayed and sent to Virginia in the beginning of the year 1617. The treasurer and

49. Stith, *Virginia*, pp. 141–45.

50. Lord Robert Rich (d. 1619), first earl of Warwick, had inherited one of the largest fortunes in England. He had a large private fleet and despite the outspoken opposition of James I to piracy he refused to give up this profitable practice (Wesley Frank Craven, "The Earl of Warwick—A Speculator in Piracy," *Hispanic American Historic Review*, X [1930], 457–79). His son Robert Rich (1587–1658), the second earl of Warwick, was destined to play a crucial role in the factional struggles that ended with the dissolution of the Virginia Company as a leader of the group attempting to oust Sir Edwin Sandys and his followers from power (Craven, *Dissolution of Virginia Company*, pp. 125–26).

Council made the necessary arrangements for the return of Pocahontas and her husband on board the admiral's ship. Mr. Rolfe was also made secretary and recorder general of Virginia, an office now first created. But at Gravesend, Pocahontas died in about the twenty-second year of her age. Her unexpected death caused not more sorrow and concern in the spectators than her religious end gave them joy. For she expired as she had lived a sincere and pious Christian. Her little son Thomas Rolfe was left at Plymouth with Sir Lewis Stucley, who desired the care and education of him. This gentleman was then vice admiral of the county of Devon, but soon after, having seized Sir Walter Raleigh and having been guilty of a notable treachery toward him, he drew upon himself the public scorn and detestation, for however hard and unjust kings and statesmen may be to those persons of their age who are of eminent parts and virtues, the public, generally more candid in their judgment, are apt to resent every ill usage to such men.[51] But Sir Lewis Stucley fell unpitied when he was afterwards detected in corrupt practices, for which he was obliged to purchase his life at the expense of his whole fortune, and at last died a poor despised and distracted beggar. As these misfortunes happened soon after this time, it is not to be supposed that young Mr. Rolfe long enjoyed the advantage of his favor and kind intentions. He was educated in London by his uncle, Mr. Henry Rolfe, and afterwards became a person of fortune and distinction in this country. But Governor Argall, with his vice admiral, Captain Ralph Hamor, pursued his voyage to Virginia, where they arrived in May. They found that all the public works and buildings in Jamestown had fallen into decay, that not more than five or six houses were fit to be inhabited, that the market place, the streets, and all other vacant spots were planted with tobacco, and the colony distributed according to the most convenient places for planting. But soon after Argall's arrival he wrote to England that the colony was in great peace and plenty and the people busily employed in preparing for their crops of corn and tobacco. With him returned Tomocomo, who in our old records is called by a third name, Tomakin. Captain Argall sent him immediately to Opechancanough, who came to Jamestown and received a present with great joy and thankfulness. Tomocomo railed violently against England and the English, and

51. Sir Lewis Stucley (d. 1620) had been commissioned by the king to arrest Sir Walter Raleigh in 1618. Although he was Raleigh's cousin, Stucley was appointed Raleigh's warden not only in his official role as vice admiral of Devonshire, but because he had a grudge against Raleigh dating back to 1584 when Raleigh allegedly deceived him on a venture involving the ship *Tiger.*

particularly against his best friend, Sir Thomas Dale. But all his reports were so clearly disproved before Opechancanough and his grandees that much to their satisfaction he was rejected and disgraced. Powhatan, leaving the care and charge of the government chiefly to Opechancanough, went about from place to place, enjoying his pleasure and visiting his different dominions. He continued in good friendship with the English. While he greatly lamented the death of his daughter, he rejoiced that her child was living and expressed a strong desire to see him, but determined that he ought not to come over from England before he should be stronger. In this year, one Mr. Lambert made a great discovery in the art of planting. For the method of curing tobacco then was in heaps, but this gentleman found out that it cured better upon lines.] [52]

[The Lord De la Warr, who had withdrawn from the government on account of his bad health, and whose commission as captain general superseded all others, being ardently wished for by the colony, was now sent by the Council and Company in a large ship with a supply of two hundred people. But meeting with contrary winds and much bad weather, many fell sick, and thirty died. In this number was the governor himself, a person of a most noble and generous disposition who had warmly embarked and expended much money in this business for his country's good. Camden [53] tells us that he had been feasted at the West India Islands and that his death was not without suspicion of poison, and Stith thinks that he has somewhere seen that he died about the mouth of Delaware Bay, which thence took its name from him. After his death, the ship was forced on the coast of New England, where was procured a recruit of wood and water and such an abundance of fish and fowl as plentifully served the crew to Virginia. On the arrival of Dale, intelligence arrived that multitudes were preparing in England to be sent to Virginia. Captain Argall called a Council and wrote to the treasurer in England the state of the colony, in which he declared what misery must ensue if provisions should not accompany the people.[54] The governor represented their want of skillful husbandmen in the colony and of plowshares, harness, and other implements for plowing. Their land was exceedingly good, and they had now about forty bulls

52. Stith, *Virginia*, pp. 145–47. Mr. Lambert found that tobacco leaves cured better when strung on lines than when sweated under piles of hay (*Brown, First Republic*, p. 260; Herndon, *Tobacco in Colonial Virginia*, p. 16).

53. William Camden (1551–1623), antiquarian and historian, published his *Annales* in 1615.

54. Argall's letter is reprinted in Brown, *First Republic*, pp. 260–61.

and oxen which were wholly idle and useless for want of knowledge how to bring them to labor. About this time, however, it is recorded some plows were set to work.

[Captain Argall was not negligent or forgetful of the grand end of his coming to Virginia but pushed on his unrighteous gains by all imaginable methods of extortion and oppression. For besides a multitude of private wrongs to particular persons, he appropriated in a manner wholly to his own use and possession whatsoever remained belonging to the public, being the fruits and relics of an expense of £80,000, so that he was loudly charged with many offenses and with depredations on the public property, with a waste of the revenues of the Company, and with grievous oppression to several private men. Sir Thomas Smith, whether in favor to Captain Argall, his kinsman, or from his real judgment, opposed the solicitation of the royal interposition against Argall lest it might prove prejudicial in the Company's power and of dangerous consequences to their liberties and give room for public scandal. He therefore substituted a milder and less clamorous way of proceeding by a letter to Argall.

[To this end, he himself, Alderman Johnson, the deputy treasurer, Sir Lionel Cranfield,[55] and others of the Council wrote Captain Argall a letter, dated August 23, 1618, charging him in very sharp and severe terms with many crimes and misdemeanors, stating that he was a heavy burden to the Company and converted the fruits of their expense to his own private use; that he was grown so proud and insolent as to scorn the title of deputy governor, declaring that he would be no man's deputy; that he wronged the magazine by his negligence and connivancy; that he had appropriated the Indian trade to himself, using the Company's frigate and other vessels together with their men to trade for his own benefit and prohibiting the trade of skins and furs to all others; that he took the old planters, who ought to be free, as well as the Company's tenants and servants, and set them upon his own employments; that he expended the public store of corn to feed his own

---

55. Alderman Robert Johnson was an important figure in the history of the Virginia Company. He had served as deputy treasurer of the Bermuda Company and was one of those who petitioned in 1623 for a royal investigation of the Company's affairs (Craven, *Dissolution of Virginia Company*, p. 258). Sir Lionel Cranfield (1575–1645), the lord treasurer of England, had demonstrated ability and loyalty and risen to a high place in the king's Council. He was one of the older adventurers in the Virginia Company and an active member of the Virginia Council and as surveyor general of the customs since 1613 had been in close touch with the colony's affairs. He was charged with settling questions regarding customs duties and the tobacco monopoly (*ibid.*, p. 232).

men; that he had for some private end and purpose of his own informed that Opechancanough and the natives intended to give the country to Mr. Rolfe's child and to withhold it from all others till he came of age; that he neither looked into nor regarded the instructions of the Company but had under pretense of their commission disposed of all the Company's cattle, against their express orders and directions, and had applied the profits thereof to his own use; that he had under color of his right as admiral seized and detained some hides unlawfully taken or purchased, for which the Company had compounded with the lord high admiral and the Spanish ambassador at the great expense of £400; and in short, that all his actions and proceedings seemed to be as if the colony was intended for his private gain and advantage, and as if he was so great, and they so mean and insensible of reason, as to let things of this public and notorious nature pass off without a strict and exact account, and upbraiding him also with these ungrateful returns to their favor and friendship in procuring him the government.[56]

[At the same time they wrote a letter to Lord De la Warr, whose death was yet unknown in England, containing the like heads of complaint and accusation against Captain Argall and informed him that by the strange insolences of his last letter, and by the informations of sundry witnesses lately come from Virginia, there was more discontent raised in the adventurers and more danger feared to the colony than had ever happened by any other thing since the first beginning of the enterprise. So that the adventurers could hardly be restrained from going to the king, although far off on a progress, and procuring His Majesty's command to fetch him home as a malefactor. But to avoid further scandal to their management and administration, they beseech his lordship to send him forthwith to England to make his personal appearance and to give his answer to such things as should be laid to his charge; and for as much as it was conceived that there would be many things for which he must make satisfaction to the Company, they desired his lordship to seize upon his tobacco, skins, furs, and other goods to be sent to them as a deposit till all matters should be satisfied and adjusted, and that he would likewise return the cattle and other public goods which he had embezzled to their proper places and owners. And at the same time, there was an order of court passed in England to sequester all Captain Argall's effects which should be sent home, to make restitution to the Company for his rapines and extortions.

56. See Kingsbury, *Records of Virginia Company*, III, 106, 119–20.

[These letters coming by Lord De la Warr's death to Captain Argall's own hands were so far from diverting or repressing his exorbitancies that they seemed only to put him upon his guard and to render him the more eager and studious to make the best of his time. For Lady De la Warr complained that he wrongfully took some of her goods from her late husband's servants without accounting for them. And indeed he had in general assumed to himself a power of ordering and disposing of his lordship's estate, employing his tenants and servants to his own work and thereby ruining and depopulating a very large and hopeful plantation begun by his lordship. But one Captain Edward Brewster, alleging Lord De la Warr's order for their being under his management and direction, endeavored to withdraw them from the governor's work and to occupy them in the maintenance of themselves and for the benefit of his lordship's heirs and fellow adventurers.[57] But one of them refused to obey him, which drew from Brewster some threatening expressions which were immediately conveyed to the governor, who being drunk with power and impatient of opposition and vexed that anyone should dare to withstand his arbitrary schemes of gain, caused Brewster to be seized, tried by a court-martial, and condemned to death.

[This proceeding was founded on an article of the martial laws of the Low Countries introduced among those sent over by Sir Thomas Smith. This decreed "that no man should offer any violence to or contemptuously resist or disobey his commander, or do any act, or speak any words, which might tend to breed disorder or mutiny, in the town or field, or disobey any principal officer's directions, upon pain of death." Although by the charter the governor might not execute martial law but in times of mutiny and rebellion, as lords lieutenant in England had done, and in all other cases, as well civil as criminal, their proceedings were to be as agreeable as conveniently might be to the laws, statutes, government, and policy of the realm of England, and it was evident that there was at that time no pretense of rebellion or smiting and that the colony enjoyed universal peace and tranquillity, yet was this innocent man's condemnation most unmercifully urged on and his life subjected to the pleasure of a furious and enraged enemy. And this not in an affair of public concern, but in a dispute of private right. It did not appear that Brewster had uttered anything against the governor but only some threatening language against a servant

57. Edward Brewster was a member of the Virginia Company and probably came to Virginia with Lord De la Warr in 1610.

who disobeyed his lawful commands. The law itself too could have no binding force or validity in the British dominions, still it must be confessed that martial law was accepted the reigning law by Virginia, to the great discouragement of the colony and to the manifest infringement of the rights and liberties of the people as British subjects. Being occasionally introduced in earlier times in a state of war and danger, it was confirmed by those bloody articles sent by Sir Thomas Smith. They were unfortunately at their coming applied to a good purpose and effect by Sir Thomas Dale in quelling certain disorderly and mutinous humors. And thus by example and authority an easy acquiescence and an ignorance of the genuine rights and privileges of subjects, it was made the standing rule of proceeding and became the custom of the country.

[When some of the court reflected on the extreme severity of these martial laws and were also moved perhaps by the particular hardship and unrighteousness of the present case of Brewster, they prevailed on the rest to go in a body and intercede for Captain Brewster's life. Being joined by such of the clergy as were at hand, they did with much entreaty and after many repulses, all allegations of Captain Argall, at last save Brewster's life, upon this express condition, that he should take a solemn oath neither directly nor indirectly in England or elsewhere to utter any contemptuous words nor do anything else that should turn to the dishonor or disparagement of Captain Argall, and that he should never return more to Virginia by any direct or indirect means. This man was a person of some figure and consideration and yet was obliged to submit to all this to respite an immediate execution. But after his return to England, being deeply sensible of this oppressive and injurious treatment and being anxious to restore his reputation and to wipe off the stain of being a condemned malefactor, he appealed from the sentence of the court-martial in Virginia to the treasurer and Company in England.] [58]

58. Stith, *Virginia*, pp. 148–53. For the Brewster decision, see Edward D. Neill, *The Virginia Company of London* (Washington, D.C., 1868), pp. 187–88. Like Stith, Randolph was unduly harsh with Argall. Whether the charges lodged against him were true or false—and most of them have been discredited—the governor rendered many important services to the colony. When Governor Argall arrived in the colony he expressed shock at "the carelessness and lawless living" of the people and their unwise confidence in the Indians. As a result, he once more invoked the *Lawes Divine, Morall and Martiall*. Since Argall's strict and strenuous regime followed a year of relaxation under Yeardley, some of the more "careless" planters, as he put it, were irked by the new rules. In addition, his frank criticism and advice no doubt annoyed some members of the Council in England. Unfortunately for Argall his administration began in 1617, a year when there

This year was memorable for the death of two persons of principal figure in the Virginian history: one was Sir Walter Raleigh, who ended his life on the scaffold, to the everlasting infamy of King James.[59] Captain Smith was requested in the Company's name to write the history of Virginia. The reasons assigned for the request were "to the end that the memory and deserts of many of her worthy undertakers, as Sir Walter Raleigh, together with divers others then living might be commended to eternal thanksgiving." The immediate composition was earnestly recommended, because a few years would devour these letters and intelligencies which yet remained in loose and neglected papers.[60]

It may be justly feared that notwithstanding this vote of justice, it has been denied to this distinguished man from a suspicion of its probable impression on the mind of his sovereign, who was exasperated against him. Seldom can such a one emerge from behind a cloud which royal authority may gather round his head; but it diminishes the luster of my country when I recollect that almost the only remembrance of him from public suffrage is to be found in the name of a parish which perished with our ecclesiastical establishment and a tavern in the city of Williamsburg, which possesses no longer one metropolitan honor.

The chief events of his life lay in Europe where the merit and demerit of his actions have been discussed and have received various judgments. With them, except as they may be connected with his benefactions to Virginia, we on the western side of the Atlantic do not intermeddle. But the celebrated Robertson has arraigned him as having become cold toward her and thereby occasioned a long dereliction of her welfare. He says that, during the remainder of Elizabeth's reign,

---

was a great mortality among the colonists and a plague among the deer, followed in 1618 by a general crop failure and the goods for the magazine arriving badly damaged by the five-month voyage to Virginia. Everyone needed a scapegoat, and Argall was their choice. As if things were not bad enough for Argall, he was caught between two opposing factions within the Council of the Company. When a new governor, Sir George Yeardley, was sent to Virginia, he had instructions to prosecute Argall. But Argall had already left for England, and even though the Sandys faction tried to put him on trial, his patron, Robert Rich, was able to prevent these proceedings (for an account of this episode, see Morton, *Colonial Virginia*, I, 45–56).

59. Sir Walter Raleigh perished by the headman's axe on Oct. 29, 1618, a victim of James I's attempt to assure Spain of his desire for peace.

60. Smith's *General History of Virginia* appeared in 1624. Although a few members of the London Council may have encouraged him, Smith did not write in the Company's name (Barbour, *Captain John Smith*, pp. 350–69).

the scheme of establishing a colony in Virginia was not resumed. Raleigh, with the most aspiring mind and extraordinary talents, enlightened by knowledge no less uncommon, had the spirit and defects of a projector. Always allured by new objects and giving the preference to such as were the most splendid, he was apt to engage in undertakings so vast and so various as to be far beyond his power of accomplishing. He was now intent on peopling and improving a large district of country in Ireland, of which he had obtained a grant from the queen.[61] He was a deep adventurer in fitting out a powerful armament against Spain in order to establish Don Antonio on the throne of Portugal.[62] He had begun to form his favorite, but visionary, project of penetrating into Guiana, where he fondly dreamed of taking possession of inexhaustible wealth flowing from the richest mines in the New World.[63] Amidst this multiplicity of objects of such promising appearance, and recommended by novelty, he naturally became cold toward his ancient and hitherto unprofitable scheme of establishing a colony in Virginia and was easily induced to assign his right of property in that country, which he had never visited, together with all the privileges contained in his patent, to Sir Thomas Smith and a company of merchants in London.[64]

It is impossible that a writer of such positive eminence as Robertson, and so painstaking a man in the search of truth, could have brought into almost the latter end of the eighteenth century the prejudices propagated under the malignity of James I to obscure the fame of Raleigh as being a projector. Columbus was conducted to his great naval experiment by a deception of the maps, which extended India farther to the east than it really is, and this suggested to him a western course in quest of it, which brought him to America—was he ever branded as a projector? Did not Raleigh confide not only in his own solid opinions on cosmography but also upon the experience of Columbus? Did he not expend his private fortune and large additional aids from royal bounty upon the expedition? When he invited cooperation, did he propose or promise anything more than every adventurer might

61. For his part in suppressing an Irish insurrection in 1580, Raleigh had received a grant of 12,000 acres in Cork and Waterford.

62. When King Henry of Portugal died childless in 1580, there were a number of claimants, including Don Antonio, the Prior of Crato; the Valois family of France; and Philip II of Spain. Philip backed his claim with force and easily routed Don Antonio. Queen Elizabeth gave her consent to two unsuccessful projects engineered by Sir Francis Drake in 1582 and again in 1589 to place Don Antonio on the throne (James A. Williamson, *The Age of Drake* [Cleveland, 1964], pp. 210–14, 372–76).

63. For Raleigh's role in the acquisition of Guiana in South America, see *ibid.*, pp. 358–70.

64. *History of America*, p. 400.

be willing to hazard upon his own speculation? Were not the voluntary subscriptions of those adventurers induced by public reports concerning America? Is it not enough to add that the rulers of Virginia, in the archives where his exertions, injuries, and expenditures are deposited, have deemed it their duty to perpetuate his agency in the success of the great work?

I pass over the charge of deism elsewhere made against Raleigh because a eulogium on patriotism is not to be measured by an orthodoxy of creed. But even this ought to be contradicted, as it may be with truth. To a Christian historian of Virginia the confronting of this imputation is consigned by the peculiar circumstance that when Locke, Bacon, and Newton have been quoted in the hearing of youth as champions of the Gospel, they have been confronted with some others, who have had a closer relation to our country. If Raleigh cannot be defended in this particular by special proofs as decisive as might be wished, it will not be rashness to observe that experience has not informed us of a man, well versed in the learning subordinate to the study of the Scriptures, not alienated from them by the opinions and examples of others, to whom his deference was unbounded; nor by his own indolence or habits of inattention; or by the seduction of some ancient frivolous system of metaphysics, the sole merit of which consists in propounding subtleties to embarrass minds not duly exercised in reflection nor by a total absorption in the business, cares, and pleasures of the world; nor by self-sufficiency; by vanity; by a frame of life which must be a source of misery if those Scriptures be true; nor by the fear or love of ridicule. Of such a man who has seriously sat down to canvass the evidences of Christianity and has not risen impressed with its authenticity, experience has not informed us; at least no reason appears in the known private history of any celebrated deist of an exception from this assertion. Raleigh in his *History of the World* has shown a competency of intellect to probe this essential topic to the bottom.[65] Until, therefore, it shall be incontestable that he was a deist, let it be denied, and even if a supposed semblance should be afforded to the idea, it will invade no rule of philosophizing on the human character to require that its probability should be tried by the tests which are here intimated. All these proclaim the contrary.[66]

The other person of great consideration with respect to Virginia

65. *The History of the World* (1614) was written during Raleigh's imprisonment in the Tower of London.
66. Robertson never mentioned Raleigh's religious beliefs.

who died about this time ⌈was Powhatan, emperor of the Indians, a prince of excellent sense and parts, and a great master of all the savage arts of government and policy. He was penetrating, crafty, insidious, and cruel, and as hard to be deceived by others as to be avoided in his own stratagems and snares. But as to the great and moral arts of policy, such as truth, faith, uprightness, and magnanimity, they seem to have been but little heeded or regarded by him. He was succeeded in his dominions, according to the regular order of succession, by his second brother Opitchapan, who is sometimes called Itoyatin and Oetan. And now upon his accession to the supreme power he again changed his name, to Sasawpen, as Opechancanough did his to Mangopeeomen. Upon what reason of custom, or dignity, or humor, these changes were made in their names cannot be said. Opitchapan, being an easy, decrepid, and inactive prince, was soon eclipsed by the superior parts and ambition of his youngest brother, Opechancanough, whose character and activity first attracted attention and at last by degrees absorbed the whole power of the government, although for some time he was content with the title of king of Chickahominy. However, they both renewed and confirmed the league with the English under the protection of which every man peaceably followed his building and planting without any remarkable accidents or interruptions for some time.⌉ [67]

67. Stith, *Virginia,* pp. 154–55.

Chapter III   From the Establishment of a Legislative Assembly to the Dissolution of the Virginia Company

We hasten to the auspicious era when many of the most interesting powers of government resulted so far within the delegation and control of the people as to enable them to provide through their representatives for their defense against savages, against the return of famine and such invasions of liberty as they had been taught to dread from their own experience and from the small though sturdy advances toward sound principles which English theory had even then made. Why during the regal government, at the very hour of organizing the constitution of our present Commonwealth, it was admitted as a principle of jurisprudence that no other of the statutes of England than those prior to the fourth [year] of James I of a general and not of a local nature should be recognized as binding is to be solved by the universal concession that from that date Virginia had a competent legislature of her own.

It would seem that the colony really wanted better guardians, than those who had hitherto been assigned to them, ⌈for after the labors of twelve years and the expenditure of many thousand pounds on her, the population did not exceed six hundred persons, nor the cattle three hundred head; the goats were few, though the hogs, whose increase speaks little in favor of public care, were indeed numerous. The land and plantations of the Company had been depopulated and ruined by Captain Argall; only three tenants and six men of those whom he called his guard were remaining upon them. The Company too had been deceived by Sir Thomas Smith, the treasurer, who represented that there was a surplus of £4,000, when their debts amounted to that sum.⌉ [1]

Had not Argall escaped before the arrival of Sir George Yeardley in Virginia, commissioned as governor, he would have been prosecuted with rigor for his outrages; for her situation had interested men in

1. Stith, *Virginia,* pp. 159–60.

power on the other side of the Atlantic. Let it be quoted as a daring treachery in him that several charters of liberties had been sent over in his charge and he was expressly instructed to convoke the General Assembly to confirm to the ancient planters all their estates and a release from personal service to the colony. His rapine and his impositions on the freemen rendered this last privilege an acquisition of great value.[2]

These charters appear to have been owing more immediately to that distinguished member of Parliament Sir Edwin Sandys, who was appointed the treasurer of the colony.[3]

After the indispensable act of remedying the scarcity of corn by a disregard of tobacco, Yeardley summoned the General Assembly, the representatives in which had been elected by townships and boroughs. [Hence that branch of the legislature (corresponding with the House of Commons in England) derived the appellation of the House of Burgesses] and so were called until the extinction of royalty in Virginia at the American Revolution.[4] [The legislature sat and debated after the manner of the Scotch Parliament, and their acts were laid before the Council in England for approbation or rejection. Of the acts of this session no record is extant; but Sandys assured the Company that they were judicious although intricate.[5] In a short time the spirit of the British constitution rooted out trials by martial law, which, as has been seen, prevailed notwithstanding the exemptions conferred on every British subject transplanted hither.][6]

2. Randolph's contention that Argall treacherously disobeyed instructions to convoke a General Assembly is not consistent with the facts. The order to call such an assembly was contained in the instructions carried to the colony by the new governor, Sir George Yeardley.

3. Randolph is referring to the instructions issued on Nov. 18, 1618, to Yeardley, described in the proceedings of the Virginia Assembly as "the commission for establishing the Counsell of Estate and the General Assembly" and "the greate Charter, or commission of privileges, orders, and laws" (Kingsbury, *Records of Virginia Company*, III, 98–109). This move was part of a general plan for reorganizing the Company and strengthening the colony conceived chiefly by Sir Thomas Smith, Sir Edwin Sandys, and Nicholas and John Ferrar (Morton, *Colonial Virginia*, I, 51).

4. The Company's instructions were to call a General Assembly consisting of two groups, the councilors chosen by the Company to assist the governor and the burgesses elected by the freemen of the colony (Kingsbury, *Records of Virginia Company*, III, 98–109).

5. By the manner of the Scotch Parliament, Randolph probably meant the practice of having the governor and the Council consult in the same house with the burgesses. The Assembly did pass a series of laws and petitions, which are reprinted in Tyler, *Narratives of Virginia*, pp. 249–78.

6. Stith, *Virginia*, pp. 160–61. Martial law was specifically terminated by the 1618 plan of reorganization.

The mortality in Virginia this year destroyed not less than three hundred of the inhabitants. The connection between the general state of health and the luxuriance of the crops is marked by no philosophic examination at the time. The fact cannot be doubted that the first harvest of wheat having been shaken and lost by the fury of the wind, a crop of rare ripe corn was raised upon the stubble.

[His Majesty had by his letters patent, bearing date May 23, 1609, granted to the Company a "freedom from all custom and subsidy for twenty-one years, excepting only 5 per cent upon all such goods and merchandise as should be imported into England or any other of His Majesty's dominions, according to the ancient trade of merchants." Notwithstanding this, which was intended for the ease and encouragement of the infant colony, the farmers of the customs, upon a general rate made of tobacco, both Spanish and Virginia, at ten shillings the pound, demanded six pence in the pound equally upon all, although Spanish tobacco was usually sold at eighteen shillings a pound, and sometimes more, and Virginia would seldom bear above three or four shillings. Mr. Jacob also, farmer of the impost upon tobacco, did most oppressively impose another six pence a pound, contrary to the clear and indubitable tenor of His Majesty's grant. And the Company in June this year importing 20,000 weight, the whole crop of the former years, had delivered it all into the customhouse, as they were required, that the tobacco might be weighed and the custom answered. But Mr. Jacob by his own authority stopped and seized the tobacco, till that impost of six pence a pound should be discharged. And this also will soon be perceived by those who are anything versed in the history of those times to be entirely consonant to the behavior of the customers then, whose insolence and arbitrary proceedings were supported by the royal authority, and were increased and carried to a greater height in the next region, and were among the chief and most visible causes of the general discontents of the nation and of the civil war which ensued.

[The Company, being thus wronged and abused, applied themselves to the lords of His Majesty's Privy Council and obtained their letter to Mr. Jacob to deliver the tobacco, upon their entering into bond to pay him whatsoever should appear to be his due upon certificate from His Majesty's learned Council within a month. But Jacob rejecting this and all other conditions offered by the Company and likewise exacting twelve pence a pound at Plymouth upon the Somer Island tobacco, it was resolved to try the strength of their charter and to enter an action against them for the damage, which was always computed at £2,500 sterling. But afterwards considering that the commodity was very perishable and that their suit could not be determined that Michaelmas term, they altered their method of proceeding; and by the advice of a great lord of the Privy Council to Sir Edwin Sandys, the Company brought their wrongs before the Council board, where, upon the attorney general's delivering his opinion clearly that by their letters patent they were free from all imposition, it was ordered, upon a full hearing of the allegations on both sides, that he should deliver the tobacco to the Company, paying all lawful duties appertaining thereto. And thus at length they regained their goods out of the hands of this harpy but were obliged to submit to the loss and damage occasioned by impairing its worth through drying and other corruption and by the fall of the price upon the sale of English tobacco made since its importation.[7]

[It was one peculiar mark and property of the Stuart family of kings that they were always craving and forever poor and in want, notwithstanding the frequent contributions of the people to some of them. King James, overcoming his natural antipathy to tobacco, began now to taste the sweets of the revenue arising from it, and therefore he demanded of the Company a duty of twelve pence per pound on theirs. But it was unanimously agreed to stand resolutely upon the privilege of their charter, which they could not give up without a breach of trust and duty. And as Virginia tobacco had never been sold for more than five shillings per pound but generally much lower, they submitted to pay three pence a pound as a custom, which was full 5 per cent on its highest price. But to avoid all contest with the king, as he had given orders for prohibiting, by proclamation, the planting of tobacco in England for five years ensuing, they agreed in return for this favor during that term, if the proclamation took effect and con-

7. The charters of both the Virginia and Bermuda companies exempted them from duties for seven years. In 1619 this provision expired for the Virginia Company, but that for the Bermuda Company still had three years to run. Nevertheless, from 1619 both companies were required to pay duties in excess of those originally provided by their charters. This decision is explained in part by the fact that when the charters were issued there was no reason to expect that imports from the colonies would be composed almost entirely of tobacco. Abraham Jacob was granted in Dec. 1621 for £8,000 a patent for the impost and right of sole importation of 60,000 weight of Spanish tobacco. The Virginia Company gained two advantages: first, a complete prohibition of tobacco growing in England; secondly, a limitation on the importation of foreign tobacco into England. The heavy taxation, the combined total being 12d. with 6d. for the impost and 6d. to the tax farmer, and the monopoly of importation established in 1620 were major factors in bankrupting the Virginia treasury (Craven, *Dissolution of Virginia Company*, pp. 224-31).

tinued so long, to add nine pence a pound more and thereby to make it up twelve pence, which was equal to the royal demand though not in the same form.

[The trade of Virginia had been thus far restrained and kept in the adventurers' hands, except where a few interlopers came in by chance; every adventurer subscribed what he thought proper to a roll, which money together with a certain sum perhaps contributed out of the public funds of the Company constituted their capital or stock. To remove therefore such a block of offense, it was now agreed to dissolve the public magazine and to leave the trade free and open to all, under this restriction, that the goods of the magazine then upon hand in Virginia should first be sold off before any of the same kinds should be vended.[8] The diligence, vigor, and fidelity of Sir Edwin Sandys, and of others of the Company, had now raised the reputation of the action very high, and an unknown person had presented a communion cup, with a cover and case, a trencher plate for the bread, a carpet of crimson velvet, and a damask tablecloth for the use of the college; and another person had given a set of plate with other rich ornaments to the church called Mrs. Mary Robinson's, who had bequeathed £200 toward the building of it; and now, in the beginning of this year, another unknown person sent £500 directed to Sir Edwin Sandys, "the faithful treasurer of Virginia." This was for the maintenance of a convenient number of young Indians, from seven or under, to twelve years of age, to be instructed in reading and the principles of the Christian religion, and then to be brought up in some trade with all gentleness and humanity, till they should attain the age of twenty-one, and after that to have and enjoy the like liberties and privileges with native English in Virginia. He likewise sent £50 to be given into the hands of two religious and worthy persons as superintendents of this duty, who should every quarter examine and certify to the treasurer in England the due execution of this design, together with the names of the children and their tutors and overseers.[9] This charity the Company thought proper not to entrust to private hands but committed the management of it to Smith's Hundred chiefly. It lay in the parts above Hampton and was so called in honor to Sir Thomas Smith. But after this Sir Thomas with the earl of Warwick and the rest of that

8. Because of financial problems the magazine was dissolved in Jan. 1620. Supplies were now to be handled by individual agreement between the Company and the merchants (Kingsbury, *Records of Virginia Company*, I, 293; Craven, *Dissolution of Virginia Company*, pp. 115–16).

9. See Kingsbury, *Records of Virginia Company*, III, 117, 575.

faction sold out their shares in this and other private plantations and only reserved their part in the Company's public stock.

[For the better procuring and retaining of the Indian children, the Company ordered a treaty and agreement to be made with Opechancanough and authorized Sir George Yeardley to make him such presents from the magazine as would be most grateful to him and would best promote the design. Mr. Nicholas Ferrar the elder also bequeathed £300 for converting infidel children in Virginia. He ordered this sum to be paid into the hands of Sir Edwin Sandys and Mr. John Ferrar at such time as it should appear by certificate that ten Indian children were placed in the college and then by them to be disposed of according to his true intent and meaning. In the meantime he obliged his executors to pay 8 per cent for the money to be given to three several honest men in Virginia of good life and fame and such as Sir Edwin Sandys and Mr. John Ferrar should approve, each to bring up one of the said children in the grounds and principles of the Christian religion.[10]

[There were at this time few clergymen in Virginia, indeed only five ministers of the church, and eleven boroughs, each of which being very distant from the others was erected into a distinct parish, although the Company had before, in their charter by Sir George Yeardley, taken care of a handsome provision for the clergy, for they had ordered that an hundred acres of land in each of the boroughs should be laid off for a glebe and that for their further maintenance a standing and certain revenue should be levied in each parish so as to make every living at least £200 sterling a year. For a further encouragement and invitation to pious, learned, and painful ministers to go over, the Company ordered six tenants to be placed on each of these glebes at the public expense and applied to the bishop of London for his help and assistance in procuring proper ministers, which his lordship readily performed, for he had ever been a great favorer and promoter of the plantation and had himself alone collected and paid in a thousand

---

10. Nicholas (1592–1637) and John Ferrar (d. 1657) were both active members of the Company and staunch supporters of Sir Edwin Sandys. John was of greater importance to the Company than his brother, but historians have usually assigned the more important role to Nicholas. The reasons for this assessment are twofold: first, Nicholas was deputy treasurer of the Company during the royal investigation of 1623; and secondly, historians have been greatly influenced by Peter Peckhard's *Memoirs of the Life of Mr. Nicholas Ferrar* (Cambridge, 1790), which was based largely on a manuscript written in 1654 by John Ferrar in commemoration of his brother (Craven, *Dissolution of Virginia Company*, p. 9; Kingsbury, *Records of Virginia Company*, III, 117, 576).

pounds toward the college. For this and his other merits toward them, he was made free of the Company and chosen one of His Majesty's Council for Virginia, and of that body his commissary usually, if not always, was one.[11]

[As the country was very defenseless and unfortified, and as the interests and improvements of the inhabitants were now much increased and become considerable, they began to grow uneasy and wrote to the treasurer and Company in England to procure them skillful engineers to raise fortifications, promising themselves to bear the charge of it. Whereupon to give them present satisfaction, and as regular fortifications to endure assault and battery were not so needful as the choosing and improving some places of natural strength and advantage, Sir Thomas Gates was entreated by the Company, as well in regard to his military skill as of his knowledge of the country, to write them his private letters of advice and direction. And he was also desired, together with Sir Nathaniel Rich, to confer with General Cecil about it, another eminent and military member of their society and youngest son to the famous Lord Treasurer Burleigh, who likewise promised, if other methods failed, to write them such particular directions and instructions that they might easily themselves proceed. To these was afterwards added Sir Horatio Vere, who was esteemed a person of the greatest military skill.[12]

[The governor and Council in Virginia had settled and allowed certain fees to the secretary, the table of which was this year sent to England for confirmation. But the treasurer and Company were become from the late exactions very jealous and cautious in that point

11. The official records have long been lost, but the names are known of some six clergymen who were incumbents of parishes in Virginia between 1607 and 1619. A glebe was land set aside for the use of a clergymen to supplement his regular salary and fees. Actually the money for a college was raised at the urging of King James I. In 1617 he ordered offerings to be taken in every parish four times a year for two years, the money collected to be forwarded to the treasurer of the London Company. In this way the Company received £1500 sterling and additional amounts later (George McClaren Brydon, *Religious Life of Virginia in the Seventeenth Century: The Faith of Our Fathers* [Williamsburg, Va., 1957], pp. 2, 3).

12. Sir Nathaniel Rich (1585?–1636), the cousin and close business associate of the earl of Warwick, often acted as a spokesman for the Warwick faction, especially in their fight against the tobacco contract of 1622 (Craven, *Dissolution of Virginia Company*, pp. 82, 244). Thomas Cecil (1542–1622) had a successful military career first in Scotland and then in the Low Countries, even serving as a volunteer aboard the fleet that fought the Spanish Armada in 1588. William Cecil, Lord Burleigh (1520–98), a distinguished and controversial political figure, was appointed lord high treasurer in 1572. Sir Horatio Vere (1565–1635) was a celebrated soldier, especially during the Thirty Years War.

and thought those fees to be oppressive and intolerable; and therefore, for the ease of the colony, they declared that the secretary should receive no fees at all, but in recompense of all services, they allotted five hundred acres of land for him and his successors with twenty tenants thereon. This was laid off on the Eastern Shore, and the grant was afterwards enlarged. But whereas Captain Argall, in the time of his suspension from the place of admiral, had deputed Abraham Peirsey, the cape merchant, to be his vice admiral, the Company declared that deputation to be utterly void and unlawful and committed the execution of that office to the governor and Council of State and to such under them as they should authorize and appoint.[13]

[Many scandalous reports had been spread (as was intimated in a private letter to Mr. Bland, a very considerable merchant of the Company)[14] of the barrenness and inferiority of the soil in Virginia. And it had been one especial piece of Captain Argall's policy in order to disgrace and dishearten the Company to vilify the country, both by himself and his instruments, and to represent it as less fertile than the most barren arable lands in England.[15] Although these aspersions were sufficiently contradicted by his own former letters and reports, yet for a fuller answer to them a commission was sent to Virginia and a return made upon oath of the strength and goodness of the soil. But as malice is more industrious than truth, these unjust scandals prevailed too much and discouraged many adventurers from making their transportations. To obviate therefore all such ill consequences, it was resolved upon motion, and committed to the care of Sir Edwin Sandys and Dr. Winston to prepare and publish a small book containing a refutation of all such scandalous reports and to subjoin an alphabetical index of the adventurers' names. This last had a double use, for in the first place it did great honor to the enterprise by showing that many of the chief persons in the nation for wisdom, fortune, and dignity were deeply concerned in and great encouragers of it; and next as this index was drawn from Sir Thomas Smith's books, which were very incorrect, it gave the alarm to all such as had paid in their monies to him and found themselves omitted in this list; and it accord-

13. Abraham Peirsey or Peirce (d. 1634), cape merchant in charge of the magazine, arrived in Virginia in Oct. 1616 with a magazine ship loaded with goods for exchange, further encouraging the colonists to plant tobacco instead of corn. In 1623 he was chosen a member of the royal commission to investigate Virginia.

14. John Bland (1573–1632), a leading supporter of the Sandys group, was chosen to the Virginia Company's Council in 1623.

15. These letters, if they were ever written, are no longer in existence.

ingly made them bring in his receipts, or bills of adventure, whereby many sums of money appeared to have been received by him which could otherwise never have been made out by his books or proved by any other method.⌉ [16]

From the account rendered by Sandys on the expiration of his office, it is recollected ⌈that there had within this year been sent out eight ships at the Company's expense and four others by private adventurers and that these ships had transported 1,261 persons, whereof 650 were for the public use and the other 611 for private plantations. He also gave them an account of the several gifts which had been made during it for pious uses and of the many patents that had passed to various private adventurers and their associates, who had undertaken to transport to Virginia great multitudes of people with much cattle. And he recounted to them the several methods which he had taken to draw the people off from their greedy and immoderate pursuit of tobacco and to turn them to other more useful and necessary commodities: that for this purpose a hundred and fifty persons had been sent to set up three ironworks; that directions had been given for making cordage as well of hemp and flax and more especially of silk grass, which grew there naturally in great abundance and was found upon experience to make the best cordage and line in the world; and that therefore each family had been ordered and obliged to set a hundred plants of it, and the governor himself five thousand; that besides, it had been recommended to them to make pitch and tar, together with pot and soap ashes.

⌈He then exhibited to the court the book of his accounts, examined and approved by five of the seven auditors of the Company, the other two being absent. And he further declared that for any business done within this year he had not left the Company, to his knowledge, one penny in debt, except perhaps the remain of some charges which had not been delivered in or were not yet become due. He declared also that he had left in stock £1,200 more than had been left to him the former year.⌉ [17]

If it should be asked how it happened that so few of the promised appearances in the growth of the colony were realized, let it be an-

16. Stith, *Virginia*, pp. 168–75. Dr. Thomas Winston (1575–1655), a graduate of Cambridge who had studied medicine at Padua, coauthored with Sandys *A Declaration of the State of the Colonie and Affaires in Virginia* (London, 1620; reprinted in Kingsbury, *Records of Virginia Company*, III, 308–65).

17. Stith, *Virginia*, pp. 176–77; for Sandys's report, see Kingsbury, *Records of Virginia Company*, I, 388–95.

swered that the manufactures of silk and of wine have been more abortive than any others.[18] While the silkworm is a native and the mulberry tree so abundant in supplying its food, we have been constantly dependent for the article of silk upon nations having fewer blessings of an extensive soil than ourselves. For a considerable time, to both silk and wine the culture of tobacco seems to have been hostile, the processes in the perfecting of either of the two first having been interrupted by the most precious article of export and never having been patiently, skillfully, or perseveringly tried upon an adequate scale. That weed of wretchedness might be redeemed from other censure, were it not that it gave a peculiarly fatal energy to an accident from tempest. A Dutch ship laden with Negroes was driven by stress of weather into a port of Virginia. They were the first of that species of man ever seen here. For retaining them as slaves there was not the semblance of piety affected by the Spanish Bishop Bartolomé de Las Casas, who in a different quarter of America had substituted them in place of the miserable natives laboring in the mines.[19] Nor yet were they suspected, as in the arrogant and impious philosophy of this day, to be in the lowest grade of human existence. The heavy timber of the wilderness, the unqualified noxiousness of a climate in which the properties of vegetable putrefaction could be corrected only by time and cultivation, the violent heats of summer, and the overwhelming indolence of white men, most of whom came hither with the allurement of amassing gold without toil, beget a suspicion that those circumstances were the avowed self-justification upon which the inhabitants purchased these Negroes as slaves and spread over the character of our country colors more indelible than the sable skin which served as a pretext for their unnatural debasement. The poison from this small event will be seen to diffuse itself in a variety of destructive shapes.

That King James should have paid no attention to such an institution as Negro slavery can be accounted for only by his excessive anxiety

18. According to Wesley Frank Craven, "it is not difficult to explain the tragic failure of Sir Edwin's program for the colony's development. The program itself, which called for heavy investment in a number of highly speculative ventures, was too ambitious and altogether out of proportion to the financial resources available for its continued support" (*Southern Colonies*, p. 145). Randolph discusses Sir Edwin's plans on pp. 98–99 below.

19. About twenty Africans were brought to Point Comfort toward the end of August 1619 by a Dutch man-of-war, probably from the West Indies where the ship had been cruising. Bishop Bartolomé de Las Casas castigated the tyranny and cruelty of Spanish native policy in his *Brevísima relación de la destrucción de las indias* (1552). In 1583 the work was translated into English under the title *The Spanish Colonies*.

to thrust himself into influence with every body of men who might be subservient to his views, meaning to combine with the revenue from tobacco the gratification of those who as proprietors of slaves might be useful to him in some intrusion into the affairs of the Company.

[At the beginning of a court held by the Company,[20] he signified through a messenger his pleasure, "out of special care and affection for the colony," that one of the four persons whom he nominated should be elected treasurer on the vacancy of Sir Edwin Sandys.[21] They had almost unanimously cast their eye upon the earl of Southampton for this appointment. He was a virtuous and zealous friend of the colony but offensive to the king as one of the leaders of the patriot party in the House of Lords. By this interposition of the king, the Company were much embarrassed. To accept his nomination was to surrender the privilege of free election. To reject it was to set the ravenous monster of prerogative at defiance. The milder course was adopted of fully, firmly, and freely representing to His Majesty the state of the colony and supplicating him not to take from them so valuable a chartered right as the freedom of choice. James, solicitous to palliate an improper act done under his command, and not disdaining even in the plenitude of his power to adopt an expedient of meanness and duplicity, disavowed the conduct of his agent, whom he blamed for suggesting to the Company the royal wish to confine their choice to some one of the persons named. He pretended to wish nothing more than that such a person should be chosen as might at all times and on all occasions have access to his presence. The earl of Southampton was thereupon elected with a unanimous vote by acclamation instead of ballot and entered into office with the assurance of his friend Sir Edwin Sandys's assistance and of support from Mr. John Ferrar, who for his integrity, diligence, and experience was appointed deputy treasurer.][22]

These transactions in England plainly announced that the tide of power in the Council was turning upon the faction there, and the

20. In the year 1620.
21. The four named were Sir Thomas Smith, Sir Thomas Roe, Mr. Alderman Johnson, and Mr. Maurice Abbot.
22. Stith, *Virginia*, pp. 178–81. Henry Wriothesley (1573–1624), third earl of Southampton, a scholarly and impetuous nobleman, is best known for his patronage of Shakespeare, frequent court brawls, and support for voyages of discovery and colonization in America. A strong supporter of Sandys, his election as treasurer brought no change in the policies nor in the real leadership of the company (Craven, *Dissolution of Virginia Company*, pp. 23, 143–44; see also Charlotte C. Stopes, *The Life of Henry, Third Earl of Southampton, Shakespeare's Patron* [Cambridge, 1922]).

next symptom of this joyous truth was that [the appeal of Captain Brewster from the sentence of the court-martial in Virginia was resumed after a long suspense, and after a bold assertion of the earl of Warwick that trial by martial law was of the noblest kind because soldiers and men of honor were the judges, the cruelty and terror to which Brewster had been a victim were reprobated as unjust, unlawful, and unwarranted in matter of form by any of the charters and the trial by martial law in time of peace as no less odious.] [23]

[The General Assembly of this year put into motion the schemes of improvements recommended by Sandys when he resigned the treasurership. Worm seed was brought from France, Italy, and Spain in large quantities, and artists who well understood the breeding of silkworms and winding off of the silk were sent over. Among the people the seed was distributed with a well-written treatise on the management of mulberry trees and of silk.[24] A select committee of merchants were also appointed to annex to several commodities reasonable prices, which on the one hand should save the Company and merchants from loss, and on the other should encourage the planters in raising them. If a project of Sir William Monson, an eminent naval commander in England and the author of the naval tracts,] had reached our times, we should probably have acquired new intelligence of the agricultural and commercial faculties of Virginia. [He offered £100 per annum and the annual importation into Virginia of twenty-five men for an exclusive right to import into Virginia for seven years two such commodities as had not been discovered or planted by any other person.] [25]

But the firmness of Virginia shows itself in a particular manner at this time. [The two original companies could not agree in the claim of Virginia for liberty to take fish at Cape Cod, which lay within the limits of the northern colony. Sir Ferdinando Gorges and others who were associates in the latter privately solicited a new patent, which should debar the former from fishing on that coast. At this the Virginia

23. Stith, *Virginia*, pp. 181–82. See Kingsbury, *Records of Virginia Company*, I, 360–63.

24. The treatise, *Observations to Be Followed . . . to Keepe Silkewormes; As Also, for the Best Manner of Planting Mulberry Trees, to Feed Them* (1620), was written by John Bonoeil, French master of the king's experiment with silk production at Oakland. Bonoeil was also a consultant for the Virginia Company and his *Observations*, with additional information on the production of wine, was reissued in 1622 for distribution to all the heads of families in Virginia.

25. Stith, *Virginia*, pp. 183–84. Sir William Monson (1569–1643), a graduate of Oxford, went to sea at age sixteen and commanded the ship *Charles* in the fleet that fought the Spanish Armada. In 1604 he rose to admiral of the narrow seas.

Company were enraged, for they had disbursed £6,000 on the fishery, which was useful in the support of Virginia and necessary to replace that expense. The patent of Gorges was indeed stopped; and the Company being brought to consider the precarious state of their privileges while they rested on the royal pleasure alone, prevailed upon Sir Edwin Sandys to undertake to secure them by a confirmation from Parliament. But the joint efforts and interest of himself and the earl of Southampton were defeated in the attempt.⌉ [26]

The factions and discord of the Company were now working the chief occasion and pretense for its dissolution. As is ordinarily the case, matter seemingly foreign and miscellaneous is interwoven in the accusation of party against party; and much if not all of the subsequent transactions in the colony, or respecting it elsewhere, may be recited in their order of time as contributing to this grand catastrophe.

All harmony of cooperation, so necessary to the well-being of the colony, was abolished. Some contests about the old magazine, really insignificant in themselves, which had been affected to be forgotten, had not lost the power of irritating.

The accounts of the late treasurer Sir Thomas Smith were still unsettled. During his office £80,000 had passed into his hands. On one side was great eagerness for compelling a liquidation; on the other equal was professed, while specious obstacles were devised to thwart it.

Captain Argall had enlisted the power and talents of his friends in protecting him from punishment due to his crimes; and the danger of himself and Sir Thomas Smith being common, a common cause was made between them.

By many needful and well-designed expenses in the importation of emigrants, the public officers were accommodated with tenants and servants, but the treasury was exhausted and never afterwards replenished. Lotteries, which had yielded £20,000, were forbidden, and the rancor attendant on reduced finances was not to be softened.

Captain Smith justly complained ⌈that although he had hazarded his fortune upon the success of Virginia, had built and rebuilt James-

26. *Ibid.,* p. 185. Sir Ferdinando Gorges (*ca.* 1566–1647), who took an active part in American affairs as long as he lived, was a member of the Virginia Company from the beginning. In Nov. 1620 he received a patent for an area encompassing most of New England. He served as governor and treasurer of the New England Council. Although it is true that the Virginia Company was never granted legal access to the fisheries, they did thereafter enjoy the desired privilege of free fishing either by an understanding with Gorges or by order of the king. For the Gorges patent, see Andrews, *Colonial Period,* I, 320–43.

town, had established four other plantations, had explored the country, and for three successive years had relieved the colony from famine by corn obtained at the peril of his life, and although every shilling which he had gained in military campaigns abroad had been cheerfully expended on Virginia and New England, he was still without compensation or retribution. The court referred him to the committee for rewarding merit.⌉ [27] Whether the case of this illustrious benefactor escaped the fate of oblivion, or he was repaid solely by the consolation of that prosperity which he had so extremely advanced, does not appear.

To aggravate the distempers of the colony, the king had insinuated himself into many of the quarrels between the Company and individuals, even to the extenuation of charges against Sir George Yeardley for having expelled from their lawful possessions many ancient planters and mechanics.

⌈Illegal impositions on tobacco were among the devices of his avarice. In all these exactions Sir Lionel Cranfield had been his principal instrument.[28] He was at first a merchant of London and then an officer in the customs, from whence he was introduced to court as a projector, which in the language of those times signified a person who could furnish expedients to the ministers to raise money in the vacation and without the assistance of Parliament. He was a dexterous officer and in this execrable function had been so useful and successful that together with the advantage of having married one of Buckingham's relations (a circumstance which was then an infallible road to the highest preferments), he had risen to the dignity of earl of Middlesex and lord high treasurer of England. He was himself an ancient adventurer in the affair of Virginia and well knew how uneasy the people there were under the pressure of the monopolies, garbling, and other illegal patents. He therefore resolved to try whether he could not make the Company consent to their own oppression and extort from them a greater profit and revenue to His Majesty by making a particular contract with themselves.

⌈To this end, he first broached the matter privately to Sir Edwin Sandys, offering a grant to the two companies of Virginia and the Somer Islands for the sole importation of tobacco into the realms of England and Ireland, reserving to His Majesty a certain rent. This he did with large professions of his love and affection to the colony of

27. Stith, *Virginia,* p. 192.
28. For Cranfield's role in the tobacco contract, see Craven, *Dissolution of Virginia Company,* pp. 221–50.

Virginia, whereof he was an ancient councilor, and declared that besides the personal duty of his place as lord high treasurer, his principal motive herein was the profit and advancement of the colonies. Sir Edwin Sandys professed his ignorance in affairs of that nature; but after some thought, he consulted with Sir Arthur Ingram,[29] another member of the Virginia Company then present, but a fast creature and retainer to the lord treasurer. At length considering that tobacco was a deceivable weed and the use of it wholly founded on a humor which might soon vanish into smoke and come to nothing, he told his lordship that to settle any great rent in money upon such an uncertain commodity might soon bankrupt the companies and utterly ruin the plantations; wherefore he conceived it much the safer way for the companies to yield His Majesty a certain proportion in specie out of the tobacco itself, whereof he thought they might give a fourth part, provided they might be discharged from all other burdens upon it. But his lordship, falling into a calculation, told him that without the grant of a third there could not be that revenue raised to His Majesty as was expected, and for the old custom of six pence a pound upon roll and four pence upon leaf tobacco, it was already granted to His Majesty's farmers and could not be reversed.

⌐After this, Sir Edwin Sandys, by his lordship's command, communicated this proposal to the Lords Southampton and Cavendish and the two deputies, who having imparted it to their Councils, brought it before the companies. Such a contract, if it could be concluded on any reasonable terms, was certainly a very great and visible advantage to the companies and colonies, for it would enable them, by having the whole commodity in their own hands, to exclude all foreign tobacco and to raise or at least to keep up the price of their own, and would as well ease them from the extortions and insults of other monopolizing patents as secure them from any further impositions.

⌐The court, as the colony advanced in strength, was loading it with impositions and kept it always staggering under the burden of taxes and imposts. This was then done solely by the king's authority without allowing to parliaments their right of giving money and laying new duties on the subject; and what was a notorious breach of faith, it was done against the plainest and most express words and tenor of former grants.

29. Sir Arthur Ingram (d. 1642), a member of Parliament and of both the East India and Virginia companies.

[However, the Company sat down peaceably under these oppressions and appointed each a committee to treat with the lord treasurer. But in the progress of the business his lordship was still throwing in new hardships upon them.

[For the last seven years the importation of tobacco into England had been only 142,085 pounds weight in each year.

[The objections of the Company were certainly sharp and home and did not a little expose the partial and most unpatriotic measures of the court. But it was the misfortune of that time that the Company dealt much in reason, and the courtiers in command. The Spanish match was still on foot; and therefore His Majesty would sacrifice any interest of his own subjects to the Spanish nation that he might gratify his ally, the king of Spain, who had been now for many years abusing him to the open mockery of all Europe. That king was fearful lest in Virginia and Bermudas should afterwards arise another England in America, of equal annoyance to New Spain with that in Europe to the old. The following agreement was however made with the king:

[1. That the sole importation of tobacco into the realms of England and Ireland should be granted to the Virginia and Somer Island companies by patent under the Great Seal of England, which grant should be drawn and construed in the most beneficial manner for the behoof of the companies and the advancement of the colonies, His Majesty's profit hereafter recited only reserved.

[2. That His Majesty should by proclamation prohibit all others from importing, as also from planting, tobacco in England and Ireland during the said contract, under grievous penalties, and that what was already planted should by virtue of the former proclamation be confiscated.

[3. That His Majesty and the lord high treasurer should take all proper methods for confiscating all tobacco unduly imported and should endeavor in all points to keep up effectually to the true intent and meaning of the contract and, particularly, that His Majesty should grant no licenses to retailers of tobacco, that the market might still remain free and open as it had hitherto done.

[4. That in consideration hereof, as also for that the companies should be discharged from all other payments on tobacco (excepting only the ancient custom in the book of rates of six pence a pound on roll tobacco, and four pence upon leaf), the said companies should pay to His Majesty the clear proceeds of a full third part of all tobacco yearly imported and landed by them in the said two realms, provided nevertheless that they should not be obliged to import more tobacco of the growth of the two colonies than they themselves thought proper.

[5. That the lord high treasurer should cause the custom to be reduced to a medium for seven years last past, ending at Michaelmas 1621, wherein should be specified how much was roll tobacco and how much was leaf, because of the different custom, and that the whole should be reduced to a certain sum of money, whereof one third to be paid by the king for his part and two thirds by the companies, and the customers to make no further demand on any tobacco either imported or exported.

[6. That His Majesty should be discharged from payment of freight and all other previous charges, but that immediately upon the arrival of the said tobacco (at which time His Majesty's interest therein would commence) he should bear the third part of all charges for landing, housing, keeping, and transporting by land, sea, or fresh water into divers parts, as also his third part of all lawsuits, of the salaries of all officers, agents, factors, and servants, and in general of all matters and businesses whatsoever incident to the said tobacco or contract.

[7. That all tobacco imported should be consigned into such hands as should be appointed by the said companies, who should in their general courts have the sole nomination of all officers, agents, factors, ministers, and servants, and the entire management of the said tobacco, yielding to His Majesty a true and perfect account thereof and paying the clear profits which should become due to His Majesty for his third and come into their hands, in which account the third of all charges should be allowed and defalcated as aforesaid.

[8. That the companies should be obliged to import not above 60,000 nor under 40,000 weight of Spanish tobacco for each of the first two years of this contract and no longer, upon condition nevertheless that the king and state of Spain did not purposely (upon knowledge of their being obliged to import so large a quantity) raise the custom or impose new burdens and charges upon their tobacco, and on condition likewise that the price of tobacco at which it was then sold in Spain be not purposely enhanced and that the markets be in all respects as free and open as formerly they have been, provided also, if any of the said quantity of Spanish tobacco do in any wise miscarry by casualties at sea, that in that case the said companies should not be bound to restore and make good the proportion so lost by any new provision and imposition.

[9. That this contract should commence at Michaelmas 1622 and continue for the space of seven years then next ensuing.[30]

[It was certainly very well and cautiously worded by Sir Edwin Sandys, who drew it; but it was at last esteemed a hard and pinching bargain upon the trade, and as a certain noble person expressed it, was not to be looked upon as a pleasant dish, well sauced and seasoned, but as a bitter potion which must of necessity be swallowed down for avoiding greater evils. The earl of Southampton therefore earnestly desired the Company duly to consider each article and not forbear to give their best counsel and advice in so weighty a business, which so nearly concerned themselves and the colonies, it being not only free for every man but demanded as a duty from him to speak his mind boldly, as his own reason should suggest. But after a long pause it appearing that nothing more could be said than had formerly been delivered, his lordship, at the Company's request, put it to the question; and it was ratified and confirmed by an almost unanimous consent, one hand only being held up against it. After which it was by Lord Cavendish, the governor, proposed to and confirmed by the Somer Island Company with the like unanimity; for the adventurers in that plantation, being about 126 in number, were all likewise members of the Virginia Company.

[But before the bargain was thoroughly concluded and ratified by the lord high treasurer, he pressed upon them an obligation to import the 40,000 weight of Spanish tobacco, in the best varinas, with a promise (which however he did not keep) not to trouble them any further, if that was granted. The Company therefore yielded to it, on condition that such a quantity of best varinas could be procured, for there had been some years when the whole importation of that kind of tobacco into Spain did not amount to 40,000 weight. But if varinas could not be had, they undertook (to give His Majesty and the lord treasurer satisfaction) to import the rest of their quantity in the best and most costly sorts of tobacco. It will doubtless be very surprising to every thinking reader to find a king thus loading and oppressing his subjects with the importation of a foreign commodity of no use or necessity but of mere luxury and wantonness, and that too in the dearest and most grievous manner, especially when that commodity might be supplied by our own colonies and must in Spain be paid for in hard cash, as the

30. This new contract of Nov. 1622 replaced the expired patent of Abraham Jacob, giving the Virginia and Bermuda companies a virtual monopoly of the tobacco trade (Craven, *Dissolution of Virginia Company*, pp. 221–50).

case then was. But to account for so unconscionable a proceeding it must still be observed that herein were answered the two grand ends which at that time lay nearest to that prince's heart, since by taking off their dearest tobaccos he did the more oblige the Spanish king and nation and threw more money into their pockets out of those of his subjects (which was in truth so much clear loss to the English nation) and did also, at the same time, advance his own profit and revenue. For as the king was by the contract to have the clear proceeds of one third of all tobacco imported, it was more to his gain and advantage to have the best Spanish tobacco, which would then sell for eighteen or twenty shillings a pound, and sometimes more, than the plantation tobacco, which would scarcely fetch two and six pence a pound.⌉ [31]

[But tobacco was at this time a sinking commodity. For although the planters magisterially forced it on the Company and others at the current price of three shillings a pound, yet it would not turn out at home after shrinkage and waste and the discharge of the duty and freight (which last alone was three pence, and sometimes four pence a pound) at above two shillings for the best, and the inferior sort at scarce eighteen pence a pound. And besides, the trade was strangely hampered and perplexed by the weak and unsteady counsels by the puny monarch then on the throne. For although in the beginning of the former year the Company had yielded to his unreasonable demands of twelve pence a pound, yet soon after, in the same summer, he issued a proclamation prohibiting a general importation of tobacco and restraining the quantity from Virginia and the Somer Islands to 55,000 weight, at the same time taking advantage of an offer of Sir Thomas Smith and Alderman Johnson in the name of the Company, but without their knowledge or authority; and so utterly disclaimed by them he granted a monopoly of solely importing tobacco, first to Sir Thomas Roe and his associates (at whose desire and instigation the proclamation above mentioned was issued) and the year after to Mr. Jacob and certain other patentees. They proceeded most injuriously against both companies, not only stinting them to too scant a proportion, but also restraining them from selling their tobacco without their seal and allowance first had, for which, under the pretense and title of garbling, they were obliged to pay four pence a pound.[32] This garbling was an ancient custom of the city of London, and an officer was appointed who

31. Stith, *Virginia*, pp. 244–50.
32. It was common practice to provide for the inspection of certain items in order to protect the king's subjects from inferior goods.

had power to enter into any shop or warehouse to view and search
drugs and spices and to garble the same, that is, to make them clean
from all garbles or trash. And it was now put into execution and
arbitrarily applied to tobacco (a new commodity in England and therefore not legally subject to garbling without an express law) in order
the more effectually to oppress the companies and plantations and to
squeeze the greater gain out of them.

[Injured as the Company thus was, they presented their petition and
representation to His Majesty for the grant of some privileges in tobacco, to which they received a gracious answer, with large professions
of his love to the colonies and that it never was his intention to grant
anything to their prejudice, but without any redress of their grievances.
It was, therefore, at last resolved to complain to the House of Commons
against the oppressions, as tending to the utter destruction and overthrow of the colonies; and as that house had called into question and
intended to suppress other monopolies, they doubted not to receive
from them full and ample redress. Mr. Bennett immediately became
the most deeply engaged and was by far the largest and most considerable adventurer of any then known in the affairs of Virginia,
whose foundations, in that early time, have continued down to the
present, for his nephew, Richard Bennett, Esq., was the first governor
of Virginia by the election of the colony, in the time of Cromwell's
usurpation, and the remain of the family now seated in Maryland is
still the richest and most wealthy, in all kinds of fortune and estate, of
any in this part of America.[33] However, no Virginia tobacco was imported into England this year, but all was carried and disposed of in
Holland.

[The news of this state of their affairs coming to Virginia, the colony
was greatly alarmed and drew up a humble petition to the king, setting
forth that His Majesty, out of his religious desire to speed the gospel of
Christ and princely ambition to enlarge his dominions, had given encouragement to such as would go to Virginia and granted them many

---

33. Edward Bennett, the founder of Bennett's Plantation and a prominent London merchant, was made a member of the Virginia Company at Sandys's request because he had
written a treatise against the importation of Spanish tobacco into England and because
he had frequently attended committee meetings which considered this business (Morton,
Colonial Virginia, I, 68). Richard Bennett, a Puritan in religious belief, had fled from
Virginia to Maryland in 1643 to escape persecution. From there he went to London,
and in Sept. 1651 returned to Virginia as a member of the royal commission assigned to
bring the royal colony of Virginia to heel. When Virginia submitted he was chosen
governor.

goodly privileges and liberties under the Great Seal of England, than which they thought no earthly assurance more firm and inviolable; that in confidence hereof, they, His Majesty's poor subjects, had adventured their lives and fortunes thither and in the prosecution of the enterprise had undergone such incredible difficulties and sufferings as would be shocking, in the relation, to His Majesty's sacred ears; that they had now by the divine assistance in some measure overcome those difficulties and brought themselves to an ability of subsisting without any other help from England than the usual course of commerce; but that they had of late been brought into danger of returning into their former, or even worse, circumstances by the sinister practices of some members of the Company at home, who pretending His Majesty's profits, but really aiming at their own exorbitant gain, had obtained a proclamation to prohibit the importation of tobacco into England; that other things of greater real value required more time than their pressing necessities would allow and more help to bring them to perfection than they had till of late been furnished withall; and that tobacco was the only commodity they had yet been able to raise in order to supply themselves and families with apparel and other needful supplements of life; that if it should be thus suppressed and prohibited, they must all of necessity perish for want of clothing and such necessaries as both nature and education required; that His Majesty would thereby not only lose so many good and loyal subjects as had adventured their lives and substance to Virginia for the promotion of those great ends, the glory of God, and His Majesty's service but must likewise be deprived of the hope and prospect of acquiring a territory as large and capable of becoming as opulent as any of those kingdoms he at present possessed. Since therefore they were assured that His Majesty tendered the lives and welfare of his subjects above thousands of gold and silver, and since his royal word was engaged and even ratified under the Great Seal of England, they besought him out of his princely compassion either to revoke that proclamation and to restore them to their ancient liberty or else to send for them home and not suffer the heathen to triumph over them.[34]

[This petition was transmitted to the treasurer and Company and seconded by a letter from Sir George Yeardley and the Council to the Company, desiring that it might be presented to His Majesty in as humble and effectual a manner as possible because they conceived the

34. See Kingsbury, *Records of Virginia Company*, II, 424–25.

very life of the colony to depend upon the success of it. But before it came to the king's hand he was become sensible of the damages that accrued to himself by the diminution of his customs. The deputy, therefore, and some others of the Company were sent for, in October of this year, and received an angry rebuke from the lords of the Privy Council for the trade opened to Holland with all their commodities.[35] An answer was demanded whether they would bring all their commodities into England or continue their trade in the Low Countries. To the former part of this inquiry, the answer was ready and obvious: that they had indeed sent their tobacco to Middelburg, not out of choice, but being constrained thereto by His Majesty's proclamation and an order of their own board. As to the latter part, concerning bringing all their commodities into England, as it was a new and unexpected proposition and a point of great weight and future consequence, they took time to consider of it and then returned a pointed and respectful answer:

[That it was a liberty and privilege generally taken and enjoyed by all His Majesty's subjects to carry their commodities to the best markets; that many commodities were now set on foot and expected soon to be returned from Virginia which although in some demand in other countries yet would not be vendible in England and nor pay the expense of freight and custom; that neither the Muscovy Company nor any other ancient corporation was under such a restraint, to whose greatest privileges and immunities they were entitled by the express words of His Majesty's charter; that the Company had granted several patents with the same privileges as they themselves enjoyed to divers persons of noble and worthy families, who had thereupon expended great sums of money, and some of them their whole estates in the plantation, and that it was not in their power, nor would it be consonant to law or equity, now to revoke or restrain them; that they conceived themselves to have no right or authority to dispose of the goods of the private planters in Virginia, who are declared by His Majesty's charter to be free as any other of his subjects, and who had merited by their long and hard services all manner of immunity and encouragement; that they could not forbid or restrain them from trading and bartering their commodities freely with such ships as carried passengers, most of which proceeded on trading voyages and returned not directly to England; that a trade had lately begun between Ireland and Virginia for cattle

35. The dispute over the sale of tobacco to Holland is discussed in Andrews, *Colonial Period*, I, 158–59.

and other necessaries, for which contracts were made in tobacco, and that this trade would hereby be nipped in the bud, to the exceeding great prejudice and the hazard of the utter ruin of the colony; and lastly, that it was not in the power of the few members of the Company then in town in the time of vacation to conclude anything positive in an affair of that vast importance wherein above a thousand adventurers in England and near four thousand inhabitants of Virginia were deeply interested and concerned. After which they concluded with assuring their lordships that they affected no foreign trade but in cases of mere necessity and for the better support and advancement of the colony, that they should always endeavor at such a mutual commerce between England and Virginia as should be consistent with the honor and benefit of both, and that next to God's glory, they chiefly aimed at the good of their country, His Majesty's honor, and the advancement of his profit and revenue, for which ends, they had out of their own private estates, besides their labor and time, expended above £100,000, without any return not only of profit but even of the least part of the principal itself to any one of the adventurers, that they knew of.[36]

[This answer gave no satisfaction to their lordships, but the Company were referred to Mr. Jacob, their old antagonist and oppressor, and were likewise ordered to give in their peremptory answer, whether they would import, not all their commodities, but all their tobacco only, into England. With Mr. Jacob, they could come to no satisfactory accommodation; and as to importing all their tobacco into England, they besought their lordships to be left at liberty either to import or not import it into England, as they should find it most beneficial to the colony. But that if they must be obliged to import all or none, they declared it was their choice to import none into England the ensuing year. But their lordships termed this an undutiful answer and commanded them at their peril to bring all their tobacco into England. The deputy and committee appointed to attend their lordships offering some reasons, they were told that they were not to dispute at that board but to obey and so were dismissed with high marks of displeasure and indignation.

[These proceedings, being reported to the Company, caused great grief and dejection among them. For the importation of Spanish and all other tobaccos was then free; and although the House of Commons in their last session had entered into some consideration about it, nothing material was done in the matter. And as to the king, out of his

36. See Kingsbury, *Records of Virginia Company*, II, 325–27.

doting fondness for the Spanish match, he was active and diligent to
protect and advance the importation of Spanish tobacco. However, the
deputy exhorted the Company not to be discouraged at these disasters.
For he hoped that God would exert himself in the protection of Virginia, who had turned for the best divers former projects which threatened the ruin and destruction of the colony. And he desired that having
put their hands to the plow, they would not now look back or be
weary of welldoing, for the action was universally confessed to be most
Christian, honorable, and glorious, and of extreme consequence to the
commonwealth and realm of England; and although they might seem
to have cast their bread upon the waters, yet after many days he
doubted not but they should find it again, to their great comfort and
advantage. And he further told them that although their exhausted
treasury had been able to do little that year for sending people to
Virginia, yet it had pleased God to stir up so many worthy minds for
the advancement of the colony that no less than twenty ships were
already gone, or ready to go, in which would be transported above a
thousand persons. But by Captain Smith's account, there were twenty-
one sail of ships sent this year, with 1,300 men, women, and children.⌐ [37]

But the greatest cause of dissatisfaction was one which nearly involved the colony in ruin. ⌐It was a cruel massacre, concerted by
Opechancanough and perpetrated by the Indians on the English in the
following manner. There was a noted Indian called Nemattanow, who
was accustomed out of bravado and parade to dress himself up in
strange, antic, and barbarous fashion with feathers, which obtained
for him among the English the name of Jack of the feathers. This
Indian was highly renowned among his countrymen for courage and
policy and was universally esteemed by them the greatest war captain
of those times. He had been in many skirmishes and engagements with
the English and bravely exposed his person, yet by his activity, conduct,
and good fortune he had always escaped without a wound. This, aided
by his craft and ambition, easily wrought in the minds of those ignorant

37. Stith, *Virginia*, pp. 198–204. During the year ending in May 1622 twenty-one ships
and 1,300 people did arrive in Virginia. In addition, they brought eighty head of cattle,
and twenty-six patents were granted to groups of associates for establishing particular
plantations in the colony (Kingsbury, *Records of Virginia Company*, III, 639–43). The
problems involved in the importation of tobacco discussed on pp. 105–10 above actually
occurred before acceptance of the tobacco contract of Nov. 1622 covered on pp. 100–105
above. This reversal in the sequence of events makes the behavior of the crown seem
even more arbitrary than does Stith's portrayal of events. It is not known whether the
copyist was in error or Randolph deliberately altered the sequence of events.

and superstitious barbarians a concert that he was invulnerable and immortal. He came to the house of one Morgan, who had many such commodities as suited the rude taste of the Indians. Being smitten with the desire of some of these baubles, he persuaded Morgan to go with him to Pamunkey, upon the promise and assurance of a certain and advantageous traffic. But, upon the way, he murdered the poor credulous Englishman and within two or three days returned again to his house. There were only two sturdy lads there, the late Morgan's servants, who, seeing him wear their master's cap, asked for their master, and Jack frankly told them he was dead. Being confirmed in their suspicion, they seized him and endeavored to carry him before a justice of the peace. But Jack so provoked them by his resistance and insolence that at last they shot him down and put him into a boat in order to carry him before the governor, who was then within seven or eight miles of the place. On the way, this immortal, feeling the pangs of death very strong upon him, earnestly entreated that two things might be granted to him: first, that it should never be made known that he was slain by a bullet; and secondly, that he should be buried among the English that the certain knowledge and monument of his mortality might be still concealed and kept from his countrymen. Such was the vanity of this poor barbarian, and so ardent was his desire of false glory in the opinion of others, against his own experience and plain conviction.

⌐Opechancanough was a haughty, politic, and bloody-minded man, ever intent on the destruction of the English and ready to catch every pretense for effecting his purpose. He had been discovered the year before tampering with a king on the Eastern Shore to furnish him with a poison to be used against the colony. He had also been accused to the governor of a design to draw together a great force under color of celebrating some funeral rites to Powhatan but really with intent to cut off all the English. But Sir George Yeardley was from this information the more watchful of his motions, so that Opechancanough was either disappointed in his scheme or else he might never have formed any such design. As to Nemattanow, Opechancanough was so far from being in his favor that he sent word to Sir George Yeardley, some time before, that he should be content if the throat of that Indian were cut. Yet being a popular man and much lamented by the Indians, Opechancanough pretended, the better to inflame and exasperate them, to be much grieved at his death and was very loud, at first, in his threats of revenge. But the reason and justice of the thing being evinced and he receiving some stern and resolute answers from the English, he cunningly dissembled his views for the present and treated the messenger sent to him about the middle of March with extreme civility and kindness, assuring him that he held the peace so firm that the sky should fall sooner than that it should be violated on his part. And such was the treachery and dissimulation of the rest of the Indians that but two days before the massacre to be related they kindly conducted the English through the woods and sent home one that lived among them to learn their language. Nay, on the very morning of that fatal day, as also the evening before, they came as at other times unarmed into the houses of the English with deer, turkey, fish, fruits, and other things to sell and in some places sat down to meals with them. Yet so general was the combination, and their plot so well laid to cut off the whole colony in one day and at the same instant, that they had all warning one from another through their most distant habitations, and every party and nation had their stations appointed and parts assigned at the plantations of the English, some being directed to one place and some to another.

⌈The English on the other hand were by this behavior as well as on other accounts lulled into a fatal security. They thought the peace sure and inviolable not so much for their solemn promises and engagements as because it was useful and necessary to the Indians themselves, for those poor, weak, and naked barbarians were in all respects benefited. By the peace they were sheltered and defended from all other enemies, were supplied with several necessary tools and utensils and other means of pleasure and entertainment, acquired a taste for civilized life, and were in no condition to withstand the superiority of the English arms, the advantage of English discipline and courage, and the skill of the English in military arts and stratagems. The English had ever treated them with the utmost humanity and kindness in the hope of alluring and bringing them to the knowledge of God and the true religion. For nothing was more earnestly recommended from England or more heartily labored by many good and pious persons of the colony than their conversion agreeably to the spirit of the Gospel and of the Protestant religion, and in the ways of gentleness and persuasion rather than by fire and sword. On all these accounts, the English were so confident and secure that in their houses a sword or a firelock was seldom kept, and most of their plantations were seated in a scattered and straggling manner as a convenient situation or a choice view of rich land dictated; it was generally thought that the farther they were from neighbors the better. All Indians were kindly received into their houses, fed at their tables, and even lodged in their bedchambers, so that they and the English seemed entirely to have coalesced and to live together as one people. So far were the English infatuated by an opinion of their simplicity and of their inclination and even interest to maintain the peace that they lent them their boats as they passed backwards and forwards to concert their measures and to consult upon the execrable design of murdering and utterly extirpating the whole English nation.

[The hour appointed being come, and the Indians, by reason of their familiarity knowing exactly in what places and quarters every Englishman was to be found, rose upon them at once, sparing neither sex nor age; and they were so quick and sudden in execution that few perceived the weapon or blow that brought them to their end. Some Indians entered the houses of the English under color of trade, others of the latter were drawn abroad upon specious pretenses, whilst the rest fell suddenly on those that were at their works and labors. And thus in one hour, and almost at the same instant, fell 347 men, women, and children, most of them by their own tools and weapons, and all by the hands of the perfidious savages. Nor were they content with their lives only, but they seized their dead bodies, defacing, dragging, and mangling them into many pieces and carrying some parts away in brutish triumph.[38]

[In this havoc, six of the Council were slain. For these bloodhounds with equal spite and barbarity murdered all before them without any remorse or pity and without having any regard to dignity or even to those persons who were best known to them or from whom they had daily received cordiality. Among these was that pious, worthy, and religious gentleman, Mr. George Thorpe, deputy to the college lands and both in command and desert one of the principal in Virginia.[39] He was a person of considerable figure in England. Yet so truly and earnestly did he aim at the conversion of the Indians that he left all at home and came over as chief manager to the college, a foundation designed principally for their education. And here he severely punished who-

---

38. The massacre took place on Good Friday, March 22, 1622. For a contemporary version, see Kingsbury, *Records of Virginia Company*, III, 550–51, 565–71. For an excellent modern account, consult Richard Beale Davis, *George Sandys: Poet-Adventurer* (London, 1955), pp. 119–62.

39. For George Thorpe, see p. 39 above.

soever under him was to them a cause of the least displeasure. He thought nothing too dear or precious for them nor ever denied them anything. In so much that, being frightened at the English mastiffs, he directed some of them to be killed in their presence, to the great grief of their owners. He also built the king a handsome house after the English fashion, in which he took such pleasure, especially in the lock and key, that he would lock and unlock his door a hundred times a day. And Thorpe would often confer with him about religion, and that treacherous infidel would seem much delighted with his discourse and company and to be desirous to requite all his courtesy and kindness. Yet did this ungrateful brood not only murder this good man but abused his dead corpse in a manner not to be related. At the very minute of executing the plot Thorpe's man, perceiving some symptoms of it, warned him to look to himself and by running off thus saved his own life. But his master was so void of suspicion and so full of confidence that he was slain before he could or would believe that any harm was intended to him. Captain Nathaniel Powell, another of the Council, who had some time been governor of the country, was also killed.[40] He was one of the first planters, a brave soldier, had deserved well in all respects, was universally valued and esteemed by all parties and factions, and was well known among the Indians. Yet they slew him and his family and afterwards cut off his head, to express their utmost height of cruelty.

[This slaughter was a deep and grievous wound to the yet weak and infant colony; but it would have been much more general and almost universal if it had not entered into the heart of a converted Indian to make a discovery. His name was Chanco, and he lived with one Richard Pace, who treated him as his own son. The night before the massacre, another Indian, his brother, lay with him; and telling him the king's command, which was to be executed the next day, he urged Chanco to rise and kill Pace, as he intended to do by Perry, *his* friend. As soon as his brother was gone, the Christian Indian rose and went and revealed the whole matter to Pace, who immediately gave notice to Captain William Powell,[41] and having secured his own house, rowed off before day to Jamestown and informed the governor of it. By these means the

40. Capt. Nathaniel Powell (d. 1622), a member of the Council in Virginia and acting governor for a few days in April 1619, his wife, and eleven others were slain at his plantation.

41. Capt. William Powell (d. 1623), a burgess from James City.

design of the Indians was prevented at Jamestown and all such plantations as could possibly get intelligence in time. For wherever they saw the English upon their guard or a single musket presented, they ran off and abandoned their attempt.

⌈Such also, at other places, as had sufficient warning to make resistance saved their lives.⌉ [42]

The news of this unexpected havoc was a stroke of death to the expectations of the Company, ⌈who censured with excessive bitterness the conduct of the governor of the colony, not being willing to acknowledge that they had constantly and expressly instructed him to win the Indians over by affability and kindness, to give them familiar entertainment in the houses of the colonists, and, if it were possible, to drive them to live together and cohabit, that is to dwell, with the English.⌉ [43] Such is the course of the world. Men in authority often give loose instructions, and discover strong tendencies of their opinions, and brand their agents with the consequences of their own errors in those instructions and opinions.

The courts of which the Company were members were in fact popular assemblies in which the factions had an opportunity to intrigue, eloquence, and clamor; and even the king stooped to bribe wicked instruments for fomenting dissensions which might bear upon persons obnoxious to his resentment. Among the rest one Samuel Wrote suddenly laid aside his character for moderation, judgment, and industry and caviled at the late proceedings of the General Court as being irregular, illegal, and fraudulent. He addressed himself to the feelings of the people on some late salaries, knowing how easy it was to asperse the most meritorious friends of the colony by arraigning them as the authors of those salaries, howsoever just and well measured they might be. He was not unmindful of the usual refuge from the animadversions of more respectable members and invited the sympathy of the General Court by giving out in speeches that he had been browbeaten and insulted for having freely delivered his conscientious opinion. He was a man of such a temper as to aspire to elevation at the expense of principle and public good. To cover rank effrontery with the guise of an obstinacy, which sometimes arises from an honest though mistaken

42. Stith, *Virginia,* pp. 208–12.

43. *Ibid.,* p. 232. The Company's letter of censure and the bitter reply by the governor and Council of Virginia are in Kingsbury, *Records of Virginia Company,* III, 666–73, and IV, 10–11.

mind, and by a mean effort to undermine others under the garb of patriotism, he offered to undertake for some inadequate pittance a work entitled to high compensation.[44]

King James's idea of prerogative was exemplified in the most striking manner by a peremptory fiat that the contract between him and the Company respecting tobacco should be void.[45]

From these circumstances sprang a more formal assertion of the right of monopoly in colonial produce. The commodities of Virginia were to be imported into England. Against this order, the Company demonstrated, stating that by the original charters and grants the inhabitants of the colony were as the rest of His Majesty's subjects and that it was not in the power of the Company to restrain them from carrying their goods to the most promising markets. They did indeed seem inclined to export directly to England such of them raised in the plantation as belonging to the Company themselves.[46] Our colonial history, had it at the beginning of the Revolution been probed to the bottom, would have shown how many of the claims of usurpation grew like this into a metropolitan right upon a mere reluctance to quarrel with the mother country.

44. Samuel Wrote, a member of the Virginia Council, was a strong critic of the tobacco contract. On Dec. 4 he and Alderman Johnson attempted to discredit those responsible for the contract by attacking the salary schedule of the Company as ordinary graft. Because of the violence of his attacks Wrote was sentenced to be forever excluded from the Council and suspended from the Company for a year. The followers of both the earl of Warwick and Sir Thomas Smith rallied to Wrote's support, and as a result of the bitterness of his trial party lines were further drawn and hardened (Craven, *Dissolution of Virginia Company,* pp. 237–38) .

45. Strong objections to the tobacco contract came from the Smith-Warwick group within the Company. At first the king's ministers were disinclined to revoke the contract, but after some weeks of urging by Smith and Warwick they rescinded it. An important reason for the Privy Council's decision was the revelation by the contract's opponents that the Company had for two years violated the ban against sending tobacco to Holland (*ibid.,* p. 243; Andrews, *Colonial Period,* I, 158–59) .

46. Randolph is in error here. After the tobacco contract was revoked a new agreement was negotiated on the most advantageous terms enjoyed by the Virginia Company since 1619. It did not return to the 12d. duties, nor did it establish a government monopoly; all tobacco from the plantations was to be brought into England at a reduced tariff of 9d. and left to the free disposal of its individual owners. Moreover, the tobacco of the plantations was to enjoy a virtual monopoly of the English market except for a limited quantity of Spanish tobacco reduced to 40,000 pounds a years from an earlier proposal of 80,000. Far from being the mere tools of the crown, the Warwick-Smith group, led by its spokesman Nathaniel Rich, had secured far more favorable terms than Sandys. Actually, the battle over the tobacco agreement was symptomatic of a larger struggle for power within the company, and the bitter opposition of Sandys's partisans toward the new contract reflected their recognition of having suffered a serious defeat (Craven, *Dissolution of Virginia Company,* pp. 243–50).

This in some measure countenanced the principle of monopoly. But it was only a principle of accommodation, not of right; at any rate, it amounted to no more than an acquiescence under the terrors of a wide prerogative. The reasoning of Sir Edwin Sandys deserves a place here. [However, he said, as the Virginians had been driven by the rigor of former contractors with the crown to such foreign markets for their commodities, so he doubted not that by general usage and good treatment they would be easily induced to return to England, their best and most natural market. But he declared it to be his opinion that to compel the colony to bring into England all their commodities without any qualification, as could be raised in the colony, and without a correspondent regulation in England concerning the same articles was oppressive and would soon bring Virginia to utter ruin.

[Mr. Rider added that the English plantations had been at first settled and since supported at the charge of private adventurers, unless it might be excepted that His Majesty, out of his great grace and favor, had granted them some lotteries and collections, the produce of which had nevertheless been expended merely for the public service, and that those vast obligations of lotteries and collections were very cheap to His Majesty, who never contributed one farthing himself to them, although he was a very great and the only gainer yet by these settlements.] [47]

This excellent reasoning and admonition of Sandys and Rider did not relax the perseverance of the Council in demanding the importation into England of all commodities made in Virginia, except that the duty of twelve pence per pound on tobacco was reduced to nine pence, not however from a better motive than that the customs, as they were called, had abated three pence per pound.

The promise of the court against the importation of more than 40,000 weight of Spanish tobacco at that day possessed no other merit than as being the alloyed coin in which factious men ought to be paid if their lot did not involve better men.

The Company were next embroiled by a stratagem not unlike that imputed to Pericles, the kindling of a war as the best means for settling accounts with the public. Alderman Johnson and Mr. Essington [48]

---

47. Stith, *Virginia*, pp. 271–72. This petition is probably the one approved by a majority of the Company's court in May 1623 (Kingsbury, *Records of Virginia Company*, II, 393–99).

48. William Essington, a London merchant, was a member of both the East India and Virginia companies.

could not disentangle themselves from the claims of the Company but by annihilating it. They therefore presented to the king, in a private manner, ⌈representations that the unity of the colonies at home was turned into civil discord and dissension and their peace abroad into massacre and hostility between the natives and the colony; and that many of the ancient adventurers and planters conceived themselves to be greatly injured, abused, and oppressed; and requesting the king to nominate some worthy persons, by commission under the Great Seal of England, who by oath or otherwise by all lawful ways and means should inquire and examine what was the true state of the colonies at the time when Sir Thomas Smith left the government of the companies, what monies had since been collected for the plantations, by whom received, and how the same had been procured and expended, and what, after so vast an expense, was the present state and condition of the colonies. That the said commissioners should also inquire into all grievances and abuses, what wrongs had been done to any of the adventurers or planters, together with the grounds and causes thereof, and should propose how the same might in time to come be prevented or reformed and how the business of the colonies might be better managed, so that, all contentions being reconciled and the authors thereof condignly punished, peace and unity restored, and the government of affairs better established, those noble works might go on and prosper with a blessing from Heaven to His Majesty's great honor and profit and to the religious and public ends for which they were at first undertaken.[49] It was supported by another statement from Nathaniel Butler, one of the faction, called "The Unmasked Face of Our Colony in Virginia as It Was in the Winter of the Year 1612."⌉ [50]

To that of Johnson the following reply was made: ⌈That in December 1618, being the twelfth year from the first settlement of the colony, after £80,000 expense and upwards of the public stock, besides other sums of private planters and adventurers, there were remaining in Virginia about six hundred persons, men, women, and children, and

49. For this petition, see Kingsbury, *Records of Virginia Company,* II, 373–74.

50. Stith, *Virginia,* pp. 276–78. Nathaniel Powell had been governor of Bermuda since 1619. His appointment to that post had been the result of strong support from Warwick, and as the earl's closest ally in America he had been attacked by Sandys on many occasions. In 1622, at the expiration of his term of office, he returned to England. However, on the return trip, presumably at the request of the Warwick group, Butler made a special visit of investigation to Virginia (Craven, *Dissolution of Virginia Company,* p. 254). Stith summarized "Virginia Unmasked" on pp. 278–80 (see also Kingsbury, *Records of Virginia Company,* II, 274–377).

of cattle about three hundred at the most, and that the Company was then left in debt near £5,000. But that at Christmas 1622, through the divine blessing, notwithstanding the late mortalities in all those parts of America and notwithstanding the massacre and the great mortality consequent thereon by the people being driven from their habitations and provisions, there were still remaining (as was computed) above 520 persons, sent over at the expense only of £30,000 of the public stock, besides the charges of particular societies and planters; that the cattle were also increased to above a thousand head, besides goats and infinite numbers of swine; and that the old debt left on the Company by Sir Thomas Smith was wholly discharged.

[That at the same time, December 1618, the only commodities of value returned from Virginia were tobacco and sassafras, whereas during the four last years great sums had been expended and care and diligence bestowed by the officers and Company for promoting various commodities and manufactures, such as ironworks, wine, silk, sawing mills, salt pans, and other things of the like nature; and that they had been particularly careful, according to His Majesty's advice and directions, to restrain the colony from their too eager pursuit of tobacco, as did abundantly appear from the frequent letters, instructions, and charters to that effect, with sundry printed books, and pamphlets made purposely and published for their use and direction.

[That as to the government, it had been within the four last years reformed according to His Majesty's original directions in the letters patent; and the people were no longer discontented and mutinous but now lived in great peace and tranquillity; and to the end that persons of worth might be allured to the places of power and profit and all occasions of rapine and extortion removed, they had raised a competent annual provision and revenue for the governor and all other officers and magistrates and particularly for the clergy, according to the degree and quality of each place. That these cares were by no means lost or ineffectual; but as they had settled the colony in perfect quiet and content, so they had raised at home so great a fame of Virginia that men now, not out of necessity as at first, but many persons of good quality and fortune had, out of choice, transported themselves thither and were daily providing to remove.

[That there had been granted in the last four years forty-four patents for lands, for each of which the patentees had undertaken to transport one hundred men at the least, whereas in the former twelve years there had not been granted above six.

⌈That, in the said time, there had been employed forty-two ships of great burden (whereof seventeen sail were, about Christmas last, in James River at once), whereas in four years before there were not above twelve employed.

⌈That in the said four last years there had come in ten times as many adventurers as had arrived in twice the time before, so that whereas before the legal number of twenty could scarce be got together to make a quarter court, it seldom now consisted of less than two hundred and sometimes of many more.

⌈That they could not omit the extraordinary blessing of God in exciting the hearts of many zealous and devout persons to extend their aid toward this glorious work, who had contributed within the four last years to the value of £1,500 for pious and religious uses, a fruit whereof the preceding years were altogether barren.

⌈That, however, it could not be denied but that the increase and prosperity of the colony had lately received a fatal blow and interruption from the Indian massacre and their peace and unity at home had been much broken and disturbed by divers troublesome oppositions. But the former, they hoped, would soon be sharply punished and revenged, and the other must with patience be borne and overcome with constancy.

⌈They concluded with beseeching His Majesty (as being the first founder and gracious supporter of this great enterprise, which would continue to all posterity a monument of his glorious name) to grant them the four hundred young men long since promised to be levied on the several counties in order to be sent to Virginia to root out the barbarous enemy and to supply the colony in parts yet defective and unsettled, and doubted not in a short time to be able to yield him so good and so real an account of the fruits of their cares and labors as might in some sort be answerable to their duty and to His Majesty's princely expectations.[51]

⌈Besides this declaration, the Lord Cavendish produced another writing containing a vindication of the late conduct of the Virginia and Somer Islands companies. His lordship had drawn this up himself for the satisfaction of some noble persons who had from sinister information conceived a harsh opinion of the Company's proceedings; and as these noblemen upon reading that discourse were fully satisfied of the justice and fairness of their actions, so he hoped it might work

51. See Kingsbury, *Records of Virginia Company,* II, 393–97.

the like effect upon His Majesty's mind. Whereupon that writing was deliberately read, and every article and branch thereof being duly weighed and considered, was put to the question, and it was ordered to be delivered to His Majesty as the Company's act and answer, there being not above three voices against any part of it and most of it being confirmed and approved by unanimous consent.⌉ [52]

For the machinations of the king were unfolding themselves by the appointment of a board of commissioners for an inquiry into the topics of complaint against the Company, as if all their rights had been already forfeited for some delinquency.[53] ⌈All their letters public and private were intercepted by his command, their books and records were sequestered by an order of the Privy Council, and two of their most faithful and able members were arrested.

⌈This was a great interruption in preparing the Company's business, which was to be laid before the commissioners. Their defense depended entirely on their books and records, from which they doubted not to make their innocence abundantly appear. And they were so sensible of the prejudice that would arise to the companies by the restraint of the deputies who were their best accountants, and from their places, the most conversant in the business of late years, that they petitioned the Privy Council so far at least to set them at liberty that they might be able to go forward with the Company's business and attend the commissioners. And their books were accordingly soon after restored, and the deputies released.

⌈But from these and other discouraging circumstances it was an easy matter to conjecture what was the final object and how things were going. And therefore the great officers of the Company, the earl of Southampton, Sir Edwin Sandys, and the two Ferrars, through whose hands all the transactions of money had for a long time passed, sued out their general acquittances in the court. Discharges were granted under the Great Seal by a cheerful and unanimous concurrence of the whole Company.

⌈The king had always been endeavoring to get such a person chosen into the post of treasurer as should be perfectly submissive to his pleasure and command. And now on the day of election the court received a letter from His Majesty signifying that he had appointed commissioners to examine into the present state of the colony of Vir-

---

52. Stith, *Virginia*, pp. 281–83; see also Kingsbury, *Records of Virginia Company*, II, 400–409.

53. The commission authorizing a royal investigation was issued on May 9, 1623.

ginia; and as he expected to receive in a few days some account of their labors therein, it was his will and pleasure that all officers should continue as they were and that they should not proceed to any new election before the morrow fortnight after at the soonest. This unexpected and mysterious order caused a long and general silence in the court. But at length, considering that they were restrained by their charters to quarter courts only for the election of officers and that all offices expiring that day, their government would become void and their patents forfeited unless something was done therein, they continued all officers in their places, not a fortnight longer, but till the next quarter court, when only an election could be made. And thus, the king never after expressed his pleasure herein and the Company to avoid misconstruction forbearing to do anything till His Majesty's pleasure was further known, the earl of Southampton and Mr. Nicholas Ferrar were, from time to time, continued in their places—till the suppression of the courts and dissolution of the Company.

[In some of the intercepted letters from Virginia, the lords of the Privy Council found great complaints of the scarcity of provisions. This had been occasioned by the massacre and the consequent war with the Indians, by which much of their corn and stocks had been destroyed and a general interruption given to the culture of their lands. Their lordships therefore called the deputy and a few more of the Company before them and commanded them to send an immediate relief to the colony. They proposed that the whole Company should be obliged to contribute toward it according to the number of each man's shares by rating them at twenty or at least ten shillings a share, and that they should be compelled to pay the same by an order of that board. But Mr. Ferrar and his associates seem not to have been perfectly convinced of the legality of such a proceeding and conceived themselves to have no power by law to lay such a general assessment on the Company without their consent. Wherefore, after much debate, they prevailed on their lordships to permit them to proceed in their usual method of voluntary subscriptions.

[But notwithstanding these lowering prospects and this unpromising situation of their affairs, the Company proceeded boldly in their defense.[54] And as soon as the commissioners were known, they deputed Sir Edward Sackville, Sir Robert Killegrew, and Sir John Danvers to wait upon them in the Company's name and to declare their joy and satisfaction in the commission. They earnestly and unanimously be-

54. See Kingsbury, *Records of Virginia Company*, II, 346–63.

sought them to take into their immediate consideration Captain Butler's information to His Majesty entitled "The Unmasked Face of the
Colony of Virginia," which had given a deadly wound to the happy
progress of the plantation, so that until by their wisdom and integrity
the truth should be discovered and the world again possessed of their
former hopes and good opinion of that colony, it must undoubtedly
languish, if not shortly perish, for want of those daily supplies which
its reputation alone had before procured in great abundance.⟧ [55]

[What the commissioners did, what inquiries they entered upon,
and what reports they made to the king, were secrets to the Company,
who in a letter to the colony acknowledged themselves to be entirely in
the dark as to what was passing or what was intended. At length, after
long waiting for the issue of their inquiries and determinations, Mr.
Deputy Ferrar with some few more of the Company were called, on
October 8, before the lords of the Privy Council, who made some
proposals to the deputy. But these being of a weighty and important
nature and Mr. Ferrar conceiving himself to have no power to give an
answer to them, they were at his request drawn up into an order of
that board that so he might under that form present them to the Company. This order of Council set forth:

[That His Majesty had taken into his princely consideration the distressed state of the colony of Virginia occasioned, as it seemed, by the
ill government of the Company; that this could not well be remedied
but by reducing the government into fewer hands, near the number of
those who were in the first patent appointed. That therein especial
provision should be made for continuing and preserving the interests
of all adventurers and private persons whatsoever. That His Majesty
had therefore resolved by a new charter to appoint a governor and
twelve assistants to be resident in England, to whom should be committed the government of the Company and colony; that the said governor and assistants should be nominated and chosen for the first time
by His Majesty. Therefore, the deputy and the others were by their
lordships required to assemble a court forthwith to resolve whether
the Company would surrender their former charters and be content to

---

55. Stith, *Virginia*, pp. 298–301. Sir Edward Sackville (1590–1652), a strong supporter
of Sir Edwin Sandys, had a varied career as a soldier, diplomat, member of Parliament,
member of several commercial companies, and privy councilor. Sir Robert Killigrew
(d. 1633), also a strong Sandys man, was a member of Parliament and later part of the
special commission appointed June 27, 1631, "for the better plantation in Virginia." Sir
John Danvers (1588–1655), a Sandys supporter, was a member of Parliament, served on
the special commission of 1631, and was one of the judges who passed sentence on
Charles I in Jan. 1649.

accept a new one with those alterations; and they were commanded to return their answer with all expedition, His Majesty being determined in default of such submission to proceed for recalling their former charters in such sort as to him should seem just and meet.[56]

[This order of the Council so struck and amazed the Company that, as if they distrusted their own ears, they caused it to be read over three several times, and after that, no man for a long time spoke a word to it. However, eight of the faction of twenty-six being present, with Sir Samuel Argall at their head, moved the Company in conformity to their lordships' order to make an immediate surrender of their charters; but far the major part of the court,][57] to the number of 112 persons, declared themselves against it. They said it was a matter of such weight and consequence that they thought themselves to have no power to give an answer to it in that ordinary court. For such courts were by their charters only permitted to treat of casual and particular occurrences of less consequence; but all weighty affairs, and particularly all things relating to government, were restrained by the precise words of their letters patent to quarter courts only; wherefore, whilst their present patents were in force, that ordinary court had no authority to determine such a matter as this, being of the highest and most important nature that had ever been propounded to them. To which it was added that in obedience to their charters they had never taken to themselves the liberty to dispose of so much as a single share of land but in their quarter courts, and they conceived themselves much more, even in conscience, bound not to betray their trust and so suddenly pass away all rights of themselves and the rest of their numerous society and of all the planters in Virginia, who were equally interested with them in their letters patent. They therefore besought their lordships that their answer might upon these just grounds be respited till the quarter court and that by that time they should have leisure to consider well of so weighty a proposition. And to this end, they ordered a very large and particular summons to be given to all the adventurers, for that day, and that their officers should give them especial notice of the business then to be treated and desire them, in the Company's name, not to fail to be present, which if they did, they would be without excuse and would have no manner of pretense to complain afterwards.[58]

---

56. See Kingsbury, *Records of Virginia Company*, II, 469.

57. Stith, *Virginia*, pp. 303–4. The faction referred to was the Warwick-Smith group. Neither Warwick, Smith, nor Rich was present at the meeting.

58. See Kingsbury, *Records of Virginia Company*, II, 471–75.

This answer, however consonant to both law and reason, gave no satisfaction to the lords of the Privy Council, who, by another act of their board dated the seventeenth of the same month of October, declared it to be merely dilatory; wherefore, as His Majesty expected a speedy account of their proceedings in the business and as it did likewise in itself require expedition, in regard of the importance and consequence thereof, they ordered and expressly charged the deputy and the rest of the Company to assemble themselves again immediately and on the Monday following to deliver a clear, direct, and final answer to that which had been before propounded and was that day reiterated unto them, viz.: Whether the Company would be content to submit and surrender their former charters and to accept a new one with the alterations intimated? And the deputy was likewise commanded to propound the question to the Company in those clear and precise terms in which it was then delivered.

In obedience to this order of the Privy Council, Mr. Ferrar called an extraordinary court, at which, by reason of the shortness of the warning, there were only seventy persons present. And he having proposed the question to them in the express terms prescribed in the act of Council, nine voices only were for submitting. But all the rest being strenuously against the surrender of their charters, an answer was accordingly returned to their lordships.[59]

These proceedings, which struck plainly at the root and foundation of all the rights and franchises of both the Company and the colony, made a great noise and gave the alarm to all such as were in any manner engaged in the action. Some ships therefore which were preparing to sail were stopped, till the issue and intent of these acts of power were further seen into and understood. But the lords of Council, being apprised of this ill consequence, made another order of their board, on October 20, importing that their lordships were that day informed there was so great a discouragement among the Virginia adventurers on account of the intended reformation and change of the government as rendered them fearful to prosecute their adventures, so that it would probably occasion some stop to those ships which were then ready freighted and bound to that country; that although their lordships much marveled that any man should so far mistake their meaning, considering the declaration that had been made at that board viva voce, as also by an act of Council and otherwise, yet for the better

59. See *ibid.*, p. 469.

satisfying of those who through their own error or the false suggestions of others had conceived any such fear or discouragement, they thereby again declared that there was no other intention than merely and only the reformation and change of the present government, whereof His Majesty had seen so many bad effects as would endanger the whole plantation if it was not corrected and amended. That nevertheless, for so much as concerned the private interest of every man, His Majesty's royal care was such that no man should receive any prejudice in his property but should have his estate fully and wholly conserved to him, and if anything was found defective, better secured, so that none need apprehend any such fears or inconveniencies, but contrariwise, cheerfully proceed. It was therefore ordered by their lordships and thought fit to be published to the Company that it was His Majesty's absolute command that the ships then intended for Virginia and in some readiness to go should be forthwith dispatched for the relief of the colony and good of the plantation without any further hindrance or stop.

What were the proceedings of the commissioners or whether His Majesty found sufficient matter, as he thought, from their reports to suppress the Company and revoke their charters is unknown. But the better to fortify this design and to raise matter of complaint and accusation, the lords of the Privy Council on October 24 appointed John Harvey, Esq. (afterwards well known as governor of Virginia by the title of Sir John Harvey), John Pory (formerly secretary and a noted tool of the earl of Warwick), Abraham Peirsey, Samuel Mathews, and John Jefferson to be their commissioners, to make particular and diligent inquiry touching divers matters which concerned the state of the colony of Virginia.[60] And that they might the better perform the orders

60. John Harvey (d. 1646), a member of the royal commission, joined the provisional government in 1625, was appointed governor in 1628, but did not take up his post in Virginia until the spring of 1630. In 1634 the governor's Council rebuked him for exceeding his power, but Harvey answered that the Council's job was only to advise with him, and then proceeded to knock out the teeth of one member and threaten the others with hanging. The following year the Council arrested Harvey, packed him off to London, and elected John West in his place. The king forced Harvey back upon Virginia, but once the point had been made that a crown representative could not be maltreated, Harvey was recalled. John Pory (1570–1636), a Cambridge M.A., traveler, man of letters, and member of Parliament, was the author of a description of life in the colony (reprinted in Tyler, *Narratives of Virginia*, pp. 281–87). He also served as speaker of the first General Assembly in 1619 and carried the report of the Harvey Commission to England (Morton, *Colonial Virginia*, I, 47, 58–59, 105). Samuel Mathews (1600?–1660) was a prominent Virginia planter and member of the General Assembly of 1624. John Jefferson did not serve.

they had received and discharge the trust committed to them, their lordships strictly willed and required the governor and Council here to yield them their best aid and assistance upon all occasions and in all matters wherein they should find cause to make use of the same. The three acts of Council also, just before recited, were committed to Mr. Pory, and particularly the last, to be published in such places in Virginia as he should judge fit for the quiet and satisfaction of the inhabitants here. Captain Harvey indeed and Mr. Pory seem to have been the most active and most trusted in this business, and therefore Captain Smith, who had probably never seen this commission and knew nothing of the others, only mentions two as sent upon this errand.[61] As for Mr. Jefferson, he never appeared in it but seems all along to have been a hearty friend to the Company and their present constitution and government. Besides, he was present at their courts in England at such times as were inconsistent with his prosecuting that commission in Virginia.[62]

But the most tremendous explosion was in the shape of a process of quo warranto against the Company.[63] To complete the train, the faction presented a petition to the lords of the Council offering to surrender the charters and praying that the refractory might be subjected to the costs of their defense against the quo warranto out of their private estates. To this the Council assented.

Notwithstanding these multiplied attacks the colony was prosperous and comfortable.

It was a meanness and injustice in James, derogatory from the royal character, to conceal from the colony the offenses charged upon them. But the General Assembly which met in February were well informed of what passed in England and in six days prepared this decisive answer:

[That, holding it a sin against God and their own sufferings to permit the world to be abused with false reports and to give to vice the reward of virtue, they, in the name of the whole colony of Virginia in their General Assembly met, many of them having been eyewitnesses

61. For John Smith's comments on the royal commission, see Tyler, *Narratives of Virginia*, pp. 399–407.

62. When the commissioners arrived in Virginia in Feb. 1624, they received a rather unfriendly reception from the colony's authorities, most of whom were agents of the Sandys faction. A year earlier letters from the colony were bitterly denouncing the Company, but now the possible overthrow of the Company raised the specter of a return to martial law and conditions as they had existed before 1618.

63. A writ of quo warranto was issued from the king's bench on Nov. 4, 1623.

and sufferers in those times, had framed out of their duty to the country and love to truth the following answer to the praises given to Sir Thomas Smith's government in the said declaration.

⌜They averred that in those twelve years of Sir Thomas Smith's government the colony for the most part remained in great want and misery under most severe and cruel laws, which were sent over in print, and were contrary to the express letter of the king's most gracious charters, and mercilessly executed here oftentimes without trial or judgment. That the allowance for a man in those times was only eight ounces of meat and half a pint of peas a day, both the one and the other being moldy, rotten, full of cobwebs and maggots, loathsome to man, and not fit for beasts, which forced many to fly to the savage enemy for relief, who being again taken, were put to sundry kinds of death, by hanging, shooting, breaking upon the wheel, and the like. That others were forced by famine to filch for their bellies, of whom one for stealing two or three pints of oatmeal had a bodkin thrust through his tongue and was chained to a tree till he starved. That if a man through sickness had not been able to work, he had no allowance at all and consequently perished. That many through these extremities dug holes in the earth and there hid themselves till they famished. That they could not for those their miseries blame their commanders here; for their sustenance was to come from England, and had they given them better allowance they must have perished in general. That their scarcity sometimes was so lamentable that they were constrained to eat dogs, cats, rats, snakes, toadstools, horsehides, and whatnot. That one man out of the misery he endured killed his wife and powdered her up to eat, for which he was burned; that many others fed on the corpses of dead men; and that one who through custom had got an insatiable appetite to that food could not be restrained till he was executed for it. And that indeed so miserable was their state that the happiest day many ever hoped to see was when the Indians had killed a mare, the people wishing as she was boiling, that Sir Thomas Smith was upon her back in the kettle.

⌜And whereas it was affirmed that very few of His Majesty's subjects were lost in those days, and those persons of the meanest rank, they replied that for one that then died, five had perished in Sir Thomas Smith's times, many being of ancient houses and born to estates of a thousand pounds a year, some less, who likewise perished by famine, that those who survived and had in ventures both their estates and persons were constrained to serve the colony seven or eight years for their freedom and underwent as hard and as servile labor as the basest fellow that was brought out of Newgate. As for the discovery, they owned that much had been discovered in those twelve years but in the four or five last years much more than formerly. That the houses and churches then built were so mean and poor by reason of these calamities that they could not stand above one or two years, the people going to work indeed, but out of the bitterness of their spirits, breathing execrable curses upon Sir Thomas Smith; neither could a blessing from God be hoped for in those buildings which were founded upon the blood of so many Christians. That the towns were only James City, Henrico, Charles Hundred, West and Shirley Hundred, and Kecoughtan; all which were ruined in those times, except ten or twelve houses in Jamestown. That at present there were four for every one then and forty times exceeding them in goodness. That of fortifications there were none against a foreign enemy, and those against the domestic foe very few and contemptible. That there was only one bridge, which also decayed in that time. That if through the aforesaid calamities many had not perished, there would doubtless have been largely above a thousand people in the country when Sir Thomas Smith left the government; but they conceived, when Sir George Yeardley arrived as governor, he found not above four hundred, most of them in want of corn and utterly destitute of cattle, swine, poultry, and other necessary provisions to nourish them; that there were some ministers to instruct the people, whose ability they would not tax, but divers of them had no orders; that they were never overfurnished with arms, powder, and ammunition, yet that in quality they were almost entirely useless. They acknowledged that in those times trial was made of divers staple commodities, which they had not means to proceed in; but they hoped that in time a better progress would be made therein; and had it not been for the massacre, many by that time would have been brought to perfection. That for boats, there was only one serviceable one left in the colony at the end of Smith's government, for which one, besides four or five ships and barks, there were not then so few as forty. That the barks and barges then built were in number so few and so weak that they soon perished. That they never knew that the natives did voluntarily yield themselves subjects to the king, took any pride in that title, or paid any contribution of corn toward the support of the colony; neither could they at any time keep them in such good correspondency as to be become mutually hopeful to each other, but contrariwise, whatever was done proceeded from fear, and not love, and their corn was got by trade or the sword.

[And now, to what a growth of perfection the colony could arrive at the end of these twelve years, they left to be judged by what had been said, and they besought His Majesty, rather than be reduced to live under the like government again, that he would send commissioners over to hang them. As to Alderman Johnson, one of the authors of the declaration, they said he had great reason to commend Sir Thomas Smith, to whose offenses and infamy he was so inseparably linked. And all this they affirmed to be true by the general report of the country which they never heard contradicted, many of them also having been eyewitnesses, or else resident in the country, when every particular here reported happened.

[This declaration was signed by Sir Francis Wyatt, the governor, Sir George Sandys, John Pott, John Pountis, Roger Smith, and Ralph Hamor, Esqrs., of the Council, and by William Tucker, William Peirce, Rawley Crashaw, Samuel Mathews, Jabez Whitaker, and others, to the number of twenty-four, of the House of Burgesses, and nearly about the full number of that house at that time.[64] For there were, three years before, eleven boroughs which had a right to send members to the Assembly, and there might be, and undoubtedly were, a few

64. See Tyler, *Narratives of Virginia*, pp. 422–26. Sir Francis Wyatt (1588–1644) arrived in Virginia in 1621 to relieve Sir George Yeardley as governor. It was during his administration that the massacre of 1622 occurred. He left Virginia in 1626 but returned to serve again as governor from 1639 to 1642. George Sandys (1578–1644) was a Latin scholar, the son of an archbishop of York, and the brother of Sir Edwin Sandys. While in Virginia he had translated portions of Ovid's *Metamorphoses* (for both Sandys and Wyatt see Davis, *George Sandys*). Dr. John Pott had accompanied Sir Francis Wyatt to Virginia as his physician and later served briefly from 1629 to 1630 as acting governor until the arrival of Sir John Harvey. In July 1630 he was tried and convicted for stealing cattle, the first trial by jury in the colony. John Pountis (d. 1624) was a member of the Council in Virginia. Roger Smith, formerly a soldier in the Netherlands, probably came to Virginia in 1616. He was appointed to the colony's Council in 1621. Capt. William Tucker was known for his expedition on May 22, 1623, to the Potomac River to release some English prisoners held by Indians there and to punish a tribe which recently had been acting hostilely. After lulling the Indians into a false sense of security with talk of peace, Tucker induced them to drink healths from poisoned containers, killing about 200 Indians (Morton, *Colonial Virginia*, I, 82). Capt. William Peirce, a planter and councilor, was described by Sir George Sandys in 1623 as "the fairest in Virginia" (*ibid.,* p. 144). Rawley Crashaw had come to Virginia in 1608 and had been a close associate of Capt. John Smith. In 1624 he served as a burgess from Elizabeth City. Jabez Whitaker, a resident of Elizabeth City County, was a member of the House of Burgesses in 1623–24 and the Council in 1626.

others since added to them. Their answer to Captain Butler's information ran in the following manner:

Most gracious Sovereign,

Whereas a copy of an information presented to Your Majesty by Captain Nathaniel Butler, entitled "The Unmasking of Virginia," is come to our hands, and whereas the same is full of notorious slanders and falsehoods, proceeding from the malice of his corrupt heart and abetted by private enmity and public division, which aim at the satisfaction of their particular spleen, although it be to the subversion of this whole colony, we the governor, Council, and colony of Virginia, in our General Assembly, out of zeal and respect to Your Majesty and this our country, not to suffer your sacred ears to be profaned with false suggestions, nor your royal thoughts to be diverted from so hopeful a plantation, which may add in time a principal flower to your diadem, do in all humbleness submit this our answer to your princely survey, annexed to the several untruths of the said informer.

1. I found the plantation generally seated, etc.

The plantations for the most part are high and pleasantly seated and the rest not low nor infested with marshes, which we wish were more frequent. The creeks are rather useful than noisome, and no bogs have been seen here by any that have lived twice as many years as he did weeks in the country, the places which he so miscalls being the richest parts of the earth if we had a sufficient force to clear their woods and to give the fresh springs which run through them a free passage. The soil is rich and restores our trust with abundance, the air is sweet, and the clime healthful, all circumstances considered, to men of sound bodies and good government.

2. I found the shores, etc.

In this he traduces one of the goodliest rivers in the habitable world, which runs for many miles together within upright banks till at length, enlarged with the receipt of others, it beats on a sandy shore and imitates the sea in greatness and majesty. It is approachable on both sides from half flood to half ebb for boats of good burden; neither is there any river in the world of this vastness, without cranes or wharfs, more commodious for landing. And it is equally contrary to truth that by wading we get violent surfeits of cold, which never leave us till we are brought to our graves.

3. The new people sent over arriving for the most part, etc.

We affirm that the winter is the only proper time for the arrival of newcomers, whereof the governor and Council have often by their letters informed the Company; and the like advice has been given to their correspondents, from time to time, by private planters, for their supply of servants. As to houses of entertainment, there was a general subscription, amounting to an unexpected sum, and workmen actually employed, to build a fair inn in James City, and every principal plantation had resolved

on the like for the entertainment of their new supplies, when it pleased
God to punish our crimes by the bloody hands of the Indians, which
obliged us to divert that care to the housing ourselves, many of us having
been unfurnished by that disaster. But buildings of late have everywhere
increased exceedingly; neither have newcomers any reason to complain,
when every man's house is without recompense open to the stranger, even
to disaccommodating [of] ourselves. So that we may with modesty boast that
no people in the world do exercise the like hospitality. As for dying under
hedges (whereof there are none in Virginia) or lying unburied in the
woods, by reason of this defect, it is utterly false. However, if such things
should sometimes be seen accidentally here, the like may and often doth
happen in the most flourishing countries of Europe.

   4. The colony was this winter in great distress, etc.

   The colony that winter was in no distress of victual, as the accuser well
knows, for he bought corn himself for eight shillings a bushel, cheaper,
as we hear, than it was then sold in England. It is true a succeeding
scarcity was feared. But what less could be expected after such a massacre,
when near half the colony were driven from their habitations in time of
planting, others straightened in their ground by receiving them, and all
interrupted in their business by supporting a sudden war? English meal,
sold, as he affirms, at thirty shillings the bushel, was only sold for ten pounds
of tobacco, for which in truck we ordinarily receive under twelve pence a
pound real value. And it is not to be supposed that any of the great should
affect scarcity in order to enrich themselves by trade, for trade has ever been
free for us all; neither have they who have brought in most corn sold it
out at unconscionable rates but have often freely imparted it to the necessity
of others without any other advantage than repayment. We agree with
that prime one who wished that corn might be under eight shillings a
bushel, meaning in tobacco at three shillings a pound, for so there would
be some proportion between the profit of making the one and the other,
and corn would thereby be planted in greater abundance.

   5. Their houses are generally the worst, etc.

   Our houses, for the most part, are rather built for use than ornament;
yet not a few for both, and fit to give entertainment to men of good quality.
If we may give credit to those who are accounted the most faithful relaters
of the West Indies, many cities of great renown there, after threescore years'
progress, are not to be compared in their buildings to ours. And so far are
they from the meanest cottages in England that many towns there have
hardly one house in them which exceeds ours in conveniency or structure.
The greatest disparagement that some of them received proceeded from his
riots and lascivious filthiness with lewd women purchased with reals of
eight and wedges of gold, the spoils of the distressed Spaniards in Bermuda,
which, as we are informed by a gentleman of good credit who casually

surveyed his inventory, did, with other treasure, amount to divers thousands. As for the interposition of creeks which men are most desirous to seat upon, where we cannot go by land we have boats and canoes for our sudden transport on any occasion.

6. I found not the least fortification, etc.

We have as yet no fortifications against a foreign enemy, although it has been endeavored by the Company, with a success unanswerable to their care and expense, and also lately by ourselves. But the work, being interrupted by the scarcity of last summer, shall proceed again, God willing, with all convenient expedition, and almost all our houses are sufficiently fortified against the Indians with strong palisadoes. His envy would not let him number truly the ordnance of James City, four demi-culverins being there mounted, and all serviceable. At Flowerdieu Hundred he makes but one of six, neither was he ever there but, according to his custom, reports the unseen as seen. The same envy would not let him see the three pieces at Newport News and those two at Elizabeth City. Two great pieces there are at Charles Hundred and seven at Henrico. Besides which, several private planters have since furnished themselves with ordnance. So that it were a desperate enterprise, and unlikely to be attempted by a man of his spirit, to beat down our houses about our ears with a bark of that burden.

7. Expecting according to their printed books, etc.

The time that this informant came over was in the winter after the massacre when those wounds were green and the earth deprived of her beauty. His ears were open to nothing but detraction, and he only inquired after the factious, of which there were none among us, and how he might gather occasions against those in the government, being as it should seem sent over for that purpose; otherwise he could not but hear of our proclamations for the advancement of staple commodities and with what alacrity and success they proceeded, vines and mulberry trees being planted throughout the whole country, the ironworks in great forwardness and shortly to receive perfection, and the glassworks labored after with all possible care, till the slaughter by the Indians and the succeeding mortality gave a ruin to some and interruption to all. So that he has nothing but our misfortunes to accuse and upbraid us with, which have obliged us still to follow that contemptible weed as well to sustain the war as to enable us again to erect those works. As for deriding the books that were sent over by the Company, it was done by himself and no other that we know of.

8. I found the ancient plantations of Henrico, etc.

Still he abuses Your Majesty with these words "I found," in places where he never was by some score of miles, having never been higher up the river than the territory of James City. Henrico was quitted in Sir Thomas Smith's time, only the church and one house remaining. Charles City, so much spoken of, never had but six houses. The soil of both is barren,

worn out, and not fit for culture. The loss of our stocks the informer has less
reason to urge, for he joined with the Indians in killing our cattle and
carried the beef aboard his ships, which would have cost him his life if
he had had his deserts.

9. Whereas according to His Majesty's gracious, etc.

The governor and Council, whom it only concerned, replied to this that
they had followed the laws and customs of England to their utmost skill;
neither could he, or any other, produce any particular wherein they had
failed. As to their ignorance, they held him to be no competent judge of
those who so far transcended him in point of learning and ability. For he
had never been bred to the law (as was not unknown to some of them) nor
yet in any other of the liberal sciences. But his principal spleen in this
article appeared to proceed from his not being admitted of the Council,
which they could by no means consistently with their instructions do.

10. There having been, as it is thought, ten thousand, etc.

His computation of ten thousand souls falls short of four thousand; and
those were, in great part, wasted by the more than Egyptian slavery and
Scythian cruelty which was exercised on us, your poor and miserable subjects, by laws written in blood and executed with all sorts of tyranny in the
time of Sir Thomas Smith's government, whereof we send Your Majesty the
true and tragical relation, from which it will appear that the pretended
confusions and private ends will strongly reflect upon him and his in-
structors. And how unfit such men are to restore that plantation, which
suffered so much under their government, we humbly refer to your princely
consideration, invoking, with him, that divine and supreme hand to protect
us from governors and their ministers who have poured out our blood
on the earth like water and have fatted themselves with our famine. And we
beseech Your Majesty to support us in this just and gentle authority
which has cherished us of late by more worthy magistrates, and we, our
wives, and poor children, as is our duty, shall ever pray to God to give you
in this world all increase of happiness and to crown you in the world to
come with immortal glory.] [65]

At this time commenced the practice in the House of Burgesses of
deputing some respectable member of their body to England to manage
the cause of the colony. [In their petition to the king by Mr. John
Pountis,[66] they declared their great joy and satisfaction that His
Majesty, notwithstanding the late unjust disparagement of this planta-

65. Stith, *Virginia*, pp. 305–12; see also Tyler, *Narratives of Virginia*, pp. 412–18.

66. John Pountis was chosen to carry a set of laws passed by the Assembly to protect
the people's needs and rights. Randolph discussed these laws on pp. 138–42 below.
Pountis died at sea, and since the king did not respond to the laws, it was assumed that he
had never received them. New copies were carried to England by Sir George Yeardley.

tion, had taken it into his nearer and more especial care. And that his royal intentions might have their due effect, they humbly besought him, being urged thereto by their duty and experience, to give no credit to the late declarations of the happy, as it was called but in truth miserable, estate of the colony during the past twelve years nor to the malicious imputations which had been laid on the government of late, but that he would be pleased to behold in miniature the true estate of both times by their relations, which they then presented by the hands of Mr. John Pountis, a worthy member of their body, and which contained nothing but the truth, without disaffection of partiality. From these they doubted not but that His Majesty would clearly understand the true condition of both times and would be pleased according to their earnest desire to continue and even further confirm the government under which they then lived. But if it should please him otherwise to determine, they besought him, by all the ties of compassion and humanity, not to suffer them, his poor subjects, to fall again into the hands of Sir Thomas Smith or his confidents, but that he would graciously protect them from those storms of faction which threatened the ruin of some persons (whose endeavors had deserved a better reward) and in general the subversion of the whole colony. And if the government must be altered, they desired, since the action was of such honor and consequence, that they might still depend upon such great and noble persons as they lately had done. And further, in consideration of the late massacre and subsequent calamities, they besought His Majesty to grant them and the Somer Islands the sole importation of tobacco, assuring him that they affected not that contemptible weed as a thing good and desirable in itself but as a present means of support. And if it should please His Majesty to send over that aid of soldiers whereof they humbly desired, that the governor and General Assembly might have a voice in their disposal, since none at that distance, by reason of accidents and emergent occasions, could direct such an affair so advantageously as they were enabled to do by their presence and experience in the country.] [67]

The commissioners who had come from England to examine the discontents in Virginia, now having discovered that the king's intention was not likely to be fulfilled by the Assembly, combined menace and artifice to extort an approbation of the revocation of the charters.

[But finding that things were going in the Assembly quite contrary

---

67. Stith, *Virginia*, pp. 312–13.

to their hopes and desires, they resolved to lay some of their powers before them, which might probably intimidate and influence them and restrain them from proceeding with much sharpness and vigor. They therefore opened a letter, importing that they supposed, in a week's time, since their publishing the orders of the lords of the Privy Council, the Assembly could not but have maturely considered the same, that therefore, for the speedier advancement of the colony in general and for the securing every man's interest in particular and that they might all by submission and thankfulness, as by obedience and sacrifice, both together ingratiate themselves and their common cause to His Majesty's renowned clemency, they as remembrancers thought it no less than their duty to propose to their consideration the form enclosed, which they hoped they would apprehend very fit to be subscribed by the whole Assembly, it being no other than what they themselves would most readily and most humbly set their hands unto. The form proposed was the following:

Whereas we understand by three acts of Council in England lately published in the General Assembly that His Majesty has signified his gracious pleasure for the universal good of this plantation, which by reason of our late calamities is in an unsettled state, to institute another form of government, whereby the colony may be upheld and prosper the better in time to come and to that end has required a surrender of the present patents, declaring his royal intention to secure to the particular members of the company such lands and privileges in the said country as, according to the proportion of each man's adventure and private interest, shall be found due unto him, we of this General Assembly do, by subscription of our names, not only profess and testify our thankfulness for that His Majesty's most gracious and tender care over us but do moreover, for our parts, in all humility and willingness submit ourselves to his princely pleasure of revoking our old charters and vouchsafing his new letters patent to those noble ends and purposes above mentioned.[68]

⌈Thus to draw the General Assembly to surrender and petition for a revocation of their charters, which the courts in England would by no means submit to, was certainly a very crafty and effectual way to disgrace the Company and to make the colony seem disaffected to them and willing to throw off their yoke and would also have given some color to the violent suppression of them afterwards.

⌈The Assembly were not inferior in dexterity of management. Being convinced that the commissioners would not have been dispatched but

68. See Brown, *First Republic*, p. 572.

for the object of canceling the charters, they endeavored to learn from them from what authority their proposals came.

[But this answer gave the commissioners great offense and drew from them a very fierce and menacing reply: that they had acknowledged, in delivering their papers, that they had neither commission nor instruction to move them to subscribe the form proposed, neither could the least shadow of any such thing be collected from their letters. That what they had proposed was out of their discretion, as wholesome counsel for the good of the colony; neither was it precipitate or sudden, but proper to the time, occasion, and persons; that the mark aimed at was no less than His Majesty's favor upon their persons and common cause, to be obtained by obedience and thankfulness. That as there needed neither commission nor instruction for them to propound the practice of so eminent a duty, so it was lawful for them as being freemen and planters to offer to the General Assembly any reasonable motion, though of far less consequence, and had they not vouchsafed to return an answer, they might justly have seemed discontented, or at least discourteous. That they had no reason, upon this occasion, to search into the depth of their authority (since their motion depended not, nor needed to depend, on their particular commission) much less to urge them to set down anything under their hands. That they could not profess that they had no further commission which might concern them besides that already put in execution, for their commissions, yet unperformed, concerned them in their houses, persons, servants, corn, cattle, arms, etc. That however they need not suspect that they would attempt anything to any man's wrong, or which they could not very well answer.[69]

[To this the Assembly calmly replied that they had already presented their humblest thanks to His Majesty for his gracious care of them and had returned their answer to the lords of the Privy Council, that when their assent to the surrender of their charters should be required by authority it would then be the most proper time to make a reply, but in the meanwhile, they conceived His Majesty's intention to change the government had proceeded from wrong information, which, they hoped, would be altered upon their more faithful declarations. But the better to enable them to take a view of the plantations and to render an exact account of the state of the colony, the Assembly ordered, upon the commissioners' application for their assistance, that

69. See *ibid.*, pp. 574–75.

the several plantations should transport them from plantation to plantation as they should desire and should accommodate them in the best manner their houses and rooms would afford. The commissioners also made the Assembly four propositions, concerning the best places of fortification and defense, the state of the colony with respect to the savages, the hopes that might be really and truly conceived of the plantation, and the properest means to attain those hopes. To all which the Assembly gave full and particular answers.[70]

[The laws of this Assembly consisted of thirty-five articles. These laws are the oldest upon our records and contain some things of especial note.[71]

[The first seven related to the church and ministry and enacted that in every plantation where the people were wont to meet for the worship of God there should be a house, or room, set apart for that purpose and not converted to any temporal use whatsoever, and that a place should be impaled and sequestered only for the burial of the dead; that whosoever should absent himself from divine service any Sunday without an allowable excuse should forfeit a pound of tobacco, and that he who absented himself a month should forfeit fifty pounds of tobacco; that there should be a uniformity in the church as near as might be, both in substance and circumstance, to the canons of the Church of England, and that all persons should yield a ready obedience to them upon pain of censure; that March 22, the day of the massacre, should be solemnized and kept holy, and that all other holidays should be observed except when two fell together in the summer season, the time of their working and crop, when the first only was to be observed, by reason of their necessities and employment; that no minister should be absent from his cure above two months in the whole year, upon penalty of forfeiting half his salary, and whosoever was absent above four months should forfeit his whole salary and his cure; that whosoever should disparage a minister without sufficient proof to justify his reports, whereby the minds of his parishioners might be alienated from him and his ministry prove the less effectual, should not only pay five hundred pounds of tobacco but should also ask the minister's forgiveness publicly in the congregation; that no man should dispose of any of his tobacco before the minister was satisfied, upon forfeiture of double his part toward the salary, and that one man of every plantation should

70. See *ibid.,* pp. 574, 576, 578.
71. These are the laws carried to England first by John Pountis and later by Sir George Yeardley.

be appointed to collect the minister's salary out of the first and best tobacco and corn.

[The eighth and ninth articles related to the governor's power: that he should not lay any taxes or impositions upon the colony, their lands, or commodities otherwise than by the authority of the General Assembly, to be levied and employed as the said Assembly should appoint. That he should not withdraw the inhabitants from their private labors to any service of his own, under any color whatsoever, and if the public service should require the employment of many hands before another General Assembly met to give order for the same, in that case the levying men should be done by the order of the governor and whole body of the Council and that in such sort as to be least burdensome of the people and most free from partiality. Thus early was the Assembly out of the memory of their past miseries and oppressions studious and careful to establish our liberties, and we had here, by the ready concurrence and cooperation of this excellent governor, a petition of right passed above four years before that matter was indubitably settled and explained in England. For these two articles contain the same in effect as that famous explanatory and fundamental law of the English constitution, viz., the firm property of the subjects' goods and estates and the liberty of their persons.

[The other articles enacted that all the old planters who were here before or came in at the last arrival of Sir Thomas Gates (in August 1611) should both themselves and their posterity, except such as were employed to command in chief, be exempted from their personal service in the wars and from all other public charges (church duties only excepted) but without the like exemption of their servants and families. That no burgess of the General Assembly should be arrested during the sitting of the Assembly and a week before and a week after, upon pain of the creditor's forfeiting his debt and such punishment upon the officer as the court should award; that there should be courts kept once a month in the corporations of Charles City and Elizabeth City for deciding suits and controversies not exceeding the value of one hundred pounds of tobacco and for punishing petty offenses; and that the commanders of the places with such others as the governor and Council should appoint by commission should be judges, the commanders to be of the quorum and sentence given by the majority of voices, with reservation nevertheless of appeal after sentence to the governor and Council, and that whosoever appealed and was cast upon such appeal, should pay double damages. That every private planter's

dividend of land should be surveyed and laid off separately, and the
bounds recorded by the surveyor, who should have ten pounds of
tobacco for every hundred acres surveyed; and that all petty differences
between neighbors about their bounds should be decided by the surveyor, but if of importance, referred to the governor and Council. That
for the people's encouragement to plant store of corn, the price should
be left free, and every man might sell it as dear as he could (for the
governor and Council did then and long afterwards set a rate yearly
upon all commodities, with penalties upon those who exceeded it);
that there should be a public granary in each parish, to which every
planter above eighteen years of age who had been in the country a
year and was alive at the crop should contribute a barrel of corn, to be
disposed of for the public uses of the parish by the major part of the
freemen, the remainder to be taken out by the owners yearly on St.
Thomas Day and the new brought and put in its room. That three
capable men of every parish should be sworn to see that every man
planted and tended corn sufficient for his family; and that those who
neglected so to do should be presented by the said three men to the
censure of the governor and Council. That all trade with the Indians
for corn, as well public as private, should be prohibited after the June
following. That every freeman should fence in a quarter of an acre of
ground before the Whitsuntide next ensuing for the planting of vines,
herb roots, and the like, under the penalty of ten pounds of tobacco a
man, but that no man for his own family should be paid for it by the
owner of the soil; and that they should also plant mulberry trees. That
the proclamations against swearing and drunkenness set forth by the
governor and Council were ratified by this Assembly; and it was
further ordered that the churchwardens should be sworn to present all
offenders to the commanders of their respective plantations, and that
they should collect the forfeitures for public uses. That a proclamation
should be read aboard every ship and afterwards fixed to the mast,
prohibiting them, without special order from the governor and Council,
to break bulk or make private sale of any commodities till they came
up to James City. That the ancient rates of commodities should be still
in force, and that men should be sworn in every plantation to censure
the tobacco (so old are the first rudiments of our tobacco law, which
nevertheless, after such long experience, raised much opposition and
disturbance). That there should be no weights or measures used but
such as were sealed by officers appointed for that purpose. That every
dwelling house should be palisadoed in for the defense against the

Indians. That no man should go or send abroad without a sufficient party well armed. That men should not go to work without their arms and a sentinel set. That the inhabitants of the plantation should not go on board ships or upon any other occasions in such numbers as thereby to weaken and endanger the plantation. That the commander of every plantation should take care that there should be sufficient powder and ammunition within his plantation and that their pieces be fixed and arms complete; that there be sufficient watch kept every night. That no commander of any plantation should either spend himself or suffer others to spend powder unnecessarily in drinking, entertainments, and the like. That such persons of condition as were found delinquent in their duty and were not fit to undergo corporal punishment might notwithstanding be imprisoned at the discretion of the commander and for greater offenses be subject to a fine, inflicted by the monthly court so that it did not exceed a certain value. That every person who had not found a man at the castle (then building at Warrosquyoake) should pay, for himself and servants, five pounds of tobacco a head toward defraying the charge of those who had their servants there. That at the beginning of July following, every corporation should fall upon their adjoining Indians and that those who should be hurt upon the service should be cured at the public expense, and if any were lamed, they should be maintained by the country according to their person and quality. That for discharging such public debts as their troubles had brought upon them, there should be levied ten pounds of tobacco upon every male above sixteen years of age, but not including such as had arrived since the beginning of July last. That no person within the colony should presume upon the rumor of any supposed change and alteration in England to be disobedient to the present government, nor servants to their private masters, officers, or overseers, at their utmost peril. And the last article related to sending Mr. Pountis to England and levying four pounds of tobacco a head to support his expenses. Most of these laws were taken from preceding proclamations and orders of the governor and Council. The governor was obliged soon after to issue a proclamation forbidding women to contract themselves to two several men at one time. For women being yet scarce and much in request, this offense had become very common, whereby great disquiet arose between parties and no small trouble to the government. It was therefore ordered that every minister should give notice in his church that what man or woman soever should use any word or speech tending to a contract of marriage to two several persons at one time, although not precise and legal yet so as might entangle or breed scruple in their consciences, should for such their offense either undergo corporal correction or else be punished by fine, or otherwise, according to the quality of the person offending.] [72]

The Company still entertained an unsuspicious confidence that the House of Commons were friendly to the colony, and therefore they presented a petition to that branch of the legislature to the following purpose.[73]

[That after divers discoveries had confirmed the opinion that Virginia was situated in a temperate and wholesome climate, that the soil was rich and fertile, the country well watered with fruitful and navigable rivers, and that their ships, through a fair sea, might have a comfortable falling in on a safe coast, it pleased God so to affect the minds of divers worthily disposed noblemen, gentlemen, and others as to think it a matter of great religion and honor to endeavor the propagation of Christianity among those barbarous people and to gain such a hopeful addition of territory to His Majesty's dominions. That His Majesty, also being informed thereof and apprehending that great honor and commodity would thence arise to this kingdom, was pleased by his most gracious letters patent of incorporation, from time to time renewed and enlarged, to confer as ample privileges and immunities, both for their assistance who should become directors of the business at home and for their comfort and encouragement that would settle and inhabit the country, as could be then foreseen or desired; that this gave so general an encouragement that noblemen, knights, gentlemen, citizens, and others, in great numbers, became adventurers, who besides their money, afforded many other helps by their industry toward the advancement and perfection of this noble work; and that, notwithstanding a multitude of accidents and disasters incident to such undertakings in a remote and savage country, yet it pleased God often to enliven their hopes and endeavors by such an undoubted probability of obtaining at least for the public and posterity so beneficial a retribution for all their pains and expense as would, in the end, crown their labors with as much glory, honor, and profit to the realm of England as could be well wished or expected.

72. Stith, *Virginia*, pp. 316–22; see also Kingsbury, *Records of Virginia Company*, IV, 580–85.

73. On April 21, 1623, Sandys, Sir Edmund Coke, and the Council and Company for Virginia drafted a long petition to the House of Commons. The king, however, forbade the Commons from dealing with the questions, declaring that all matters pertaining to Virginia were under the advisement of the Privy Council.

[They then proceeded to recount the several emoluments and advantages to England which they have in their view and expectation. 1. The conversion of the savages to Christianity and establishing the first colony of the reformed religion. 2. The discharging the overplus of necessitous people, which administered fuel to dangerous insurrections, and the leaving greater plenty for those who remained. 3. The gaining a large territory already known to be great, and which might prove much greater, whose fertility of soil and temperature of clime agreed well with the English and produced by nature and industry whatever useful commodities were found in any known country. 4. The beneficial fisheries discovered, which together with the continual intercourse and commerce between people of the same nation, would contribute exceedingly to the increase of the English trade and navigation. 5. The vast quantity of timber and materials for building and setting forth ships, whereof there was a great scarcity throughout all Europe. 6. The assurance that many rich trades might be found out there and driven on to the incredible benefit of the nation, besides the no small hopes of our easy and short passage to the South Sea, either by sea or land. 7. The inestimable advantage that would be gained in case of war, both for the easy assaulting the Spanish West Indies and for the relieving and succoring of all ships and men of war, the want whereof had, in former times, disappointed and overthrown so many voyages. But hereby the benefit to the English would be certain and the enemy's loss and annoyance inevitable. After which they went on in the following manner:

[But so it is that now, when the natural difficulties incident to all new plantations are by diligence and tract of time, but most especially by the blessing of Almighty God, in a great measure overcome, yet there have arisen other unnatural impediments, proceeding from faction and discord, from the cunning courses and practices of some persons who tended wholly to their own profit, from misemployment of the public stock, false accounts, and the like corruptions and diversions from the main business; and that these were so increased of late and supported by strong hand as threatened speed ruin and destruction to that excellent work if remedies were not timely applied; that they, the Council and Company of Virginia, differed not a little from other companies, as well in their composition, consisting of principal noblemen, gentlemen, merchants, and others, as in the ends for which they were established, being not simply for matter of trade but for things of a higher and more public nature; that nevertheless finding them-

selves in their body, as it was then distempered, unable to be their
own physicians without higher assistance, they thought it their duty as
well to clear their own reputation, as in discharge of their consciences
and of the trust reposed in them to represent to the Parliament this
child of the nation, exposed, as in the wilderness, to extreme danger
and then fainting, as it were, and laboring for life.

[They therefore humbly entreated that honorable house to take into
their commiseration the distressed colony and oppressed Company and
to receive an account from such of His Majesty's Council for Virginia
as being members of their house had been appointed by the Company
to give them a full and exact relation of all their grievances and oppressions, which though of sundry kinds yet had received (as they
doubted not to make evident) either their original or strength from
the lord high treasurer out of his private and unjust designs, not only
to almost the overthrow of the colony but also to the deception of His
Majesty in his profit and revenue, to the great prejudice of the whole
kingdom in matter of trade, and even to points of dangerous consequence to the liberty of the subject.[74]

[This proceeding was certainly no ways grateful to the king, who
conceived himself much injured and affronted if the Parliament entered
upon any consideration which was not recommended to them by himself. For he looked upon them not as the grand council of the nation
but of the king and expected that they should proceed with the abject
adulation and submission of his Privy Council and never touch upon
any disagreeable subjects. But above all matters of grievance were the
points on which he was most tender and touchy and would often wince
grievously, and although the thing was disguised, and even praises were
given him in some parts of this petition, yet it was evidently leveled
in the main against him and his ministers. However, as His Majesty had
called this Parliament with quite different views and treated it in a
quite different manner from the last, he took no notice of it but permitted it to take its course in the house. Its reception was also secured
by the complaints in the latter part against the lord high treasurer,
whom Buckingham and the prince were at this time pulling down and
tearing, as it were, with great violence from the king's side, not without
very great pain and grief to His Majesty.

[This petition was committed to the deputy and such others of the
Council as were also members of the House of Commons, to present
to their house in the name of the Council and Company of Virginia. It

74. See Kingsbury, *Records of Virginia Company,* II, 526–28.

was received by the Commons very acceptably, notwithstanding some opposition at first; and a committee was appointed to hear and examine their grievances and oppressions, to which all of the Company that were members of the house were admitted to come and to hear, but not to have any voice. But conceiving that counsel at law could not be so fully informed of all passages as was requisite and would not perhaps be so cordially concerned or favorably heard, they divided their grievances into four several heads and committed them to the following gentlemen to deliver and speak to them: 1. The case of their tobacco, with all the oppressions and impositions upon it, was committed to Mr. Deputy Treasurer Nicholas Ferrar. 2. The business of the contract, to Sir Edwin Sandys. 3. The proceedings of the commissioners, to Lord Cavendish. 4. All passages and measures since, to Sir John Danvers. And all these gentlemen, but especially the Lord Cavendish, did very nobly and cheerfully undertake to perform and make good their several parts.

[It was the misfortune of these affairs to be brought into Parliament very late in the sessions, and they were besides of a very tender and delicate nature. For in their process and issue, they must have turned to a plain arraignment of the weakness and unfairness or even the downright injustice and oppressiveness of the king's conduct toward the Company and colony. The main business therefore of their oppressions and grievances did not proceed in Parliament but was waived and slurred over in silence. But the particular case of tobacco, by the exceeding care and wisdom of Sir Edwin Sandys assisted by Lord Cavendish and the other gentlemen of the Company who had seats in Parliament, was brought to a happy issue. For the importation of foreign tobacco was put as one of the nine grievances of the realm in point of trade which this session presented to His Majesty for relief. And although this was done professedly for the good of England, without any mention or relation to Virginia, yet the deputy told the Company that he doubted not but the whole house had, in their hearts, an especial regard to the advancement of the colonies. And as this course was as effectual for the exclusion of Spanish tobacco as if it had been done by bill, so was it much better, than as if it had been done by the bill which was drawn during the last Parliament. For since that time, the state and price of tobacco was so much altered that it could then no ways bear the twelve pence a pound duty which that bill laid upon it but must thereby have been as certainly ruined and overthrown as by any other course. This second mode brought with it all the good of the bill and

left out all its evil. Wherefore, he said, it could not be too much commended, nor Sir Edwin Sandys, to whom they were beholden for it,
sufficiently thanked.] [75]

On July 15, 1624, when every sentence was ripe, or rather when the
king had contracted an indifference to public opinion as connected
with pure right, he by a proclamation suppressed the holding of the
courts of the Company in England and instituted a temporary government. The quo warranto was however tried *pro forma* and decided
against the Company.

Thus terminated the Virginia Company.

Thus we have detailed the principal events and polity of Virginia
for the first eighteen years of her settlement, conscious at the same
time of our inability to give them all the pleasantness of color and
shape which, with some slight departure from the real history, fancy
might have approved, and taste would not have condemned. But whatever may be the defects of the foregoing narrative, an estimate may be
made of the faculties or qualities which the colony actually possessed
in the year 1624 and which might have remained as a basis of hope
and expectation to the adventurers.

1. Nature had withheld from the soil the precious metals but had
bestowed richer treasures in its luxuriance and rapidity of vegetation.
The repetition too of crops in the same year, the kindness of the
climate to grains and plants imported from the Old World, the resources in some native vegetables and animals which were peculiar,
numerous species of valuable timber, ores adapted to the calls of labor
and genius opened prospects more truly splendid than those which
dazzled, seduced, and corrupted the Spanish conquerors in the south.
But science was at this time too imperfect for an enumeration of the
positive advantages of Virginia with fidelity, although the human intellect could not be so dull as to be insensible to the visions of profits
so soon to be realized. The patient industry of the English character had
given a direction to those natural benefits which nothing but the tur-
bulence of a paltry and misjudged ambition could destroy.

2. The general temper and habits of the emigrants, coinciding with
the views and opinions of the king on religion, produced a total dependence upon England for every comfort of manufacture and a sympathy with most of the political sentiments of the English nation. He
was the monarch of one entire people, although one portion of them
was separated into another hemisphere, and even at this early day were

75. Stith, *Virginia*, pp. 324–28.

the rudiments laid for preserving their identity on almost every subject.

3. Without pronouncing a judgment upon the outrage committed by the king under the forms of law upon the charters, it is some cause for wonder that it caused an agitation so little serious. But wise men, especially those who are weak, forbear with the constituted authorities, rather than yield to every gust of passion or discontent. The ground for insurrection was ample; the stake was great; and among the members of the Company were to be found fire and intelligence enough for any emergency. But it is a lesson not unworthy of adoption in seasons even the most enlightened to count the cost of popular tumult before it is excited and clearly to see the effect of war before it is waged.

4. During this period we see a people proud of English blood, equally aloof from the frenzy of reform and the abjectness of vassalage, attached to a limited monarchy and the Church of England which diffused their influence without seeming to be active.

5. The emigrants discovered a hardihood beyond example in settling in feeble bodies among tribes of savages in a wilderness in which they could not but expect the heaviest disasters, nay at sometimes to abandon the colony and at others to be almost cut off or to combat famine approaching to desperation.

6. They were warlike, except when perverted or weakened by factions, and quick in resenting supposed encroachments from power.

7. They manifest the awe which the character of a truly great and patriotic man (as Captain John Smith was) will have upon the sturdy sons of labor and of courage.

8. They sink indeed too often into the then English vices: they indulged the pride or at any rate an ostentatious hospitality of the English character; but the charities of human nature were not forgotten or neglected.

9. The censures which Dr. Robertson casts upon Stith for his preference of the proprietor's government under the treasurer and Company ought to have been spared.[76] But is not Stith manifestly superior when the peace and happiness of society are consulted? Ought any

---

76. Robertson argued that some writers, particularly Stith, whom he praised as "the most intelligent and best informed historian of Virginia," viewed the dissolution of the Company as a disastrous event because their liberal sentiments made them indignant at the arbitrary proceedings of James I. However, according to Robertson, their indignation "rendered them incapable of contemplating its effects with discernment and candor. There is not perhaps any mode of governing an infant colony less friendly to its liberty than the dominion of an exclusive corporation possessed of all the powers which James conferred upon the company of adventurers in Virginia" (*History of America*, p. 417).

power upon earth but particularly a sovereign, morally bound by his own charters to maintain certain rights to his subjects, to scan the defects of those charters and upon professions of a loose philosophy to say to them that as their destinies would be meliorated by a change in the dynasty or constitution, they should accept a new order of things against their will and express remonstrances? It was usurpation in the king and a precedent for transplanting to Virginia the harshest principles of the Tudors and Stuarts.

After all, be these elements of our nation good or bad, they will in the sequel of this work exhibit a frequency, if not a constancy, of operation closely allied to the national character.

The Surrender of Virginia to Cromwell

 Reasons were assigned in the preface why much liberty would be taken in pretermitting the farrago of colonial records and in selecting such parts only of their matter as would excite an interest not merely local or merely transitory. That liberty I now use in passing from the year 1624 to the charter granted to Lord Baltimore for Maryland in 1632, which however constitutes a branch of an important event subsequent to the surrender of Virginia to the arms of Cromwell in 1651.[1]

That at this time the territory of Virginia, rude and chiefly destitute also of the fossil treasures of Mexico, with a population not exceeding seven thousand souls, should have fallen within the scope of Cromwell's lust of power would create no small surprise, if for inordinate ambition like his, any prize was too small. To stoop to so distant a mile of value so small was not untinctured by the vanity of holding without mutilation the rights which he had wrested with blood from the lawful prince. From this cause, the caprice of licentious fortune, or a desire to chastise Virginia for the steady loyalty of her past conduct, a force was dispatched from England to reduce her to the will of the usurper.[2] To have resisted with obstinacy would have been a vain and fatal

1. Sir George Calvert (*ca.* 1580–1632), first Lord Baltimore of the Irish peerage, had been a subscriber to the Virginia Company, a member of the New England Council, and the promoter of a settlement in Newfoundland prior to developing plans for a colony on the upper Chesapeake. Maryland drew its name from the French Catholic Queen of Charles I (Craven, *Southern Colonies*, p. 184). Randolph did not fulfill his promise to discuss the founding of Maryland.

2. Charles I was beheaded on Jan. 30, 1649. In July the Council of State sent a notice to the colonists demanding their obedience to the Commonwealth. Upon receiving this notice the General Assembly of Virginia, meeting at Jamestown on Oct. 10, 1649, made its stand perfectly clear by proclaiming Prince Charles king and declaring that anyone expressing any doubt of the right of succession of Charles II would be guilty of high treason (W. W. Hening, ed., *Statutes at Large; Being a Collection of All the Laws of Virginia from the First Session of the Legislature in the Year 1619* [Richmond and Philadelphia, 1809–23], I, 359–61). In 1652 four commissioners and a strong military force arrived in Virginia.

defiance of that power, which with so much ease could have been accumulated on our shores, and might have been almost too impolitic to be justified, even by the noble principle of defending our country to the last extremity, especially as the terms conceded to her flowed from a respect for her prowess and a reluctance to provoke to desperation her love of liberty.

The following are the "Articles agreed on and concluded at James City in Virginia for the surrendering and settling of that plantation under the obedience and government of the Commonwealth of England by the Commissioners of the Council of State and by authority of the Parliament of England and by the Grand Assembly of the governor, Council, and burgesses of that country."

First it is agreed and constituted that the plantation of Virginia and all the inhabitants thereof shall be and remain in due obedience and subjection to the Commonwealth of England, according to the laws there established, and that this submission and subscription be acknowledged a voluntary act not forced nor constrained by a conquest upon the country, and that they shall have and enjoy such freedoms and privileges as belong to the freeborn people of England, and that the former government by the commissions and instructions be void and null.

2. Secondly that the Grand Assembly as formerly shall convene and transact the affairs of Virginia, wherein nothing is to be acted or done contrary to the government of the Commonwealth of England and the laws there established.

3. That there shall be a full and total remission and indemnity of all acts, words, or writings done or spoken against the Parliament of England in relation to the same.

4. That Virginia shall have and enjoy the ancient bounds and limits granted by the charters of the former kings, and that we shall seek a new charter from the Parliament to that purpose against any that have entrenched upon the rights thereof.

5. That all the patents of land granted under the colony seal by any of the precedent governors shall be and remain in their full force and strength.

6. That the privilege of having fifty acres of land for every person transported in the colony shall continue as formerly granted.

7. That the people of Virginia have free trade as the people of England do enjoy to all places and with all nations according to the laws of that Commonwealth, and that Virginia shall enjoy all privileges equally with any English plantations in America.

8. That Virginia shall be free from all taxes, customs, and impositions whatsoever, and none to be imposed on them without consent of the Grand Assembly. And so that neither forts nor castles be erected or garrisons maintained without their consent.

9. That no charge shall be required from this country in respect of this present fleet.

10. That for the future settlement of the country in their due obedience, the Engagement shall be tendered to all the inhabitants according to act of Parliament, made to that purpose; that all persons who shall refuse to subscribe the said Engagement shall have a year's time if they please to remove themselves and their estates out of Virginia, and in the meantime during the said year to have equal justice as formerly.

11. That the use of the Book of Common Prayer shall be permitted for one year ensuing with reference to the consent of the major part of the parishes, provided that those things which relate to kingship or that government be not used publicly; and the continuance of ministers in their places, they not misdemeaning themselves, and the payment of their accustomed dues and agreements made with them respectively shall be left as they now stand during this ensuing year.

12. That no man's cattle shall be questioned as the company's unless such as have been entrusted with them or have disposed of them without order.

13. That all ammunition, powder, and arms, other than for private use, shall be delivered up, security being given to make satisfaction for it.

14. That all goods already brought hither by the Dutch or others are now on shore shall be free from reprisal.

15. That the quitrents granted unto us by the late kings for seven years be confirmed.

16. That the commissioners for the Parliament subscribing these articles engaged themselves and the honor of Parliament for the full performance thereof; and that the present governor and the Council and the burgesses do likewise subscribe and engage the whole colony on their parts.

Rich. Bennett—seal
Wm. Claiborne—seal
Edmund Curtis—seal [3]

3. *Ibid.*, 363–68. These three men were members of the parliamentary commission. Richard Bennett was appointed the first governor under the new regime. William Claiborne (*ca.* 1587–*ca.* 1677) had come to the colony as surveyor for the Virginia Company and remained to become a successful fur trader, Indian fighter, and colonizer. He sponsored a settlement on the Pamunkey River that grew into a county in 1654, which he named New Kent. Claiborne was appointed secretary of state and councilor in the new government, next in rank to Governor Bennett (Nathaniel C. Hale, *Virginia Venturer, A Historical Biography of William Claiborne, 1600–1677* [Richmond, 1951], pp. 297–98). Capt. Edmund Curtis acted as an alternate for another commissioner, Capt. Robert Dennis, commander of the fleet who was lost on the voyage to Virginia. The other commissioner was Thomas Stagg, a London merchant, shipowner, and planter who divided his time between England and Virginia. Randolph may well have found the terms of the agreement in Thomas Jefferson, *Notes on the State of Virginia* (Paris, 1785; London, 1787; Thomas P. Abernethy, New York, 1964), pp. 108–9.

There was a magnanimity in stipulating against the imputation of conquest and the consequences of such a doctrine. The semblance of disgrace was wiped off when Virginia disdained the humiliation to which the mother country had been subjected. Even when an adherence to the Commonwealth of England was stipulated, the continuance of the spirit of the laws of England was understood and expected. Chartered rights were protected against the royal prerogative by which our territory had been abridged, and effectually to deny to Cromwell an authority which had been tolerated in the overwhelmed Charles was no small trial of Cromwell's forbearance.

The security to landed titles under grants from former royal governors was a bold struggle for stability against the temper and violence of a tyrant.

Universal free trade and equal privileges with those of any English plantations in America, an exemption from all imposts not laid with the consent of the General Assembly, and the prohibition of forts without a similar consent were of the essence of liberty.

The permission to the discontented to retire from Virginia with their property, or to remain and enjoy equal justice, the free use of the Book of Common Prayer, in which kingship is incorporated with religion, safety to the goods imported by the Dutch, the confirmation of the royal grant of quitrents for seven years, the act of general oblivion, besides many inferior considerations in conjunction with the preceding, bespoke, to the honor of our country, such inherent principles of freedom as without convulsion or irresistible force must grow with our growth and strengthen with time. They formed a stepping stone at least from which the transition to sound and permanent government was easy.

It is probable indeed that in all these particulars good faith was not inviolably observed,[4] but they present the stamina of free souls, capable in the first instance of withstanding the solicitations and influence of Sir William Berkeley,[5] the governor (an ancient cavalier with an urbanity of manners which strikes deep when descending from the at-

4. Randolph may have been referring to Governor Bennett's opposition to the House of Burgesses' choice of a speaker in the summer of 1653. The quarrel ended when the Burgesses withdrew the speaker-elect, but not without protest. A more serious problem occurred in 1658 when the governor and the Council attempted to dissolve the Assembly. The Burgesses took the position that the governor and the Council had no such legal right and responded by declaring the governorship vacant. After a two-year dispute the house compromised by specifying a two-year term for the governor (Craven, *Southern Colonies*, pp. 263–64).

5. Sir William Berkeley (1606–1677), an M.A. from Merton College, Oxford, well connected in England, and a devoted follower of Charles I, had become governor in 1642. As a royalist, he was replaced in 1652 by Richard Bennett but was reappointed by Charles

titude of a chief magistrate), and afterwards of exacting terms from an inexorable despot. It is probable that the regulation of our external trade with foreign nations by the Parliament was not immediately complained of because not distinctly analyzed. Still these articles argue a strong, awakened sense of right and of the necessity of future security. The spirit which they display is the native spirit of Virginia. But little of the contagion of the Royalist party in England had yet communicated itself to the bosoms of the people here.

After passing this fiery trial Virginia rose in dignity, riches, and importance. Her pretensions to learning were not very exalted. The best sort had been acquired, that of applying sound sense to private and public welfare. Manners had received a polish which without enfeebling courage, moderates that ferocity which suspicion sometimes ascribes to the rough inhabitants of a newly cultivated desert.

Virginia was exempt from pollution by the fanaticism and hypocrisy of Cromwell and from the poison of the licentiousness of the second Charles.

Bacon's Rebellion

In 1676 the commotion which was denominated Bacon's Rebellion threatened the subversion of the government of Virginia.

It has lately received a historical gloss, the object of which is to metamorphose it into one of those daring efforts which gross misrule sometimes suggests, if it may not strictly vindicate.[6] But the whole force of precedent having been already obtained in the successful resistance of the American colonies to Great Britain, we ought not to sanction a new case in which tyranny is less palpable or less clearly meditated. Let the transaction therefore be seen in its real character.

II after the Restoration. Virginia's inhabitants had supported the governor's opposition to the Commonwealth, but once terms were offered they resisted his blandishments (Morton, *Colonial Virginia*, I, 169–73; Marcia Brownell Bready, "A Cavalier in Virginia— The Right Hon. Sir William Berkeley, His Majesty's Governor," *Wm. and Mary Qtly.*, 1st ser., XVIII [1910], 115–29).

6. Randolph was referring to John Daly Burk's *History of Virginia* (Petersburg, Va., 1804–5). Burk regarded Bacon's Rebellion as a struggle for freedom, arguing that under more auspicious circumstances Bacon might have been the Brutus or Cromwell of his country. For a discussion of the historiography of Bacon's Rebellion, including Randolph, see Wilcomb Washburn, *The Governor and the Rebel: A History of Bacon's Rebellion in Virginia* (Chapel Hill, N.C., 1957), pp. 1–16.

There is no doubt that much dissatisfaction was felt by the colony from several pressures both abroad and at home.

1. However the rights of charters may be indefensible in behalf of the first discoverer of a new country, as between the aboriginal possessors and foreign nations; yet as between the sovereigns who grant and the subjects who accept them, they assume the validity of compacts in being not subject on general principles to defalcation except with the mutual consent of the parties. In the year 1628, as we have seen, Lord Baltimore had explored the tract of country called Maryland, in which he was desirous of settling a colony of Roman Catholics, and his son Cecilius in 1632 obtained a grant for it. Ineffectual petitions were presented against it to the king,[7] and the colonists were reconciled, notwithstanding their antipathy to neighbors with religious principles so offensive and with pretensions so encroaching and in some private instances oppressive. But the embers of opposition not being absolutely extinguished, enough remained for a flame, if industriously fed.

2. By restrictions in England on the planting of tobacco, the only easy substitute for money in Virginia was withdrawn.[8]

3. The terror of Indian hostility was upon every tongue and every heart.[9] Many years had now elapsed since the colony had experienced any degree of that personal security without which government is worthless and life a burden. Hence upon any irruption of the savages it was not difficult to inflame the people into a belief that their rulers were inattentive to their protection in the most critical and most exposed parts of the country.

While to these things the sensibility of the colony was in a condition to be directed, Nathaniel Bacon the younger, well educated in England and bred to the profession of the law, was a member of the king's Council in Virginia and a perfect master of colonial politics and feelings.[10] From his official station he could detect, if not sometimes create,

7. William Claiborne had been sent to England with a petition opposing the establishment of a colony of Maryland.

8. Randolph no doubt meant those revenues on tobacco which most planters regarded as onerous (Morton, *Colonial Virginia*, I, 216).

9. An Indian war had erupted in July 1675.

10. Nathaniel Bacon, Jr. (1647–76), was a young man in his twenties when he arrived in Virginia in 1674. After he attended Cambridge for two and one-half years, his father withdrew him for having "broken into some extravagancies." His involvement in a scheme to defraud a young neighbor of his inheritance led his father to send him to Virginia (Washburn, *Governor and Rebel*, pp. 17–18). Bacon's elevation to the Council was probably due to his being a cousin of Governor Berkeley.

the vulnerable parts in the conduct of the governor. A nefarious ambition prompted him to blazon them abroad; and by his eloquence and spirit of enterprise, he attracted the weak, the furious, the men of ruined fortunes, who would hazard any change, upon schemes possessing no other merit than that of being specious while untried. It is obvious therefore upon what a fund of inflammable materials such a penetrating demagogue as Bacon could now operate. From physical force beyond the Atlantic he feared nothing; even Cromwell had in our capitulation submitted to terms beneath his character, temper, and apparent power.

Bacon's first measures were most natural and successful. Numbers and unanimity were his resources, high excitement his immediate agent. The massacres by the savages and the clamors of every portion of the colony whose protection was not complete against surprise supplied to men, women, and children themes of abuse of the governor. For what, it was asked, was this exposure endured? Was it for a country which might be their own or that of some papist or minion, as the monarch should will? Or was it for a sort of which the very fertility invited the government to debar the laborer from the humble privilege of consulting his own interest in cultivating it?

As soon as Bacon was surrounded by followers willing to wield arms upon these complaints, he charged the governor with imbecility, with unfitness to lead the colony in any work of self-defense, or of attack, which might be incidental to it. To arrogate the supreme command by an immediate stride was too extravagant even for Bacon. He therefore contented himself with turning the ardor of his associates to the point of soliciting from the governor a commission for himself as general. This was of course refused, upon every idea of safe and regular government. Immediately Bacon was magnified to the skies, and the governor vilified to the lowest region of contempt. That Bacon was born to save the people was, if not the creed, at least the gasconade of many of the most respectable and powerful.

As the governor persisted in his denial of the commission, Bacon appealed to the necessity of self-preservation and erected his standards as against the savages. Some of his acts fortified the impression which he made upon the people, and the governor began to tremble at the progress of his popularity. Berkeley, being foiled in his attempts to cajole and deceive, denounced with penalties Bacon and his party. To a man of Bacon's decision, temporizing or fluctuation was impossible, and he immediately invested with force the residence of the governor at Jamestown and dictated to the executive and legislature various laws and orders consonant with his views.[11]

But he had no sooner retired with his army from the town than all the proceedings under his influence were solemnly annulled and he himself was proclaimed a traitor.[12]

Civil war was now inevitable. Bacon threw off all mask and restraint, exhibiting himself as the depository of all authority. But while he was advancing most powerfully upon the party of government, his death opened a season of jubilee, exultation, and cruelty.[13] His memory was pursued with every rigor of attainder, and his rebellion was almost purged away by the wanton and perfidious indulgence of the governor in bloodshed and revenge. But is rebellion unseen amidst these facts? A legitimate government existed. It was honest in the measures of general defense. Bacon branded them as being inadequate, remonstrated, and finding remonstrance ineffectual, he took up arms to prescribe and enforce a wiser conduct, pretending that the ordinary, constitutional modes of redress or punishment would come too late, but at the same time criminating the governor with that deliberate wickedness which sometimes justifies a revolution. In a country like ours, where the will of the people justly predominates, let us not lend a sanction to any perversion of that will by approving a resort to arms until all which ought to be endured shall have been endured, and redress be sought in every legal, constitutional, and reasonable shape. Our own Revolution was not without its clouds, hardships, and impoverishment, and who can assert that the price of another will not be dearer? This exhortation will be more heartfelt by those who have witnessed the gradation of political theories from the first eruption of our troubles. For some time the ebullitions in France maintained an ascendancy which all the good sense and experience subsequent have not yet so completely eradicated as to leave nothing to be still effaced by the detestation of what passed afterwards in that country. Perhaps however some illusions may be occasionally imported or drawn from countries not resembling our own, which it may be necessary to dissipate with an unsparing hand. In the descent to revolutions, the path is easy; in the attempt to rise again lies the difficulty.

In a few years after this rebellion one of the pretended causes of it

11. This series of twenty statutes, often referred to as "Bacon's laws," were passed in June 1676 (see Hening, *Statutes*, II, 341–65).

12. *Ibid.*, p. 380.

13. Bacon died of exposure and exhaustion in Oct. 1676.

was repeated in a more alarming degree, by a grant from the crown of what was and yet is called the Northern Neck to the family under whom the late Lord Fairfax held it until his death.[14] It comprehended the territory lying between the rivers Potomac and Rappahannock and in words conferred a barony or seigniory little short of an *imperium in imperio*. However, notwithstanding these objections, it melted away into a calm, moderate, and satisfactory exercise of power, not incompatible with the general sovereignty of the colony. It is the happiness of Virginia character hardly ever to push to extremity any theory which by practical relations may not be accommodated. In a further instance, too, this spirit was exemplified, where for the sake of harmony, many plausible animadversions on the grant were waived. The titled under it are now no less solid than those on the south side of the Rappahannock, or no less definite.

Revolution in England of 1688

Threatening, however, as the rebellion of Bacon had been to the order, peace, and existence of the government of Virginia, it was an evil not without some mixture of good. It warned the people of the dangers from faction and an excessive credulity in the captivating professions of an insidious demagogue. A body of hardy adventurers were taught to feel their rising importance, as individuals and as a society. They were, at the same time, brought to reflect upon principles which from their intercourse with the mother country, they had in a manner, although imperfectly and superficially, caught from Locke, Sidney, Harrington, and Hooker, and which served as stations from whence to begin a career of political thought. With great promptness therefore they entered into a full sympathy with the English nation when they voted the abdication of James II, the accession of William III, and that noble system of liberty which sprang from a small number of fundamental

14. Charles II, while in exile in 1649, granted the Northern Neck of Virginia (between the Potomac and Rappahannock rivers) to seven friends who had remained faithful. One of these, Thomas Lord Culpeper, secured the interests of the others and received a perpetual charter to the region on Sept. 28, 1688. The Fairfax family acquired the patent when Catherine, daughter of Lord Culpeper, married the fifth Lord Fairfax. The Northern Neck was not a proprietary colony since Lord Fairfax had no powers of government, and the area remained under the political control of the Virginia government (Robinson, *Land Grants in Virginia*, pp. 66–74; Andrews, *Colonial Period*, II, 234–37).

maxims and have become lessons of instruction wherever and whenever sound government has been contemplated.[15] To part with the
Stuarts was no violence to any affection of Virginia; to be relieved from
the hauntings of popery was a jewel for which scarcely any price was
deemed too great.[16] The crime of treason was no longer a nest of snares.
Positive statutes, it is true, were still scourges to the preaching and
assembling of dissenters, but a spirit of mildness was an antidote to the
licensed severity of laws. Virginia may be said to have been inoculated
by the revolution without the poison of those prejudices which still ran
unmitigated in the bosom of England.

The Pistole Fee Controversy

Under all these influences, Virginia was politically happy. For I do not
class among political disturbances the acts of governors or of kings
which were either too limited in their sphere or too short-lived to have
any other effect than to rouse the people to observation and vigilance.
With a uniformity resulting from these causes in all their shapes of action and reaction, Virginia continued to flourish until the time of Sir
Robert Walpole, [when] the merchants in England began to wanton
in the spoils of that confidence which the Virginia planter placed in
them in the sales of their tobacco shipped thither.[17]

A question of excise which in this year agitated the British nation
was essentially different from that which in later days has vexed the

15. For discussions of the impact of the Glorious Revolution on Virginia, see Richard
Morton, *Struggle against Tyranny, and the Beginning of a New Era: Virginia, 1677–1699*
(Williamsburg, Va., 1957), valuable for a good bibliography of contemporary and
secondary works; and Thomas Jefferson Wertenbaker, *Virginia under the Stuarts* (Princeton, N.J., 1914).

16. The Virginia Council, headed by Nathaniel Bacon, Sr. (1620–92), proclaimed on
April 26, 1689, the accession of King William and Mary, and named May 23 as the day
for the proclaiming of Their Majesties at every courthouse in the colony.

17. Sir Robert Walpole (1676–1745), the king's chief adviser and administrator from
1721 to 1742, left colonial affairs largely to the direction of Thomas Pelham-Holles, first
duke of Newcastle (1693–1768), whose policy of loose control has been dubbed the period
of "salutary neglect." However, this did not prevent interference by British merchants in
the affairs of the colony. They pulled wires to get their friends appointed to the Virginia Council and frequently used their influence in bringing royal vetoes to acts of
the Virginia Assembly and in proposing measures in their own interest which were det-
rimental to the colonists (Morton, *Colonial Virginia*, II, 506–7).

United States. Walpole professed to abolish the duty called customs except the subsidy of three farthings per pound on tobacco, from a conviction that those customs with that exception exposed the revenue to serious losses from fraud and the fair trader to injury. He was desirous of substituting an excise to be paid before the delivery of the commodity from the warehouses for consumption. Whether this project was intended as a decoy into the adoption of a general excise, or not, belongs not to our inquiry. He fostered it with the most ardent affection and did not usher it into the world until with parental care he had made the best preparation in his power for its auspicious reception. As far back as the year 1731, we trace him operating upon the governor of Virginia. In the journal of the Council this entry occurs:

The governor communicated to the Council a scheme projected in Great Britain for putting the tobacco under an excise, instead of the present method of paying the duties thereof, and desired their opinion thereon. Whereupon the board are of the opinion that the scheme proposed would be greatly for the interest of His Majesty, in securing his customs, would prevent the running of tobacco, and prove very beneficial to the inhabitants of the country. But forasmuch as this matter is of very great moment, and divers members of the board being absent, the Council are of opinion that if the weather will permit, a full Council be called to meet here on the twenty-third of December, or otherwise that the governor will be pleased to send copies of the scheme aforesaid to the several absent members and receive their sentiments thereon and accordingly transmit their answer to the person from whom he received the project.[18]

The concealment of the author's name justifies the suspicion of Alderman Perry [19] in the House of Commons that Sir Robert Walpole, the then prime minister, employed every engine to stamp popularity on his wishes. What was done by the Council and House of Burgesses does not appear on record further than that John Randolph was charged with a representation from the General Assembly to the House

18. See H. R. McIlwaine, ed., *Executive Journals of the Council of Virginia* (Richmond, 1925–40), IV, Dec. 15, 1731, 258–59.

19. Micajah Perry, alderman of the city of London, former Lord Mayor and a member of the House of Commons, headed an organization of London merchants trading in Virginia who fought every move that might lessen their profits in the tobacco trade. Consequently they opposed the creation of an excise tax on tobacco (Morton, *Colonial Virginia*, II, 519). For Perry and his firm, see Elizabeth Donnon, "Eighteenth-Century English Merchants: Micajah Perry," *Journal of Economic and Business History*, IV (1932), 70–98.

of Commons in support of the scheme, but for certain prudential reasons which his country afterwards approved, it was not made to that body.[20] It is probable that the public odium overwhelmed the measure, or Walpole foresaw that he must abandon it.[21] In a speech from Walpole it was, however, warmly advocated:

In discussing this subject, it will be necessary (he says) to advert to the condition of the planters of tobacco in America. If they are to be believed, they are reduced to the utmost extremity, even almost to a state of despair, by the many frauds which have been committed in that trade and by the ill usage which they have sustained from their factors and correspondents in England, who from being their servants, have become their tyrants. These unfortunate people have sent home many representations of the bad state of their affairs and have lately deputed a gentleman with a remonstrance setting forth their grievances and praying for some speedy relief. This they may obtain by the scheme I intend to propose. I believe it is from that alone that they can expect any relief.

To discuss the merits of it would now be useless, but let not Virginia be abused for her countenance to this solitary excise on tobacco with an improper coalition in the views of Walpole. Safety to her property dictated her measures. Her own liberty could not be affected by the scheme, nor would it have forged any shackle on the liberty of the mother country. Such too has been the voice of her posterity.

However difficult it may be to trace the causes of national character, or even to avoid the danger of mistaking the momentary impulse of a people for a permanent feeling, Virginia now wears an aspect which has never varied. The preceding history contains repeated instances of loyalty debased by no servile compliance and of a patriotic watch-

20. The burgesses and Council of Virginia passed a petition in 1732 entitled *The Case of the Planters in Virginia,* which included *A Vindication of the Said Presentation,* both published in London in 1733. The petition was written by Sir John Randolph (*ca.* 1693–1737), attorney general, speaker of the House of Burgesses, and the only native Virginian during the colonial period ever to be knighted. Randolph was chosen by the Assembly to present the petition to the British authorities and lobby for its adoption (Maude H. Woodfin, "Sir John Randolph," *DAB;* Morton, *Colonial Virginia,* II, 518; St. George Leakin Sioussat, "Virginia and the English Commercial System, 1730–1733," American Historical Association, *Annual Report for the Year 1905* [Washington, D.C., 1906], pp. 71–97).

21. The measure was presented to Parliament and according to Richard Morton "brought about one of the most notable debates in the history of the House of Commons" (*Colonial Virginia,* II, 520). The bill even passed on the first reading, but the opposition was so great that the motion to print failed by a narrow margin, and Walpole was forced to let it die. The prime minister relied upon John Randolph for counsel, and it was as consolation for the failure of his mission that he was knighted.

fulness never degenerating into the mere petulance of complaint. The event to be now registered is in unison with this encomium.

The government of Virginia, the next in emolument to Ireland and Jamaica, and in a political view inferior to no other colony, was often delegated to some needy favorite and administered by some lieutenant, the favorite of that favorite. At this time Lord Albemarle was the governor, and Robert Dinwiddie, who had recently been the master of a little vessel trading in the rivers, his deputy. Possessing neither science nor just ambition, unexpectedly raised to a power within the grasp of which when [sic] perverted riches obviously lay, and burning with an inordinate desire for more, he refused his signature to many thousand patents for vacant lands until a fee of one pistole on each should be paid into his private purse.[22] The lands were said to be the property of the king, as lord paramount, and subject in their disposal to his will. By this reasoning an upright Council was bewildered into an approbation of the demand.

The House of Burgesses revolted against an extortion hitherto unknown and dispatched Peyton Randolph, the then attorney general, to impress its iniquity and unconstitutionality upon the mind of His Majesty.[23]

In behalf of the governor the debate was conducted by Murray, afterwards the earl of Mansfield, and Hume Campbell; in behalf of the

22. William Anne Keppel, Lord Albemarle (1702–54), a soldier who had distinguished himself in the Netherlands, onetime ambassador to France, and privy councilor, was the absentee governor of Virginia from 1737 to 1754. During his tenure every office in the colony was given away in England (*ibid.*, p. 507). Robert Dinwiddie (1693–1770) was a member of an ancient Scottish family long engaged in trade. Unlike his predecessors he was not a soldier but had won recognition as a public servant, dealing largely with trade and public revenue. This background in business probably explains his zeal while governor in collecting revenue and his strong emphasis on the royal prerogative. It is difficult to accept Randolph's strictures against Dinwiddie as a man who "was burning with an inordinate desire" for money. According to Richard Morton the Governor was a prosperous man who apparently did not need to build his fortune at the expense of the colonists" (*ibid.*, pp. 599–600, 632–34). The pistole fee was required for the signing of land grants of 100 acres. A Spanish pistole was probably worth about £16 8d. sterling. For discussions of the controversy, see Jack P. Greene, "Landon Carter and the Pistole Fee Dispute," *Wm. and Mary Qtly.*, 3d ser., XIV (1957), 66–69; Glenn Curtiss Smith, "The Affair of the Pistole Fee, Virginia, 1752–55," *Va. Mag. of Hist. and Biog.*, XLVIII (1940), 209–21; and Louis K. Koontz, *Robert Dinwiddie: His Career in American Colonial Government and Westward Expansion* (Glendale, Calif., 1941), pp. 201–35.

23. Peyton Randolph (*ca.* 1721–75) was a burgess for the College of William and Mary, speaker of the House of Burgesses, attorney general, president of the Virginia Conventions of 1774 and 1775, and of the Continental Congress in 1774 and 1775 (Maude H. Woodfin, "Peyton Randolph," *DAB*).

colony, by Henley, since Lord Northington, and Forrester.[24] With an indelicacy foreign to the temper and manners of Murray and with a brutal insolence congenial with those of Campbell, the exaction was palliated by their genius and finally supported by the Council of the king. The king was at one time compared to a private landholder who might modify his terms with the mercenary dexterity of a huckster. But where the trustee of Virginia was for her domains, how he could affix a real tax upon them without the assent of the legislature was forgotten to be proved, if indeed it was not designedly waived by the illustrious Mansfield. Campbell remembered that the mere name of rebellion might be a worthy cause or operative resource of argument. He did not hesitate to change Virginia, tractable as she was, with entertaining views beyond the rescinding of a paltry fee.

We have no recorded details of the result of this controversy, but it is certain that the pistole was required until the increasing discontents caused it to be reduced one-half.[25]

The governor was wounded to the soul, and personal revenge was his weapon. He suspended Peyton Randolph from the office of attorney general and appointed George Wythe in his room.[26] But as the habits of a seducing and not of a wholly unambitious profession never warped him from friendship or patriotism, he accepted the commission with

24. William Murray (1705–93), a lawyer and judge, variously served as king's counsel, as a member of both the House of Commons and House of Lords, and as attorney general. At the time of the pistole fee controversy he was a leader in the House of Commons. Alexander Hume Campbell, an attorney for Dinwiddie and his interests, was at various times king's counsel, chancellor of the Duchy of Lancaster Chamber, and a member of Parliament. Robert Henley (1708?–72), a lawyer and M.P., was later to serve as attorney general, a member of the privy council, and lord chancellor. Both Arthur Forrester, later an M.P. for three cities, and Henley argued that the taking of the fee was contrary to the Virginia constitution. Contemporary Virginians must have known Campbell's actual words because Peyton Randolph, as agent for the colony, was present at the proceedings (Jack P. Greene, ed., "The Case of the Pistole Fee: The Report of a Hearing on the Pistole Fee Dispute before the Privy Council, June 18, 1754," *Va. Mag. of Hist. and Biog.,* LXVI [1958], 399–422).

25. Although both sides finally tired of the affair, more effective in ending the dispute was the news that the Privy Council had technically decided in Dinwiddie's favor. However, the governor was denied a complete victory by the Council's findings; no fees were to be charged on patents of 100 acres or less, for lands of imported families, for lands beyond the mountains, and for patents which had been initiated before April 22, 1752 (Morton, *Colonial Virginia,* II, 631–32).

26. George Wythe (1726–1806), an eminent lawyer, jurist, burgess, and signer of the Declaration of Independence, was best known as a professor of law at the College of William and Mary and the mentor of Thomas Jefferson, James Monroe, and Henry Clay (Theodore S. Cox, "George Wythe," *DAB*). Governor Dinwiddie reluctantly reappointed Peyton Randolph attorney general on instructions from the Board of Trade.

the customary professions of gratitude, not disclosing his secret and honorable determination that he would resign it to his predecessor on his return. It is possible, however, that it had been intimated to the governor from England that he was to be restored. Without such an instruction even this obdurate ruler would not have dared to contemn the lofty tones of the people. The House of Burgesses were as bold as the time would permit. Their opposition would have been folly had a resort to force constituted a part of it: to know when to complain with truth and how to complain with dignity was characteristic of watchful patriots and ample for the only end which could be then projected.

The French War of 1755

The plan of France for connecting Canada with Louisiana now began to develop itself. By the encroachments on Virginia, France roused her lieutenant governor to demand its abandonment.[27] To be the bearer of a message on this subject to the French commander on the river Ohio, through all obstacles and dangers, was an enterprise committed to George Washington, who had recently attained manhood.[28] The answer from that commander being unsatisfactory, a regiment of three hundred men was levied by the Virginia Assembly and the command of it given to Colonel Fry of Virginia.[29] Washington, his lieutenant colonel, succeeded Fry upon his death and surprised a French encampment a few miles west of the Great Meadows. There, having erected a small fortification called Fort Necessity to secure the pro-

27. The lieutenant governor was Robert Dinwiddie. France had answered the challenge of the Ohio Company's entrance into that valley with Céloron's expedition in 1749 down the Ohio. In 1753 the Marquis Duquesne, governor general of New France, sent an expedition to occupy the valley by constructing three forts, one on Lake Erie, Fort Le Boeuf on French Creek, and Fort Verango on the Allegheny River (Lawrence H. Gipson, *The British Empire before the American Revolution* [Caldwell, Idaho, and New York, 1936–67], IV, 265–75; see also Kenneth P. Bailey, *The Ohio Company of Virginia and the Westward Movement, 1748–1792* [Glendale, Calif., 1939]).

28. George Washington (1732–99), at the time a major and adjutant of the Southern District of Virginia, set out from Williamsburg on Oct. 30, 1753.

29. Joshua Fry (1700–54), a graduate of Oxford university, had been forced by the economic necessity of a growing family to leave his chair of mathematics at the College of William and Mary for the Virginia frontier as a surveyor and land speculator. He led the Virginians against the French in 1754 and died during the campaign (Richard L. Morton, "Joshua Fry," *DAB*).

visions and horses, he was proceeding to Fort Duquesne at the junction of the Allegheny and Ohio rivers, with the intention of dislodging the French. Their movements, however, imposed upon Washington a retreat to Fort Necessity. On his march he was attacked by de Villiers, a French general at the head of fifteen hundred men, and capitulated, and in the articles of capitulation, written in the French language, which was not understood by Washington, the death or loss of one Jumonville, another French officer, was mentioned as an assassination.[30] A more egregious artifice was never practiced against plain facts and the declaration of Washington himself.

Shortly after this, the British government manifested extreme ignorance of Indian warfare in supposing that officers of American appointment must be so far inferior in skill and military qualities to those commissioned by the crown that when coming into contact, the latter ought to take precedence of the former. To those who are now acquainted with Washington's acute and unchangeable sense of military honor, it will not appear surprising that he should resent this degradation and resign his regiment. It was not prophetic, but it was almost a species of prevision that this single act should be a link in those feelings which at the distance of more than twenty years brought brighter triumphs to America over Great Britain.

General Braddock took the command of the American forces against the French and Indians.[31] It was said that the duke of Cumberland, the generalissimo of Great Britain, had selected him, as a man who could fight the devil, misapprehending the nature of the service so as to conceive that undauntedly to face death was of itself competency against an enemy trained in the stratagems and retreats suggested by a wilderness uncleared and almost untrodden by an European foot.

Braddock, fearing nothing so much as a departure from long-established military rules, could not, however, but be struck with a glimpse of the difference between war in a country like this and war in the open countries of Europe, and having heard of Washington's

30. Coylon de Villiers was a captain. Washington did have a Capt. Jacob Van Braam with him to act as interpreter, but his knowledge of French was limited. Jumonville, the French commander defeated by Washington in the battle at Great Meadows, along with nine other Frenchmen, was scalped by Washington's Indian allies.

31. Although Maj. Gen Edward Braddock (1695–1755) had served forty-five years in the famous Coldstream Guards he had little experience in actual warfare (Stanley M. Pargellis, "Braddock's Defeat," *American Historical Review*, XLI [1935–36], 253–70). William Augustus, duke of Cumberland (1721–65), capt. gen. of the British army, persuaded the king, against his earlier wishes, to approve Governor Dinwiddie's request for troops.

merit in a command against Indians and his disgust with an arrangement of rank so arbitrary and unreasonable, he invited him into his family as a volunteer aide-de-camp.

His immediate advice to Braddock was to disencumber himself of artillery and heavy baggage and to march with all rapidity to the Ohio, before the succors expected by the French could arrive.

This advice was not entirely acceded to until after Braddock had moved a short distance from Alexandria. Then the necessity of exchanging wagons for packhorses gave to Washington's opinion complete effect. The army consisted of two British regiments and a few corps of provincials.

But instead of pushing on with vigor they halted to level every molehill and to erect bridges over every brook, advancing not more than nineteen miles in four days. Washington, being seized with a violent fever, was commanded in peremptory terms by Braddock to remain on the route behind until he should go through a medical course. But on July 8, 1755, his impatience under absence from the field carried him to the army then on the Monongahela, though scarcely able to ride on horseback. There he found Braddock preparing to attack Fort Duquesne, on the next day, and immediately resumed the duties of his station. On his march thither, Braddock was attacked in a plain overgrown with trees, sufficient to conceal the assailants. To an enemy invisible, he exhibited himself on horseback and his whole force in regular military style. Sixty out of eighty officers were killed or wounded. Washington was unhurt, after having lost two horses from under him and received several balls through his clothes. Braddock was mortally wounded, and his army retreated.

Thus was frustrated an attempt which under bravery equal to that of Braddock, regulated by the prudence and knowledge of Washington, would probably have inflicted a decisive blow on France in the vantage ground which she professed at the confluence of the two rivers. Thus too was lost the confidence necessary to our tranquillity and once reposed in British soldiery. The frontiers were deserted with precipitation. A panic spread itself almost to the Atlantic coast. So violent and diffusive was it that a hundred volunteers under Peyton Randolph, the attorney general of Virginia, quit their beds of ease to meet the Indian enemy. From discipline or high military exertion little could be hoped for. A smaller number of riflemen would have been more effective. But the first who set an example of spirit among the people are almost the authors of the defense which grows out of it. That defense, though in

this case tardy from the inattention of the governor and General Assembly to the expostulations of Washington, was not abandoned but
was only absorbed in the memorable scenes which occupied in Europe
and the northern parts of America the space between Braddock's defeat
and the Treaty of Paris in 1763.

This treaty and the royal proclamation which followed it form essential ingredients in the history of Virginian territory. The treaty is
perhaps the basis of a history of higher order. It is almost a book of
prophecy: in it are ceded states—and possibly powers whose destinies
may alarm America or modify her ultimate fate.[32]

The Stamp Act Crisis

This is an era illustrious indeed in the annals of Virginia. Without an
immediate oppression, without a cause depending so much on hasty
feeling as theoretic reasoning, without a distaste for monarchy, with
loyalty to the reigning prince, with fraternal attachment to the transatlantic members of the empire, with an admiration of their genius,
learning, and virtues, with a subserviency in cultivating their manners
and their fashions, in a word with England as a model of all which was
great and venerable—the House of Burgesses in the year 1765 gave
utterance to principles which within ten years were to expand into a
revolution.[33]

The charters had shown that the first adventurers demanded and
were allowed to possess the rights of English subjects. The English
constitution was at once the standard and bulwark of their liberty.
Under its protection they had contested the usurpations of kings, Parliaments, and governors. The specific doctrine which condemned taxation without representation had been often quoted as a fundamental
one of colonial freedom, and every generation of lawyers imbibed it in
their studies.

32. The Peace of Paris concluded the Seven Years or French and Indian War. Faced
by the added responsibilities of new provinces secured from France in the peace treaty, the
British administration prepared a royal proclamation on Oct. 7, 1763, forbidding anyone to purchase land or to settle beyond the Allegheny watershed, land reserved for the
Indians.

33. For an excellent discussion of the Stamp Act controversy, see Edmund S. and
Helen M. Morgan, *The Stamp Act Crisis: Prologue to Revolution* (Chapel Hill, N.C.,
1953).

The details of government and the subjects of legislation in Virginia were few and circumscribed in comparison with those of an independent empire. Hence Virginian politics did not go beyond general principles and a jealousy of the rights most dear. It was understood that to hold the purse was a check upon the sword itself.

Corruption was making gigantic strides in England, and America was a field in which necessitous partisans might be pampered at the expense of American labor. American property therefore had no other security than the mercy of Parliament, if they could enact laws of revenue without the assent of the colonies. Virtual representation was sophistry at best, if we give it its highest character.[34] Scarcely in any state of Virginia opinion could sentiments like these have been restrained where there was the slightest appearance of parliamentary taxation. But when intelligence arrived of parliamentary resolutions preparatory to the Stamp Act,[35] a corps of members in the House of Burgesses whose habits and expectations had no relation to men in power had increased without being discovered by the aristocratic part of the house, or by those members themselves: From the lower counties, fortune, rank, and perhaps fashion had often sent representatives; but the repeated divisions of the upper counties drew representatives from humble walks. A collision between the two classes caused them to diverge from each other as widely in their sentiments in granting public money as in their incomes and expenses. While one would pay a public servant upon a strict calculation of the labor to be performed, the other would augment the stipend for the sake of dignity. A rivalship was the consequence; but the new party had hitherto been able only to vote and to be counted. They wanted a leader. At this critical moment, Patrick Henry appeared as a member from the county of Louisa.[36]

From birth he derived neither splendor nor opulence. But from a pious and virtuous example, he imbibed a disposition to religion and

34. The doctrine of virtual representation was articulated by Thomas Whately, a subordinate of Lord Grenville, in response to colonial objections to the proposed stamp act. Whately contended that even though the colonists could not actually vote for any member of the House of Commons, neither could many Englishmen who were excluded by property qualifications or by residence in boroughs that sent no member. These Englishmen and the colonists, argued Whately, were virtually represented because every member of Parliament represented the whole Empire and not merely the few electors who chose him (Edmund S. Morgan, *The Birth of the Republic, 1763–1789* [Chicago, 1956], pp. 18–19).

35. Parliament enacted the Stamp Act in March 1765.

36. Patrick Henry (1736–99) entered the House of Burgesses in 1765 (Robert Douthat Meade, *Patrick Henry: Patriot in the Making* [Philadelphia, 1957]).

virtue, which when formed in youth fails not in good fruit in maturer age.

The mildness of his temper, coinciding with this example, rendered him amiable. Of classical erudition he neglected the scanty opportunities which were afforded to him for the chase, for conversation, and for his own reflection. He sounded the recesses and depths of the human heart. On the facts thus collected he suffered his vast genius and unbounded imagination to brood, unfettered by scholastic rules. His memory was faithful and prompt.

At first he devoted himself to merchandise, and from an aversion to drudgery and with no fondness for labor, he could not be otherwise than unsuccessful.

Having experienced his command in social discourse, he took refuge in the study and practice of the law. In black-letter precedents he was never profound, in general principles he had no reason to shrink from a struggle with any man. Not always grammatical, and sometimes coarse in his language, he taught his hearers how to forget his inaccuracies by his action, his varying countenance and voice.

Crowning these popular qualities with the universal belief that he understood the condition of the Virginian planters and was completely embarked in their fate, he was naturally hailed as the democratic chief.

Sir Robert Walpole, the celebrated premier of Great Britain, is said to have declared in the year 1739, when to tax the colonies for revenue was proposed to him, that he had not courage for such an experiment. He was not ignorant of their growing ability or of the wants of the parent country. But upon this subject he had learned from the history of Virginia that while she never withheld due submission to government, her patience had its just limits. The ministry in 1765 did not discover these plain signs but calculated that our black population and our propensities would paralyze rebellion and that a tumult stirred in haste would subside after a momentary ferment.

However these things may be, on May 29, 1765, Mr. Henry plucked the veil from the shrine of parliamentary omnipotence. He inveighed against the usurpation of Parliament in their avowed purpose at a future day of changing stamp and other duties in the colonies without their consent.

It was judicious in Mr. Henry to suspend his resolutions denouncing this usurpation until a day or two before the close of the session. At this stage of business those who would be most averse to an absence from home, merely to guard against evils in speculation, had retired. Those who were left behind were exempt from this restlessness. They clung to Mr. Henry, and some others classed on the other side in the controversy were not unmoved by the crisis.

The resolutions offered by Mr. Henry are understood to have been written by Mr. John Fleming, a member from Cumberland County distinguished for his patriotism and the strength of his mind; and they were seconded by Mr. George Johnston from Fairfax County.[37]

It is unknown whether the friends of Henry's resolutions were impressed by the inconsistency of permitting taxes for the regulation of external trades and rejecting internal taxes for the purpose of revenue. If they were, they probably extricated themselves by pleading the infancy of political reasoning, which had conceded the distinction to a certain mystical dependence of a colony on the mother country. Had Henry boldly cut the knot by reprobating both species of taxation equally, and the latter as having been submitted to from an unconsciousness of the nerve of manhood, a reluctance to excite discontents, or an overpowering idolatry to parliamentary power, the frankness and truth of the concession would have destroyed its force.

In his harangue, he certainly indulged a strain never before heard in the royal Capitol. This circumstance passed while he was speaking: "Caesar," cried he, "had his Brutus; Charles the first his Cromwell; and George the third—" "Treason, sir," exclaimed the speaker, to which Henry instantly replied, "and George the third, may he never have either." This dexterous escape or retreat, if it did not savor of lively eloquence, was of itself a victory.[38] He carried through

---

37. John Fleming, Jr. (d. 1767), was a lawyer who represented Cumberland County in the House of Burgesses. George Johnston (d. 1766) was an eminent lawyer from Fairfax County and a burgess from 1758 to 1765. In a strong speech he seconded Henry's resolutions. According to Robert D. Meade (*ibid.*, p. 169), Henry wrote the resolutions himself but did show them to Fleming and Johnston for comment. Their support of the resolutions indicates that they had encouraged Henry. For the text of Henry's "Virginia Resolves," see Samuel Eliot Morison, ed., *Sources and Documents Illustrating the American Revolution* (London, 1962), pp. 17–18.

38. In no part of this History, have I drawn any character to its size, as it appeared at the time. Accordingly, in the year 1774 Mr. Henry's is resumed, retouched, and enlarged perhaps with a few repetitions—RANDOLPH'S NOTE (see below, pp. 178–81).

There is still some doubt about the forcefulness of Henry's speech. Randolph's account is almost an exact reproduction of John Daly Burk's written a few years earlier, and William Wirt, whose *Life of Patrick Henry* (1817) was most responsible for Henry's reputation, followed both Burk and Randolph almost word for word. But the Morgans have used the diary of an eyewitness, possibly the chevalier d'Annemours, which was discovered in the archives of the Service Hydographique de la Marine at Paris and published in the *American Historical Review* (XXVI [1921], 726–47, XXVII [1922], 70–89), as evidence "to deflate the legend of Henry's daring" (*Stamp Act Crisis*, pp. 122–23). How-the committee of the whole house all the resolutions which he proposed. But on the succeeding day, when they were reported to the house itself, the two last, as being too inflammatory, were laid aside; and the rest which were adopted, being more correspondent with the general sentiment, were by the severance of those two better guarantees of a stable opposition to Parliament.[39] The governor, after the public business, omitted the civility of a parting speech and dissolved the House of Burgesses by a simple fiat.[40] Thus by the suspicion attending colonial management and an excessive confidence in their own security did the British ministry become the pioneers to the dismemberment of the empire.

If Walpole was more corrupt than they, he was certainly more wise, and had his apprehensions in 1739 been renewed in the statesmen of 1764 who are now to be judged by posterity, they might be forgotten without execration from their own country.

Were it not for the pure character of Lord Botetourt, the governor in 1769, it might be a problem whether he was selected for his fascinating manners as an instrument to inveigle the docility and beguile the credulity of Virginia.[41]

If from birth and education he had not been a courtier, his dependence on the crown for the revival of an extinguished title must have generated habits to conciliate and please. He came hither not only with the grace of polished life but also with the predilections of the

ever, Meade, who also cited the same French traveler, still feels that the eyewitness reports of Thomas Jefferson and John Tyler are reliable enough to support the traditional account of the speech. Although he is willing to accept the Frenchman's word that Henry offered an apology to the speaker for his remarks, Meade argues that such apologies were customary. "If Henry did speak any apologetic words, they were doubtless uttered almost tongue in check to give him some legal protection" (*Patrick Henry*, pp. 175–81).

39. These two resolutions were either not offered or if presented, were rejected. One maintained that the inhabitants of Virginia were not to obey any law designated to impose taxation other than those passed by the General Assembly, and the other provided that any person asserting that anyone other than the General Assembly had the right to lay any taxation would be deemed an enemy of the state.

40. The governor, or lieutenant governor, was Francis Fauquier (1704–68), described by Thomas Jefferson as the ablest man who ever filled the chair of government in Williamsburg (Fairfax Harrison, "A Portrait of Governor Fauquier," *Fauquier Historical Society Bulletin*, No. 4 [1924], 343–50).

41. Norborne Berkeley, baron de Botetourt (1718–70), a court favorite impoverished by gambling and a diligent Tory member of the House of Commons, replaced General Amherst as governor. Amherst, a protégé of Pitt, had engaged this fat sinecure in absentia while Lieutenant Governor Fauquier shouldered the work and responsibility of governing. Botetourt was to become an extremely popular governor (Dumas Malone, *Jefferson the Virginian* [Boston, 1948], pp. 128–29).

people, who were proud in being no longer governed by a deputy. His predecessors Fauquier, Dinwiddie,[42] Gooch, Spotswood, Nott, Nicholson, and Drysdale had been the vehicles of sinecures to some principals who never cast an eye or thought on Virginia.[43] Through Botetourt the colony was assured by the king that as a mark of honor to it, the residence of the chief governor there should never be dispensed with in future.

Always accessible on business, adhering without a single deviation to the resolution of sleeping every night in the metropolis, affable to the humblest visitor, in social circles easy himself and contributing to the ease of others, he was sincerely and universally beloved.

In his public functions his purity and punctuality confirmed the attachment which his qualities as a gentleman had begun. By his patronage he inspired the youth of William and Mary College with ardor and emulation, and by his daily example in the observance of religion he acquired a kind of sacred ascendancy over the public mind.

But the affection and admiration of Virginia were wound up to the highest pitch, when in 1769 he opened the General Assembly with a speech containing these strong expressions:

I think myself peculiarly fortunate to be able to inform you that in a letter dated May 13 I have been assured by the earl of Hillsborough that His Majesty's present administration have at no time entertained a design

42. For Dinwiddie and Fauquier, see notes 22 and 40 above respectively.

43. William Gooch (1681–1751), a soldier who had served with distinction in Queen Anne's War, was governor of Virginia from 1727 to 1749 (Percy Scott Flippin, "William Gooch," *DAB*). Alexander Spotswood (1676–1740), son of an army physician, was born in the English military outpost in Tangier, North Africa. Bred in the army, he turned early to a career as a professional soldier. He served as governor from 1710 to 1722 (Jack P. Greene, "The Opposition to Lieutenant Governor Alexander Spotswood, 1718," *Va. Mag. of Hist. and Biog.*, LXX [1962], 35–42; and Leonidas Dodson, *Alexander Spotswood, Governor of Colonial Virginia, 1710–1722* [Philadelphia, 1939]). There is a blank space in the manuscript following Spotswood's name, but it can be assumed that Randolph meant to include Edward Nott (1654–1706). Nott, governor from 1705 to 1706, was sent to Virginia to rule for the absentee governor-in-chief George Hamilton, earl of Orkney, who remained in England enjoying a good salary with no responsibility for forty years (Morton, *Colonial Virginia*, I, 388). Francis Nicholson (1655–1728), a professional soldier and able administrator, served not only as governor of Virginia in 1690–92 and 1698–1705 but also as governor of New York, Nova Scotia, South Carolina, and Maryland (Stephen Saunders Webb, "The Strange Career of Francis Nicholson," *Wm. and Mary Qtly.*, 3d ser., XXIII [1966], 513–48; and Leonard W. Labaree, "Francis Nicholson," *DAB*). Hugh Drysdale (d. 1726), governor from 1722 to 1726, won the good will of Virginians by his considerate treatment of their wishes and by his tact in exercising the royal prerogative. Botetourt was the first governor in chief during the eighteenth century actually to assume his duties in Virginia.

to propose to Parliament to lay any further taxes upon America for the purpose of raising a revenue, and that it is their intention to propose in the next session of Parliament to take off the duties upon glass, paper, and colors upon consideration of such duties having been laid contrary to the true spirit of commerce.[44]

It may be possibly objected that as His Majesty's present administration are not immortal, their successors may be inclined to undo what the present ministers shall have attempted to perform; and to that objection, I can give but this answer, that it is my firm opinion that the plan I have stated to you will certainly take place, and that it never will be departed from, and so determined am I forever to abide by it that I will be content to be declared infamous if I do not to the last hour of my life, and at all times and in all places, and upon all occasions, exert every power with which I am, or ever shall be, legally invested in order to obtain and maintain for the continent of America that satisfaction which I have been authorized to promise this day by the confidential servants of our gracious sovereign, who, to my certain knowledge, rates his honor so high that he would rather part with his crown than preserve it by deceit.[45]

A most humble and dutiful address was immediately voted, in which his lordship's popularity holds a conspicuous place:

Your lordship's great regard and attention to the welfare and true interests of this colony had before endeared you to us all, but your generous and noble declarations upon this occasion demand our warmest and most grateful acknowledgments. We assure your lordship, we shall think ourselves supremely happy, if in conducting the arduous and momentous affairs of this great country, we should in the end receive the approbation of a ruler we so very cordially honor and esteem.[46]

As Botetourt was advanced in life and had resolved to spend the remainder of it in Virginia, he might probably have administered the government to the latest period of the British dominion, had not death interrupted the prospect. Among the lamentations on his demise, one was that the pledge in his speech would have bound him to exert himself in removing all cause of alarm and in establishing the American

44. This reference is to a letter from the earl of Hillsborough (1718–93), secretary of state for the colonies, notifying the American colonists that he was going to recommend repeal of all the Townshend duties except the one on tea. Months later, in March 1770, Parliament redeemed his pledge.

45. H. R. McIlwaine and J. P. Kennedy, eds., *Journals of the House of Burgesses* (Williamsburg, Va., 1905–15), *1766–1769*, p. 227.

46. *Ibid.*, p. 234.

principle. But how great is the difficulty to believe that he would have renounced every hope from the honors in acquiring which he had exhausted very many years and much of his fortune. That a devotion to monarchy, with every tie to the mother country and not one to this, should suddenly transform himself into an American partisan; that a man to whose ear the term omnipotence, as applied to his country, conveyed neither the harshness of blasphemy nor a suspicion of credulity should become an exile from England among a people to him, as it were, alien. Human nature forbids such expectations. I rejoice therefore that he died so timely. For himself, he perhaps avoided humiliation. Virginia was not mortified by the regret of questioning or doubting that he was spotless and erected to his memory a statue not more admired for its exquisite workmanship than for being a memorial of a statesman more than great, because truly honest.

And yet subsequent events force us to retrace some peculiarities in the letter of Hillsborough, bordering upon artifice. A badge of slavery was to be preserved, if it were only a fragment. The article of tea was withheld from proscription for inflaming the New World, and perhaps in its ultimate effects for embroiling, if not destroying, the Old.

With the saving of the duty on tea and the act of Parliament asserting a right to bind the colonies in all cases whatsoever,[47] the first was abundant for a devouring flame, even after the repeal of the Stamp Act. The wisdom of the ministry consisted in the use of expedients and finesse, and pride was manifested in their conduct, as if America had been a nation of rivals, instead of a nation of children and friends.

The death of John Robinson, the speaker of the House of Burgesses and treasurer of the colony, produced great agitation. These offices had been generally united in the same person. The chair, as the presidency of that house was called, was the seat of the prolocutor, and being without a salary derived the support of its dignity, as far as money was necessary to it, from the emoluments attached to the treasury.

This gentleman was a native, educated wholly in Virginia. His reputation was great for sound political knowledge and an acquaintance with parliamentary forms, a benevolence which created friends and a sincerity which never lost one. Then only had he an enemy when the private individual was to be sunk in the public office.

When he presided the decorum of the house outshone that of the

47. Randolph was doubtless referring to the Declaratory Act of 1766, which reaffirmed Parliament's right to tax the colonies.

British House of Commons, even with Onslow at their head.[48] When he propounded a question, his comprehension and perspicuity brought it equally to the most humble and the most polished understanding. To committees he nominated the members best qualified. He stated to the house the contents of every bill and showed himself to be a perfect master of the subject. When he pronounced the rules of order, he convinced the reluctant. When on the floor of a committee of the whole house, he opened the debate, he submitted resolutions and enforced them with simplicity and might. In the limited sphere of colonial politics, he was a column.

Hence he was for a long time elevated above the criticism of his faults. The thousand little flattering attentions which can be scattered from the chair operated as a delicious incense. When he was suspected of mismanaging the treasury, he could probably have sheltered himself by some handy resolution; but he met the charge with an air of magnanimity and defense and appointed his very enemies to investigate it. Exculpated by their report, he continued triumphant until his death unlocked the truth. Immediately on his decease a suspicion stalked abroad, and a large deficit was ascertained in the treasury.[49]

In the Assembly a board of five commissioners, rather than a single treasurer, was urged by several leading members; but the unnecessary expense and the confidence in Mr. Nicholas, whom the governor had appointed treasurer for the time, confirmed him in the post. He was allowed a commission on the monies received; and Peyton Randolph, the speaker, a salary of £500 sterling per annum. Mr. Robinson's arrearage has been discharged. The only apology which can be framed for the supineness of the legislature in not more frequently and more minutely examining the treasury is founded in human nature. A seeming captious jealousy is painful. Addresses to the heart are too apt to silence the admonitions of the understanding, and patriotism itself is sometimes checked by the generosity of abhorring the semblance of persecution.

48. Arthur Onslow (1691–1768) was unanimously elected speaker of the House of Commons in 1728, an office to which he was reelected in 1735, 1741, 1747, and 1754.

49. John Robinson (1704–66) received in 1738 dual appointments as treasurer of Virginia and speaker of the House of Burgesses, posts which he held until his death. "Although many writers have confidently assumed," writes David J. Mays, "that the real purpose of the loan office scheme of 1765 was to repay loans already made from the Treasury, and to save Robinson, no convincing evidence has been presented to sustain their assertions. Possibly they were correct. But the evidence now available points the other way" (*Edmund Pendleton, 1721–1802, A Biography* [Cambridge, Mass., 1952], I, 174–208).

The intermediate period between this time and the beginning of the year 1774 resembled that season between two old friends when the language begins to be embittered and the heart is gnawed, a rupture is dreaded but the cause is not forgiven.

Chapter V   Introduction to That Part of the History Embracing the Revolution, Including Biographies of Some Leading Men

We have seen that until the era of the Stamp Act almost every political sentiment, every fashion in Virginia appeared to be imperfect unless it bore a resemblance to some precedent in England. The spirit, however, which she had caught from the charters, the English laws, the English constitution, English theories at that time had diminished her almost idolatrous deference to the mother country and taught her to begin to think for herself.[1]

It was no small elevation of character in Virginia to have learned to renounce the idea of parliamentary omnipotence; and from this stand assumed in the year 1765, she was driven into the contemplation of higher objects by injuries, insults, and contempt, which, whether real or supposed, were in the season of general equality a powerful ferment in bringing odium upon the British ministry.

But this first struggle against our ancient prepossessions, although it was of some magnitude, demanded no sacrifice of feelings like that which the present conjuncture exacted. The remonstrances against the Stamp Act breathed loyalty and prays for the continuance of the relation of subjects. In former disputes, harmony had been restored without difficulty, and to state rights with force did not seem to verge in the smallest degree toward an opposition beyond that of mere words. Now indeed, on the opening of the year 1774, a deeper tone broke forth. The public mind had been familiarized to an appeal to arms at first as only a possible event, which was sincerely deprecated, and afterwards, as a probable one, which might be imposed by necessity. It had daily received fresh excitement from brooding over the causes of discontent and with avidity converted into matter of inflammation truth as well as exaggerated rumors.

1. For the approach of the Revolution in Virginia, see Thad W. Tate, "The Coming of the Revolution in Virginia: Britain's Challenges to Virginia's Ruling Class, 1763–1776," *Wm. and Mary Qtly.*, 3d ser., XIX (1962), 323–43; and Hamilton J. Eckenrode, *The Revolution in Virginia* (New York, 1916).

This new state of things may perhaps be said to have originated more peculiarly with the people than almost any other of which history affords an example, and which was not kindled by palpable oppression. It was cherished, it is true, by some of the most distinguished citizens, was opposed by no check from executive influence, and as far as religion was enlisted into the service, was fostered by most of its ministerial professors. But that it should have been indulged to the extent of a resolution not to reject even force from the catalogue of the means of redress will evince to those who shall understand our resources the existence of a public sentiment pervading the colony, which was neither the offspring of transient caprice nor to be alarmed by strict calculations of danger, a principle too, which upheld order, notwithstanding the relaxation of long-established authority emanating from the crown, and which confined the temper growing out of public dissensions within limits of moderation, in the intercourse between man and man.

The pride of Virginia had so long been a topic of discourse in the other colonies that it had almost grown into a proverb. Being the earliest among the British settlements in North America, having been soon withdrawn from the humiliation of proprietary dependence to the dignity of a government immediately under the crown, advancing rapidly into wealth from her extensive territory and the luxuriant production of her staple commodities, the sons of the most opulent families trained by education and habits acquired in England and hence perhaps arrogating some superiority over the provinces not so distinguished, she was charged with manifesting a cons[c]iousness that she had more nearly approached the British model . . . [torn] of excellence, and what was claimed as an attribute of character in a government readily diffused itself among the individuals who were members of it. Hence it happened that the few offices to which the king or his vicegerent could nominate conferred a luster upon their incumbents and their connections and placed them in the attitude of expecting from the rest of the community an attention which is the proper tribute of public merit. But as soon as the favor of the British court generated a suspicion inconsistent with the purity of Virginian patriotism, and more particularly, when it was foreseen that if battles were to be fought, they were to be fought by men who had no other stake or hope than their own country, the old standard of distinction was abolished and a new one substituted on the single foundation of fitness for the rising exigency. Although therefore many of those whom I shall portray as they presented themselves to the public eye at the present period, either for the purposes of immediate utility or as affording prognostics of future splendor (the vanity of pedigree was now justly sunk in the positive force of character), were from their fortune, birth, and station high on the scale of the aristocracy of the day, they were stripped of every consideration and attachment which virtue, talents, and patriotism did not beget. It is not expected that the reader will avoid comparisons between these men and the heroes and sages of the Old World whose situation in life can be deemed in the least degree similar, nor can it be certainly affirmed that the correctness and fullness of European annals may not shed on the latter an effulgence of which in the American patriots are deprived by the loss of the opportunities of discriminating and recording their separate eloquence and counsels. But it will not be deemed rash to enter into any such comparison assuming which for its basis this principle: that at this season which tried men's souls (to use the phrase of a celebrated popular writer) [2] Virginia produced public agents suitable to every crisis and service.[3]

To Patrick Henry the first place is due, as being the first who broke the influence of that aristocracy. Little and feeble as it was, and incapable of daring to assert any privilege, clashing with the right of the people at large, it was no small exertion in him to surprise them with the fact that a new path was opened to the temple of honor, besides that which led through the favor of the king. He was respectable in his parentage, but the patrimony of his ancestors and of himself was too scanty to feed ostentation or luxury. From education he derived those manners which belonged to the real Virginian planter and which were his ornament, in no less disdaining an abridgment of personal independence than in observing every decorum interwoven with the comfort of society. With his years the unbought means of popularity increased. Identified with the people, they clothed him with the confidence of a favorite son. Until his resolutions on the Stamp Act, he had been unknown, except to those with whom he had associated in

2. This reference is to Thomas Paine's famous phrase from the first of thirteen pamphlets entitled *The American Crisis.*

3. For discussions of Virginia's ruling gentry, see Lyon G. Tyler, "The Leadership of Virginia in the War of the Revolution," *Wm. and Mary Qtly.,* 1st ser., XVIII (1910), 145–64; Jack P. Greene, "Foundations of Political Power in the Virginia House of Burgesses, 1720–1776," *ibid.,* 3d. ser., XVI (1959), 485–506; Charles Sydnor, *Gentleman Freeholders: Political Practices in Washington's Virginia* (Chapel Hill, N.C., 1952), and Keith B. Berwick, "Moderates in Crisis: The Trials of Leadership in Revolutionary Virginia" (Ph.D. dissertation, University of Chicago, 1959).

the hardy sports of the field and the avowed neglect of literature. Still he did not escape notice, as occasionally retiring within himself in silent reflection, and sometimes descanting with peculiar emphasis on the martyrs in the cause of liberty. This enthusiasm was nourished by his partiality for the dissenters from the Established Church. He often listened to them while they were waging their steady and finally effectual war against the burdens of that church, and from a repetition of his sympathy with the history of their sufferings, he unlocked the human heart and transferred into civil discussions many of the bold licenses which prevailed in the religions. If he was not a constant hearer and admirer of that stupendous master of the human passions, George Whitefield, he was a follower, a devotee of some of his most powerful disciples at least.

All these advantages he employed by a demeanor inoffensive, conciliating, and abounding in good humor. For a short time he practiced the law in an humble sphere, too humble for the real height of his powers. He then took a seat at the bar of the General Court, the supreme tribunal of Virginia, among a constellation of eminent lawyers and scholars and was in great request even on questions for which he had not been prepared by much previous erudition. Upon the theater of legislation, he entered regardless of that criticism which was profusely bestowed on his language, pronunciation, and gesture. Nor was he absolutely exempt from an irregularity in his language, a certain homespun pronunciation, and a degree of awkwardness in the cold commencement of his gesture. But the corresponding looks and emotions of those whom he addressed speedily announced that language may be sometimes peculiar and even quaint, while it is at the same time expressive and appropriate; that a pronunciation which might disgust in a drawing room may yet find access to the hearts of a popular assembly; and that a gesture at first too much the effect of indolence may expand itself in the progress of delivery into forms which would be above the rule and compass but strictly within the prompting of nature. Compared with any of his more refined contemporaries and rivals, he by his imagination, which painted to the soul, eclipsed the sparklings of art, and knowing what chord of the heart would sound in unison with his immediate purpose, and with what strength or peculiarity it ought to be touched, he had scarcely ever languished in a minority at the time up to which his character is now brought. Contrasted with the most renowned of British orators, the older William

Pitt, he was not inferior to him in the intrepidity of metaphor.[4] Like him he possessed a vein of sportive ridicule, but without arrogance or dictatorial malignity. In Henry's exordium there was a simplicity and even carelessness, which to a stranger, who had never before heard him, promised little. A formal division of his intended discourse he never made; but even the first distance, which he took from his main ground, was not so remote as to obscure it, or to require any distortion of his course to reach it. With an eye which possessed neither positive beauty nor acuteness, and which he fixed upon the moderator of the assembly addressed without straying in quest of applause, he contrived to be the focus to which every person present was directed, even at the moment of the apparent languor of his opening. He transfused into the breast of others the earnestness depicted in his own features, which ever forbade a doubt of sincerity. In others rhetorical artifice and un-meaning expletives have been often employed as scouts to seize the wandering attention of the audience; in him the absence of trick con-stituted the triumph of nature. His was the only monotony which I ever heard reconcilable with true eloquence; its chief note was melo-dious, but the sameness was diversified by a mixture of sensations which a dramatic versatility of action and of countenance produced. His pauses, which for their length might sometimes be feared to dispel the attention, riveted it the more by raising the expectation of renewed brilliancy. In pure reasoning, he encountered many successful com-petitors; in the wisdom of looks, many superiors; but although he might be inconclusive, he was never frivolous; and arguments which at first seemed strange were afterwards discovered to be select in their kind, because adapted to some peculiarity in his audience. His style of oratory was vehement, without transporting him beyond the power of self-command or wounding his opponents by deliberate offense: after a debate had ceased, he was surrounded by them on the first occasion with pleasantry on some of its incidents. His figures of speech, when borrowed, were often borrowed from the Scriptures. The proto-types of others were the sublime scenes and objects of nature; and an occurrence at the same instant he never failed to employ with all the energy of which it was capable. His lightning consisted in quick suc-

4. William Pitt, first earl of Chatham (1707–78), the "Great Commoner," took com-mand of the British government during the Seven Years War when the nation's fortunes were at a low ebb and proceeded to become the chief architect of France's humiliating de-feat. From the beginning of the Anglo-American controversy he opposed taxing the colonies.

cessive flashes, which rested only to alarm the more. His ability as a writer cannot be insisted on, nor was he fond of a length of details; but for grand impressions in the defense of liberty, the Western world has not yet been able to exhibit a rival. His nature had probably denied to him, under any circumstances, the capacity of becoming Pitt, while Pitt himself would have been but a defective instrument in a revolution the essence of which was deep and pervading popular sentiment.

In this embryo state of the Revolution, deep research into the ancient treasures of political learning might well be dispensed with. It was enough to feel, to remember some general maxims coeval with the colony and inculcated frequently afterwards. With principles like these, Mr. Henry need not dread to encounter the usurpation threatened by Parliament, for although even his powerful eloquence could not create public sentiment, he could apply the torch of opposition so as fortunately to perceive that in every vicissitude of event, he concurred with his country.[5]

As yet Thomas Jefferson had not attained a marked grade in politics.[6] Until about the age of twenty-five years he had pursued general science, with which he mingled the law, as a profession, with an eager industry and unabated thirst. His manners could never be harsh, but they were reserved toward the world at large. To his intimate friends he showed a peculiar sweetness of temper and by them was admired and beloved. In mathematics and experimental philosophy, he was a proficient, assiduously taught by Dr. Small of William and Mary College, whose name was not concealed among the literati of Europe.[7] He panted after the fine arts and discovered a taste in them not easily satisfied with such scanty means as existed in a colony whose chief ambition looked to the general system of education in England as the ultimate point of excellence. But it constituted a part of Mr. Jefferson's pride to run before the times in which he lived. Prudent himself, he did not waste his resources in gratifications to which they were incom-

---

5. At the end of this part of the history, some of the characters now described will be resumed to the time of their death—RANDOLPH'S NOTE. (This portion of the *History* was either lost or never completed.)

6. The best account of Thomas Jefferson's (1743–1826) career during the period covered by Randolph is to be found in Malone, *Jefferson the Virginian*.

7. William Small (d. 1775), a Scotsman by birth, taught at the College of William and Mary from 1758 until 1764, when he returned to England. He was the friend of such men as Joseph Priestley, James Watt, and Erasmus Darwin (Brooke Hindle, *The Pursuit of Science in Revolutionary America, 1735–1789* [Chapel Hill, N.C., 1956], pp. 91–92).

petent, but being an admirer of elegance and convenience, and venerated by his contemporaries who were within the scope of his example, he diffused a style of living much more refined that that which had been handed down to them by his and their ancestors. He had been ambitious to collect a library, not merely amassing *number* of books, but distinguishing authors of merit and assembling them in subordination to every art and science; and notwithstanding losses by fire, this library was at this time more happily calculated than any other private one to direct to objects of utility and taste, to present to genius the scaffolding upon which its future eminence might be built, and to reprove the restless appetite, which is too apt to seize the mere gatherer of books.

The theories of human rights he had drawn from Locke, Harrington, Sidney, English history, and Montesquieu he had maturely investigated in all their aspects, and was versed in the republican doctrines and effusions which conducted the first Charles to the scaffold.[8] With this fund of knowledge, he was ripe for stronger measures than the public voice was conceived to demand. But he had not gained a sufficient ascendancy to quicken or retard the progress of the popular current.

Indefatigable and methodical in whatever he undertook, he spoke with ease, perspicuity, and elegance. His style in writing was more impassioned, and although often incorrect, was too glowing not to be acquitted as venial to departures from rigid rules. Without being an overwhelming orator, he was an impressive speaker, who fixed the attention. On two signal arguments before the General Court, in which Mr. Henry and himself were coadjutors, each characterized himself—

8. Jefferson placed John Locke (1632–1704) alongside Sir Isaac Newton and Sir Francis Bacon in his trinity of immortals (Malone, *Jefferson the Virginian*, p. 101). Algernon Sidney (1622–83), famous as a republican writer, became a whig martyr when he used his trial and speech of Dec. 7, 1683, on the scaffold awaiting execution to proclaim publicly his belief in the legality of armed resistance to tyranny. His *Discourses concerning Government* (1689) became a textbook of revolution in America. An estimate of Sidney's popularity in America can be found in Caroline Robbins, *The Eighteenth-Century Commonwealthmen* (Cambridge, Mass., 1959), p. 45. James Harrington (1611–77), political theorist and author of *The Commonwealth of Oceana* (1656), was referred to by the patriots with the same respect as they had for Sidney, if with less understanding (Bernard Bailyn, *The Ideological Origins of the American Revolution* [Cambridge, Mass., 1967], p. 34). Richard Hooker (1554?–1600), theologian, is best known for his *Lawes of Ecclesiasticall Politie* (1593), in which he argued that human conduct was to be guided by "all the sources of light and truth which man finds himself encompassed" and that the universe is governed by natural law which was not expounded in the Scriptures but can be ascertained by man's reason. For Jefferson's reading of English history, see H. Trevor Colbourn, *The Lamp of Experience: Whig History and the Intellectual Origins of the American Revolution* (Chapel Hill, N.C., 1965), pp. 158–84.

Mr. Jefferson drew copiously from the depths of the law, Mr. Henry from the recesses of the human heart.

When Mr. Jefferson first attracted notice, Christianity was directly denied in Virginia only by a few. He was adept, however, in the ensnaring subtleties of deism and gave it, among the rising generation, a philosophical patronage, which repudiates as falsehoods things unsusceptible of strict demonstration. It is believed that while such tenets as are in contempt of the Gospel inevitably terminate in espousing the fullest latitude in religious freedom, Mr. Jefferson's love of liberty would itself have produced the same effects. But his opinions against restraints on conscience ingratiated him with the enemies of the establishment, who did not stop to inquire how far those opinions might border on skepticism or infidelity. Parties in religion and politics rarely scan with nicety the peculiar private opinions of their adherents.

When he entered upon the practice of the law, he chose a residence, and traveled to a distance, which enabled him to display his great literary endowments and to establish advantageous connections among those classes of men who were daily rising in weight.

In official rank and ostensible importance, Peyton Randolph stood foremost in the band of patriots.[9] He held a post of the highest popular celebrity under the royal dominion, being speaker of the House of Burgesses. But his diffidence prevented him from affecting any personal preeminence over those who were hailed for their bustling activity. He enjoyed without intrigue that portion of general esteem to which he thought himself entitled (and more he did not wish). What he did enjoy was permanent. He had in early life been chosen into that branch of the legislature for the College of William and Mary and was afterwards the constant member for the city of Williamsburg, the place of his nativity. Although a servant of the crown as attorney general, he was so firmly planted in the affections of his countrymen that the General Assembly deputed him to defend them before the king in Council against the arbitrary exaction of a pistole as a fee for every patent for land granted by Governor Dinwiddie. We have seen with what manly fidelity he executed this mission, with what asperity he was treated by that governor, how his office under the crown was wrested from him and reluctantly restored under the impulse of public feelings.

When France was circumvesting our western frontier, he, in the crudeness of military skill, engaged a company of men of opulence and

9. For Peyton Randolph, see p. 161 above.

ease in a warlike expedition, patriotic in its cause and useful in its example, but ineffectual in its result. On the great American question he halted not for a moment, although it was intimated to him that the governor would exercise his prerogative in refusing to receive him as speaker when he should be presented to him according to ancient usage. At this time a rejection of this sort might have been a painful diminution of his annual income. Every measure deemed conducive to American success he advocated with zeal. His uniformity added force to the soundness of his character; and the amiableness of his demeanor with the steadiness of his friendship recommended the suggestions of his judgment, however little illuminated by eloquence.

In the quarter of Virginia included in the proprietorship of the Northern Neck, Richard Henry Lee had gained the palm of a species of oratory rare among a people backward in refinement.[10] He had attuned his voice with so much care that one unmusical cadence could scarcely be pardoned by his ear. He was reported to have formed before a mirror his gesture, which was not unsuitable even to a court. His speech was diffusive, without the hackneyed formulas, and he charmed wheresoever he opened his lips. In political reading he was conversant, and on the popular topics dispersed through the debates of Parliament, his recollection was rapid and correct. Malice had hastily involved him in censure for a supposed inconsistency of conduct upon the Stamp Act; but the vigor and perseverance of his patriotism extorted from his enemies a confession that he deserved the general confidence which was afterwards conceded to him.

The then treasurer of Virginia was Robert Carter Nicholas, whose popularity, though less effulgent, gave light and heat to the American cause.[11] He was bred in the bosom of piety, and his youthful reading impressed upon his mind a predilection for the Established Church, though he selected the law as his profession. The propriety and purity of his life were often quoted, to stimulate the old and to invite the young to emulation, and in an avocation thickly beset with seductions, he knew them only as he repelled them with the quickness of instinct. In speaking of him, I should distrust the warping of personal affection,

10. Richard Henry Lee (1732–94) served as a burgess, member of the Committee of Correspondence and the Convention of 1775, and delegate to the Continental Congress (Burton J. Hedrick, *The Lees of Virginia: Biography of a Family* [Boston, 1935]).

11. Robert Carter Nicholas (1728–1780), besides being a burgess and the treasurer, was a member of the Virginia Revolutionary Convention and the House of Delegates, 1777–79, and judge of the Court of Chancery and the Court of Appeals (Thomas P. Abernethy, "Robert Carter Nicholas," *DAB*).

if all Virginia were not in some measure my witness; and I should unwillingly incur the supposition of a tacit insinuation against the bar in general by laying so great stress on *his* virtue, were it not that in the hour of temptation the best men find a refuge and succor in asking themselves how some individual spotless in morality and sincere in Christianity would act on a similar occasion. By nature, he was of a complacent temper; in all his actions he was benevolent and liberal. But he appeared to many who did not thoroughly understand him to be haughty and austere, because they could not appreciate the preference of gravity to levity, when in conversation the sacredness of religion was involved in ridicule or language forgot its chastity. When upon the death of Mr. John Robinson, who had been speaker of the House of Burgesses and the treasurer of Virginia, it was intimated to Mr. Nicholas that the governor was about to consign the care of the public money to a person not unexceptionable merely because no successor better qualified could be procured, that magistrate was confounded by the unusual address, but wholesome lecture, which Mr. Nicholas delivered to him: "I am told, sir, that the treasury is likely to be conferred on a man in whose hands it would not be safe, and that the reason assigned for such an appointment is that an adequate candidate is not within your knowledge. Of myself I shall say no more than that if you deem me equal to the public expectation, I will abandon my profession, superior as it is in emolument." The dignity of truth and virtue subdued with awe the royal vicegerent. For many years the official accounts of Mr. Nicholas had been scrutinized without the detection or existence of the most minute deficiency.

He was slow in the adoption of expedients, howsoever dazzling with their novelty, or forced into an undue magnitude by the arts of enthusiasm. But he lingered not behind the most strenuous in proposing and pushing measures commensurate with the times.

Edmund Pendleton held a high station as counsel, refuting by his success every symptom of aristocratic depression, even in the sons of a cottage where virtue and talents concur.[12] At the bar, his influence was justly great. In the legislature, he for many years had assisted with his habits of business every burgess who was a stranger to parliamentary forms or unacquainted with debate. With a pen which scat-

12. Edmund Pendleton (1721–1803), a burgess, one of the organizers of the Committee of Correspondence, and a member of the Conventions of 1775 and 1776, drafted the Virginia Constitution of 1776 and served in the Continental Congress (Mays, *Edmund Pendleton*).

tered no classical decorations and with an education which debarred him from thorough grammatical accuracy, he performed the most substantial service by the perspicuity and comprehensiveness of his numerous resolutions, reports, and laws. Labor was his delight, although vivacity and pleasantry were never suppressed in their due place. His amiableness bordered on familiarity without detracting from personal dignity. He lived at home with the unadulterated simplicity of a republican; from abroad he imported into his family no fondness for show. He was not rich because from his own purse he had reared into respectability a body of collateral relations, without much regard to the admonitions of a narrow revenue.

If in his public conduct he was ever questionable, it was supposed to be in presenting no bounds to his gratitude for his primary patron, Mr. Robinson, the former speaker and treasurer, whose death, as we have seen, discovered a chasm in the public coffers. It is true that Mr. Pendleton's exertions sheltered his memory from much obloquy, but it is not less true that he was active and fortunate as one of his administrators in replacing the deficit.

Mr. Pendleton was master of the principles of opposition to the ministry, and his heart followed with warmth what his head thus suggested.

That George Washington has been postponed to this period of our patriotic catalogue is owing solely to the circumstance that at the beginning of the year 1774, to which these sketches of characters are as yet limited, some others were more prominent.[13] It could not have been then truly foretold that ever those germs of his solid worth, which afterwards overspread our land with illustrious fruit, would elevate him very far above many of the friends of the Revolution. But take him as he even then was.

From various causes the biography of Virginia must be mutilated or confused in its earliest lives at least, until public records succeeded to oral tradition. The unlettered state of our society in general at that beginning of the last century, the inaptitude of individuals for the observation of character, the feeble hold which is taken by the memory of transactions not striking, the imperfect talent of combination and inductions, the dispersion of the inhabitants of a new country, and ignorance of the names of those who could testify, and the advanced age at which any Virginian born as late as the year 1732 could prob-

13. For Washington, see Douglas S. Freeman, *George Washington, A Biography* (New York, 1948–57).

ably deserve a large page even in a colonial story deprive us of those prognostics which when referred to manhood almost create a rule for a kind of prophecy. Hence even Washington is a partial prey to the corrosion of time.

His youth had developed no flattering symptoms of what the world calls genius, but he had been conspicuous for firmness, for a judgment which discriminated the materials gathered by others of a quicker and more fertile invention, and for a prudence which no frivolousness had ever checkered. He possessed a fund of qualities which had no specific direction to any particular calling but were instruments for any crisis.

By nature, by his attention to agriculture, an exposure of himself in the chase, and his occupation of a surveyor of land, he was remarkably robust and athletic. It had been the lot of Washington, at the age of nineteen years, as the sequel of his history when resumed will show, to have been at the most vigorous era of his life the only man whose total fitness pointed him out for a mission which first introduced him to public notice. When France had made some progress in the completion of a scheme to surround the British colonies by a line of posts from the lakes to the river Ohio, the governor of Virginia had resolved to remonstrate against the encroachments and to demand the removal of them. The very journey through a wilderness without a track opened by civilized man and infested by Indians not friendly to the English was truly formidable from its dangers and fatigues. But the grandeur of the enterprise animated Washington to commence it on the very day of receiving his commission and instructions. Among the lovers of ease and those who in the lap of luxury regarded the territory as doomed to a perpetual savage rudeness, Washington was mentioned as an adventurer, meritorious indeed, but below competition or envy. In the hands of Washington the expedition did not droop; in the hands of any other it would probably have perished. With what applause he fulfilled his errand of defiance is recorded by his country; and in the journal which, on short notice, he composed, and the publication of which his modesty induced him to desire to be withheld, he evidenced a perspicuity and skill in composition which diffused a reverence for his powers of varied utility.[14] It was impossible to peruse

14. Washington's journal of his mission to carry Governor Dinwiddie's warning to the French commandant at Fort Le Beouf, M. de St. Pierre, to leave the Ohio Valley was first published in Williamsburg by William Hunter in 1754 (reprinted as *The Journal of Major George Washington*, ed. James R. Short and Thaddeus W. Tate, Jr. [Charlottesville, Va., 1963]).

it without emotions like these: the quickness of his movements; the patience with which he encountered the inclemencies of the weather; the military acuteness with which he surveyed the lands in the fork of the Monongahela and Ohio, where Pittsburgh has been since erected, and compared that site with Logstown; his accuracy in the computation of distances; his success in the acquirement of the intelligence to be procured; his management in obtaining secret interviews with the half king [15] and extracting from him all that he knew; his discernment in ascertaining when to yield and when to resist importunities; his escape from French snares; his treasuring up the imprudent discoveries made by the French officers; his conciliation of respect from those who were hostile to his business; his observance of all attention toward even savage princes, whose favor might be beneficial to his country; and the anxiety, which pervaded his whole journey, to do his duty in everything. All these traits when brought together gave reason for the anticipation that no trial could exhaust such a fund of qualities, but that they would supply every call.

Being a member of the House of Burgesses after his return from the Ohio, the speaker was charged to express to him the thanks of that body. That officer by the august solemnity of his manners would probably have embarrassed most men in their attempt to reply to the compliments with which he covered Mr. Washington, for while they soothed, they awed him. When the address from the chair was concluded, he could not articulate without difficulty. This being perceived by Mr. Robinson, he did honor to himself, and relieved Mr. Washington, by crying out at the instant, "Sit down, Mr. Washington. Your modesty is equal to your merit, in the description of which words must fall short." [16]

Of a regiment raised for the defense of the frontiers, the command had been given to a Mr. Fry,[17] and Mr. Washington had been ap-

15. Since Washington had been instructed to confer with the Indian chiefs on the Ohio he traveled to Logstown by way of the fork of the Ohio River. There he added Chief Half King and three other Indians to his party. The title "half king" stems from the fact that the chief was subordinate to the chiefs of the Six Nations in New York.

16. An account of this incident can be found in Mason Locke Weems, *The Life of Washington*, ed. Marcus Cunliffe (Cambridge, Mass., 1962), p. 32. Originally published as an eighty-page pamphlet entitled *The Life and Memorable Actions of George Washington* (1800), Weems's work quickly attained immense popularity and has unquestionably become the most influential book in the history of American folklore. In 1806 a so-called fifth edition was published which contained for the first time the tale of George Washington and the cherry tree.

17. For Joshua Fry, see p. 163 above.

pointed lieutenant colonel. Upon the death of Fry, Mr. Washington succeeded to the command and was unfortunate at the Great Meadows, but it is remarkable that in no adversity had his honor as a soldier or a man been ever stained.

He was himself a pattern of subordination, for when orders of the most preposterous and destructive nature were given to him, he remonstrated indeed, but began to execute them as far as it was in his power.

A new arrangement of rank, which humiliated the provincial officers of the highest grade to the command of the lowest commissioned officer of the crown, rendered his continuance in the regiment too harsh to be endured. He retired to Mount Vernon, which his brother by the paternal side, passing by his own full blood, had bequeathed to him.[18] His economy, without which virtue itself is always in hazard, afforded nutriment to his character.

But he did not long indulge himself in the occupation of his farm. General Braddock, who had been sent by the duke of Cumberland, the commander in chief, to head the forces employed against the Indians and French, invited him into his family as a volunteer aide-de-camp. The fate of that brave but rash general, who had been taught a system unpliant to all reasoning which could accommodate itself to local circumstances and exceptions, might have been averted, if Washington's advice had been received. As it was, he in his debilitated state could accomplish nothing more than by his valor and to lead from the field of slaughter into security the remains of the British army.

Washington now was no longer forbidden by any rule of honor to accept the command of a new regiment raised by Virginia. In his intercourse with Braddock and his first and second military officers, he continued to add to the inferences from the whole of the former conduct instances of vigilance, courage, comprehensiveness of purpose, and delicacy of feeling, and in the enthusiastic language of a Presbyterian minister,[19] he was announced as a hero born to be the future savior of his country.

It was the custom of the king to enroll in the Council of State in Virginia men with fortunes, which classed them in the aristocracy of

18. Washington inherited Mount Vernon when the widow of his elder half-brother Lawrence died in 1761.
19. Randolph probably meant Weems, an Episcopalian, not a Presbyterian, minister.

the colony. The proprietor of the Northern Neck, Lord Fairfax,[20] had been importunate for the promotion of Colonel Washington to a seat at that board, and he would have been gratified long before if four of his tenants and one of his own name had not been already in the same corps. That this honor awaited him, Colonel Washington well knew, but the probability that the event was not far distant could not abate his sympathy with his country's wrongs, and he promptly associated his name with every patriotic stress and idea.

Richard Bland, who was a general scholar, was noted as an antiquary in colonial learning.[21] He had enlightened the people by a pamphlet overflowing with historical facts, which reinforced the opposition to the ministry.[22] He attacked with boldness every assumption of power and had combated every ancient usage of the secretary of Virginia to appoint the clerks of the county courts. This was an earnest of his sincerity in his present career.

Another favorite of the day was Benjamin Harrison.[23] With strong sense and a temper not disposed to compromise with ministerial power, he scrupled not to utter any [un]truth. During a long service in the House of Burgesses, his frankness, though sometimes tinctured with bitterness, was the source of considerable attachment.

George Wythe is said to have been indebted to his mother for the literary distinction which he attained.[24] But it is more probable that she was by chance capable of assisting him in the rudiments of the Latin tongue, and that he became a scholar by the indispensable progress of his own industry in his closet. Preceptors lay the cornerstone; but the edifice can be finished only by the pupil himself, under the auspices of good taste. Mr. Wythe not only labored through an apprenticeship but almost through a life in the dead languages. In his

20. Thomas Lord Fairfax (1691–1781) was heir to the Northern Neck of Virginia through his mother Catherine, the only daughter and heiress of Thomas Lord Culpeper (Stuart E. Brown, Jr., *Virginia Baron: the Story of Thomas Sixth Lord Fairfax* [Berryville, Va., 1965]).

21. Richard Bland (1710–76), a burgess for thirty-three years, was a member of the Virginia Conventions of 1775 and 1776, the Committee of Correspondence, and Continental Congress in 1774 and 1775. See Clinton Rossiter, "Richard Bland: The Whig in America," *Wm. and Mary Qtly.*, 3d ser., X (1953), 33–79.

22. *An Enquiry into the Rights of the British Colonies* (1776). For a modern edition, see Earl G. Swem, ed., *An Enquiry* (Richmond, 1922), which includes some introductory remarks on Bland.

23. Benjamin Harrison (1726?–91), prominent in the Revolutionary struggle, succeeded Thomas Nelson as governor of Virginia on Nov. 30, 1781, a post he held until Nov. 1784 (Edmund C. Burnett, "Benjamin Harrison," *DAB*).

24. For George Wythe, see p. 162 above.

pleadings at the bar, it was a foible to intersperse such frequent cita-
tions from the classics. But he argued ably and profoundly. The temptations of the law never raised a doubt on his purity, and though long
habituated to the patronage and friendship of royal governors, in every
conflict with them he adhered to his country. He acted upon the maxim
that genuine riches consisted in having few wants. A natural instability
he held with a tight rein. On an alarm of hostility from the last
British governor, he sallied forth with his hunting shirt and musket,
at an age when his patriotism would have sustained no shock had he
remained at home. But his character, rather than his actions, rendered
him a valuable resource to the infant Revolution. Upon the death of
Peyton Randolph he was called, as the most beloved citizen, to represent the city of Williamsburg.

John Blair was born of Scotch parents, educated in Great Britain,
connected in Scotland by marriage, and chief adviser of his father, who
as president of the royal Council had been thrice temporary governor.[25]
He was himself the clerk of that Council, under the gift of the governor
during pleasure. If the habits of monarchy could have disqualified him
for the part of a republican, he must have been alienated from the
cause of democracy. But without parade he was steadfast and alert in
it. He lived without suspicion, in those precarious days, of having betrayed a syllable of what passed at the Council board. On the other
hand he vindicated the rights of man, not with declamation or in a
visionary sense, but in one coinciding with practical happiness. His
suavity of manners, which is often a veil for hypocrisy, was with him an
affusion of nature. He was adept in classical learning, mathematics,
divinity, various branches of natural philosophy, belles lettres, and the
law. A discerning foreigner once observed of him that his only fault was
that he was such pure gold that a little alloy was necessary to the
finishing of him as a perfect practical man.

Thomas L. Lee, who had been tutored for no department of public
speaking, was by accident banished from the lists of the softer oratory.[26]

25. John Blair (1687–1771), nephew of James Blair, the founder of the College of
William and Mary, had been a burgess for Williamsburg, member of the Council, 1743–71,
and as Council president, acting governor, Jan.–June 1758 and March–Oct. 1768 (Earl G.
Swem, "John Blair," *DAB*).

26. Thomas Ludwell Lee (1730–78), brother of Richard Henry, William, and Arthur Lee,
a lawyer and judge, represented Stafford County in the House of Burgesses and in the
Conventions of 1775 and 1776. He served on the committee which drew up the Virginia
bill of rights and the plan for an independent state and was one of the five men appointed
in 1777 to revise the state constitution (Hedrick, *Lees of Virginia*).

A friend of his was assailed in the House of Burgesses, and he rose in his defense; but Lee's sensibility checked his utterance and extinguished his courage ever again to rise on any other occasion than to be counted. But when the formality of a public body did not agitate him, he was a real orator. He enraptured with his grace every private society. In the subordinate committees he struck the point with a promptness which excited a wonder how he could ever be destitute of confidence in himself. By fair reasoning out of the house, he satisfied political skeptics and fortified the wavering.

Among the numbers who in their small circles were propagating with activity the American doctrines was George Mason in the shade of retirement.[27] He extended their grasp upon the opinions and affections of those with whom he conversed. How he learned his indifference for distinction, endowed as he was with ability to mount in any line, or whence he contracted his hatred for pomp, with a fortune competent to any expense and a disposition not averse from hospitality, can be solved only from that philosophical spirit which despised the adulterated means of cultivating happiness. He was behind none of the sons of Virginia in knowledge of her history and interest. At a glance he saw to the bottom of every proposition which affected her. His elocution was manly sometimes, but not wantonly sarcastic.

About this time Charles Lee was greatly admired in Virginia.[28] He was an officer in the British army, having brought with him a reputation for literature and arms. His disgust with the British government, which had pretermitted him in promotion, had given birth to various productions from his pen, much to the annoyance of the ministry. When he came hither, this crime of neglect had not been expiated, and he arraigned the radical vices of the English constitution, the exercise of its power, and the jeopardy of colonial liberty. Without any restraint from controversial replies, he satiated his revenge in a new and more fatal shape. With the rough exterior of a veteran soldier, he was domesticated in most of the principal families, whom wit and pith of remark could entertain. Eccentric and anomalous, he was agreeable

27. George Mason (1725–92), a Tidewater gentleman, had drafted the "Virginia Resolves" of May 1769, and as a member of the May 1776 Convention he helped frame the Virginia bill of rights and constitution (Robert A. Rutland, *George Mason, Reluctant Statesman* [Williamsburg, Va., 1961]).

28. Gen. Charles Lee (1731–82), a veteran British-born officer who had served in America and in Portugal during the Seven Years War, returned to America in the fall of 1773 and gave his allegiance to the patriot cause (John R. Alden, *General Charles Lee: Traitor or Patriot?* [Baton Rouge, La., 1951], pp. 62–65).

everywhere. He well played the part of a republican, though born under a monarchy and educated in an army. And without a particle of religion, he simulated an attachment to it. It was believed however that from a sternness of principle he would perform with fidelity every requisition of duty or promise in his profession, and that his rancor against the ministry was unextinguishable.

It has been stated that Mr. John Mercer was the first in Virginia who distinctly elucidated upon paper the principles which justified the opposition to the Stamp Act.[29] He showed them in manuscript to his friends. They spread rapidly so as to produce a groundwork for and uniformity of popular sentiment.

This selection of characters does not exhaust that store of faculties which contributed their proportion to the impending scenes. From these it may be calculated how deeply rooted in Virginia must have been the American cause. Of some others who lived to enforce and adorn the Revolution, a sketch may be exhibited in a future page.

Many circumstances existed favorable to the propagating of a contagion of free opinion, although every class of men cannot be supposed to have been aided by extensive literary views: 1. The system of slavery, howsoever baneful to virtue, begat a pride which nourished a quick and acute sense of the rights of freemen. 2. Whether there was any peculiar facility in the mutual intercourse of the people or a greater frequency of occasion for numerous public assemblies, the Virginians seemed to catch the full spirit of the theories which at the fountainhead were known only to men of studious retirement. 3. The hospitality and even convivial circles, which were the natural offspring of living, perhaps a certain fluency of speech, which marked the character of Virginians, pushed into motion many adventurous doctrines,

29. John Mercer (1704–68), born in Dublin, Ireland, and educated at Trinity College, was a prominent Stafford County attorney, an active businessman, a member of the Ohio Company speculating in western lands, and the author of *An Extract Abridgement of All the Public Acts of Virginia* (Williamsburg, Va., 1737) and its *Continuation* (1739). Richard Beale Davis regards Mercer as one of several possible candidates for authorship of a group of poems, prose glossaries, and quasi-dialectical letters referred to as the "Dinwiddinae," written between 1754 and 1757. These writings presented views diametrically opposed to those of Lieutenant Governor Robert Dinwiddie and, among other things, discussed the question of taxation ("The Colonial Virginia Satirist: Mid-Eighteenth-Century Commentaries on Politics, Religion, and Society," American Philosophical Society, *Transactions*, new ser., LVII, pt. 1 [March 1967], 8–17). Randolph's remarks would seem to strengthen the case for Mercer. Descriptions and characterizations of most of the men discussed in these pages can be found in Hugh Blair Grigsby, *The Virginia Convention of 1776* (Richmond, 1855), and *History of the Virginia Federal Convention of 1788* (Richmond, 1890–91).

which in a different situation of affairs might have lain dormant much longer and might have been limited to a much narrowed sphere. 4. Nor ought it to be forgotten that even if the fancied division into something like ranks, not actually coalescing with each other, had been really formed, the opinions of every denomination or cast would have diffused themselves on every side by means of the professions of priest, lawyer, and physician, who visited the houses of the ostentatious as well as the cottages of the planters. 5. The season too for counting the possessors of the right of suffrage often returned and of course afforded opportunities for unreserved interchange of ideas between candidates and electors and among electors themselves.

6. Obvious as it was that the dissenters, as they were called, could be animated with a zeal inferior to that of no partisan of general liberty, it was yet impracticable for the mother country or the colony to incorporate religion into the controversy, further than as public fasting and prayer might always in the hands of the latter make an impression against power, branded with the charge of oppression, and as the Church of England might have been assured that the Established Church as such could not hope in a revolution for a better boon than to retain the *status quo* of ancient privilege. If the church and the dissenters could have been brought to such an issue that the Establishment was in danger, the band of union might not have been totally free from fracture. But the two sects were contrasted by some striking circumstances. The Presbyterian clergy were indefatigable. Not depending upon the dead letter of written sermons they understood the mechanism of haranguing and had often been whetted in disputes on religious liberty so nearly allied to civil.

Those of the Church of England were planted on glebes, with comfortable houses, decent salaries, some perquisites, and a species of rank which was not wholly destitute of unction. To him who acquitted himself of parochial functions, those comforts were secure, whether he ever converted a deist or softened the pangs of a sinner. He never asked himself whether he was felt by his audience. To this charge of lukewarmness there were some shining exceptions, and there were even a few who did not hesitate to confront the consequences of a revolution which boded no stability to them. The dissenters, on the other hand, were fed and clothed only as they merited the gratitude of their congregations. A change or modification of the ancient regime carried no terrors to their imagination.

Notwithstanding these advantages of solid character and religious votaries on the side of the people, although in so favorable a soil the spirit of freedom was not obstructed by a weed, which their frown did not eradicate, and every thwarting movement of government heaped fresh odium on its head, the British partisans administered some cautions, which put to the test the principles then inflaming the colony. Her feelings were wounded by an insinuation that a revolution was coveted only by those whose desperate fortunes might be disencumbered by an abolition of debts.[30] But this was contradicted by a loyalty without being immovable and by the certainty of a general pecuniary ability which could not be by a delay of collection for the risk of an untried order of things.

It was, however, clearly foreseen that sooner or later the sword of America must be drawn, even to obtain a reconciliation not destructive in its sacrifices; but it could not without difficulty be conceived how subjects could repel their sovereigns in war and yet restrict their triumphs to the literal restoration of their ancient relations.

Deprived too of an intercourse with England, the chief market for her supplies and for the sale of her raw materials and the sole nursery of her credit; with a dearth of manufactures, occasioned by British prohibitions and regulations; relying on British bottoms for her navigation; estranged from the thought of a compact with foreign nations, as a substitute for the inevitable stoppage of commerce with Great Britain; without military stores; without discipline in the militia, to whom no war was known, except that waged with the savages in the woods, and even that confined to the western frontier; without a man who had inspired an absolute confidence in him as a military leader upon a large or scientific scale; with a conviction that the merciless tomahawk would be uplifted against her; and with the anticipation that a more dangerous, because a domestic, enemy might butcher their masters and their families, instigated by promises of emancipation— Virginia, had she been languid or fluctuating, could not have been unmoved by the menaces of a government then extolled as the most formidable in Europe. But from her nerve, which contemned consequences, she was ready to launch into an ocean unexplored, provided with no chart of actual experience and resting upon general maxims

---

30. This reference is to the large indebtedness of most Virginia planters to English and Scottish merchants (see Emory G. Evans, "Planter Indebtedness and the Coming of the Revolution in Virginia," *Wm. and Mary Qtly.*, 3d ser., XIX [1962], 511–33).

of liberty. Her latest partiality for Great Britain did not exaggerate as too grievous the price of liberty nor spread a gloom too thick to be dissipated by men resolved to be free.

These obstacles being overcome, others from the patronage or personal weight of the chief executive magistrate were insignificant.

It has been stated that the governor at this time was John, earl of Dunmore, a native and peer of Scotland, who once sat in the British House of Lords.[31] Among the manifold errors of the British government in their policy toward Virginia was that of not discerning that soon without a cessation or relaxation of their principles, a degree of complacency, at least, might have effected much on the public mind by the choice of such a governor as Botetourt had been, in suavity and frankness of manner, in exemplary virtue, and a warm patronage of learning and religion. But Dunmore, generally preferring the crooked path, possessed not the genius to conceive, nor the temper to seek, the plain and direct way which nature opens to the human heart through those cheap courtesies which were in the power of the vicegerent, the fountain of honors to be bestowed. On his translation from the government of New York to that of Virginia, he was accompanied by Edward Foy, as his confidential inmate, counselor, and private secretary. This gentleman exacted for his civil talents the homage due to his military merit as a captain of artillery at the battle of Minden in Germany. The consequence was that the imperviousness of the army officer was added to the arrogance of a pedant and cynic.

The only two offices of value to which Dunmore could permanently appoint were the clerkships of the Council and of the House of Burgesses. In the appointment to every other of moment, he was controllable by the advice of the Council or was the mere organ of recommendation to the pleasure of his royal master. For the clergy of the Church of England, he had no other allurement than the employment of his interest with the bishop of London (to whose diocese Virginia belonged), for a single commissaryship with an annual salary of £100 sterling, a vacancy occurring not much oftener than once in the usual term of life and generally conferred on some minister whose mind, activity, and persuasiveness were small, while his affectation of dignity was everything.[32]

31. John Murray, earl of Dunmore, (1732–1809), assumed the governorship of Virginia in 1771. He had received many honors, but the spirited Virginians resented his haughty airs (Malone, *Jefferson the Virginian*, p. 169).

32. The need for some kind of ecclesiastical supervision over the churches in the colonies had induced Henry Compton, bishop of London from 1675 to 1713, to establish

Dunmore flattered himself that the devotion of the people to the mother country would supply the defect of patronage, but he forgot that a high sense of personal independence was universal. A governor who could withstand a popular current must possess more than ordinary qualifications. But of those which shed a beam of false luster, and certainly of those of an exalted kind, Dunmore was wholly destitute. In stature he was low, and though muscular and healthful he bore on his head hoary symptoms of probably a greater age than he had reached. To external accomplishment he pretended not, and his manners and sentiments did not surpass substantial barbarism, a barbarism which was not palliated by a particle of native genius nor regulated by one ingredient of religion. His propensities were coarse and depraved.

But it must be confessed that probably no British vicegerent, not Botetourt himself, had he been on earth, could have gained ten revolters from their country's cause.

End of the Introduction

---

representatives in some of the colonies. Since Virginia was not part of any diocese, Compton could not send over an archdeacon or suffragan bishop. He therefore sent over a commissary to represent him, the first being James Blair, later founder and first president of the College of William and Mary. For a full discussion, see Arthur Lyon Cross, *The American Episcopate and the American Colonies* (Cambridge, Mass., 1902), pp. 25–51.

Chapter VI   The History of the Revolution

 The facts which at the beginning of this year were preying upon the recollection and patience of the thinking part of the colony were principally these: that their submission to the mutilation of their rights under the charter of 1609,[1] by grants of land from the king to Lord Baltimore,[2] the Culpeper family, and other favorites; the victories which the avarice of some of the royal governors in a summary mode of extorting money had gained from the approbation of the crown; [3] and the parliamentary declaration of a right to bind the colonies in all cases whatsoever were swelling into a gigantic mass of precedent, which at a future day might be turned to the destruction of their liberties. The duty also on tea, too paltry to justify incurring the hazard of general discontent, bespoke a raging appetite for colonial revenue.[4] Every day intelligence arrived from England of authorized contempts of American prowess and courage and of a callousness to American remonstrances. The British officers on board of the vessels stationed on our coast echoed the insulting expressions which had been imported and drew from the people a countervehemence, which amounted to a pledge against yielding or shrinking. Aspersions on a nation are not divided, as responsibility is, among a multitude of individuals, each assuming to himself only his fraction, but rather resemble in their effect the ancient mode of battle, in which every man made the common cause his own peculiar case. Virginia read with composure the denunciations against the colonies, acquired hourly a more precise and determined sense of colonial rights, and wafted incense across the Atlantic to that phalanx of orators in

1. For the charter of 1609 and its consequences, see pp. 32–35 above.

2. The grant establishing the colony of Maryland on the upper reaches of the Chesapeake was issued on June 30, 1632. On p. 154 above Randolph refers to the establishment of Maryland as one of the sources of frustration that led to Bacon's Rebellion, especially since it was a colony of Roman Catholics.

3. One such instance of "extorting money," according to Randolph, was the pistole fee. See above, pp. 161–63.

4. When the other Townshend duties were repealed in 1770 the tax on tea was retained.

Parliament, who, besides our gratitude and adoration, had some reward in using the complaints of America as banners under which they attacked the ministry. The veil of sanctity had been roughly torn from the king and his most conspicuous servants, and the corruption of Parliament had been probed by the letters of Junius, whose concealment seemed to be a lucky refuge from an impotent prosecution of those who by office were bound to seem to labor for a discovery of their author.[5]

In times of general sensibility, almost every public event is tortured into an affinity with the predominant passions. The law which established the fees of the ministerial officers attending the courts and the costs of litigation had been originally temporary and constantly renewed before the day limited for its expiration.[6] But from the dissolution of the General Assembly, the usual opportunity of prolonging it beyond the stated termination of its existence had passed away, and a suspension which from this cause took place in the proceedings of the courts on April 12, 1774, proclaimed a derangement in the machine of government which was immediately converted into the misrule of the king. But notwithstanding this relaxation of law, order was maintained, and licentiousness discouraged by general morality. Independent companies had separated themselves from the militia at large, were clothed in uniforms, and yet professed obedience to the militia laws. George Washington had accepted the command of many of them.[7] The old who had seen service in the Indian war of 1755 roused the young to resist the ministry; and the sons, who had committed themselves by strong military declarations, reacted on their fathers with new opinions, new demands, and new prospects; and yet this military ardor thus unrestrained interfered not with a forbearance toward those who repined at the loss of the government of England. It left the point to

---

5. Junius was the pen name of an unknown English political satirist who had defended the cause of John Wilkes and attacked such important personages as Grafton, Bedford, and George III. Widely quoted in America, Junius's most notable series appeared in the *London Public Advertiser* from Jan. 1769 to Jan. 1772. For a modern edition, see C. W. Everett, ed., *The Letters of Junius* (London, 1927).

6. On May 5, 1774, in response to the news of Parliament's passage of the Boston Port Act, the House of Burgesses resolved that a day of prayer and fasting be set aside for June 1, the day the act was to go into force (*Burgesses, Journals, 1773–1776*, p. 124). Two days later Governor Dunmore dissolved the Assembly (Charles R. Lingley, *The Transition in Virginia from Colony to Commonwealth* [New York, 1910], p. 65).

7. Several counties raised companies during the fall of 1774, and by the summer of 1775 at least thirty volunteer companies had been organized. Prince William County had asked Washington to be their commander (Lingley, *Transition*, pp. 106–7).

which the general temper was insensibly advancing, the severance of
the colonies from the parent state, as an evil which either need not be
apprehended or might be arrested at any moment. It caused the people
to overlook the train of combustible materials which were at hand and
which a single spark might at any time kindle into an explosion.

In May, the General Assembly met, and in reply to a speech of
empty professions from the governor, they avowed their loyalty to the
king and their good will to Dunmore. They say "that the fatherly
attention of their most gracious sovereign to the *happiness* of his subjects, in making the good of his people the first object of his thoughts,
cannot but impress their minds with the liveliest sense of duty and
gratitude." They proceed thus: "It will ever afford us much pleasure
to observe an increase of your lordship's domestic felicity, and with the
greatest cordiality we embrace the first opportunity to congratulate
your lordship on the arrival of the amiable and most respectable Lady
Dunmore, with so many branches of your noble family, an event which
we consider as having brought with it the surest pledges of our mutual
happiness." [8] To aim at a reform of the mere etiquette of public language is perhaps little less than knight-errantry, but to infect with the
compliments of ordinary discourse the genuine dignity of a legislature
ill accords with that sincerity of principle upon which they then claimed
the merit of acting. They expected nothing good from Dunmore. They
had seen reason to fear much mischief from him.

This address was received by him as the harbinger of success to his
stratagems, and anxious to hold at his disposal a military force, he
worked a dispute of boundary between Virginia and Pennsylvania into
a topic of great irritation. In a message to the House of Burgesses, he
informs them that a considerable body of His Majesty's subjects had
settled in Virginia, contiguous to the western boundary of Pennsylvania; that he had appointed militia officers to defend them on any
emergency and magistrates to preserve order; that the governor of
Pennsylvania pretended a claim to that country; that he (Dunmore)
had taken steps to enforce the authority of Virginia in that district; and
that he submits to the house, as the governor of Pennsylvania meant
to obstruct by every possible means the government of this colony in
the disputed district, whether provisions be not necessary to render the
legal power of the officers and magistrates there effectual.[9]

---

8. For Governor Dunmore's speech and the Burgesses' reply, see *Burgesses, Journal,
1773–1776*, pp. 73–74, 77–78.

9. See *Burgesses, Journal, 1773–1776*, pp. 90–91. The boundary dispute with Pennsylvania,
involving the curious knob which, as part of West Virginia, still projects northward

On the day following the message, inflammatory letters from John Connolly, a man of intrigue and hardihood of enterprise, and devoted to Dunmore, were communicated by him to the house, as fuel to the fury projected against the province of Pennsylvania and as an alarm from Indian hostility.[10] Cautious as the house were, they could not wholly shun the snare spread for them. They were no less averse to the very semblance of submission to usurpation than to a precipitate quarrel with a sister colony. While therefore they express their regret at such a dissension, they declared it to be their duty to protect the people of Virginia from oppression, let it arise from what quarter it might, but that to inflict the punishment of imprisonment or death on the officers of either government on account of an unsettled line was to deviate from the plain and simple plan of accommodation observed in former contests of this nature. They then requested the governor to fix a temporary boundary line, until the king should act, and to exert his powers under the laws against invasions and insurrections, which they did not doubt would for the present be sufficient to repel the attacks of the Indians, who had perfidiously commenced hostilities.[11]

The prudence and calmness of these sentiments, and the reluctance to organize a corps of regular soldiers, were answered by an affected acquiescence, while Dunmore lamented the difference of opinion upon the inadequacy of the militia.

To charge him with a scheme for embroiling Virginia with Pennsylvania and thus to paralyze the energy of both in the threatened rupture with Great Britain might perhaps be unjust. The outrages from the governor of Pennsylvania [12] could not pass without animadversion, and he is protected from the fullness of censure by the assent of the House of Burgesses to the employment of *some* force.[13] But the unnecessarily appointed officers whose functions would clash with those of the officers of Pennsylvania, when in a few months an appeal to the

---

between Ohio and Pennsylvania and is called "the Panhandle," was not settled until 1779 (Jack M. Sosin, *The Revolutionary Frontier, 1763–1783* [New York, 1967], pp. 56–60).

10. John Connolly (*ca.* 1743–1813), born in Lancaster, Pa., had studied medicine and moved to Pittsburgh. Having been granted land by Virginia, and with an eye to making a fortune in speculation, he sided against his native province by becoming an agent of Governor Dunmore and playing an important part in instigating Dunmore's War (1774). During the Revolution he was a Loyalist and engineered a conspiracy to launch an invasion in the west with Loyalists and Indians.

11. See *Burgesses, Journal, 1773–1776*, p. 93.

12. John Penn (1729–95), the grandson of William Penn.

13. See *ibid.*, p. 97. The Assembly rejected Dunmore's appeal for troops to meet the Pennsylvanians and punish the Indians who were attacking outlying settlers.

king would have adjusted the controversy. It would therefore not be excessively harsh to suspect a man who labored to subjugate the colony and whose bitterness toward Virginia increased every day. The proclamations of Penn and Dunmore are strictly parallel in disregarding every consideration of peace, and notwithstanding the exasperation of these individuals regardless of the fatherly care chief magistrates should exercise over the people committed to their superintendence, the conduct of the Virginia Assembly on this occasion was a striking instance of the happiness springing from the wisdom of a legislature not divested by executive influence from pursuing its dictates and the interest of their constituents.

Amidst the agitations of the times, the Assembly were not unmindful of agriculture and were desirous of increasing the facilities of the farmer in a speedy preparation of his crops of wheat for market. That baneful weed tobacco, which had stained our country with all the pollutions and cruelties of slavery, had exhausted the fertility of our soil, had swallowed up in its large plantations vast territories, which if distributed into portions were best adapted to favor population, was yet the only commodity which could command money for the planter at a short notice and the only one from which the dexterity of the British merchant could extract such various emoluments and was therefore with him a choice subject of trade. But it had become obvious that the staff of life was entitled to legislative stimulus, and a reward of £100 was voted to John Hobday for the invention of a machine which pressed out the wheat with ribbed cylinders put into circular motion by horses.[14] In nothing was the tardiness of Virginia in improving machinery more visible than in the long dormant state of this important, though in its first stage certainly crude, combination of mechanical power. It might be too great a refinement to connect as cause and effect the cessation of that spirit which coveted tobacco as the greatest blessing of our state with the most promising effort which had been ever made in the legislature for a complete toleration of Protestant dissenters. Let it be some apology for Virginia that this indulgence had not in practice been long before conceded in England, and that for more than a century and a half the depositaries of public authority had revered the Church of England as the safeguard of tranquillity, which in the mother country had been once radically disturbed by the extravagances of her enemies. The history of the English Revolution in 1688 had not universally imparted its entire essence here, counter-

14. See *ibid.*, pp. 116–17; Hindle, *Science in Revolutionary America*, pp. 213–14.

acted as it was by the established clergy, most of whom delighted rather in the lethargy of fixed salaries than in the trouble of thought, learning, and research, which a vigorous dissenting minister, no longer depressed, might occasion. The law, however, which was on its passage, was defeated by the dissolution of the Assembly, in consequence of the fast now to be mentioned.[15]

The town of Boston in Massachusetts, being esteemed the focus of rebellion, was the peculiar victim of ministerial vengeance. A statute had been enacted annihilating her ports after June 1, 1774, abolishing her mart of foreign commerce, and stirring up the neighboring towns to share in her plunder, by the exclusive possession of privileges which Boston had enjoyed and which were now to be transferred to her rivals.[16] Men mad in the career of power seldom delay to consult the human heart. They overlook the sympathies which act upon nations sincerely sisters for general purposes and which cannot be torpid, although the distance of place and an exemption from instantaneous suffering may for a moment deceive with the expectation of at least an indifference on their part.

Mr. Jefferson, and Charles Lee, may be said to have originated a fast to electrify the people from the pulpit. Such is the constitution of things that an act of public devotion will receive no opposition from those who believe in its effect to appease offended heaven and is registered in the cabinet of the politician as an allowable trick of political warfare. Those gentlemen, knowing that Robert Carter Nicholas, the chairman of the committee of religion, was no less zealous than themselves against the attempt to starve thousands of the American people into a subservience to the ministry, easily persuaded him to put forth the strength of his character on an occasion which he thought to be

15. The position of the Established Church in Virginia would not have been seriously challenged but for the rise of the dissenting sects (Hamilton J. Eckenrode, *Separation of Church and State in Virginia* [Richmond, 1910], chap. 3). In 1772 the committee on religion of the Burgesses was ordered to draw up a bill to satisfy a petition by the Baptists for toleration, but the bill as drafted was never passed. The principal opposition came from the Baptists, who objected to a provision which prohibited meetings at the "night season" when their members could "be better spared from the necessary duties of their callings" (Meade, *Patrick Henry*, p. 250). The committee on religion was assigned to draw up a new bill, but their work was cut short when Governor Dunmore dissolved the Assembly. An act of toleration was finally enacted in June 1776 (see H. R. McIlwaine, *The Struggle of Protestant Dissenters for Religious Toleration in Virginia* [Baltimore, 1894]). Randolph discussed the law of 1776 on pp. 263–64 below.

16. The closing of the port of Boston by one of the so-called Coercive Acts of March and April 1774 was the ministry's angry response to the Boston Tea Party of Dec. 16, 1773, an event which Randolph curiously leaves unmentioned.

pious and to move for a fast to be observed on the first day of June, which few besides himself could so well delineate as a hopeful appeal to the deity and over which his reputation as a religionist spread popularity.[17]

The style in which the fast was recommended was too bold to be neglected by the governor as an effusion which would evaporate on paper. It was a cement among the colonies, unconnected as they were in situation and dissimilar as they were in manners, habits, ideas of religion, and government from the states abounding in slaves. It brought home to the bosom of each colony the apprehensions of every other; and if in the hour of reflection the ministry could have foreseen the approach of a closer union among the colonies, these resolutions might have been well interpreted into the seed of a revolution. The governor therefore resorted to his power of dissolving the Assembly, a power which hindered the circulation of offensive matter under the legislative seal but inoculated the whole colony with the poison against which it was directed.

The burgesses immediately after the dissolution assembled with Peyton Randolph at their head; made the cause of Boston their own; protested with indignation against the taxation of America in the British Parliament and the baseness of tampering with one section of the colony, to sever itself from the general sentiment for the sake of the sports of another. A congress of deputies from each province had been discussed in town meetings in New York and Boston and was now consigned to the committee of correspondence for execution. A convention was also voted to be held in the latter part of the summer.[18]

The fast was obeyed throughout Virginia with such rigor and scruples as to interdict the tasting of food between the rising and setting sun. With the remembrance of the king, horror was associated; and in churches as well as in the circles of social conversation, he seemed to stalk like the archenemy of mankind.

The counties and corporations elected with alacrity representatives, or delegates as they were called, to that Convention.[19] Their powers were to take under their consideration the present critical and alarming situation of the continent of North America. Thomas Jefferson, who was one of those elected, was prevented by indisposition from attend-

17. See *Burgesses, Journal, 1773–1776*, p. 124. Jefferson was the author of the resolution, but he wisely persuaded Robert Carter Nicholas, a man of great piety, to move the necessary resolution, which was promptly passed on May 24, 1774 (Mays, *Edmund Pendleton*, I, 270).
18. See *Burgesses, Journal, 1773–1776*, p. 138.
19. The convention which met at Williamsburg in August 1774.

ing. But he forwarded by express for the consideration of its members a series of resolutions.[20] I distinctly recollect the applause bestowed on the most of them when they were read to a large company at the house of Peyton Randolph, to whom they were addressed. Of all, the approbation was not equal. From the celebrated *Letters of the Pennsylvania Farmer* (John Dickinson) we had been instructed to bow to the external taxation of Parliament, as resulting from our migration and a necessary dependence on the mother country.[21] But this composition of Mr. Jefferson shook this conceded principle, although it had been confirmed by a still more celebrated pamphlet, written by Daniel Dulany of Maryland and cited by Lord Chatham as a textbook of American rights.[22] The young ascended with Mr. Jefferson to the source of those rights; the old required time for consideration before they could tread this lofty ground, which, if it had not been abandoned, at least had not been fully occupied throughout America. From what cause it happened that the resolutions were not printed by the order of the Convention does not appear, but as they were not adopted, several of the author's admirers subscribed to their publication.[23] When the

20. *A Summary View of the Rights of British America.* As resolutions they were never acted on officially, but they were printed in Williamsburg, Philadelphia, and England that same year. Jefferson did not supply the title, and his name did not appear on these publications (Malone, *Jefferson the Virginian*, p. 181).

21. John Dickinson (1732–1808), hailed as "the penman of the American Revolution," was the author of the widely acclaimed and influential *Letters from a Farmer in Pennsylvania to the Inhabitants of the British Colonies* (1767–68). For a discussion of Dickinson's views, see Colbourn, *Lamp of Experience*, pp. 107–19. Until the appearance of the Morgans' *Stamp Act Crisis*, the traditional view of the colonial response to the Stamp Act was that the colonists drew a distinction between internal and external taxation, conveniently shifting their position when confronted by the Townshend duties. The Morgans maintain that Dickinson, who drafted the resolutions of the Stamp Act Congress, used the *Letters* to answer English charges that the colonists were inconsistent because they had abandoned the distinction between internal and external taxation (*Stamp Act Crisis*, p. 154). Dickinson quoted the resolves and then pointed out that there in fact was "no distinction made between internal and external taxes." It is interesting to note that Randolph, an eyewitness to the Virginia Convention of 1774, believed such a distinction had indeed been made.

22. Daniel Dulany the younger (1722–97) of Maryland was the author of *Considerations on the Propriety of Imposing Taxes in the British Colonies, for the Purpose of Raising a Revenue, by Act of Parliament* (1765). Randolph's view that Dulany accepted external taxation probably resulted from the latter's distinction between taxation and legislation. The power to legislate, according to Dulany, meant that Parliament could regulate the commerce of the Empire.

23. According to Dumas Malone, the resolutions were not endorsed because "the intemperance of Jefferson's language would have made his resolutions unacceptable as the official statement of a responsible group desiring to accommodate a dispute, and he himself recognized that his paper was too strong for the Virginia Convention" (*Jefferson the Virginian*, p. 182).

time of writing is remembered, a range of inquiry not then very frequent, and marching far beyond the politics of the day, will surely be allowed to them. Mr. Jefferson was, however, disappointed in a seat at the first session of Congress. His presence at the Convention would probably have multiplied the suffrages in his favor, but the seven who were nominated to that new assembly had the advantage of being better known, of possessing more extensive connections, and of being older servants of the public. The successful candidates were Peyton Randolph, Richard Henry Lee, George Washington, Patrick Henry, Richard Bland, Benjamin Harrison, and Edmund Pendleton, in the order in which they are here named. Some of the tickets on the ballot assigned reasons for the choice expressed in them. These were that Randolph should preside in Congress, that Lee and Henry should display the different kinds of eloquence for which they were renowned, that Washington should command the army, if an army should be raised, that Bland should open the treasures of ancient colonial learning, that Harrison should utter plain truths, and that Pendleton should be the penman for business. Perhaps characters were never better discriminated.

In defining the objects of the Congress the Convention of Virginia did not soar so high as the electing bodies of some of the other states. Virginia kept out of sight a truth which time never fails to bring to light, that when subjects question a power asserted by a mother country their measures will be elevated in their progress further than was at first expected. Virginia instructed her deputies so to touch our commercial connection as to "procure redress for the most injured province of Massachusetts Bay, to secure British America from the ravage and ruin of arbitrary taxes, and speedily obtain that harmony and union so beneficial to the whole empire and so ardently desired by all British America." [24]

Until Congress should act, and their proceedings should be divulged, the people deemed it unadvisable to make any movement collectively; but the opposition to the ministry retained its fire. Vigilance was alone necessary in the meantime with respect to their enemies. After those proceedings were disclosed, an opportunity did not present itself for a revision of them in a convention, until that which met at Richmond in March 1775. But the mouths of all were filled with eulogiums on the patriotic, enlightened, and manly conduct of Congress.

24. See Peter Force, ed., *American Archives . . . A Documentary History of . . . the North American Colonies* (Washington, D.C., 1837–53), 4th ser., I, 689–90.

In the enthusiasm of the day, this body was supposed to be honored by a comparison of it with some of the august assemblies of antiquity. So natural is it to court for modern times a luster reflected through the medium of antiquity. But America desires no other tribute of applause for this illustrious body than that their agency corresponded with the character of their constituents, ambitious to shine in the annals of liberty.

But before the posture given to our affairs by Congress had undergone a discussion in the Convention, Dunmore had been gratified in his vehement lust for embodying a large army of expert riflemen and woodsmen from the militia of the western frontiers. He had collected under cover of the standing law providing against Indian hostilities a brave yeomanry, which if not convertible under his authority to other purposes, unsuspected and unjustifiable, might at least be more immediately within the sphere of his influence from those blandishments which a commander in chief can liberally disperse. If they could be detached from the rest of their countrymen, the most hardy and most experienced in war of the sons of Virginia would be cast into the scale of Great Britain; if he miscarried, as he in fact did, the necessity of chastising the Indians would always be a veil over his original views.[25] His conduct of this little army was mysterious to a degree of folly. Instead of prostrating, as he might, all the Indian enemy by a concentrated application of his strength, he divided it into two parts, one of which he confided to Colonel Andrew Lewis, to be led to the mouth of Kanawha River, and with the other, far superior, he moved to a point on the Ohio River, distant more than seventy miles, making seasonable cooperation impracticable. Lewis, notwithstanding the bravery of himself, his officers, and men at Point Pleasant, the place of his destination, was defeated by the Shawnees, Delawares, Mingoes, and Tawas and mortally wounded.[26] His surviving compatriots, eager to avenge the death of their friends, were on the wing for the destruction of the Shawnee villages when tidings of peace, on the condition of the cessation of the Indian lands on the eastern side of the Ohio,

25. Dunmore was responding to the outbreak in 1774 of hostilities with the Indians of western Virginia. The governor was probably more mindful of defending his land speculations in the area than raising an army to defend the British cause in Virginia (Meade, *Patrick Henry*, p. 336). However, in early 1775 the governor did begin forming independent companies of militia (Malone, *Jefferson the Virginian*, p. 194).

26. According to a note written in the margin of the manuscript by Hugh Blair Grigsby: "Colonel Lewis was not killed. He died in Bedford in 1780. General Lewis expelled Dunmore in 1775. It was Colonel Charles Lewis who was killed at Point Pleasant."

surrendering their prisoners, and delivering hostages on performance, gave Dunmore by a false éclat, a feather for his vanity.[27]

The dissolution of the Assembly in the preceding year had demonstrated that it was no security against the repetition of the same offenses to the governor. He had therefore intermitted to call one, careless whether anarchy had ensued or not from the derangement of our police. In March 1775 the indications were stronger still, and a convention was held in the town of Richmond.[28] Among the members were Peyton Randolph, Thomas Jefferson, Edmund Pendleton, Benjamin Harrison, George Washington, Patrick Henry, Robert Carter Nicholas, Richard Bland, and Richard Henry Lee, who have been already drawn to the size of character which they had then unfolded. To show in what numbers Virginia might feel an assurance, others were associated with them, whose respectability, virtue, and good sense made and fixed proselytes, by conviction inculcated in private when they were averse to address their compatriots in public. Among these were John Harvie, Thomas Lewis, Henry Tazewell, John Nicholas, Paul Carrington, Archibald Cary, William Fleming, John Banister, William Fitzhugh, Charles Carter, Francis Peyton, Meriwether Smith, Thomas Marshall, James Mercer, Joseph Jones, Thomas Walker, Edmund Berkeley, Lemuel Riddick, Willis Riddick, Burwell Bassett, Thomas Newton, William Robinson, Henry Lee, Thomas Blackburn, Edwin Gray, James Taylor, Mann Page of Spotsylvania, Dudley Digges, Thomas Nelson, Jr., of York, Champion Travis, and Joseph Hutchings.[29] All of them had at

27. The war with the Indians, or Dunmore's War, began early in 1774 when John Connolly took Fort Pitt and initiated retaliatory actions against the Indians of the region for their recent attacks against settlers. Dunmore seemed to welcome hostilities with the Indians as a diversion from the controversy between Virginia and Pennsylvania over this disputed territory. The Shawnee chief Cornstalk mobilized 1,000 Miami, Shawnee, Wyandots (Hurons), and Ottawas to attack Lewis. Of the Virginians 81 men were killed and 140 wounded, but the Indians withdrew across the river with few losses. Dunmore then marched his combined forces overland to the Shawnee villages on the Scioto where the greatly outnumbered Indians sued for peace and agreed to remain north and west of the Ohio River (Sosin, *Revolutionary Frontier*, pp. 84–87).

28. For the Richmond Convention of 1775, see Lingley, *Transition*, pp. 110–36.

29. John Harvie (1742–1807), a native of Scotland who had emigrated to Virginia at an early age, settled in Albemarle County where he practiced law. He represented West Augusta County in the Virginia Conventions of 1775 and 1776, was elected to the Continental Congress in 1777, and was a signer of the Articles of Confederation. Thomas Lewis (1718–90) was a member of the Conventions of 1775 and 1776, a commissioner to negotiate with the Indians in 1778, and a delegate to the Virginia Ratifying Convention of 1788. Henry Tazewell (1735–99), a prominent lawyer, served in the legislature from 1775 to 1785 where he promoted the abolition of primogeniture and entail and the separation of church and state. He was also a member of the committee that reported

stake fortunes which were affluent or competent and families which were dear to them; neither of these blessings would they have jeopardized upon a political speculation in which their souls were not deeply engaged. If some misguided historian should at a future day revive the exploded calumny of evil motives which agitated this Convention, let these names be adduced as monuments of absolute refutation.

The first resolution of the Convention was unanimously entirely and cordially to approve the proceedings and resolutions of the Continental Congress; to consider the whole continent as under the highest obliga-

---

the Declaration of Rights and the state constitution. John Nicholas, Albemarle County clerk from 1749 to 1815, was a burgess from 1756–1768 and a member of the Conventions of 1774 and 1775. Paul Carrington (1733–1818), a lawyer and king's attorney for Bedford County, represented Charlotte County in the House of Burgesses from its formation in 1765 to 1775 and as a member of the Conventions of 1774, 1775, and 1776. Archibald Cary (1721–87) of Chesterfield County served in every Assembly from 1756 to 1776, and in the Revolutionary Conventions of 1774, 1775, and 1776. As chairman of the committee of the whole he read to the Convention on May 15, 1776, Virginia's Resolution for Independence. William Fleming (1736–1824) was a lawyer and a member of the House of Burgesses for Cumberland. John Banister (d. 1787), educated in England where he studied law at the Temple, a burgess for Dinwiddie County and a member of Continental Congress, was one of the framers and signers of the Articles of Confederation. William Fitzhugh (1741–1809) was a burgess from King George County and a member of the Continental Congress from 1779 to 1780. Charles Carter (1732–1806), a burgess from Lancaster County, was a member of the Convention of 1775 and in 1776 of the first state Council. Francis Peyton was a burgess from Loudoun County and a member of the Conventions of 1775 and 1776. Meriwether Smith (1730–94) of Essex County was a member of the House of Burgesses, the Conventions of 1775 and 1776, a delegate to Continental Congress from 1778 to 1782, and the Virginia Convention that ratified the Federal Constitution. Thomas Marshall (1730–1802), a lieutenant in the French and Indian War, represented Fauquier County in the Burgesses and in the Conventions of 1774, 1775, and 1776. He served as a colonel of the Third Virginia Regiment in the Continental army. James Mercer (1736–93) of Marlborough, a graduate of the College of William and Mary, was a member of the House of Burgesses in 1765 and again in 1774, a delegate to the Convention of 1775 and the Constitutional Convention of 1776, and in 1779–80 a representative to the Continental Congress. Joseph Jones (1727–1805) represented King George County in the Assembly from 1772 to 1775, as a member of the Committee of Safety in 1775, and in the Conventions of 1774, 1775, and 1776. He was also a delegate to Continental Congress, a judge of the General Court, a member of the Ratifying Convention of 1788, and a major general in the Virginia militia. Dr. Thomas Walker (1715–94), educated at William and Mary, one of the country's foremost physicians and a land speculator, had represented Louisa, Hampshire, and Albemarle counties in the House of Burgesses and in the Conventions of 1775 and 1776. Edmund Berkeley was a burgess and member of the Conventions of 1774, 1775, and 1776 from Middlesex County. Lemuel Riddick and Willis Riddick (1711–75), probably father and son, were both burgesses from Nansemond County and members of the Convention of March 20, 1775. Burwell Bassett (1734–93) represented New Kent in the House of Burgesses from 1762 to 1775 and at the Conventions of 1774 and 1776. William Robinson (d. 1777) was probably the burgess from King George County in the Assembly from 1766 to 1772. Henry Lee (1729–87),

tion to them for the wisdom of their counsels and their unremitted endeavors to maintain and preserve inviolate the just rights and liberties of His Majesty's dutiful and loyal subjects in America. In correspondence with this resolution a second was passed for the warmest thanks to the delegates from Virginia for their cheerful undertaking and faithful discharge of the very important trust reposed in them.[30] We here perceive Virginia concerned in branding with injustice, cruelty, and oppression the late acts of Parliament involving Massachusetts Bay; in annulling an obedience to them as the attempts of a wicked administration to enslave America; in countenancing that province in the support of all officers who should refuse to carry into execution the others of courts held by judges who were appointed with any other tenure than that which the charter and laws directed; in approving the payment of the public revenue of that province into the hands of the provincial treasurer, until government should be placed upon a constitutional foundation, or it should be otherwise ordered by the provincial congress; in exhorting the people of Massachusetts to act upon the defensive merely as long as such conduct might be vindicated by reason and the principle of self-preservation and no longer; and in applauding the assumption of various powers in the present crisis. In

---

justice of the peace, county lieutenant, and burgess, represented Prince William County in the Conventions of 1774, 1775, and 1776. He was the father of "Light-Horse Harry" Lee. Thomas Blackburn (1740–1804), burgess and delegate to the March and July Conventions of 1775 from Prince William County, was afterwards lieutenant colonel of the Second Virginia Regiment and an aide to General Washington. Edwin Gray of Southampton County served as a burgess from 1769 to 1776, as a member of the Conventions of 1774, 1775, and 1776, the House of Delegates, and the State Senate. Mann Page (1749–81), a graduate of William and Mary, was a delegate to Continental Congress in 1777. Dudley Digges (1718–90), a lawyer and burgess for York County from 1752 to 1776, was a member of the Committee of Correspondence in 1773 and of all the Revolutionary Conventions. Thomas Nelson (1739–89), a close friend of Jefferson, was educated in England, receiving his A.B. at Trinity College, Cambridge. He then returned to Virginia in 1761 and was immediately elected to the House of Burgesses from York County. Nelson was a member of the Conventions of 1774, 1775, and 1776, served in Continental Congress, was a signer of the Declaration of Independence, and held a commission as a general of militia which he commanded in the siege of Yorktown. He was elected governor on June 12, 1781, and when he resigned on Nov. 30 he was accused of maladministration for assuming dictatorial powers but was exonerated by the state legislature. Champion Travis was a member of the Conventions of 1775 and 1776, colonel of the state regiment in 1775, naval commissioner in 1776, and justice and sheriff of James City County. Joseph Hutchings represented Norfolk Borough in the House of Burgesses almost continuously from 1761 to 1776 and in the Conventions of March and July, 1775. For a complete list of delegates, see Force, *Archives*, 4th ser., II, 165–66.

30. See *ibid.*, p. 167.

a word, Virginia pledged herself to Massachusetts for upholding her in all measures which she might think expedient.[31]

The most conspicuous acts of Congress, which the Convention thus recognized, were: 1. a letter to General Gage, the British commander in Boston, requiring him to discontinue the fortifications there; 2. a declaration of American rights, which is a copious summary of them; 3. an association against exportation, consumption, and importation under certain limitations; 4. an address to the people of Great Britain; 5. a memorial to the inhabitants of the British colonies; 6. a letter to the colonies of St. John, Nova Scotia, Georgia, East and West Florida; 7. an address to the inhabitants of Quebec; and, 8. an address to the king.[32]

With these acts, this history has no further concern than as enunciations of those doctrines to which the conviction of Virginia had arrived and as an earnest of measures which might flow from them. Now when passion no longer taints the original question, it probably will not be doubted by any that an internal taxation of the colonies by the authority of Parliament was a violation of their rights. In the association nothing was done but innocently and without bloodshed to do as a nation what every individual had a right to be as an individual British subject. As the ministry would have hastened the pace of military vengeance, if the pulse of the British people had beaten as strongly as their own pride and their hunger for items of revenue, the address to that people was a just retort of the example of *divide et impera,* and may be also ranked with the evidences of our anxiety to continue brethren of the same government. The address to the king, whose personal character and situation effaced every hope of rousing him to think or act in contradiction to his advisers, was a deference to the American people, who could not relinquish the slightest prospect of returning harmony. And this line of conduct rescued Congress from the imputation, to which the letter to the island of St. John, West Florida, and Quebec might give birth, of a wish to convulse and dismember the British Empire. True perhaps it is that Virginia now was resolved to follow whithersoever these doctrines and these measures should lead, and that had she been asked what she had in reserve, upon the final failure of all overtures of reconciliation, a consistent answer could have been only that it would have been better not to have stirred

31. For the proceedings of the Convention, see *ibid.,* pp. 165–72.
32. See *ibid.,* I, 909, 910–12, 913–16, 917–21, 921–28, 929, 930–34, 934–37.

at all than to be reduced to slavery, aggravated by the disgrace of pompous and hollow professions.

Accordingly a resolution was passed for immediately putting the colony into a posture of defense and for preparing a plan of embodying and disciplining such a number of men as might be sufficient for that purpose.[33] Henry moved and Richard Henry Lee seconded it. The fangs of European criticism might be challenged to spread themselves against the eloquence of that awful day. It was a proud one to a Virginian, feeling and acting with his country. Demosthenes invigorated the timid, and Cicero charmed the backward. The multitude, many of whom had traveled to the Convention from a distance, could not suppress their emotion. Henry was his pure self. Those who had toiled in the artifices of scholastic rhetoric were involuntarily driven into an inquiry within themselves, whether rules and forms and niceties of elocution would not have choked his native fire. It blazed so as to warm the coldest heart. In the sacred place of meeting, the church,[34] the imagination had no difficulty to conceive, when he launched forth in solemn tones various causes of scruple against oppressors, that the British king was lying prostrate from the thunder of heaven. Henry was thought in his attitudes to resemble Saint Paul while preaching at Athens and to speak as man was never known to speak before. After every illusion had vanished, a prodigy yet remained. It was Patrick Henry, born in obscurity, poor, and without the advantages of literature, rousing the genius of his country and binding a band of patriots together to hurl defiance at the tyranny of so formidable a nation as Great Britain. This enchantment was spontaneous obedience to the workings of the soul. When he uttered what commanded respect for himself, he solicited no admiring looks from those who surrounded him. If he had, he must have been abashed by meeting every eye fixed upon him. He paused, but he paused full of some rising eruption of eloquence. When he sat down, his sounds vibrated so loudly, if not in the ears, at least in the memory of his audience, that no other member, not even his friend who was to second him, was yet adventurous enough to interfere with that voice which had so recently subdued and captivated.[35] After a few minutes Richard Henry Lee fanned and refreshed with a gale of pleasure, but the vessel of the Revolution was still under the impulse of the

33. See *ibid.*, II, 168; Lingley, *Transition,* pp. 129–32.

34. The Richmond Convention held its meetings at Old Saint John's Church.

35. It was at the Richmond Convention that Patrick Henry uttered his famous cry, "Give me liberty, or give me death" (see William Wirt Henry, *Patrick Henry: Life, Correspondence, and Speeches* [New York, 1891], I, 254–72).

tempest which Henry had created. Artificial oratory fell in copious streams from the mouth of Lee, and rules of persuasion accomplished everything which rules could effect. If elegance had been personified, the person of Lee would have been chosen. But Henry trampled upon rules and yet triumphed, at this time perhaps beyond his own expectation. Jefferson was not silent. He argued closely, profoundly, and warmly on the same side. The post in this revolutionary debate belonging to him was that at which the theories of republicanism were deposited. Washington was prominent, though silent. His looks bespoke a mind absorbed in meditation on his country's fate, but a positive concert between him and Henry could not more effectually have exhibited him to view than when Henry with indignation ridiculed the idea of peace "when there was no peace" and enlarged on the duty of preparing for war.

The generous and noble-minded Thomas Nelson, who now for the first time took a more than common part in a great discussion, convulsed the moderate by an ardent exclamation in which he called God to witness that if any British troops should be landed within the county of which he was the lieutenant, he would wait for no orders and would obey none which should forbid him to summon his militia and repel the invaders at the water edge. His temper, though it was sanguine and had been manifested in no less scenes of opposition, seemed to be more than ordinarily excited. His example told those who were happy in ease and wealth that to shrink was to be dishonored.[36]

The Convention instructed the Committee of Correspondence to procure authentic information whether the House of Representatives of New York had deserted the union with the other colonies, what the real sense of the people of that province was, to ascertain the names of the individuals who might have concurred in the votes derogating from that union.[37] In the progress of a revolution we must be satisfied if the simple charities of human nature are preserved. But courtesy or delicacy toward individuals or bodies suspected will never shelter them from an intrusive scrutiny.

Provision was made for the collection of supplies for the relief of Boston, and the administration of justice was interrupted. Volunteer companies of infantry and troops of horse were recommended to be

---

36. The proceedings of the Convention of March 20–27, 1775, were published in the *Virginia Gazette,* April 1, 1775.

37. See Force, *Archives,* 4th ser., II, 168. It had been reported that the New York House of Representatives had deserted the Continental Association.

raised and to be in constant training and readiness for action on any emergency. Money also was recommended to be raised for ammunition.

Although adulation from public bodies for some expedient of policy is supposed not to tarnish the individuals who compose them, we ought not to palliate our surprise that a convention possessing such a force of character as this did should pollute itself by an unfelt eulogium on Dunmore. It was no secret that his late expedition against the Indians was suggested by the belief that he could intimidate them, and by intimidating them, direct their tomahawk against the frontiers most open to their ravages; and yet it was resolved unanimously "that the most cordial thanks of the people of this colony are a tribute justly due to our *worthy* governor, Lord Dunmore, for his truly noble, wise, and spirited conduct on the late expedition against our Indian enemy—a conduct which at once evinces His Excellency's attention to the true interest of this colony and a zeal in the executive department which no dangers can divert or difficulties hinder from achieving the most important services to the people who have the *happiness* to live under his administration." Perhaps this glaring sacrifice of sincerity would not have been made, had it not been for the wretched practice of presuming the commander in chief, even in the teeth of every rule of presumption, to be the efficient cause of successes obtained by his officers and soldiers. On them undoubtedly thanks could not be misspent. Foy sneered. Dunmore clutched with avidity this item of mischievous popularity, which he would apply, if possible, to the annoyance of Virginia. No man can say that complimentary acts of public bodies, howsoever neutral they may seem to be, may not be wrested with evil, unless they certainly steer to some good.[38]

Contemporaneously with the arrangements for defense were adopted resolutions for encouraging manufactures, which had they been executed with spirit and perseverance, would have established independence on a rock, unmovable to British capital. In the plan proposed are a frank confession of the inability of Virginia to furnish to herself articles of the first necessity and magnanimity in encountering on the principle of liberty the most painful privations. It inculcates too a useful and instructive truth, that when a people devoted to liberty once entertain an apprehension for its safety, they overleap the calculations of what in ordinary life would be called prudence.

Woolen, cotton, and linen manufactures were to be promoted in as

---

38. See *ibid.,* p. 170.

many different branches as possible. Except in some small instances, in which poor industrious families spun and wove their own clothing, the foreign merchant annually supplied those manufactures for the slaves and their masters.

Flax, hemp, and cotton were to be cultivated not only for the use of each family but for the accommodation of others on moderate terms. Cotton had been hitherto made in quantities not much exceeding a scanty domestic consumption, and flax and hemp were not frequent or very abundant below the heads of our great rivers.

Saltworks were to be established. We had depended for salt on importation from abroad. The art of making it, simple as it is, was then a mystery in chemistry; and the great waters adjoining the sea, which were alone adapted to its production in the eastern quarter of Virginia, might be visited in all their recesses by any British cockboat. The salt springs in the west were too remote for the wants of the lower country.

Saltpeter was to be collected and refined, as well as sulphur; and elementary ingredients of gunpowder had been always bought more cheaply than they could be made.

Gunpowder was to be made, the compounding of which had been practiced only by the riflemen of the upper country and had not become an article of merchandise to be capable of a competition with that which was imported.

Nails, wire, and other necessary articles of iron were to be manufactured. Many of these had been prohibited by Parliament, and a slitting mill or tilt hammer had never been erected; even hoes and axes were imported. Steel was to be made upon an extensive scale. The process, though not difficult, was unknown in use.

Different kinds of paper were to be made. Only one experiment had been made in Virginia, and that was abortive.

Wool combs, cotton, and wool cards, hemp and flax heckles were to be made.

Fulling mills and mills for breaking, swingling, and softening hemp and flax were to be erected. Grindstones, although the rough material was daily before our eyes, had been neglected to be made.

Malt liquors made in Virginia were to be substituted for foreign, and hops and barley were to be encouraged.[39]

Had these recommendations been observed as closely as they might have been, without inconvenience to the planter, farmer, and mechanic,

39. See *ibid.*, pp. 170–71; Lingley, *Transition*, p. 134.

this country, the climate and soil of which promised to industry an ample profit, would not have been behind any state in improvement or dependent on any nation for its manufactures.

How Virginia had fallen into this dearth of things so easily attainable is to be solved by the peculiarities of her situation from an ancient date. As soon as that noxious weed tobacco had obtained the currency of fashion in Europe and the introduction of slavery had sheltered the white population from the labor and exposure incidental to its cultivation, it was seen that the raw materials of manufacture could be invested with greater profit in purchasing what she wanted from England, where labor was cheap, the arts subdivided, capital existed for every valuable business, and science and experience had astonished with new facilities and improvements, than in the application of her manual force to the tedious progress of manufactures. They must be nurtured from the lowest state of infancy, without funds at double expense and without the collateral aids which each manufacture requires from many others. Besides, the woolen, cotton, and linen fabrics of England had become the standards of taste and necessity in Virginia. To similar sources and to the tumult of war may be traced the tardiness in seizing the first moments of self-government for the exercise of self-denial. Nature had been too propitious to Virginia to generate the noble art of living upon little. Comfort sprang up, was luxuriant, but was also an opiate to the activity of native invention, little short of the effect of possessing mines of gold and silver.

What course of reflection these facts and others like them, known to exist elsewhere in the colonies, excited in the minds of many, eminent for learning and philanthropy, but novices in the feelings of the New World, threatened with chains and mounting to some high but dubious destiny, is exemplified in a letter of the celebrated historian Dr. Robertson, written in October 1775. Speaking of the colonies, he says that

the ministry have been trifling for two years, when they should have been serious, until they have rendered a very simple piece of business extremely perplexed. They have permitted colonies disjoined by nature and situation to consolidate themselves into a regular systematical confederacy, and when a few regiments stationed in each capital would have rendered it impossible from them to take arms, they have suffered them quietly to levy and train forces, as if they had not known and seen against whom they were prepared. . . . This (that is the liberty to buy and sell, where and with whom they

please) they will one day attain, but not just now, if there be any degree of
political wisdom or vigor remaining. At the same time, one cannot but regret that prosperous and growing states should be checked in their career.

Be it right or wrong, the Convention was struck with R. H. Lee's
quotation from Scripture, that the race was not to the swift, nor the
battle to the strong, and believed that those were doubly armed whose
cause was just. May the cause of liberty be ever conducted with prudence, but never benumbed by too frigid estimates of difficulty or
danger.

One of the last acts of the Convention was dictated by a proclamation of the governor. He was as humble a proficient in the season as in
the wisdom of doing things. That proclamation, in declaring that the
king had given orders that all vacant lands should be put up in lots at
public sale, that the purchasers should hold them, subject to a reservation of one halfpenny sterling per acre by way of annual quitrent,
augmented the preexisting inflammation. It was an innovation on the
established usage of granting lands within the colony [and] announced
that revenue was to be hunted for in disregard of charters and ancient
habits and to be embraced in its minutest shapes. To attack this new
head of the hydra of precedent, a committee was appointed of Patrick
Henry, Richard Bland, Thomas Jefferson, Robert Carter Nicholas,
and Edmund Pendleton to inquire whether His Majesty may of right
advance the terms of granting lands in this colony, and to make report
to the next General Assembly or Convention. But this affair was lost in
the subsequent events, and at any other time would probably have
died away with those numerous thoughtless acquiescences with which
our history is strewed, in exercises of doubtful prerogative.[40]

It being apprehended that Peyton Randolph, who with his former
colleagues had been elected to the succeeding Congress held in Philadelphia in May 1775, might be detained by sickness or his duties as the
speaker of the House of Burgesses, Thomas Jefferson was named as
his eventual successor.[41]

The Convention then considered the delegation of its members as
at an end and recommended to the people to choose delegates to represent them for one year.[42] In civil commotions it has always been the
artifice of parties to invent for their opponents names to which odium

40. See Force, *Archives*, 4th ser., II, 171–72.
41. See *ibid.*, p. 172.
42. See *ibid.*

or ridicule is attached. The Neri and Branchi of Florence; the Guelfs and Ghibellines of France; and the Whigs and Tories of England were the offspring of this species of stratagem. The enemies to parliamentary taxation and the ministry stigmatized those who favored either as Tories and assumed to themselves the appellation of Whigs.[43] The origin of these distinctions, Hume in his *History of England* describes thus:

Factions indeed were at this time extremely animated against each other. The very names by which each party denominated its antagonist discover the virulence and rancor which prevailed. For besides petitioner and abhorrer, appellations which were soon forgotten, this year [1680] is remarkable for being the epoch of the well-known epithets of Whig and Tory, by which, and sometimes without any material difference, this island has been so long divided. The court party reproached their antagonists with their affinity to the fanatical conventiclers in Scotland, who were known by the name of Whigs; the country party found a resemblance between the courtiers and the popish banditti in Ireland, to whom the appellation of Tory was affixed. And after this manner, these foolish terms of reproach came into public and general use; and even at present seem not nearer their end than when they were first invented.[44]

Mr. Jefferson in his *Notes on Virginia,* page 285, remarks that a Tory has been properly defined to be a traitor in thought but not in deed.[45] In some cases it may have been the harsh language of the most violent

43. The Neri and Branchi were the designations for the two major power factions in early fourteenth-century Florence. In 1302 the Neri or Blacks, an aristocratic group, seized power from the Branchi or Whites, the faction representing the middle class, and many were exiled including the poet Dante. Guelph and Ghibelline were the names used to identify the opposing groups in the great struggles of the twelfth and thirteenth centuries between the Holy Roman emperors and the papacy. The first were supporters of the pope and the latter of the emperor. Although these names are most commonly associated with factions in the Italian city-states, they were also used in France. Whigs and Tories are applied here to the rival groups in the struggle between parliamentarians and royalists in seventeenth-century England.

44. David Hume (1711–76), the Scottish philosopher and historian, published his six-volume *History of England* in the years from 1754 to 1761. At this point the manuscript has a blank page with the following note: "here copy from Hume's Hist. of England Vol. VIII, Ch. 68 p. 126." So as to render the *History* as close to the author's intent as possible this passage from Hume has been included ([London, 1796], VIII, 126; for Hume, see J. B. Black, *The Art of History: A Study of Four Great Historians of the Eighteenth Century* [New York, 1965], pp. 77–116).

45. Jefferson, *Notes on Virginia,* ed. Abernethy, pp. 148–49. In the section entitled "Query XVI: The measures taken with regard to the estates and possessions of the Rebels, Commonly called Tories," Jefferson attempted to justify the confiscation of Loyalist property.

and intemperate, but it cannot be admitted that thinking men, who valued free will as a gift of heaven, were thus indiscriminate in their severity. What multitudes could now be cited, who, confounded by the new order of things suddenly flashing upon their minds and still entangled by the habits of many years, were branded as Tories, though spotless as to treason even in thought; who could not comprehend what was to be the issue of provoking the fury of the British nation and were yet innocent even as to wishes of harm to their country; who believed in a chance of reconciliation, if excesses were spared; who might feel sufficient irritation at the distant danger of an abstract principle. It is the glory of our country that the influence of a contrary sentiment, while it might diminish cordiality, left without molestation very many men to adorn and profit the republic.

In April 1775, Dunmore, eager to acquit himself with some noise toward his royal master and misconceiving action, whether well or ill directed, to be synonymous with duty, adopted a measure which in any aspect could not promote his interest, as a scheme to deprive the city of Williamsburg of ammunition and arms must inevitably precipitate a general tumult. There was a paltry magazine in that city, the then metropolis, which had served as a receptacle for a few military stores of government and for the gunpowder of the merchants there, who from caution retained but small quantities for the course of retail. These were, by Dunmore's order, secretly, in the night, conveyed on board of a vessel of war; thus adopting a policy in one sense groveling, and in another not far removed from assassination, as it was believed at the time, and more strongly suspected from what happened afterwards, that he designed, by disarming the people, to weaken the means of opposing an insurrection of the slaves, whom he purposed to invite to his standard, and for a protection against whom in part the magazine was at first built. The citizens ran to arms as soon as the rapine was detected and would have assaulted the governor in his residence had they not been dissuaded by the calmer counsels of Peyton Randolph and Robert Carter Nicholas. The violence projected was, however, rather suspended than extinguished. It was suspended to afford to the governor an opportunity of promising to replace the gunpowder, in conformity with an address from the corporation. But instead of the candor and frankness incumbent on official stations, he replied with evasion and falsehood. Public office, if it cannot gratify with pleasant things, ought at least not to sap confidence by the desertion of truth. Dunmore says that "hearing of an insurrection in a neighboring county, he had removed the gunpowder from the magazine, where he did not think it secure, to a place of perfect security, and that upon his word and honor, whenever it was wanted in any insurrection, it should be delivered in half an hour; that he was surprised to hear that the people were under arms on this occasion, and that he should not think it prudent to put powder into their hands in such a situation." [46] The impetuosity of a multitude, once arrested, does not instantly return to its former extravagance, although their demands may not be completely satisfied; and now, after some further effervescence, it gradually subsided into perfect tranquillity.

In other parts of Virginia, Dunmore's excuse for the removal of the powder was spurned at with indignation for its departure from the fact and his equivocation about an insurrection, the interpretation of which when it might happen he reserved to himself. In the county of Hanover, in which Patrick Henry lived, the standing committee created by the Convention and the armed volunteer company refused to acquiesce; and Henry at the head of the latter marched to extort from the king's receiver general, Richard Corbin, out of the royal coffer, the value of the powder.[47] That officer drew a bill of exchange on London for the amount, being upward of £300 sterling, which sum was paid into the treasury. It was Henry's ulterior intention to visit Williamsburg with his company of men, and in some manner or other, to hold Dunmore responsible for the restitution of the powder. But when he had advanced within fifteen miles of that city, he was met by Robert Carter Nicholas and Thomas Nelson, who represented to him that as his object had been accomplished in the bill of exchange, he and his party would best consult the peace of Virginia by returning in peace, and they prevailed upon him to return. Of itself the money was of no account, but the occurrence disrobed the regal government of superstitious reverence and thereby forwarded a most essential branch of the impending Revolution. Henry was proclaimed a traitor by Dunmore, and his personal safety was thereby incorporated with the American cause.[48] It conferred upon him a degree of military prominence, which might be a basis for future elevation in any line.

46. Dunmore's proclamation is in Force, *Archives,* 4th ser., II, 372. For a discussion of the Williamsburg episode, see Eckenrode, *Revolution in Virginia,* pp. 49–51.

47. Richard Corbin (1708–90), a burgess from Middlesex County, was appointed to the Council in 1751 and remained a member until the Revolution. During the controversy over the removal of the powder from Williamsburg, Corbin was the king's deputy receiver general. Though he remained sympathetic to Great Britain he retired to his country home and took no part in the war.

48. See Force, *Archives,* 4th ser., II, 516.

Dunmore caught the glimpse of greater pliability in a new Assembly than in that which had been dissolved. The joint address of the two houses of Parliament to the king, his answer, and the resolution of the House of Commons on February 7, 1775, had been transmitted to him with rapidity, and he summoned the legislature for June 1, 1775. In his speech to them at the commencement of the session he tells them that the joint address and answer no longer permit a doubt that their well-founded grievances properly represented would meet with that attention and regard which are justly due to them; that the resolution of the Commons will, he trusts, have the effect of removing the jealousy which has been the principal source of disquiet and uneasiness in the minds of the people; that he therefore entertains the strongest hopes that nothing will remain, after a just consideration of the nature and tendency of that resolution, to prevent their seriously exerting themselves to bring the disputes which have unhappily raged between the mother country and the colonies to a good end, to which the step already taken by the House of Commons must be considered as a benevolent tender and an auspicious advance on the part of the parent state. He then adds that

It must now be manifest to all dispassionate people that the Parliament, the high and supreme legislature of the empire, far from having entertained thoughts so inconsistent with the wisdom and public virtue, which have distinguished that august body, of oppressing the people of the colonies or of promoting the interest of one at the expense of another part of their fellow subjects, have only been extending their care that the whole, in consideration of the enjoyment of equal rights, privileges, and advantages, should be obliged, according to their abilities and situations, to contribute a portion toward the burdens necessary for the support of the civil government and common defense.[49]

The tenor of these overtures from Parliament will best appear from the perusal of them:

That it is earnestly hoped by all the real friends of the Americans that the terms expressed in the resolution of the twentieth of February last will be accepted by all the colonies who have the least affection for their king and country, or a just sense of their own interest.

That these terms are honorable for Great Britain and safe for the colonies.

That if the colonies are not blinded by faction, these terms will remove every grievance relative to taxation and be the basis of a compact between the colonies and the mother country.

49. See *Burgesses, Journals, 1773–1776,* pp. 174–75.

That the people in America ought, on every consideration, to be satisfied with them.

That no further relaxation can be admitted.

The temper and spirit of the nation are so much against concessions that if it were the intention of Administration, they could not carry the question.

But Administration have no such intention, as they are fully and firmly persuaded that further concessions would be injurious to the colonies as well as to Great Britain.

That there is not the least probability of a change of Administration.

That they are perfectly united in opinion and determined to pursue the most effectual measures and to use the whole force of the kingdom, if it be found necessary, to reduce the rebellious and refractory provinces and colonies.

There is so great a spirit in the nation against the Congress that the people will bear the temporary distresses of a stoppage of the American trade.

They may depend on this to be true.[50]

The answer of the House of Burgesses is a manly repulse of the snare.

To His Excellency, the Right Hon. John, earl of Dunmore, Governor of Virginia, etc., etc.

My Lord,

We His Majesty's dutiful and loyal subjects, the burgesses of Virginia, now met in General Assembly, have taken into our consideration the joint address of the two houses of Parliament, His Majesty's answer, and the Resolution of the Commons, which your lordship has been pleased to lay before us. Wishing nothing so sincerely as the perpetual continuance of that brotherly love which we bear to our fellow subjects of Great Britain, and still continuing to hope and believe that they do not approve the measures which have so long oppressed their brethren in America, we were pleased to receive your lordship's notification that a benevolent tender has at length been made by the British House of Commons toward bringing to a good end our unhappy disputes with the mother country. Next to the possession of liberty, my lord, we should consider such a reconciliation as the greatest of all human blessings. With these dispositions, we entered into consideration of that resolution; we examined it minutely; we viewed it in every point of light in which we were able to place it; and with pain and disappointment, we must ultimately declare it only changes the form of oppression without lightening its burden. We cannot, my lord, close with the terms of that resolution, for these reasons:

Because the British Parliament has no right to intermeddle with the

50. See Force, *Archives*, 4th ser., II, 1840. These overtures were an offer of reconciliation by Frederick Lord North (1732–92), prime minister of Great Britain from 1770 until 1782.

support of civil government in the colonies. For us, not for them, has government been established here. Agreeable to our ideas, provision has been made for such officers as we think necessary for the administration of public affairs, and we cannot conceive that any other legislature has a right to prescribe either the number or pecuniary appointments of our officers. As a proof that the claim of Parliament to interfere in the necessary provisions for support of civil government is novel, and of a late date, we take leave to refer to an act of our Assembly, passed so long since as the thirty-second year of the reign of King Charles II, entitled, "An act for raising a public revenue, and for the better support of this His Majesty's colony of Virginia." This act was brought over by Lord Culpeper, then governor, under the Great Seal of England and was enacted in the name of the king's most excellent Majesty, by and with the consent of the General Assembly.[51]

Because, to render perpetual our exemption from an unjust taxation, we must saddle ourselves with a perpetual tax, adequate to the expectations and subject to the disposal of Parliament alone, whereas we have a right to give our money, as the Parliament do theirs, without coercion, from time to time, as public exigencies may require. We conceive that we alone are the judges of the condition, circumstances, and situation of our people, as the Parliament are of theirs. It is not merely the mode of raising but the freedom of granting our money for which we have contended. Without this, we possess no check on the royal prerogative; and what must be lamented by dutiful and loyal subjects, we should be stripped of the only means as well of recommending this country to the favors of our most gracious sovereign as of strengthening those bands of amity with our fellow subjects which we would wish to remain indissoluble.

Because, on our undertaking to grant money, as is proposed, the Commons only resolve to forbear levying pecuniary taxes on us, still leaving unrepealed their several acts passed for the purpose of restraining the trade and altering the form of government of the eastern colonies,[52] extending the boundaries and changing the government and religion of Quebec,[53] enlarging the jurisdiction of the courts of admiralty, taking from us the right of trial by jury, and transporting us into other countries to be tried for criminal offenses.[54] Standing armies too are still to be kept among

51. Thomas Lord Culpeper (1635–89) was governor of Virginia from 1677 to 1683. For a discussion of the revenue bill and the struggle over its passage, see Wertenbaker, *Virginia under the Stuarts*, pp. 226–31.

52. The Coercive Acts of 1774.

53. The Quebec Act of 1774 extended the boundaries of the province into the Mississippi Valley as far south as the Ohio River, established a civil government with no representative assembly, and granted special privileges for the Catholic church.

54. The Sugar Act of 1764 provided that violations of the Navigation Acts be tried in admiralty courts, which operated without juries. In 1768 parliamentary leaders exhumed a forgotten act passed during the reign of Henry VIII in the sixteenth century to justify transporting American agitators to England for trial.

us; and the other numerous grievances, of which ourselves and sister colonies, separately and by our representatives in general Congress, have so often complained, are still to continue without redress.

Because at the very time of requiring from us grants of monies, they are making disposition to invade us with large armaments by sea and land, which is a style of asking gifts not reconcilable to our freedom. They are also proceeding to a repetition of injury, by passing acts for restraining the commerce and fisheries of the provinces of New England and for prohibiting the trade of the other colonies with all parts of the world, except the islands of Great Britain, Ireland, and the West Indies. This seems to bespeak no intention to discontinue the exercise of this usurped power over us in future.

Because, on our agreeing to contribute our proportion toward the common defense, they do not propose to lay open to us a free trade with all the world; whereas, to us, it appears just that those who bear equally the burdens of government should equally participate of its benefits. Either be contented with the monopoly of our trade, which brings greater loss to us, and benefit to them, than the amount of our proportional contributions to the common defense; or, if the latter be preferred, relinquish the former; and do not propose, by holding both, to exact from us double contributions. Yet we would remind government that on former emergencies, when called upon as a free people, however cramped by this monopoly, in our resources of wealth, we have liberally contributed to the common defense. Be assured, then, that we shall be generous in future as in past times, disdaining the shackles of proportion when called to our free station in the general system of the empire.

Because the proposition now made to us involves the interest of all the other colonies, we are now represented in general congress by members approved by this house, where our former union, it is hoped, will be so strongly cemented that no partial applications can produce the slightest departure from the common cause. We consider ourselves as bound in honor, as well as interest, to share one general fate with our sister colonies, and should hold ourselves base deserters of that union to which we have acceded were we to agree on any measures distinct and apart from them.

There was, indeed, a plan of accommodation offered in Parliament, which, though not entirely equal to the terms we had a right to ask, yet differed but in few points from what the general Congress had held out. Had Parliament been disposed sincerely, as we are, to bring about a reconciliation, reasonable men had hoped that by meeting us on this ground, something might have been done. Lord Chatham's bill, on the report, and the terms of the Congress on the other, would have formed a basis for negotiation, which a spirit of accommodation, on both sides, might perhaps have reconciled. It came recommended, too, from one whose successful experience in the art of government should have ensured to it some attention from those to whom it was rendered. He had shown to the world that Great Britain, with her colonies united firmly under a just and honest government, formed a power which might bid defiance to the most potent enemies. With a change of ministers, however, a total change of measures took place: the component parts of the empire have, from that moment, been falling asunder; and a total annihilation of its weight, in the political scale of the world, seems justly to be apprehended.

These, my lord, are our sentiments on this important subject, which we offer only as an individual part of the whole empire. Final determination we leave to the general Congress, now sitting, before whom we shall lay the papers your lordship has communicated to us. To their wisdom we commit the improvement of this important advance. If it can be wrought into any good we are assured they will do it. To them also we refer the discovery of that proper method of representing our well-founded grievances, which, your lordship assures us, will meet with the attention and regard so justly due to them. For ourselves we have exhausted every mode of application which our invention could suggest as proper and promising. We have decently remonstrated with Parliament; they have added new injuries to the old. We have wearied our king with supplications; he has not deigned to answer us. We have appealed to the native honor and justice of the British nation; their efforts in our favor have been hitherto ineffectual. What then remains to be done? That we commit our injuries to the evenhanded justice of that Being who doth no wrong, earnestly beseeching him to illuminate the councils and prosper the endeavors of those to whom America has confided her hopes; that, through their wise direction, we may again see, reunited, the blessings of liberty and property and the most permanent harmony with Great Britain.

June 14, 1775 [55]

It may, however, at first sight be supposed that when this answer speaks of a free trade with all the world, it coincides with Dr. Robertson's suspicion and prediction; but it is obvious from the context that it is hinted at only as a condition for the concessions required from the colonies.[56]

It was a dexterous management of the affections of the British subjects on both sides of the Atlantic to refer to the bill of Lord Chatham as susceptible with a modification of being made the ground of reconciliation. His name was engraved on the hearts of them all, and in America he was greeted as the chief of her friends. How he would have extricated himself in fair argument from the embarrassments of his

55. See *Burgesses, Journal, 1773–76*, pp. 219–21.
56. See above, pp. 216–17.

distinction between an external regulation of trade and internal taxation, his eloquence alone could say, and it is problematical whether, if the American controversy had been accommodated upon that principle, his popularity or his consistency would not have been wrecked in the vindication of it in practice. While he denominated his bill a bill of concession to America, he claimed for it the name of a bill asserting the rights of the mother country.[57]

But from an inquiry instituted into the plunder of the gunpowder, symptoms of exasperation were appearing, not absolutely exempt from a pretext that Dunmore and his family were in danger at least of insult. He therefore retreated with them on board of a frigate of war lying at Yorktown about twelve miles below Williamsburg. He was frivolous enough to submit to the choice of the Assembly either to forward to him on board the business in which he would have participated on shore or to adjourn to Yorktown, which on another occasion the commander of the frigate had threatened (with perfect power to execute the threat) to batter down, if a body of marines, which he had landed as guards to the governor in his palace, should be interrupted in their march thither.[58]

The result of this inquiry was a voluminous farrago of bitterness against the governor.[59] I shall not comment on it further, because it was much the child of licentiousness, as being without a rein upon it from cross-examination. But with it the Assembly and all the acts which had been matured up to the governor's exodus died; and with this abortive Assembly, the regal government breathed its last, except for the disturbance of the peace of Virginia. Dunmore not only gathered troops from ships of war and enlisted a few malcontent white persons but proclaimed emancipation to the slaves.[60]

In July 1775 the Convention [61] passed an ordinance appointing a committee of safety for the more effectual carrying into execution the several rules and regulations established by that body for the protection of the colony. They were a temporary executive for one year, or

57. Lord Chatham presented a bill to the House of Lords on Feb. 1, 1775, entitled "A Provisional Act for settling the Troubles in America and for asserting the supreme legislative authority and superintending power of Great Britain over the Colonies." After a heated debate the bill was defeated by a vote of 61 to 32 (Force, *Archives,* 4th ser., I, 1503–14).

58. See *ibid.,* II, 371, 975.

59. See *ibid.,* p. 1209.

60. See *ibid.,* III, 1385.

61. In response to the resolution of the Convention of March 1775, new elections were held to choose delegates for a convention which met in July 1775.

until the then next Convention. Thus did the colony glide from monarchy into self-government, without a convulsion or a single clog to its wheels from its novelty or from disaffection. Thus too were falsified all the predictions of Dean Tucker, the most inveterate of America's enemies, that to withdraw from the Western Hemisphere the superintending sun of Great Britain would involve it in darkness and misery.[62]

The intelligence of the bloodshed at Lexington and Bunker Hill in the neighborhood of Boston had in Virginia changed the figure of Great Britain from an unrelenting parent into that of a merciless enemy, whose malice was the more severe, as her affection had been the more earnestly courted. George Washington had been unanimously elected by Congress as captain general and commander in chief of the American army. The Convention had organized a large corps of militia, styled minutemen, who were to be trained at convenient seasons and ready for service at all times. Two regiments of regular infantry had been also raised, the command of which was given to Patrick Henry, then a member of Congress sitting in Philadelphia. Officers with military experience were rare: Virginia was compelled to rely principally on those elements of character which were indispensable in a soldier. Henry was seconded by men who had been active in the French and Indian War of 1755, and their imperfect lessons promised to render him with his ambition and attention an able defender of liberty in the field, as he had been in the forum.

The navy of Dunmore was supposed to consist of three vessels of war of twenty, sixteen, and fourteen guns, and his army of two companies of a British regiment and about one hundred Negroes.[63] He fed his vanity with menaces of destruction to every town and building on the eastern waters and fancied that he was evincing a species of Roman heroism when he warned the inhabitants of Hampton, a little village near the mouth of James River, that he would burn it in reprisal for two schooners, which the Virginians had captured.[64]

These inhabitants communicated their defenseless state to the Com-

62. Josiah Tucker (1712–99), dean of Gloucester, wrote several political tracts in which he advocated strong military force as the best means for repressing the insurrection in America. Randolph was referring to Tucker's *Four Tracts, together with Two Sermons on Political and Commercial Subjects* (Gloucester, 1774).

63. Dunmore's plans included both an attempt to enlist Negro slaves in the king's service and a scheme to bring Ohio Valley Indians down upon the western frontier of Virginia (John R. Alden, *The American Revolution, 1775–1783* [New York, 1954], p. 77).

64. For a discussion of Dunmore's military activities, see Christopher Ward, *The War of the Revolution* (New York, 1952), II, 845–49.

mittee of Safety, who are represented by Burk, a late historian, to have canvassed the question, whether the lower country should not be abandoned as untenable.[65] From what disclosure this fact is handed to us cannot be conjectured, as that body sat with closed doors and under injunctions of secrecy, and it was not rumored abroad, until it appeared under the authority of his name. I do not with the assurance of knowledge peremptorily contradict it. It perhaps might have been very honestly discussed in the scantiness of military skill, and while raw militia alone were to sustain the charge of disciplined troops, and so long a line of coasts was accessible to the cannon of vessels of war. But crude counsels never confirmed by a majority of the acting rulers, quickly renounced, and blotted out by contrary conduct detract from neither the patriotism nor firmness of the committee. The names of the members attending at this conjuncture are at present unknown; but of the eleven who constituted it, seven possessed large estates within the district intended to be derelict, and it may be concluded that if so baneful and disgraceful an idea escaped the mind in which it was generated, it must have been the hasty excrescence of a brain disturbed from the perplexity of the moment, but recovering itself after more mature reflection. Howsoever this may be, it is certain that under the orders of that very committee, in seven hours after the request of aid had arrived in Williamsburg, a company of regulars, of which George Nicholas, the eldest son of Robert Carter Nicholas, and a company of minutemen, of whom George Lyne was the captain, and one hundred riflemen commanded by Colonel William Woodford were seen in Hampton after a march of thirty-six miles.[66] The enemy's little fleet enfiladed the town; but from the position taken by the riflemen, no man could stand at the helm, or show himself in the management of the sails, without being immediately devoted to slaughter. From the shyness and inactivity which fear had caused in the sailors, a part of the fleet was driven on shore, and the rest fled to Norfolk. Thus was the enemy repulsed with loss and ignominy to them and with glory to the Virginians—a glory probably not of excessive splendor in military records, but of immense utility in this stage of the Revolution, which

65. Burk, *Virginia*, III, 432.

66. George Nicholas (1754?–1799), an accomplished and experienced parliamentarian, was later to distinguish himself as one of the most formidable proponents of the Constitution. Capt. George Lyne was commander of a company of minutemen from King and Queen County. William Woodford (1734–80), a burgess from Caroline County, was to distinguish himself as a general in the Continental army.

was fettered with a general sentiment that the British navy was in its humblest shape invincible and militia but sport for British regulars.

Dunmore on his part made an excursion into Princess Anne County to destroy some cannon. The same spirit which produced the defeat at Hampton stimulated Colonel John Hutchings, the commander of Norfolk County, to raise his militia and to endeavor by an ambush to intercept the motley corps of the governor.[67] Dunmore fell into the snare but was extricated by a panic, which could not be accounted for and put the militia to flight after the first discharge of their musketry, leaving their colonel a prisoner.

The crest of Dunmore was now as high as that of the Virginians after the affair at Hampton. Hearing that a large body of them were in motion to attack him, he advanced some miles to the Great Bridge to receive them. Woodford was detached to dislodge him but was impeded by accidents which he could not control and by information that Dunmore was hastening to Suffolk, a town on Nansemond River about twenty miles from Norfolk, to receive submissions and scatter his proclamations commanding the people to repair to the royal standard.[68] He therefore sent Lieutenant Colonel Charles Scott and Major Thomas Marshall, with 215 light troops, of whom 103 were expert riflemen, to intercept him. At the same time he requested a reinforcement of at least 100 men, with further supplies, necessary for the equipment of the volunteers who were joining him daily. Without delay his wishes were complied with, and Colonel Thomas Bullitt, celebrated in the Indian war, was dispatched to aid Woodford with his experience.[69] Scott and Marshall did not overtake Dunmore in his predatory retreat, but surprised a body of Tories on their way to the Great Bridge and disarmed many who had renewed their allegiance to the king.

67. John Hutchings had raised 170 men in Princess Anne County and was moving up to join Colonel Woodford when he was met and crushed by a superior force that Dunmore had put ashore at Kemp's Landing.

68. Dunmore's army included two or three hundred Negroes under the name of Lord Dunmore's Ethiopians, a group of whites called the Queen's Own Loyal Virginians, and a small force of regulars, a total army of about 1,200 men. Colonel Woodford had under his command one of Virginia's two regular regiments (with John Marshall as a lieutenant of militiamen) and about 200 volunteer riflemen (Ward, *War of the Revolution*, II, 847; for a discussion of "Dunmore's Ethiopian Regiment," see Benjamin Quarles, *The Negro in the American Revolution* [Chapel Hill, N.C., 1961], pp. 19–32) .

69. Charles Scott (*ca.* 1739–1813) , a noncommissioned officer under Washington in Braddock's expedition, was a member of the Continental army from the beginning of the war, eventually rising to the rank of general. Thomas Bullitt (d. 1778) was a planter in Fauquier County and adjutant general of Virginia. For Marshall, see n. 29 above.

To describe the position of small forts and redoubts and to narrate all the humility of the warfare of that day satisfies none of the desiderata of history. The bulk of such an inert mass cannot be enlivened by one particle of interest to those who read now the tales of those ancient times. But let it not be forgotten that at the Great Bridge the Virginians faced like veterans the blaze of danger and drove the enemy into a post of security; the companies of Nicholas and Walker Taliaferro [70] were on the point of storming the fort when the enemy deserted in confusion. Bullitt was solicitous for an assault of the strongest entrenchment and strongest ground occupied by the enemy. He was transported into the most decided confidence in the heroism of his inflamed countrymen. But the prudence of Woodford held fast the fame which had been recently acquired, knowing the importance of it as an incentive to future exertion and a passport to future victory. With inferior numbers did the detachment under Woodford kill or wound every officer and private of Dunmore's forces, and the injury to his own corps was confined to a single private wounded. I record, however, with great pleasure the humanity of the Virginians: They had been branded with opprobrious name of rebels, had been outraged as unworthy of the rights of war, and had fought under a conviction that the gibbet was already prepared for them in Dunmore's mind, should they be conquered. And yet did they not hesitate between a manly oblivion or resentment and the indulgence of ferocious passion. Their tenderness to the unfortunate was acknowledged by the British themselves.[71]

The news of this disaster was a deathblow to the most aspiring hopes of Dunmore, whose compunctions were the more tormenting as he had impressed or inveigled into his army a body of Highland Scotch, who under his auspices had emigrated to America to establish themselves as tillers of the earth, many of whose families were now bereft of bread, in a foreign land not friendly to them, except from motives of compassion. Dunmore had considered it as a stroke of profound and lucky policy to recruit the able-bodied men among this tribe of wretches, indifferent about the probable consequence of their catching the feelings of citizens, whose aim was to plant their wives and children in a

70. Walker Taliaferro was a burgess from Caroline County and a member of the conventions of 1774, 1775, and 1776.

71. Although the patriots hung no Tories, with the striking exception of runaway slaves who had joined the governor, Woodford's proposal that they be held prisoner, subject to the judgment of the Convention, was unacceptable. Most of those who fought with Dunmore chose to sail with the British warships rather than face these terms (Eckenrode, *Revolution in Virginia*, p. 85).

soil more promising than that of their native land. Pure vengeance was the aliment of his soul and blunted his understanding. He himself took refuge on board of his own ship, and the remains of his army in Norfolk; the Highlanders were neglected by him as outcasts doomed to perish by nakedness or famine. Coals of fire must have been heaped on his head when he heard that those whom he classed with traitors administered to their necessities and equipped them for a journey to and settlement in North Carolina, for which province they were destined when they embarked from Scotland.[72] Indeed in no state of exasperation was the conduct of any public body marked with a severity or obduracy disproportioned to the just suggestions of self-preservation. The Convention had by a special resolution protected the resident British merchants, factors, and agents who did not manifest enmity to the common cause in the enjoyment of their civil rights and liberty, and discountenancing all national reflections; and when this extreme courtesy and tolerance had been grievously abused, they repealed it, but not without a license to those who had taken up arms against the country or been inimical to leave it. It was reserved for the honor of an American nation to observe Christianlike forbearance during the rage of civil war.[73]

Upon the junction of Colonel Robert Howe [74] and his regiment from North Carolina, he and Woodford advanced with their whole force to Norfolk. As soon as they appeared, Dunmore, to efface the defeat at the Great Bridge and to intimidate the opposition to the supplies of wood and water which had been refused to him, drew up his squadron before the town; but this measure was so far from producing the intended effect that it taught the Virginians that even the British navy could not be secure in all situations. The riflemen were so stationed as to reach with their bullets the man who ventured to appear in their

72. As recent arrivals in the colonies the Highlanders had little chance of becoming Americanized, especially since they continued to live in clans. Moreover, they were grateful to the British government which had given them a new beginning and land in America (Wallace Brown, *The King's Friends: The Composition and Motives of the American Loyalist Claimants* [Providence, 1965], pp. 205–8).

73. As early as 1776 men active in behalf of the crown were declared subject to imprisonment or death and loss of property. In 1777 those who merely refused to take an oath of allegiance were disenfranchised, denied the right to sue for debts and to acquire land, and taxed doubly. In 1779 the state began general confiscation and sale of property belonging to Tories and British-born persons (John R. Alden, *South in the Revolution, 1763–1789* [Baton Rouge, La., 1957], pp. 323–24; see also Isaac S. Harrell, *Loyalism in Virginia; Chapters in the Economic History of the Revolution* [Durham, N.C., 1926]).

74. Robert Howe (1732–86), a colonel in 1775, eventually rose to the rank of major general and command of an American army in the South.

ships. The naval commander thereupon commenced a bombardment of the town and landed parties, which set fire to several houses near the river. The Virginian army rushed through the smoke and fires and drove the British to their boats. Thus the essence of Dunmore's prowess and talents served only to familiarize our raw troops to danger and to inspire them with contempt for the terror of British power. War was not longer unnerved by vain expectations of peace. Such too was the temper of the Convention which met in Richmond on December 1, 1775, breathing the spirit of a nation invaded and no longer halting between the torpor of reconciliation and the exigencies of the crisis.

Dunmore determined to try the last resort of his nominal office of governor. He proclaimed martial law, beckoned to his standard, under the penalty of treason, every man capable of bearing arms, and emancipated all slaves of a similar description. So little were the Convention alarmed by this scheme of domestic murder that they contented themselves with a determination to repel force by force and promised pardon to such slaves as should return to their duty in ten days. That kindness of providence which is displayed in antidotes for the poison of almost every climate is most peculiarly exhibited in giving to the general mind of a nation roused by oppression an elasticity by which it may rise from its depression above almost every terror.

Virginia committed but few errors in the selection of men to whom she committed her interests. But she was not equally fortunate in the repudiation of a father and his three sons, of the name of Goodrich.[75] They were so original and happy in their genius of shipbuilding that from the construction of vessels adapted to all the waters of this colony, many cargoes escaped capture and relieved the most urgent wants of the navy and of the people. But upon a doubt whether upon some occasion they had acted correctly, they were suspected of being unfaithful to the country and forced into the condition of enemies. Their hostility was not to be appeased. Their faculties were so applied as to enable them to intercept every vessel which they could discern in the shallowest water and most intricate navigation. It was said that the whole British navy had scarcely made prizes of Virginia ownership to an equal amount with theirs. Fertile as revolutions generally are in

---

75. John Goodrich, a Nansemond planter and shipowner, had served the colony well in the early stages of the conflict by bringing vitally needed powder from the West Indies. But Goodrich apparently was intimidated by Dunmore; at any rate, he began to act on the British side as a commander of an armed sloop which captured several prizes. Finally captured, he was judged guilty and sent to the interior, and his estates were seized (Eckenrode, *Revolution in Virginia*, p. 138).

character equal to every growing necessity, Virginia never repaired the loss which she sustained in these men. They had explored every vulnerable point and weakness in Virginia; and their hatred kept pace with their knowledge. Whether they were guilty or not of the first imputations was decided by the voice of the public, according to the temperament of him who judged. But a cloud may suddenly envelop well-disposed and capable men, which they may not easily pierce, or which if lessened is never wholly dissipated. They may be forgiven, and the attainder of their reputation may be proclaimed to be unjust, but the suspicion infects every struggle toward full and delicate confidence. The cause of these men I pretend not perfectly to understand or to advocate. But it is a superfluous function of history to warn a republic to avoid temerity in condemning, without the highest proof, her servants who until the hour of darkness shone with luster in her service.

The Convention closed their labors for supporting the war without expressing in any act a yearning to independence; and yet they had ascended an eminence from which independence was visible in all the surrounding horizon. An army had been levied, the regal government was laid aside, Virginia had exercised the rights of a nation, with reference only to the power granted by the conventions. Still, if the most influential members of these bodies had in terms moved for independence, the exceptions would have been few to a universal clamor against it.

However, Thomas Paine, an Englishman by birth and possessing an imagination which happily combined political topics, poured forth a style hitherto unknown on this side of the Atlantic for the ease with which it insinuated itself into the hearts of the people who were unlearned, or of the learned, who were not callous to the feelings of man. From his pen issued the pamphlet of *Common Sense*,[76] pregnant with the most captivating figures of speech; with the abuses of the British government not before seen in America in so gross and palpable forms; with proud republican theories, which flattered human nature; with contempts of British power, which had appalled the most sanguine calculations; and with compliments on the docility of patriots in all the arts of war by land and by sea. It was published under the reputed sanction of Dr. Benjamin Franklin and was a textbook from which many of the most respectable officers in our army warmed the coldest among their civil friends. Under all these advantages, the public

76. *Common Sense* was published in Jan. 1776.

sentiment, which a few weeks before had shuddered at the tremendous obstacles with which independence was environed, overleaped every barrier.

The Convention of 1776

The election of delegates for the Convention, the stated meeting of which was to be in May 1776, was now depended in very many, if not in a majority, of the counties upon their candidates pledging themselves or being understood to be resolved to sever, as far as their voices could extend, the colonies from Great Britain. But in truth, this pamphlet put the torch to combustibles which have been deposited by different gusts of fury, excited by successive acts of the ministry and those who were their agents. The effect on this body of inflammable materials was so rapid and instantaneous that all previous indications were either concealed from or discredited by the most acute statesman. Franklin, it is true, was adored for political wisdom, and Paine entranced our understandings; but independence would have rested in the womb of time, had not its birth been, as it were, studiously quickened by the excesses of the ministry, demonstrating that a peaceful reunion with embittered enemies who treated Americans as vassals of the mother country was impossible. In fact, therefore, independence was imposed upon us by the misdeeds of the British government.

In the Convention of May, the members who filled the most space in the public eye were Edmund Pendleton, who presided, Patrick Henry, who had from some disgust resigned his command of the First Virginia Regiment, in time to be elected, George Mason, James Mercer, Robert Carter Nicholas, James Madison of Orange, Richard Bland, Thomas Ludwell Lee, Richard Henry Lee, Thomas Nelson, George Wythe, and John Blair. These were associated with numbers whose fortunes and unobtrusive good sense supported the ardor of the more active in the theater of business. Madison, even then, attracted great notice.[77] Until the meeting of this convention he was unknown at the metropolis. He was educated at Princeton College in New Jersey and had been laborious in his studies, which ranged beyond strict academic limits but were of that elementary cast, subservient in their general principle to any science which he might choose to cultivate in

77. For James Madison (1751–1836), see Irving Brant, *James Madison* (Indianapolis, 1941–61).

detail. As a classical scholar, he was mature; as a student of belles lettres, his fancy animated his judgment, and his judgment, without damping his fancy, excluded by the soundness of criticism every propensity to tinsel and glitter. It still glowed, but it glowed without glare. His diffidence went hand in hand with his morals, which repelled vice, howsoever fashionable. In convention debate his lips were never unsealed, except to some member who happened to sit near him; and he who had once partaken of the rich banquet of his remarks did not fail to wish daily to sit within the reach of his conversation. It could not be otherwise, for although his age and the deference which in private circles had been paid to him were apt to tincture him with pedantry, he delivered himself without affectation upon Grecian, Roman, and English history from a well-digested fund, a sure presage of eminence. A very sensible foreigner observed of him that he never uttered anything which was not appropriate and not connected with some general principle of importance. Even when he commented upon the dignity with which Pendleton filled the chair, it was in that philosophic spirit which looks for personal dignity in officers of a republic as well as of a monarchy. While he thrilled with the ecstasies of Henry's eloquence and extolled his skill in commanding the audience, he detected what might be faulty in his reasoning. Madison was enviable in being among the few young men who were not inflated by early flattery and could content themselves with throwing out in social discourse jewels which the artifice of a barren mind would have treasured up for gaudy occasions.

At this date commences the difficult alternative of either discarding from this history all connection with that of the United States or of torturing the latter into an alliance with the former. The best course seems to be to give each state its separate rights of reputation, where separate rights have been acquired by particular exertions, or even by the decisive merits of its particular citizens. But as an extensive national operation combines a number of minutiae, which contribute almost imperceptibly to its final success, and even undistinguishably every measure and every battle, which obviously tends to the consummation of the great object, may be appropriated by any state to its own history, as members of the same grand union, care being taken to prevent the abuse of repeating the whole revolutionary history of the United States as if it were naturally capable of combining with that of the particular state without any diminution. But this connection between the United States and Virginia shall be postponed until after the end of the year 1781.

Chapter VII Continental Events, etc., but More Properly the Revolutionary History of the United States as Interwoven with That of Virginia

 This portion of the revolutionary history of the United States is engrossed by civil events and military transactions. The former rather indicate the temper of the belligerent parties; the latter their relative power or the approach of each to its proposed object: of the king of England to conquest or subjugation; of the United States to the recognition of their independence.

Prior, however, to the first eminent consolidated act of *power* under the United Colonies, the appointment of George Washington to the command of the American army, a few circumstances seem more peculiarly to belong to individual states.

Copiously to extract these instances, as well as others which follow until the end of the war, from the only authentic history of that period, the *Life of George Washington* by Chief Justice Marshall,[1] might with difficulty escape the charge of plagiarism, or of piracy, as it is sometimes expressed. I risk, too, the less in merely giving what I wish to call the philosophy of that period, as I profess nothing didactic in the military art.

1. The posts of Ticonderoga and Crown Point were captured by an American force, principally from Connecticut under their own authority, and principally on their own credit and expense.[2] The military stores which fell into our hands there were a seasonable supply for the prosecution of more enlarged views; and in addition to these succors, the seizure of a sloop of war at St. Johns conferred on us the command of the lakes. These achievements teemed with the most solemn presages to the enemy.

1. John Marshall's *Life of George Washington* (Philadelphia, 1804–7), less a life of Washington than a history of the United States, was just coming off the press as Randolph was working on his *History*. Randolph quoted extensively from Marshall's *Washington*.

2. On May 9, 1775, a force commanded by Ethan Allen (1738–89) and Benedict Arnold (1741–1801) captured Ticonderoga; two days later one of Allen's detachments under Seth Warner seized Crown Point, which the English had demolished and evacuated (Willard M. Wallace, *Appeal to Arms* [Chicago, 1964], pp. 30–31).

2. The king had banished all hope of reconciliation by announcing to Parliament a daring spirit of resistance in Massachusetts and his determination to maintain the supreme authority of the British legislature over all his dominions. Both houses adopted the royal infatuation and pride. These the eloquence and influence of even Chatham, covered with the mantle of superstition which his rapid descent to the grave seemed already to spread over his virtues, if not his very feelings, could not subdue or abate.

3. The battle of Concord and that of Lexington, which formed the first entrance, as it were, into arms, was most propitious to the American cause.[3]

4. On the eve of a revolution, trifles often weigh much in the estimate of human actions. The reprisals in Virginia for the gunpowder removed by the British governor became a universal pledge that to resist a governor in such circumstances should not be dreaded as treason.[4]

5. An American cannot believe that it was material to our success whether the first onset of British hostility came on the east or any other geographical division of America. Still he cannot refuse his assent to the probability that there were portions of the colonies in which the position and army of the British General Gage [5] might for a time have produced a more unfavorable impression than at Boston. In the preparations for resistance at Bunker or Breed's Hill, farmers and laborers, accustomed to no other use of gunpowder than for amusement or explosions to remove obstacles, were on a sudden to confront the highest order of discipline and terror in the enemy. They not only planted themselves in support of the breastwork, thrown up in haste and in the most unscientific manner during the preceding night, but numbers also were mowed down by the cross fire of two ships of war as the Americans were passing the isthmus to the rampart. There the unusual resort to cannon was soon so familiar to them that with their skill and bravery in managing it they staggered the British veterans in their approach, caused the general to halt and hold a council and afterwards to arrest his movements, until reinforcements should arrive from

3. The battles at Lexington and Concord were fought on April 19, 1775 (see Arthur B. Tourtellot, *Lexington and Concord: The Beginning of the War of the American Revolution* [New York, 1963]).

4. On April 20, 1775, Dunmore seized twenty kegs of powder from the provincial magazine at Williamsburg for fear that they were destined for rebel guns.

5. Gen. Thomas Gage (1721–87), commander in chief of the British army in America, was appointed governor of Massachusetts to enforce the Coercive Acts of 1774 (see John R. Alden, *General Gage in America* [Baton Rouge, La., 1948]).

Boston. The chief leader of these provincials was not recommended to them by a confidence in his military experience or reflection on war. His profession and habits lay in the medical art.[6] They asked themselves only whether he was patriotic and brave. Besides this good fortune, they had, from the long contemplation of dangers inevitable from the British army, made up their minds to face extremities, when the other colonies perhaps had just begun to think seriously and awfully upon the prospect. Be the cause what it may, to the luster of the day at Bunker Hill we may trace much of our future splendor and success. It gave character and banished one of the parents of fear in war, an idea of self-humiliation in comparison with an army.

6. The contagion of heroic example would of itself have aroused Virginia to repel the British squadron in its invasion of Hampton and animated her to the distinguished defeat of Dunmore at the Great Bridge.

7. Among the deferences paid to Virginia in the early Congresses, it was natural that her pretensions to give a commander in chief of the army should be consulted. But independently of this motive, one of her sons enjoyed as high a character for military experience and acquirement as any inhabitant of another colony. This was George Washington, whose fame was as fair for so hazardous an experiment as could be found in America. He was a native, with habits hardy, bold, and active. His fortune was suitable to any station and superior to every influence. He had been a disciple in the British school of Indian warfare and a witness of the fatality of rashness in a general. In a word, the title to public confidence was complete in him alone. Colonel Charles Lee and Major Horatio Gates [7] were Britons and British soldiers.

Upon the notification to him of his appointment, he in his reply of acceptance manifested that he was secure from arrogance and presumption and was neither hasty in overlooking difficulties nor would be too flexible in yielding to them. Discernment and patriotism may be said to have concurred in the appointment as the best in the power of Congress.[8]

8. The work was, however, begun only. Large bodies of troops ar-

6. Dr. Joseph Warren (1741–75), a leader of the rebels in Massachusetts.

7. Horatio Gates (1727–1806) had sold his commission in the British army and emigrated from England to the Shenandoah Valley in 1772. He was appointed adjutant general of the Continental army (George A. Billias "Horatio Gates: Professional Soldier," in Billias, ed., *George Washington's General* [New York, 1964]).

8. Washington was appointed commander in chief by the Continental Congress on June 15, 1775.

rived from England; the governor of Massachusetts proclaimed martial law and excepted from an act of indemnity and pardon two of the most distinguished citizens, Samuel Adams and John Hancock.[9] This lesson, that safety was to be sought only in arms, dictated the immediate necessity of emitting paper money, collecting military stores, and raising an army according to our best energies.

9. The constitution of the army existing under the states was so far sound that from its patriotism and bodily ability a hope was inspired of its capacity to be well organized. But it was impossible from the manner and circumstances of assembling it that it should be other than a crude mass, compounded of corps distracted by various and independent authorities. The appointment of some of the most indispensable officers was omitted; even a quartermaster general, a commissary general, engineers, and many officers of the staff were unknown. The terms of enlistment, being unequal in duration, forbade a coincidence of operation for any length of time. The roads were crowded with some returning home after short tours of duty and others going to camp for a moment, as it were, under the charm of novelty of military display. The equality in the intercourse of fellow citizens, necessary in the cultivation of a revolution, unnerved the army which was to support it. The unshrinking temper maintained by the friends of the war in this condition of things proclaimed that the cause was deeply seated in the heart. It countenanced in some respects, indeed, the prediction of our friends in England that attempts to conquer us were desperate, but rendered the ministry callous.

10. To defend lines as extensive as those with which Boston was necessarily invested, when numbers, materials, and ammunition were so defective; to substitute enthusiasm and native courage for military habits and experience; and to efface by a preference of military life a predilection for the comforts left at home; to meet under all these disadvantages a large, well-disciplined, well-provided enemy, enjoying every facility of transportation by water, could not escape the penetration, though they did not alarm the breast, of any officer. But it was unaccountable that experienced British generals, of whose character activity was the essence, should adopt a species of defensive warfare. For a considerable time, understanding, as it was believed, our situation as well from the disaffected, as from facts of notoriety, our wide-stretched lines were permitted to remain as if they had been works indeed, when

9. Samuel Adams (1722–1803) and John Hancock (1737–93) were, of course, the leaders of the Boston patriots.

the only semblance of their impregnability arose perhaps from the suspicion excited at Bunker Hill that to flee before British cannon was no American attribute. Of a great importance was this early promise of prowess.[10]

11. It seemed to be the fate of England to mistake her policy and means of annoyance. The destruction of the town of Falmouth in Massachusetts denoted a cruelty regardless of the usages of civilized war.[11] It unintentionally but decisively added fuel to the American flame. Letters of marque and reprisal were now granted, and under them vessels of great value were captured, having on board articles of the first necessity.[12] Supplies of provisions to Bermuda and the West Indies were intercepted, and the insidious popularity of several of the British governors now ceased to deceive: their persons were no longer held sacred, and the consequences of arresting them had fallen into contempt.

12. In the face of an enemy who upon an ordinary calculation was able to destroy with ease was our army to be reenlisted, after the contrast of a camp had given to domestic life a zest and regret. This was undertaken with momentary expedients, with temporary enlistments, in the spirit of the times, not in the wisdom of Congress, with men wanting both fuel and clothing in the latitude of Boston, with the militia and soldiery around that town visited by the smallpox.

13. But it was a noble trait in Congress to be ignorant of depression from adversity and even amidst real weakness to adopt measures of retaliation for infractions of the law of nations. It was a noble concealment which patriotism stretched over some of our most vulnerable parts. It was an illustrious effect that in March 1776 the enemy should be compelled to evacuate Boston. This step uttered the most explicit language, inviting America to confide and persevere. Our very disasters in Canada exhorted with the same strength.[13] To be partially defeated and even to retreat is not to be subjugated. Light enough

10. For a discussion of the siege of Boston, see Ward, *War of the Revolution,* I, 52–124. The battle of Bunker Hill occurred in June 1775; see Thomas J. Fleming, *Now We Are Enemies: The Story of Bunker Hill* (New York, 1960).

11. Falmouth (Maine) was burned by British sailors in the late fall of 1775.

12. Before the end of 1775 Washington had commissioned several craft, and Congress had created the Navy and the Marine Corps. By 1778 about 10,000 Americans were engaged in privateering (see Henry Steele Commager and Richard B. Morris, ed., *The Spirit of Seventy-Six: The Story of the Revolution as Told by Participants* [New York, 1958], II, 964–81).

13. The Americans had launched an invasion of Canada in 1775. After experiencing some early successes, the American army was repulsed at Quebec, and although another army captured Montreal, they were forced to retreat by smallpox and expiring enlistments (see Kenneth Roberts, *March to Quebec* [New York, 1938; rev. ed., 1940]).

broke through this gloom in Canada to penetrate all but British blind-
ness, and inspire America with fresh vigor and alacrity. Various cheer-
ing rays were floating elsewhere. The British naval armament had been
repulsed at Fort Moultrie in South Carolina, and a body of Highland emigrants who had risen on the side of England was dispersed.[14]

14. As Congress were not to be heart-stricken by misfortune,
neither were they to be puffed into bravado. When they declared that
foreign aid was attainable, the assertion was ridiculed on the British
side, and the British nation was duped by the arts or ignorance of their
own diplomatists.

The Declaration of Independence, though calculated to bring the
temper of foreign nations to the test, for some time amounted only to
an additional evidence that America was resolved to evince the sincerity of her purpose by a dependence on herself—alone, if necessary.

15. A stormy season succeeded. We evacuated Long Island and New
York. Fort Washington had been carried; [15] the weakness of the American army and the impracticability of a general stimulus to the militia
compelled our general to retreat through Jersey until he was covered
by the river Delaware and possessed an open passage to the interior
of the country. When he had thus far eluded the pursuit of his overwhelming antagonist, we were relieved by a confused hope that all
was not lost, although it was indistinctly murmured by the most sanguine what were the means reserved by providence for our deliverance.
General Charles Lee too had incautiously exposed himself to a surprise
and with malignant injustice was charged with being perfidious.[16]
But it was a war of the people's choice, to which they were pledged by
the highest sanctions.

16. The successes therefore at Trenton and Princeton were not insulated events but formed an epoch from which the reputation and
safety of America may take a new date.[17] The intelligence shot through
America with electrical rapidity and scattered wonder in its train how

14. A British invasion fleet arrived at Charleston on June 1, 1776, but after a strenuous
effort was repulsed (Ward, *War of the Revolution*, II, 665–78).

15. The British army under Gen. Sir William Howe (1729–1814) forced Washington to
evacuate New York in Sept. 1776 but missed a golden opportunity to crush the American
army (Piers Mackesy, *The War for America, 1775–1783* [Cambridge, 1964], pp. 87–93).
Fort Washington, located at the northern end of Long Island, with a garrison of almost
three thousand men, was captured by the British on Nov. 16, 1776.

16. Captured by a British scouting party, Gen. Charles Lee was later court-martialed for
allegedly disobeying orders and angrily left the American service.

17. The victory at Trenton was the result of Washington's famous crossing of the
Delaware River on the night of Dec. 25, 1776. In Jan. 1777, Washington was able to out-
maneuver an attacking British army by slipping out of Trenton under cover of darkness
to safety at Princeton, N.J.

those brilliant acts could have been achieved. To hear that Washington had emerged from behind the Delaware, when it was supposed that he could seize and clutch a position of safety, as the best fortune which could then attend him, and had assumed the very ground on which he had declined open battle seemed at first one of those fictions which those who pant for news can forge so easily and circulate with so shameful a disregard to truth.

17. The defeat of Arnold on the lakes produced no extraordinary sensation at any great distance from the scene of action, although had he not miscarried no ministry could have withstood the impression which he would have made in England.[18] It was a refuge from our disappointment to see, not to feel.

18. In the calamitous and prosperous events of our Revolution, it will be perceived that many were so neutral in their operation as in America to excite no other sensation than that of surprise, or in England to inflame opposition to the ministry. These are not within our plan of incorporation with this history of Virginia. Hence we pass over the reduction of the town of Newport in Rhode Island by General Clinton and Admiral Parker,[19] and other transactions of a similar minor kind, when considered in relation to the war at large.

19. To our enemy, however, admonition upon admonition was of little avail. Otherwise a striking catalogue with no very great intervals, if it did not disturb the repose, certainly deserved the attention of the ministry. The final view of independence was never to be relinquished. The bloody alliance of Great Britain with the Indians of the Six Nations was severed by the management of General Schuyler.[20] Colonel Connolly had been intercepted in his traverse through the western frontiers, and his machinations of Indian hostility frustrated.[21] The system of retaliation marked out by Congress was not in the parade of threat

18. In Oct. 1776 Benedict Arnold led out a "mosquito fleet" to win control of Lake Champlain, and though he fought skillfully he was decisively defeated on Oct. 13 off Valcour Island (see Willard M. Wallace, *Traitorous Hero: The Life and Fortunes of Benedict Arnold* [New York, 1954], pp. 110–20).

19. Maj. Gen. Henry Clinton (*ca.* 1738–95), the son of a British admiral and colonial governor of New York, had captured Newport, R.I., in Dec. 1776. Adm. Sir Peter Parker (1721–1811) was the commander of the British fleet that in 1776 had found Charleston so unhospitable.

20. Gen. Philip Schuyler (1733–1804) of New York was the commander of the expedition against Canada. The Six Nations were the federation of Iroquois tribes centered in New York, northern Ohio, and western Pennsylvania (see Don R. Gerlach, *Philip Schuyler and the American Revolution in New York, 1733–1777* [Lincoln, Nebr., 1964]).

21. John Connolly had been authorized by Governor Dunmore to raise a regiment of Loyalists in the backcountry of Pennsylvania and Virginia. Connolly also went to General Gage in Boston and received authority to recruit a regiment to be called the Queen's

but in a spirit which, while it might be appeased by equality and justice, was not to be intimidated. The British power on sea, in the midst of terror, had been shown to be resistable on many occasions and liable to be eluded on many more. Prizes had been taken in the year 1776 equal in amount to a million of dollars, and of the most precious qualities for war, and our particular necessities under it.

20. In other parts of our revolutionary picture the darkness was considerable, and nothing short of most fervid patriotism could enlighten it.

21. Paper money had been emitted by Congress without funds of their own, without taxation, or even a pointed nominal pledge of redemption. In the Anglo-American family, such an anomaly had been hitherto a stranger. But legitimated by necessity, it was received into use with some cordiality. The disaffected to our cause inveighed against the spuriousness of its value, and caution and avarice denied to it hospitality. But the child waxed strong and was protected in its existence, until its original constitution was lost and to be connected with it was to hazard fortune.

Is there any principle of religion or morality which forbade a weak infant nation, driven into war for the avoidance of slavery, to arm itself by the best means in its power?

It was scarcely possible, indeed, that depreciation should not be foreseen. The degree of it and its havoc probably were not. Yet to stop would have been political suicide. Thus what in established governments might have been fraud, in ours, which without final success must have been annihilated, was explained, nay justified by its situation. A redemption dollar for dollar, if practicable, would have overpaid almost every holder of paper currency. It might have been heroically romantic. It would have gone beyond the most sublime precedents of any revolution. The patchwork of Congress did not arraign their wisdom, so much as it proved the difficulty of devising a remedy.[22]

The sternness of American virtue was exemplified in the fewness of the instances of defection among the people from the Revolution.

Royal Rangers, equip an expedition to Detroit, and launch an offensive that would capture Fort Pitt and Alexandria before joining Dunmore for the reconquest of Virginia. However, he was arrested in Maryland and at the order of the Continental Congress he was confined in jail at Philadelphia and then Baltimore. Finally exchanged in October 1780, he attempted to organize a Loyalist uprising around Pittsburgh and served with Cornwallis in Virginia (Carl Van Doren, *Secret History of the American Revolution* [New York, 1941], pp. 23–26).

22. For a discussion of the problems of paper money during the Revolutionary War, see John C. Miller, *Triumph of Freedom, 1775–1783* (Boston, 1948), and E. James Ferguson, *The Power of the Purse* (Chapel Hill, N.C., 1961).

Where the enemy appeared, they committed devastation. They were too often cruel and in the consternation of fire and sword obtained professions of returning allegiance from small numbers of those whose families and property were unprotected from military vengeance; but the furrow of the keel on the ocean was scarcely less permanent.

22. Every day discovered some defect in the militia, at such a time and in such a service considered as a resource of perfect safety against invasion. It was rather a depository of pure purpose and partaker of the same feelings with the people at large.

23. Even the regular forces were in a manner for a time in serious danger in the hospitals, whither they had gone to extinguish by one effort the prevailing alarms from the smallpox. Hence the state of the army was low and perilous.

24. The recruiting service too proceeded heavily, almost every state acting with a solicitude to retain its force within its own limits.

25. The dispersion of our army at Brandywine [23] must, in the mind of the enemy, have been productive of such pernicious consequences, had it been pursued with rigor, as to oblige America to summon up against despair all her recollections of the recovery of her affairs by the successes of Trenton and Princeton.

26. The éclat of possessing Philadelphia, the banishment of Congress to Lancaster,[24] our failure in the battle of Germantown, the evacuation of Ticonderoga, and the loss of our stores were hurrying the public mind into a painful abyss, when it was revived by the surrender of Burgoyne and his army.[25] This opened the second seal in the volume of independence, so as to be legible by Great Britain. In truth it gave to America a strong foothold for her grand work. It supported with joyful anticipation our army amidst the huts of Valley Forge, the combinations for supplanting Washington, the privations and nakedness of American soldiery.[26]

23. In Sept. 1777 General Howe defeated Washington's forces along the Brandywine at Chadd's Ford on the Philadelphia road.

24. General Howe took up quarters at Philadelphia in the winter of 1777 while Congress fled to Lancaster, Pa.

25. Gen. John Burgoyne (1722–92) had captured Saratoga, but on Oct. 17, 1777, he was forced to surrender his army to the Americans. As a result, the British were forced to evacuate Fort Ticonderoga (see Hoffman Nickerson, *The Turning Point of the Revolution; or, Burgoyne in America* [Boston and New York, 1928], esp. pp. 129–57).

26. While the British army enjoyed the comforts of Philadelphia, Washington's troops suffered through the winter of 1777 at Valley Forge, Pa. (see John Joseph Stoudt, *Ordeal at Valley Forge: A Day-By-Day Chronicle from December 17, 1777, to June 18, 1778, Compiled from the Sources* [Philadelphia, 1963]).

27. No doubt Great Britain fancied that our appetite for independence was reduced below arrogance when she offered through her second commissioners the reconciliation, which could be received for consideration at best only *pro forma*, and for final acceptance had passed over the time many years. It was the fatality of all British overtures to ensure their rejection by their tardiness.[27]

28. But if we could have wanted encouragement and refreshment, they came most seasonably in our treaty of alliance with France, in the evacuation of Philadelphia by the British army, in the expedition of Clark against Detroit, and in the great stroke meditated by Washington at Monmouth, which, if executed as planned by him, would, to use a phrase of his own, "have crippled the enemy." [28]

29. Here let us be permitted to remark that in estimating the vicissitudes of the war, our disasters, though they may be sometimes detailed in frightful numbers, were, with a few exceptions, not formidable in magnitude, never treated by Congress or by Washington beyond the reach of repair, while many of our successes spoke directly as fiats to American independence.

30. In the former class we rank the divisions of party in Congress, the reduction of Georgia,[29] the insurrection of the Tories in South Carolina,[30] the invasion of Virginia by Mathews, the British general,[31] and the discontents of the army.[32]

27. The British government had made two efforts at reconciliation after the commencement of hostilities. The brothers Howe, Gen. William and Adm. Viscount Richard (1726–99), were authorized to open peace negotiations but to offer nothing more than pardons for the rebels. Again in 1778 a peace commission was sent to America with a proposal for home rule without recognizing American independence or the withdrawal of British troops. However, the American states had already entered into an alliance with France (Mackesy, *War for America*, pp. 73–89, 186–89; for the brothers Howe, see Troyer Anderson, *The Command of the Howe Brothers during the American Revolution* [New York, 1936]).

28. During the summer of 1778 George Rogers Clark (1752–1818) led a band of 175 frontiersmen on an expedition to Detroit. Although they were unable to take Detroit they did capture Kaskaskia, Cahokia, and Vincennes and eventually succeeded in breaking British power in the west (see John Bakeless, *Background to Glory; the Life of George Rogers Clark* [Philadelphia, 1957], pp. 67–98; and Sosin, *Revolutionary Frontier*, pp. 117–21; see also below, pp. 271–72). The battle of Monmouth (June 1778) was indecisive with equal casualties on both sides.

29. The British attacked Georgia in 1778 and by early 1779 the state was securely in British hands.

30. When Charleston surrendered in 1780 Loyalists in the interior flocked to the British colors.

31. Maj. Gen. Edward Mathews led a force of about 1,800 men to Virginia in May 1779.

32. In Jan. 1781 dangerous mutinies broke out among Pennsylvania and New Jersey

31. In the latter the reduction of Stony Point rises above the surface of ordinary events.[33]

32. Paulus Hook witnessed a grandeur of military enterprise and merit.[34]

33. The capture of St. Vincent and Grenada [35] and the victory over the Six Nations [36] detracted something from British hostility.

34. The war with Spain brought accessions, which the British government well understood and felt.[37] Tarleton was defeated by Colonel Washington.[38]

35. Then, indeed, we are stunned by the surrender of Fort Moultrie, the capitulation of Lincoln, the settlement of the British government by Clinton in South Carolina and Georgia, the defeat of Gates at Camden,[39] the slothful proceedings of the states in the discharge of

---

troops. They were ultimately suppressed only by lavish promises, much cajoling, and the threat of attack by faithful regiments (see Carl Van Doren, *Mutiny in January* [New York, 1943]).

33. Stony Point was a "defiant promontory" thrust out into the Hudson River near West Point. Led by Anthony Wayne, the Americans captured the Point in July 1779. Although this victory held little military value, it had an inspiring effect upon the American army and upon the general public (Ward, *War of the Revolution*, II, 602-3).

34. Paulus Hook was a low-lying, blunt point of sandy land projecting into the Hudson River directly opposite New York City. On August 19, 1779, a force of Americans led by "Light-Horse Harry" Lee took the Hook from British troops. The victory had little value except as encouragement to the rebels (*ibid.*, 604-10).

35. St. Vincent and Grenada were islands in the West Indies captured by the French in 1774. Both islands were restored to Great Britain in 1783 by the Treaty of Peace.

36. In 1779 Gen. John Sullivan (1740-95) with 5,000 troops leveled forty Iroquois villages in northern Pennsylvania and western New York.

37. Spain entered the war against Britain as France's ally in 1779.

38. Lt. Col. Banastre Tarleton (1754-1833), a British officer in command of a force of Loyalists and Redcoats during the few months preceding Yorktown, was defeated by Continentals and Virginia milita at Cowpens on Jan. 17, 1781. William Washington (1752-1810) commanded a small force of 125 mounted men in the army of Gen. Daniel Morgan (for Tarleton, see Robert D. Bass, *The Green Dragon: The Lives of Banastre Tarleton and Mary Robinson* [New York, 1957]).

39. Fort Moultrie (Sullivans Island) in Charleston Harbor fell to a British force invading South Carolina in the spring of 1780. Maj. Gen. Benjamin Lincoln (1733-1810) of Mass. had been appointed by Congress in Sept. 1778 as commander of the Southern Department. On May 9, 1780, Lincoln was forced to surrender Charleston and hand over 5,000 Continentals (see Clifford Shipton, "Benjamin Lincoln: Old Reliable" in Billias, ed., *Washington's Generals*). Because of the stunning success of the southern campaign, Sir James Wright, the last royal governor of Georgia, was sent back to Savannah to resume his duties. He was able to maintain a British civil regime there for about three years. Gen. Horatio Gates lost to the forces of General Cornwallis on Aug. 17, 1779, at Camden, S.C. John R. Alden calls Camden "the most disastrous defeat ever inflicted upon an American army." As a result Gates lost "North Carolina—if not Virginia—and his whole army" (*American Revolution*, p. 234).

their federal duties,[40] and the height to which parties were carried in Congress.

36. The armed neutrality and the consequent war with Holland, being nearer to the British home, were nearer to the British bosom.[41] The American war and American agency were such strong ingredients in it that it was obviously an engine in our labors for independence.

37. What remains of the capital events and circumstances of the war, except the battles of the Cowpens, Guilford, and Eutaw, are comprised in the body of the history from the defeat of Ferguson.[42] See Marshall's *Life of Washington,* 4th vol., p. 342.

It may possibly be thought that this continental history has been compressed or strained into membership with a general history of Virginia. But surely the latter must have appeared mutilated, if those acts and counsels in which she virtually always and most effectually often bore a part had been pretermitted.

38. Were political speculations to combine the various events of the war which contributed to the confirmation of our independence, they would probably terminate in some or other of these ideas.

1. Disguise the source as we may, Virginia in common with other colonies received from the parent country an original stamina, perhaps I might add something phlegmatic in her temper, which inclined her to regulated liberty by saving her from those ebullitions which teem with violence and insubordination.

40. Randolph was doubtless referring to the states' reluctance to fulfill their financial obligations to the Continental government.

41. When the Netherlands was preparing to join the League of Armed Neutrality, Great Britain demanded that Dutch merchants cease selling naval stores to France and Spain. Britain sent an ultimatum to the Hague in Nov. 1780 followed in Dec. by armed attacks on Dutch shipping. The League of Armed Neutrality, formed in 1780 by a group of neutrals—Russia, Sweden, and Denmark—declared the Baltic closed to warships of the fighting nations. With the support of France and Spain the League acquired adherents until, by 1783, all the major and most of the minor European states had joined (Alden, *American Revolution,* p. 192).

42. Gen. Nathaniel Greene (1742–86) was defeated by a British force at Guilford Court House (March 15, 1781) (see M. F. Treacy, *Prelude to Yorktown: the Southern Campaign of Nathaniel Greene, 1780–1781* [Chapel Hill, N.C., 1963], pp. 142–88). Patrick Ferguson (1744–80), the son of a Scottish judge, was the inventor of a breech-loading rifle which could be fired five or six times a minute, at least twenty-five times as fast as a muzzle-loading rifle when its barrel became fouled. When Clinton sent an expedition south in 1779, Ferguson was allowed to raise his own corps of riflemen, American Tories, called the American Volunteers (Ward, *War of the Revolution,* II, 740). He was killed on Oct. 7, 1781, at the Battle of Kings Mountain, S.C. His Tories had bravely resisted attack but crumbled when Ferguson fell. General Greene defeated a force under Col. Alexander Stuart in Eutaw Springs, S.C., on Sept. 8, 1781 (*ibid.,* 823–34).

2. From an elevation of character, she was incapable of being seduced by the artifices of the British government.

3. Her associations in the more recent opposition to Great Britain were cool and deliberate suggestions of the people themselves, not impulses of ambition or of faction.

4. Her portion of merit, as a state, in accomplishing the Revolution, may be estimated from her character, her wealth, her readiness to coalesce with other states upon principles of fraternity in danger and object.

5. In her concessions of interest in territory and of political power in the Confederation, her archives will show that she always deserved the confidence and never the obloquy or suspicion of her sister states.[43]

We may justly question whether our American general ever was deceived by indulging himself too warmly in the flattery of some military prospect or by too great confidence in the appearance of a devotion to the American cause, unsound at the bottom. After the defeat of Gates at Camden, Cornwallis viewed the two Carolinas, not as to be subdued, but as to be protected and preserved as actual British territory. For this purpose he sent Major Ferguson into the western part of North Carolina near the mountains. He was to be supported in his communication with Cornwallis by Tarleton's Legion; but his messengers, announcing the approach of danger from several corps of American militia, were intercepted, and he was compelled to choose his ground for defense and wait an attack on Kings Mountain. There Ferguson was slain, and with him expired the courage of his corps. The second in command immediately demanded quarter. Of British troops eight hundred and ten surrendered themselves, and fifteen hundred stand of arms were also taken.

Hence Cornwallis was disabled from an expedition into North Carolina and was obliged to wait for reinforcements from New York. General Clinton dispatched General Leslie not so much with succors as with augmented means to press Virginia.[44] Portsmouth on Elizabeth River was fortified, but Cornwallis ordered him to repair to Charleston. There, for military objects, fresh troops were constantly thrown in,

43. On Jan. 2, 1781, the Virginia Assembly formally ceded the states' claim to the Northwest Territory with the provision that Congress void all land company purchases in the region. Congress did not accept the Virginia cession until March 1784, after the Virginia legislature had ceded the area (Dec. 1783) without specific requirements.

44. Gen. Alexander Leslie (1740–94) had been sent by Cornwallis to raid the valley of the James River and to ravage Richmond and Petersburg in order to cut the flow of supplies and troops to the American Army of the South.

until Cornwallis marched himself to Petersburg and took the command, compelled thereto by the various miscarriages and disappointments which had befallen the British arms, though at first seduced by a supposed brilliancy of prosperity.

Although undoubtedly Cornwallis was sooner or later destined for Virginia, yet was it a striking peculiarity of events which brought him hither at the time of his coming and under circumstances which at the beginning of the year he little apprehended. But whether from a want of skill, the necessity of obedience to superior command, or a misconstruction of orders, he took his final position at Yorktown; the location of him at that spot was pregnant with his overthrow. Washington's anxiety seems to have been constantly on the watch and daily employed in admonishing Lafayette [45] lest Cornwallis should escape from Virginia. In York, therefore, he was invested, and the elements defeated his only attempt to escape. We are not unwilling to confess that without the French fleet, and perhaps without the French army, our success might not have been so quick and so complete in producing the capitulation of Cornwallis and his army. But our pride is supported by justice when we assert that America was competent to her own salvation. Had not the enemy discovered this truth, the abandonment of his hopes after the downfall at Yorktown would not have accorded with his exasperation against unnatural rebels, nor would it have been much promoted by a dread of our ally, who was dragged into the war by a regard to interest, not to the sacredness of our cause.

Having thus dispatched in brief the military part of the continental history, I resume the peculiar one of Virginia from the period at which that continental history was first taken up, intending to carry down to the adoption of the Constitution of the United States what remains to be executed of my original plan.

45. The Marquis de Lafayette (1757–1834) had little real military experience. Motivated by romantic ideas of the American revolt, sharing the French desire for revenge against England, and thirsting for glory, he arrived in America with a party of other adventurers on June 13, 1777. On July 31 Congress commissioned him a maj. gen. without command. The best accounts of Lafayette's activities are Louis Gottschalk, *Lafayette Comes to America* (Chicago, 1935), and *Lafayette and the Close of the American Revolution* (Chicago, 1936, 1942).

Chapter VIII   The Revolution in Virginia

When the disposition of the people as exhibited by their representatives could not be mistaken, Henry had full indulgence of his own private judgment, and he concerted with Nelson[1] that he, Nelson, should introduce the question of independence and that Henry should enforce it. Nelson affected nothing of oratory except what ardent feelings might inspire; and characteristic of himself, he had no fear of his own with which to temporize, and supposing that others ought to have none, he passed over the probabilities of foreign aid, stepped lightly over the difficulties of procuring military stores and the inexperience of officers and soldiers, but pressed a declaration of independence upon what, with him, were incontrovertible grounds, that we were oppressed, had humbly supplicated a redress of grievances, which had been refused with insult, and that to return from battle against the sovereign with the cordiality of subjects was absurd. It was expected that a declaration of independence would certainly be pressed, and for obvious reasons Mr. Henry seemed allotted to crown his political conduct with this supreme stroke. And yet for a considerable time he talked of the subject as being critical, but without committing himself by a pointed avowal in its favor or a pointed repudiation of it. He thought that a cause which put at stake the lives and fortunes of the people should appear to be their own act, and that he ought not to place upon the responsibility of his eloquence a revolution of which the people might be wearied after the present stimulus should cease to operate. But after some time he appeared in an element for which he was born. To cut the knot, which calm prudence was puzzled to untie, was worthy of the magnificence of his genius. He entered into no subtlety of reasoning but was roused by the now apparent spirit of the people as a pillar of fire, which notwithstanding the darkness of the prospect would conduct to the promised land. He inflamed, and was followed by, the

1. Thomas Nelson

Convention. The vote was unanimous for independence, except in the instance of Robert Carter Nicholas, who demonstrated his title to popularity by despising it, when it demanded a sacrifice of his judgment. He offered himself as a victim to conscience, being dubious of the competency of America in so arduous a contest. He alone had fortitude enough to yield to his fears on this awful occasion, although there was reason to believe that he was not singular in their conception. But immediately after he had absolved his obligation of duty, he declared that he would rise or fall with his country and proposed a plan for drawing forth all its energies in support of that very independence. May every man acting like him receive the like reward of an increase of popularity, which in the opinion of timeserving parasites would be annihilated by such boldness. The principles of Paine's pamphlet [2] now stalked in triumph under the sanction of the most extensive, richest, and most commanding colony in America. The event had been vehemently desired by a majority of Congress, who would not venture to originate it with themselves.[3] They were aware of its favorable influence on the affairs of America with respect to foreign nations.

As soon as the Convention had pronounced the vote of independence, the formation of a constitution or frame of government followed of course.[4] For with the royal authority, the existing organs of police and the laws ceased, and the tranquillity of society was floating upon the will of popular committees and the virtue of the people.

To this work then unprecedented in America, talents were requisite of a higher order than those which could foment a revolution. Patriotism, firmness, and a just foresight of the dangers to be encountered were sufficient to dissolve an empire. But the deepest research which had then been made here into the theory of government seemed too short for those scenes which the new order of things was to unfold and for those evils which human passions with new opportunities and solicitations must beget.

Mr. Jefferson, who was in Congress, urged a youthful friend in the Convention to oppose a *permanent* constitution until the people should elect deputies for the special purpose. He denied the power of the body elected (as he conceived them to be agents for the management of the

2. *Common Sense* (1776)

3. On May 15 the Virginia Convention instructed its delegation in Congress to push for a declaration of independence (Mays, *Edmund Pendleton*, II, 106–11).

4. For discussions of the Virginia Constitutional Convention of 1776, see Lingley, *Transition*, pp. 158–77; Malone, *Jefferson the Virginian*, pp. 235–46; Alden, *South in the Revolution*, pp. 306–28; and Grigsby, *Virginia Convention of 1776*.

war) to exceed some temporary regimen. The member alluded to communicated the ideas of Mr. Jefferson to some of the leaders in the
house, Edmund Pendleton, Patrick Henry, and George Mason. These
gentlemen saw no distinction between the conceded power to declare
independence and its necessary consequence, the fencing of society by
the institution of government. Nor were they sure that to be backward
in this act of sovereignty might not imply a distrust whether the rule
had been wrested from the king. The attempt to postpone the formation of a constitution until a commission of greater latitude and one
more specific should be given by the people was a task too hardy for an
inexperienced young man.

A very large committee was nominated to prepare the proper instruments, and many projects of a bill of rights and constitution discovered the ardor for political notice rather than a ripeness in political
wisdom. That proposed by George Mason swallowed up all the rest
by fixing the grounds and plan, which after great discussion and correction were finally ratified.

The celebrated *Notes on Virginia* have since become the vehicle of
the former objections of its author made *in limine:* "When the enemy
shall be expelled from our bowels, when peace shall be established, and
leisure given us for entrenching within good forms the rights for which
we have bled, let no man be found indolent enough to decline a little
more trouble for placing them beyond the reach of question, if anything more be requisite to produce a conviction of the expediency of
calling a convention at a proper season to *fix* our form of government,"
etc. "The ordinary legislature may alter the constitution itself." [5]
There are indeed defects in it of magnitude; and there is, no doubt,
a power resident in the people to change it, as they please. If Mr.
Jefferson's observations have contributed to some degree or restlessness
under it, they ought if just to be adverted to. They have been disarmed
of the possibility of mischief by the solemn recognitions in our courts
of the validity of the constitution. It would be useless to revive a discussion which has been thus put to sleep, though it may be yet asked
whether the confirmation of the people by their acquiescence for so
many years be no argument against the unhinging of such various authorities which have been exercised under it, and possibly of some
rights which have been derived from it? Is it nothing that independence
was established with as little premonition to the people as the consti-

5. *Notes on Virginia,* ed., Abernethy, pp. 110–24, contains Jefferson's remarks on the constitution of 1776.

tution was, and that the constitution considered only as temporary, until a more legitimate one shall be adopted (which is the extent of his demand), can no more be revoked by the legislature, which is the creature of it, appointed to execute it, than the trustees of power can transcend their instructions? But happily, practical utility will always exterminate questions too refined for public safety.

It has been often doubted, too, whether a written constitution has any superiority over one unwritten. This is a point of comparison between the English constitution and that of Virginia. An unwritten constitution can, upon the appearance of a defect, be amended, without agitating the people. A written one is a standing ark, to which first principles can be brought on to a test. Whatever merit is due to either opinion, it should not be forgotten that the spirit of a people will in construction frequently bend words seemingly inflexible and derange the organizations of power. This has happened in Virginia, where the line of partition between the legislative and judicial departments has been so remote from vulgar apprehension, or plausible necessity has driven such considerations before it.

The bill of rights and the constitution are monuments which deserve the attention of every republican, as containing some things which we may wish to be retrenched and others which cannot be too much admired.

The declaration in the first article of the bill of rights that all men are by nature equally free and independent was opposed by Robert Carter Nicholas, as being the forerunner or pretext of civil convulsion. It was answered, perhaps with too great an indifference to futurity, and not without inconsistency, that with arms in our hands, asserting the general rights of man, we ought not to be too nice and too much restricted in the delineation of them; but that slaves, not being constituent members of our society, could never pretend to any benefit from such a maxim.

The second article derives all powers from the people and declares magistrates to be always amenable to them.

The third article affirms the supremacy of a majority in a community.

The fourth explodes an inheritance in office.

The fifth separates the legislative, executive, and judicial functions and reduces the members of the two former at fixed periods to private stations.

One part of the sixth provides for the freedom of elections, and another confers the right of suffrage on all having sufficient evidence of a permanent common interest with and of attachment to the community. But it did not intend to leave this right to the will of the legislature according to capricious views of expediency. It reserved a more specific provision for the constitution.

The seventh, against the suspension of laws by any other authority than that of the representatives of the people, was suggested by an arbitrary practice of the king of England before the Revolution in 1688.

The eighth reenacts in substance modes of defense for accused persons similar to those under the English law.

The ninth, against excessive bail and excessive fines, was also borrowed from England, with additional reprobation of cruel and unusual punishments.

The tenth, against general warrants, was dictated by the remembrance of the seizure of Wilkes's papers under a warrant from a secretary of state.[6]

The eleventh, preserving the trial by jury, was not considered as a mandate to legislatures without the possibility of exception.

The twelfth, securing the freedom of the press, and the thirteenth, preferring militia to standing armies, were the fruits of genuine democracy and historical experience.

The fourteenth, prohibiting the erection of a government within the limits of Virginia, proceeded partly from local circumstances, when the chartered boundaries of Virginia were abridged by royal fiats in favor of Lord Baltimore and Lord Fairfax, much to the discontent of the people, and partly from recent commotions in the west.

The fifteenth, recommending an adherence and frequent recurrence to fundamental principles, and the sixteenth, unfettering the exercise of religion, were proposed by Mr. Henry. The latter, coming from a gentleman who was supposed to be a dissenter, caused an appeal to him whether it was designed as a prelude to an attack on the Established Church, and he disclaimed such an object.[7]

6. This reference is to John Wilkes (1727–97), an English radical who had been arrested in 1763 and convicted of seditious libel for his authorship of the famous *North Briton* No. 45. The fact that Wilkes had been arrested on a general warrant and his argument that the seizure of his private papers constituted a threat to the right of property were familiar to colonists protesting taxation without representation (see Pauline Maier, "John Wilkes and American Disillusionment with Britain," *Wm. and Mary Qtly.*, 3d ser., XX [1963], 373–95).

7. The thirteenth article provided for a militia and declared that "standing armies in time of peace should be avoided as dangerous to liberty; and that in all cases the military should be under strict subordination to, and governed by, the civil power." For the text of the Virginia Bill of Rights, see Morison, *Documents of the Revolution*, pp. 149–52.

An article prohibiting bills of attainder was defeated by Henry, who with a terrifying picture of some towering public offender against whom ordinary laws would be impotent saved that dread power from being expressly proscribed.

In the formation of this bill of rights two objects were contemplated: one, that the legislature should not in their acts violate any of those canons; the other, that in all the revolutions of time, of human opinion, and of government, a perpetual standard should be erected, around which the people might rally and by a notorious record be forever admonished to be watchful, firm, and virtuous.

The cornerstone being thus laid, a constitution delegating portions of power to different organs under certain modifications was of course to be raised upon it.[8] The most enlightened in the Convention confessed their want of perfect information, while some who were absorbed in their inveteracy against Great Britain condensed every merit of such a composition in a total abhorrence of the British constitution, not one trait of which would they adopt, unless it had been so long naturalized in practice as to give it the complexion of Virginian growth. Thus custom and habit, revolting against the pruning knife of reformation, transplanted into the constitution of Virginia many valuable things, which perhaps might have been discarded, had they not previously appeared in a Virginian garb. A governor, therefore, a senate, and a house of delegates were the more easily admitted from their resemblance to ancient arrangements under the regal government. But this fluctuation between old prepossessions and recent hatred destroyed a solicitude for a diligent extraction of whatsoever good might be found in the British constitution, or for a careful rejection of some improprieties to which time had reconciled us.

After creating the office of governor, the convention gave way to their horror of a *powerful* chief magistrate without waiting to reflect how much stronger a governor might be made for the benefit of the people, and yet be held with a republican bridle. These were not times of terror indeed, but every hint of a power which might be stigmatized as being of royal origin obscured, for a time, a part of that patriotic splendor with which the mover had before shone. No member but Henry could with impunity to his popularity have contended as strenuously as he did for an executive veto on the acts of the two houses of legislation. Those who knew him to be indolent in literary investigations were astonished at the manner in which he exhausted this topic, unaided as he was believed to be by any of the treatises on government

8. For the text of the Virginia Constitution of 1776, see *ibid.*, pp. 152–56.

except Montesquieu. Amongst other arguments he averred that a governor would be a mere phantom, unable to defend his office from the usurpation of the legislature, unless he could interpose on a vehement impulse or ferment in that body, and that he would otherwise be ultimately a dependent instead of a coordinate branch of power. His eloquence, however, had an effect only personal to himself: it only stopped the wheel of popular favor, while as to him in this respect it was inclining to roll backwards.

It may surprise posterity that in the midst of the most pointed declamations in the Convention against the inequality of representation in the British House of Commons, it was submitted to in Virginia without a murmur and even without a proposition to the contrary. The fact was that the countries to the eastward of the Blue Ridge, in which that inequality was the most glaring, were too numerous to be irritated, and it was tacitly understood that every body and individual came into the Revolution with their rights and was to continue to enjoy them as they existed under the former government, except in the example of the antiquated and reduced borough of Jamestown and the College of William and Mary, which were now to be stripped of the honors of representation.

That the qualification of electors to the General Assembly should be restricted to freeholds was the natural effect of Virginia having been habituated to it for very many years, more than a century. The members of the Convention were themselves freeholders and from this circumstance felt a proud attachment to the country in which the ownership of the soil was a certain source of comfort. It is not recollected that a hint was uttered in contravention of this principle. There can be no doubt that if it had been, it would have soon perished under a discussion.

The elementary idea of a right of suffrage in the election of a legislative deputy is that the elector possess as nearly as may be free will and a common interest with the persons to be represented. Were we to suppose a society small enough to be managed by a pure democracy, every member of it having free will would have an equal vote. Not that a single subject would be committed to the charge of the elected, but because, notwithstanding the variety of rights which some individuals might possess (for example, although besides the rights merely relative to their persons, to which all are equally entitled, others may have other rights in property, which may be affected by legislation), yet the difficulty, if not impracticability, of graduating them in a fit ratio would impose upon the society the necessity of making some general compromise among the pretensions of the whole, by acting upon a conjecture, in the gross, that all have the same interest. It would concede nothing in the argument concerning universal suffrage were it to be added that if only a single source of suffrage were to be consulted, the equal interest of all in the preservation of merely personal rights would stand most forward for acceptance.

However, the interests of the members of every civilized society are various, some of them possessing rights merely personal, others those arising from property, the latter of which require protection and watchfulness as much as the former. Here, too, the impracticability of a due gradation is equally strong. It does not follow that the same gross rule is to be observed, since the refusal to adopt it might amount to a stoppage of the movements of the democracy, for to select among rights might exclude some who did not possess them. The gross rule already stated is therefore necessarily adhered to. In this dilemma no solution presents itself but to allow to each society the right of establishing that qualification which approaches nearest to the common interest, which is the desideratum. Compare then the rights of suffrage founded on permanent property with that founded on the contribution of revenue in the way of taxes or of personal service in defense of the country.

I am not unapprised that circumstances may perhaps exist in which this attention to a common interest may require a more latitudinary right of suffrage than that accompanying a freehold, but the supposition of such circumstances may at present be laid aside. But the choice in the comparison may be contrasted thus: With a freehold a man is bound to defend his country and must pay, at least, indirect taxes. But a freehold fixes a man to his country more than a merely personal or movable right, which travels with him at any instant and in any direction. Alienations of land cannot be so rapid as the transfer of a personal chattel. There is consciousness of independence, growing from the knowledge that personal labor expended upon the soil will raise the possessor above want. The possession of soil naturally turns the attention to its cultivation, and generally speaking, men who are occupied by labor in the country are more exempt from the vices prevailing in towns. Experience in America cannot be peremptorily affirmed to be decisive either way; but it has shown one evil, at least, of which freeholders have afforded but few instances: combinations have been formed with more ease among those who want them than among those who vote with them.

The sarcasm contained in the associating of the title of George III as king of Great Britain and Ireland with that of elector of Hanover was perhaps the littleness of a partisan, rather than the dignity of a nation in arms. Its apology must be sought in the *high-toned* temper of a revolution.

In England the origination of money bills only was interdicted to the second branch of legislation. Our jealousy extended the interdiction to the unreasonable exclusion of the senate from the origination of *any* law.

By a further analysis of the constitution, a lesson will be taught that the most expanded mind, as that of George Mason was, who sketched the constitution, cannot secure itself from oversights and negligences in the tumult of heterogeneous and indistinct ideas of government circulating in a popular body unaccustomed to much abstraction.

The choice of a governor was lodged in the House of Delegates and Senate, exercising a concurrent vote. These could not fail to be formidable to him, by his dependence for an annual election, which could be made of the same person only for three successive years in a term of four, for the quantum of salary, and the terrors of impeachment. He was clogged with a council of state, who were to be elected by that Assembly and to court them for their favor, on the triennial ostracism of two of them.

Instead of permitting to the Assembly the power of instituting and abolishing courts of law according to the calls of the times, they were improvidently trammeled in respect to their reforms by inserting in the constitution as a species of favorites courts of special denominations.

The subordinate business of Virginia next received the attention of the Convention.

Two different works were established at public expense for the manufacture of salt.

The common law of England, all statutes and acts of Parliament made in aid of the common law prior to the fourth year of the reign of King James I of a general nature, and not local to that kingdom, together with the several acts of the General Assembly then in force, so far as they might consist with the several ordinances, declarations, and resolutions of the general convention, were considered as in full force. In what books and at what dates the common law was to be found, how real and necessary improvements and corrections by statutes posterior to that era were to be neglected, while ancient rigor was to be enforced, was left to the discretion of the judges.

The British ministry had threatened our western frontiers with the ravages of Indian warfare, and John Connolly had been the emissary of Dunmore to engage their tomahawk in immediate massacre. The Convention to divert their vengeance did not scruple to open a treaty for two hundred of their warriors, who were to march to the assistance of our regular forces on the eastern quarter. Nor ought they to have scrupled; so plainly distinguishable was the morality of our purely defensive conduct from that which for offense could let loose the horrors of savage warfare.

On the petition of one Richard Henderson and his associates, a great question in the law of nations as applied to America was agitated and decided by the Convention: whether a purchase by individuals of lands, to which the Indians claimed title, by their manner of occupancy was binding upon Virginia, within whose limits they lay.[9] She in terms annulled every such purchase not confirmed by the government existing at the time. She supposed that it was no less absurd to recognize the extravagant hunting rights of savages than the idle assumption of the Pope to grant the Western world between two nations. Henderson's party thought that for western lands the present was a moment of pure indifference, or that the policy of conciliating American citizens would be instrumental in their gratification. But in both were they disappointed. Virginia persisted in denying the principle of such titles as under the law of nations. The charters and practice under them had preoccupied the subject.

The Convention proposed to Pennsylvania a temporary boundary, to assuage the heat which the proprietary governor of that province from interest and Dunmore from rancor to Virginia had contrived to raise between them.[10]

---

9. Richard Henderson (1735–85), a North Carolinian and a judge with an astute understanding of legal problems, had formed in August in 1774 the Louisa Company, renamed five months later the Transylvania Company. The company purchased from the Cherokee nation at a great congress in March 1775 a huge area stretching from the Ohio and the Kentucky rivers to the southern edge of the Cumberland River watershed. With his fellow North Carolinian Daniel Boone, he helped lay the groundwork for the state of Kentucky. However, settlers who relied upon his titles soon discovered that they were not so firmly founded. When Henderson sought legal recognition the Virginia authorities refused his claim and asserted the state's sovereignty over an area as far west as the Mississippi (Alden, *South in the Revolution*, pp. 136–37, 282).

10. On June 15, 1776, the Virginia Convention proposed a settlement of the boundary dispute with a specific proposal and appointment of Virginia's delegates to the Continental Congress as negotiators (Force, *American Archives*, 5th ser., II, 40–42). The dispute was finally settled by a joint commission in 1779 (*ibid.*, 4th ser., II, 684; and Allan Nevins, *The American States during and after the American Revolution, 1775–1789* [New York, 1927], p. 591).

The persons nominated as candidates for the office of governor were Patrick Henry; Thomas Nelson, the president; and John Page, a member of the royal Council.[11] Nelson had long been secretary of the colony and ranked high in the aristocracy, who propagated with zeal the expediency of accommodating ancient prejudices by electing a man whose pretensions to the chief magistry were obvious from his now being nominally the governor under the old order of things; and out of one hundred and eleven members, forty-five were caught by the desire of bringing all parties together, although Mr. Nelson had not been at all prominent in the Revolution. From every period of Henry's life, something of a democratic and patriotic cast was collected, so as to accumulate a rate of merit too strong for this last expiring act of aristocracy.

Page had the virtue and felicity, though enrolled from birth, fortune, and station in the aristocratic ranks, to enjoy the confidence of every good man and to be respected even by the bad, whether a royalist or republican.

General Charles Lee took an early opportunity, after the introduction of the new government, of expressing to Governor Henry his anxiety to see the title of Excellency, which had been appropriated to former governors who were not deputies, buried in the Revolution. Some titles designating offices force themselves into popular language, while others which are pompous distinctions having no intelligible analogy to the duties of the office have been created by flattery. It is natural that a governor or a judge should hear his name coupled with his office, but Excellency and Honorable spring from vague allowances of merit, as necessarily attached to certain posts. It was expected at the commencement of our revolutionary government that these gaudy trappings would be abandoned. They were retained indeed by usage, not by an authoritative recognition, nor yet from any admiration of the empty baubles in the country of our origin, or an antirepublican tendency in the people; but they may be ascribed to a degree of pride, which would not suffer the new government to carry with it fewer testimonies of public devotion than the old. This is verified by the total contempt of trifles by the officers themselves.

At the beginning of this year, the town of Norfolk, the fine harbor

11. John Page (1744–1808), one of Thomas Jefferson's oldest friends, was a descendant of "King" Carter and Mann Page, both prominent Tidewater landowners. The reference to John Page as a royal councilor may either be to his ancestor Mann Page or a mistake since he did serve as the first president of the Council under the new constitution and as lieutenant governor (Malone, *Jefferson the Virginian*, pp. 58–59).

of which on Elizabeth River and its neighborhood to the outlet of James River into the bay of Chesapeake destined in time to be the most distinguished emporium in the colonies south of Potomac River, was destroyed by fire.[12] Even when the conflagration was but of recent date, impartiality could not decide who were its authors. The Americans dwelt with bitterness on this outrage on the laws of civilized nations, imputed to the British, while these retorted the charge of at least promoting the progress of the havoc, when it might have been stopped but for their studied interference in carrying it to its greatest height. The blame was that of neither party exclusively. The enemy, embittered with their discomfiture in Norfolk and its vicinity, were strenuous in combining revenge with the scattering of terror. The Americans had fancied that it would pamper the enemy if such a station and asylum, as Norfolk was to them under the cover of their navy, should not be broken up; and the Convention with the concurrence of Colonel Robert Howe, the then commander of the Virginia forces, ordered the destruction of the remainder of the buildings, after the fire had raged for some days. A popular assembly and an inexperienced field officer were thus the dupes of a momentary impulse.

Virginia, counting with certainty on the unquenchable spirit of America and buoyed up with hope, emitted large sums of paper money, without the pledge of adequate specific funds for its redemption.[13] As a medium it circulated freely, and its conveniencies resembled the facilities of that struck by the old government. We believed, because from enthusiasm we felt, what reason would have pronounced to be impossible, that good faith would at last redeem with an equivalent in specie every paper dollar, according to its nominal import, which the utmost industry of the printing presses and the extreme of public necessity would produce. A fatal error for many an honest patriot; an instrument of fraud in many a designing and unprincipled man; but a vital principle in the arduous contest. There was no man daring enough to traffic upon an avowal of a disparity between the precious

12. The destruction of Norfolk took place in Jan. 1776. Gen. Robert Howe had ordered the burning of the remaining buildings so they could offer no cover for the enemy.

13. On Aug. 17, 1775, the Committee of Safety created an additional £350,000 in treasury notes, and the Convention of 1776 issued an additional £100,000. By the spring of 1781 the state had aggregated £45,000,000. The inevitable consequence was that the notes became almost worthless, and just after the surrender of Cornwallis the passage of a sweeping measure of repudiation annulled all the state's promises to pay in full. Holders of paper money were to receive a loan office certificate for one dollar in return for every $1,000 surrendered (Nevins, *American States*, pp. 93, 136, 486).

metals and paper money, although commodities imported from beyond [the] sea were from their increasing scarcity somewhat advanced beyond the regular prices of tranquil times, and under this cloak of a fair augmentation, mercantile sagacity had spread a secret distrust of paper credit. Dexterities, however, of this sort are not confined to revolutionary times.

Not a vestige of the emblems of royalty was tolerated where the public voice could be brought to act upon it. The wall of the House of Burgesses, which was now transferred to the Convention, was decorated with several of them. The chair in which the speaker sat, now filled by the president of the Convention, had a frontispiece commemorative of the relation between the mother country and colony. These had been criticized before any formal act of reprobation was taken, and all of them were at different times effaced. Nay, so irrational was the fury of some that the noble statue which public affection had erected to the memory of Lord Botetourt, who by his patronage and example had fostered religion and learning in Virginia, was with difficulty saved from a midnight attack. To her honor be it known that all her authorities contradicted on this occasion the trite calumny of ingratitude in republics.

Everything which had been done in the Convention of May [14] was hailed as masterpieces of political wisdom and acted upon with a cheerfulness and submission which naturally resulted from this first demonstration of popular self-government. The young boasted that they were treading upon the republican ground of Greece and Rome and contracted a sovereign contempt for British institutions. With them to recede from those institutions with abomination was the perfection of political philosophy. Not a murmur was heard against the incompetency of the Convention to frame the constitution according to its full extent. Nay, so captivating were its charms that it was many years before some of its defects, even upon the theory of democracy itself, were allowed or detected.

Whatsoever may be the general opinion as to the inefficacy of test laws in restraining a people from adhering to an enemy, Dunmore had by oaths of allegiance deterred many who were mild and inactive in their nature from a union with their country. The Convention employed a similar security for fidelity to the republic.[15] To compel good

14. The Constitutional Convention of 1776.
15. In May 1777 the Assembly passed a law requiring all males over sixteen years of age to take an oath of allegiance to "the Commonwealth of Virginia as a free and independent state" (Eckenrode, *Revolution in Virginia*, p. 182).

will may in general be vain; in revolutions an oath of fidelity mixes religion with fear.

Although Virginia from the first assumption of arms had submitted herself to the united counsels of America in Congress, yet she now acted a lofty part in the exercise of sovereignty. In fact, it was problematical what species of government the jealousy of the separate states would concede to any general council or congress. To mention the surrender of one atom of sovereignty, as a contribution to a continental reservoir, was to awaken a serious alarm. Some state legislatures or other state authorities, even at this early period, were guilty of heresies with respect to the faith which they had agreed to place in Congress; and they were strong, because Congress was the puppet of requisitions without energy. But Virginia unanimously adopted the primitive Confederation.

The Convention of May assembled in November as the regular legislature under the constitution.[16]

It has been seen that the friends of the Established Church were apprehensive of the force of their own principles, to which they had assented in the bill of rights, and how they were quieted by the assurances of Mr. Henry. But they were patriots who dreaded nothing so much as a schism among the people and thought the American principle too pure to be adulterated by religious dissension. They therefore did in truth cast the Establishment at the feet of its enemies, not extending their views to times when Mr. Henry might not be able to confirm his word by stemming the torrent of opposition, nor having sufficiently learned that if secular interests impel when they rule by themselves, they overthrow all resistance when allied with religion. An indiscriminate taxation for a long series of years had been laid upon dissenters, who renounced all hopes of ascending to salvation through the gates of the church. The sums drawn from their pockets, though small and not harshly inconvenient in the periods of payment, were certainly unjust and oppressive. The dissenters were no less ambitious than the members of the church and were eclipsed by them. Henry was in the executive chair and therefore was disqualified to vindicate his former assurances to the church, though probably he might have acquiesced in the insidious form which a projected law was assuming. It did not *profess* to *abolish* the Establishment, but it sapped it by

16. The Convention, which came to an end on July 5, 1776, arranged for the election of senators and then adjourned to meet as the first House of Delegates under the new constitution on "the first Monday in October next" (Hening, *Statutes*, IX, 53; Force, *Archives*, 4th ser., VI, 1616; Lingley, *Transition*, pp. 137–38, 177).

suspending the stipends of the clergy.[17] The first fracture in a chain forged by an unjust principle cannot easily be closed. In support of this law, the severest persecutions in England were ransacked for colors in which to paint the burdens and scourges of freedom in religion; and antiquated laws in England, against the exercise of which the people would even there have recoiled, were summoned up as so many demons hovering over every scrupulous conscience not bending to the church. The votaries of that church were entrapped by an expectation that the new land would be a permanent anchor to its existence, although the parochial salaries might never be revived. In this they were sacrificed to the poverty of their own intellect in not discerning the nature and condition of their own sect. It had almost always been on the side of the monarchy, while the hearts of the dissenters might truly be said to be in covenant with those who were clamorous against the threats of civil oppression. The lower country was the principal residence of the protectors of the Establishment, and it was apparent that these must soon be outnumbered in the legislature, where petitions were readily granted for the division of the upper counties, and the consequent multiplication of the representation of dissenters. The advocates for the church were apparently unconscious of its imbecility. It was enervated by mental inactivity, and it was palpable that a blow like this must stun it into a state of lingering, from which it could never wholly recover.

At this session, the old usage of preambles indicating the principal objects of laws had not yet been discontinued. They had always been committed to the pen of skillful men, who comprehended their entire subject and believed that there might be as much merit in deliberation and care as in an affectation of expedition and brevity. This remark arises from the striking contrast which the two laws now to be treated of exhibit with such as are ushered into the public code without the decency of expounding to the people the motives of their enaction. It is true that the enacting words ought to be so explicit as to render it unnecessary to resort to a key from an introduction, which may be injurious if it does not cover with accuracy the whole of the matter enacted; but we have experienced in many English statutes, and in the best models of Virginia statutes, that preambles well drawn are auxil-

17. This reference is to a law of Dec. 9, 1776, which did not disestablish the Anglican church but did much to relieve dissenters by exempting them from taxes in support of the Established Church and suspending the act providing a fixed salary for ministers (Hening, *Statutes*, IX, 164–67; Malone, *Jefferson the Virginian*, pp. 276–80; and Lingley, *Transition*, pp. 190–201).

iary to sound construction, the old frivolous contest whether a preamble be a part of the law to which it is affixed being now settled upon rational and convenient principles.

The first of those acts directs a revision of the laws. The report of that work will be found in the proceedings of the legislature of [the] years 1785 and 1786.[18] As the necessity of such a revision must be admitted by those who consider that the subordinate wheels of government ought to be in unison with the great machine, so will homage be paid to the comprehensive scheme delineated in that law, drawn by Mr. Jefferson.

The other law abolished entails and converted tenants in tail into tenants in fee simple.[19] At first the doctrine of entails in Virginia depended upon the English statute *De donis conditionabus*. But afterwards, she specially prohibited the docking of entails, except by an act of Assembly or the inquisition of a jury deciding the value of the property to be docked to be less than £200 sterling. The practice under the former mode was often nothing but mockery, for although an equivalent was supposed to be settled on the issue in tail, it instructs us that legislative bodies have no diligence and sometimes too much indifference in their inquiries which relate to the distribution of private property. It has several times happened that an heir in tail has been obliged to accept as a substitute for the ample benevolence of an ancestor some *caput mortuum* in soil, which was an encumbrance, attested, however, in point of form to the Assembly as being of equivalent worth. Thus was plucked up by the roots one of the firmest props of aristocracy and was testified a sincere attachment to the republican system, zeal for the suppression of false credit between man and man, and a discouragement to filial disobedience.

18. For the text of the bill for the revision of the laws, see Hening, *Statutes*, IX, 175–77; Julian P. Boyd, ed., *The Papers of Thomas Jefferson* (Princeton, 1950–), I, 562–63. This act, moved and presented to the Convention by Thomas Jefferson, was the basis for the work of the revisal of the laws of Virginia conducted by a committee consisting of Edmund Pendleton, George Wythe, George Mason, Thomas Ludwell Lee, and Jefferson as chairman. They began their work in 1777 and finally submitted a report in 1779 with 126 suggested changes. A few of these were translated into law immediately, but due to the exigencies of war the report as a whole was deferred. During the next two years James Madison succeeded in transforming approximately half the bills into law (Malone, *Jefferson the Virginian*, pp. 262–63; for the report of the Committee of Revisions, see Boyd, *Papers of Jefferson*, II, 305–657).

19. Under the rules of primogeniture and entail all the land went in bulk to the eldest son. This bill to abolish entail passed by the Delegates on Oct. 23 and by the Senate on Nov. 1, 1776, was the work of Jefferson (Hening, *Statutes*, IX, 226–27; Malone, *Jefferson the Virginian*, pp. 251–60; Boyd, *Papers of Jefferson*, I, 560–62).

Since the days of Bacon in 1676, a case of that species of treason
which may ensnare the unwary and sacrifice the innocent had probably
not occurred in Virginia. But the slaughter which the loose description
of that crime had once committed in England admonished the Assembly
to adopt the definition upon which that country now rested much of
the personal safety of its people.[20] It was an offense sounding too horrible
in the ears of government not to be punished with death. But although
death was made the penalty here, the dower and distributive shares
of widows were sheltered from forfeiture and an attainder no longer
worked a corruption of blood. The laws disabled the executive from
granting full mercy but referred the question of pardon to the succeeding Assembly, until the meeting of which execution might be respited.
The line is not clearly marked between this law and the one for the
punishment of certain offenses: maliciously and advisedly to endeavor
to excite the people to resist the government, or to persuade them to
return to a dependence on the crown of Great Britain, or to excite
and raise tumults and disorders in the state may at some time or other
be found to be too little distinct from the law of treason.

It will be recollected that what I have called the continental history
of the United States, as connected with that of Virginia, will be found
in an appendix, prepared with a view to be incorporated by the reader
with this history.

To the latter the following additions may with propriety be made
in the following year.

1. The Virginia Assembly unanimously approved the Articles of
Confederation, thus testifying by immense sacrifices how highly they
valued union among the states.[21]

2. The corroding tooth of depreciation had so deeply eaten into the
credit of paper money and the variety and magnitude of public expense had poured from the press such torrents of this medium that
the Assembly could no longer abstain from the delicate subject of
taxation. Not only were the emissions of Virginia to be redeemed, but
her quota also of the Continental paper. The data for a system of
finance were few and badly arranged. To the amount wanted, taxes
could not be strained, as had formerly been the case. In their journey
into the treasury, a part of their product in the value collected was

20. See Hening, *Statutes*, IX, 168.

21. After making concessions in 1778 on ownership of the Northwest Territory and
boundary claims with Maryland, Virginia ratified the Articles of Confederation. For a
complete discussion of this and other problems associated with union, see Merrill Jensen,
Articles of Confederation; and *The New Nation: A History of the United States During
the Confederation* (New York, 1950).

by depreciation exposed to be lopped off, and political arithmetic was a mystery. But fortunately disproportion excited no murmurs, while ease to the payer grew with the quantity of paper emitted. Taxation was begun.[22]

3. It must be the wish of every friend to our national character that when from a state of public inflammation, the rulers may rely with certainty upon a full sympathy from the people, and more especially when the national will under no control from abroad meets with no obstacle to divert it from the strict path of integrity, all public acts should stand upon the base of national honor. Remarks like these would not have been made had the law of sequestration in this year never been pushed further than itself, and for the present will be dropped here after a mere reference to that law and vindicating it as far as it goes, even against the suggestions of impropriety upon the soundest principles of national law and right.[23] For although many British subjects had lived in Virginia upon the faith of ancient harmony and membership in the same empire, had brought fortunes and credit hither, and here had centered all their hopes of happiness and gathered capitals expected to be used here for life, yet the government was rent asunder by misrule, and the adherents to either party must share in the fate of that which they elected, as subjects under the general law of nations. The review of this topic may present in 1779 another aspect.

Under the regal administration, there had been a court of superior jurisdiction called the General Court and composed of twelve judges, members of the Privy Council, besides the governor. Among them generally sat a commissary of the bishop of London, within whose diocese Virginia lay. Their jurisdiction was univeral in subject and place; their decisions incapable of appeal under the sum of £500 sterling. Professional men now were substituted in the larger judicial arrangements.[24]

22. A general property tax of 10*s.* on the £100, and a like tax on cash capital; a tax of 2*s.* on the pound on annuities or income from money at interest; a tax of 10*s.* on the £100 on salaried income; a poll tax of 5*s.* on every tithable, with certain exceptions, above twenty-one; 4*d.* a head on all meat cattle; an export tax of 10*s.* on every hogshead of tobacco; and excise and license taxes (Hening, *Statutes,* IX, 349; Nevins, *American States,* p. 495).

23. The sequestration act of 1777 permitted people to pay off British debts in depreciated currency by payments into the state loan office (Hening, *Statutes,* IX, 377–80; see also below, p. 273.

24. A reorganization of the legal system began on Oct. 11, 1776, with the appointment of a committee chaired by Thomas Jefferson with instructions to write a bill establishing courts of justice (Lingley, *Transition,* pp. 178–79).

The discomfiture at the battle of Brandywine instead of producing despair awakened vigor.

Virginia persevered in active military preparations. She raised volunteers for the grand army, a regiment of cavalry, a battalion for garrison duty, recruits to fill up deficiencies by loss, and pecuniary supplies of public exigencies; and she retouched with force the laws providing against invasions and insurrections.

But the nerve which constantly showed itself against the British enemy now struck a serious blow at the administration of justice. It was generally believed that a banditti in the neighborhood of Norfolk had availed themselves of the cover and aid which a British squadron and British forces had lately afforded them for plunder and revenge by various atrocities on many citizens. One Josiah Philips, an alert and audacious leader, had eluded every attempt to capture him.[25] Terrible he certainly was, and his arrest would have merited a high reward. But the General Assembly, without other evidence than general rumor of his guilt, or the insufficiency of legal process in taking him into custody, on the motion of a member attainted him of high treason, unless he should surrender by a given day. In a very august Assembly of Virginia, it was contended that, as he deserved to die, it was unimportant whether he fell according to the technicality of legal proceeding or not. Probably he deserved death, although if a judgment can be formed of this by subsequent facts, the prosecution against him being as against a robber, not a traitor, he was an offender less heinous than he was conceived to be. His apology, too, was not perhaps admissible, although it was that he had never for a moment acquiesced in the Revolution or in the opposition to Great Britain and that his

25. Josiah Philips (d. 1778), a laborer living in Lynnhaven Parish, Princess Anne County, had accepted a commission from Dunmore. He gathered a small band of whites and runaway slaves and began to plunder the isolated area on the border of Virginia and North Carolina. Fearing an insurrection in the Norfolk region, the legislature passed a bill of attainder designating June 30, 1778, as the last day of grace. When Philips was captured the government decided to disregard the attainder and convicted him in a general court. He was executed on Dec. 4, 1778 (see William P. Trent, "The Case of Josiah Philips," *American Historical Review*, I [1896], 444–54). In 1788, at the Virginia Ratifying Convention, Randolph cited the Philips case as a "striking and shocking" violation of the Declaration of Rights. Philips, he argued, had been the victim of an act of attainder, under which he had suffered death. Randolph was attorney general at the time and should have remembered that the bill of attainder was not actually used. The outlaw had been tried and condemned by regular legal processes. Stranger yet, the next day Patrick Henry, governor at the time of the episode, defended the execution of Philips under the attainder, forgetting the regular trial (Malone, *Jefferson the Virginian*, p. 292; Eckenrode, *Revolution in Virginia*, pp. 190–93).

loyalty was not for a moment concealed, but he received on the first opportunity, and acted under, a military commission from the crown. He did not surrender himself within the time prescribed and was exposed, on being arrested, to the single question whether he was the person attainted and upon the establishment of the affirmative to be led to execution. He waived his apology because he would not exasperate his jury in his defense against robbery. What was his peril, while he was roving abroad, devoted by a legislature to death unless he should surrender himself, ought not to have been withdrawn from the view of those whose duty it was to fence the constitution against noxious precedents. Nor is it an expiation of this hasty measure of wrath that the previous alternative was offered to him of submitting to trial. The denunciation of a government is almost the sure harbinger of condemnation. Let it be conceded, as it ought, that virtuous men were the authors of this terror to peace and happiness. But examples are more fatal when they proceed from respected sources, and the victim selected will have the more cause to tremble as the precedent is the act of pure hearts. An attainder may probably exist in the sphere of Virginian legislative power, as an attribute to legislation itself, or from some connection with the character of grand inquest of the Commonwealth. But it is a dread attribute at best, to be deprecated as confounding, in defiance of the bill of rights, judicial with legislative authority.

We have seen how in the year 1620 an accidental importation of African slaves began this blot in our population and morals. For many ships loaded with these wretches had been sent to Virginia by the capitals of British merchants, who favored their friends by high commissions on the sales. The plantations were crowded with them and their descendants. At length, laws were passed by the Assembly for discouraging the importation by duties on each slave imported. But the influence of the dealers in human flesh, who resided near the British ministry, baffled the voice of humanity and policy.[26] Hence as soon as Virginia became mistress of herself, she forbade further importations under a penalty of money and of emancipation of the slave.[27] This law has always found ready advocates for its execution, although the importation to be animadverted on should be from one of our sister states.

Under the regal government, the only final tribunal of judicial sen-

---

26. In 1710 and again in 1723 the Virginia Assembly levied a tax on each slave imported. After strong protests by British merchants the law was repealed by the king in Council (Morton, *Colonial Virginia*, II, 491–92).
27. See Hening, *Statutes*, IX, 471–72.

tences rendered in Virginia was the king in council, for sums not less than £500 sterling. With the renewal of the judicial functions in the year 1777, a court of appeals was not immediately instituted; but at this time (October 1778) it was compounded of the three judges of the High Court of Chancery, the five of the General Court, and the three of the admiralty, each set of judges being excluded from sitting in causes decided in their own courts.[28] The number was too large for adequate expedition if the causes should be multiplied, and let the talents of the whole be what they might, it would seem that such a tribunal ought to have been selected from abilities of peculiar fitness for the field of general jurisprudence rather than to be the accommodating result of bringing members from different benches, evidently, in some instances, demanding different and inferior powers of mind. In this court an *esprit de corps* was in theory to be apprehended, as well as perhaps an occasional irritation from one class of judges to another.

On the northwestern side of the river Ohio, within the territory of Virginia, several British posts had been reduced by the militia of Virginia, and the inhabitants had acknowledged themselves citizens of Virginia and taken the oath of fidelity to her. This called for the exercise of a new duty in legislation, to provide for the government of a conquered country. It was exercised in a style not generally observed in the Old World. A county appendant to Virginia was erected, with every salutary and convenient arrangement which the peculiarity of its population could demand.[29]

There was another flattering assay of the military genius of Virginia, to which from the loss of the Virginia records it is impossible at this late day to do justice. This is to be lamented the more as the nature of the expedition bespoke in George Rogers Clark, the leader of it, energies and skill for which no military preferment would have been excessive. Our only gratification therefore must be to give an account of it in the words of Chief Justice Marshall's history of it in the 3rd volume of his *Life of George Washington*, page 565.[30]

⌜While the frontiers of New York and Pennsylvania were thus suffering the calamities incident to savage warfare, a fate equally severe

28. See *ibid.*, 522–25.

29. This new area, formerly in Augusta County and a part of the territory ceded by Virginia in 1783, was called Illinois County. The area had been taken from the British in 1778 by George Rogers Clark and his Virginia riflemen (Martha W. Hiden, *How Justice Grew: Virginia Counties, An Abstract of Their Formation* [Williamsburg, Va., 1957], pp. 41, 44).

30. Passages cited from Marshall are designated by special brackets.

seems to have been destined for Virginia. The western militia of that
state had made some successful incursions into the country northwest
of the Ohio and had taken some British posts on the Mississippi. These,
by an act of the legislature, were erected into a county, called the county
of the Illinois; and a regiment of infantry with a troop of cavalry, to
be commanded by Colonel George Rogers Clark, a gentleman whose
great courage, uncommon hardihood, and capacity for Indian warfare
had given him repeated success in enterprises against the savages, were
ordered to be recruited for its protection.

⌈This corps was divided into several detachments, the principal of
which remained with Colonel Clark at Kaskaskia. Colonel Hamilton,
the governor of Detroit,[31] who was understood to have been extremely
active in fomenting Indian hostility, was at Vincennes, with about six
hundred men, principally Indians, projecting an expedition, first
against the post at Kaskaskia and then up the Ohio to Pittsburgh,
after which he proposed to desolate the frontiers of Virginia, when
Clark anticipated and defeated his design by one of those bold and
decisive measures which, whether formed on a great or small scale,
with many thousand or a few hundred troops, mark the military and
enterprising genius of the man who plans and executes them.

⌈Clark was too far removed from the inhabited country to hope for
support and was too weak to expect to maintain Kaskaskia and the
Illinois against the regular force, aided by the whole body of Indians
from the lakes to the mouth of the Ohio, by whom he was to be attacked
at the first commencement of the season for action. Yet he made every
preparation in his power for defense. While thus employed, he received
unquestionable information from a Spanish merchant that Hamilton,
who supposed himself to be in a state of perfect security at Vincennes,
had detached his Indians to block up the Ohio and to harass the
frontiers, reserving at the post he occupied only about eighty regular
troops, with three pieces of cannon and some swivels mounted. Clark
at once resolved to seize this favorable moment for preserving himself
from the impending danger. He detached a small galley which he
had fitted out, mounting two four-pounders and four swivels, manned

31. Henry Hamilton, the lieutenant governor of Detroit, had attempted in 1775 to
organize a large-scale offensive in the upper Ohio Valley that never quite came to pass.
However, numerous small bands of Indians often moved in the direction of Pitts-
burgh from Detroit and other British posts in 1775, 1776, and 1777 (Ward, *War of the
Revolution*, II, 850–51; John D. Barnhardt, ed., *Henry Hamilton and George Rogers
Clark in the Revolution with the Unpublished Journal of Lieutenant Governor Henry
Hamilton* [Crawfordsville, Ind., 1951], pp. 21–36).

with a company of soldiers, and having on board stores for his troops, with orders to force her way up the Wabash and take her station a few miles below Vincennes, permitting nothing whatever to pass her. Having made this arrangement, he set out in the depth of winter with one hundred and thirty men, the whole force he could collect, to march across the country from Kaskaskia to Vincennes. On this march through the woods and over high waters, sixteen days were employed. They were five days crossing the drowned lands of the Wabash in the neighborhood of the fort and were under the necessity of wading about five miles in water, frequently up to the breast. After subduing these difficulties, which had been supposed insurmountable, this little party appeared before the town, which was completely surprised and readily consented to change its master. Hamilton defended the fort a short time and then surrendered himself and his garrison prisoners of war. With a few of his immediate agents and counselors, who had been instrumental in the savage barbarities he had encouraged, he was by order of the executive of Virginia put in irons and confined in a jail.

[This small expedition was very important in its consequences. It entirely broke the plan which threatened to pour destruction, the ensuing campaign, on the whole country west of the Allegheny Mountains; it detached from the British interest very many of those numerous tribes of Indians south of the waters immediately communicating with the Great Lakes and had, most probably, a material influence in fixing the western boundary of the United States.]

The Assembly met in May. The charter of Virginia had appropriated to her many millions of acres of land from the Atlantic Ocean on the east to a line dividing the Mississippi, under the Treaty of Paris in 1763. But notwithstanding the prohibition contained in the royal proclamation against settlements on wastelands above the heads of the rivers, multitudes of hardy adventurers had before the Revolution defied the law and savages and settled on them. It was foreseen that they could not be disturbed without some convulsion; and indeed as far as men ought to be encouraged who act deliberately against law, they had laid in a stock of merit in forming a barrier against the incursions of the Indians.

Virginia discovered that she had hardly a choice between an acquiescence in the rights acquired by the hardihood of occupancy to the vacant western lands and the daily diminution of that important fund for her public debt. After satisfying therefore those sturdy claimants and adjusting some legal pretensions long before existing, a land office was opened upon a scale which nourished speculation, although it was productive of revenue. In the passage of one of the laws upon this subject,[32] a member of the Assembly who was honorably interested in charter importation rights was pursued by another who hated him with a violence which nothing could satiate but the expurging of the rights from the list of such as were to be confirmed. The other, sensible that a direct attack upon them would be too gross, assaulted the surveys, by which they had been located upon particular rich lands, for some mistake in form, upon which a vote was obtained declaring them to be void. Elated by this victory and poorly versed in the subject, this hunter after formal defects did not see the force of a small amendment in a part of the bill remote from the clause which had been defeated. Thus justice was protected by dexterity from malicious ignorance; thus an impotency of character cheats itself with a momentary flash of triumph and teaches us not to confide in a legislator who does not view the whole ground and persevere to the last, as the same consequence might have followed in a better cause.

No fact had transpired in the conduct of Great Britain varying the principles which had been professed in the act of sequestration in the year 1777. Hostility had expended all its horrors, but it had not risen on her part to confiscation, which was the specific condition prescribed by the legislature to itself on that subject. The reasons assigned for not continuing British property longer in the situation in which it then was were not without plausibility; but may not a moralist be permitted to ask whether this confiscation is not better justified by the concessions of the enemy in the negotiation of the peace than by an observance of uniformity of principle in ourselves?[33]

Jamestown, situated about fifty miles above the mouth of James

32. See Hening, *Statutes*, X, 35–65.

33. Article five of the Treaty of Peace required the government of the United States to "earnestly recommend" that the various legislatures restore all estates, rights, and properties confiscated from British subjects. Loyalists were to have the right to go to any part of the United States and remain a year for the purpose of recovering their estates and properties. Article six stipulated that there be no further confiscations of British or Loyalist property and no further prosecutions of Loyalists (the treaty is reprinted in Samuel Flagg Bemis, *Diplomacy of the American Revolution* [New York, 1935], pp. 259–64). Randolph included a note to refer here to Jay's Treaty. In article six of that treaty, signed at London on Nov. 19, 1794, all debts were to be paid, and where their value and security had been impaired, then the "United States will make full and complete compensation" (for a reprint of Jay's Treaty, see Bemis, *Jay's Treaty: A Study in Commerce and Diplomacy* [New Haven, 1962], pp. 453–84). A discussion of planter indebtedness can be found in Emory G. Evans, "Planter Indebtedness and the Coming of the Revolution in Virginia," *Wm. and Mary Qtly.*, 3d ser., XVIII (1962), 511–33.

River, was the first metropolis of the colony. But when Commissary Blair,[34] who [sic] by grants and bounties in England, had been able to build the College of William and Mary at the Middle Plantation, now the city of Williamsburg, he inculcated the opinion that as youth ought to study men, as well as books, this double benefit could not be so effectually attained as by the removal of the seat of government to the vicinity of the college. The prospect was surely at Williamsburg a very barren one for a metropolis. Its navigation consisted in two small creeks, one of which emptied into York, and the other into James River at the distance of about four or five miles. In speaking of sites at that day, the capacities which the subsequent spirit of improvement has suggested were foreign to our minds. But Williamsburg in its utmost splendor could be recommended as a position for the seat of government only by the dryness of its soil. During the regal government it was a serious labor to invent arguments for preferring it as the resort for the general business of the colony. As population moved to the westward, the truth spread with it that it was an unreasonable deference to the lower country for the inhabitants of the upper to haven within a few miles of the bay of Chesapeake for access to the supreme court, to the legislature, and to the executive. Many considerations of different complexions had anchored the metropolis at Williamsburg. The two public edifices of the Capitol and college had been engrafted on the public mind by the expensiveness of them and were considered as ornaments not to be disregarded, even if the dignity of a metropolis should be consulted. The aristocracy, whose estates and residence were convenient to it, were a little phalanx around it; a superstitious reverence for time was one of its defenders; and its enemies, after they were powerful enough to shake this allegiance to Williamsburg, were at variance as to the spot to which the metropolitan offices should be transported. The royal veto was always an asylum to Williamsburg. But the Revolution spoiled the metropolis of its false glory by discovering that there the public archives were open to plunder from the crews of hostile ships, public business to interruption from similar causes, and that its distance from our western borders was a grievance to their inhabitants. The town of Richmond at the falls of James River,

34. James Blair (1655–1743), a young Scottish minister, had come to Virginia in 1685 as the representative or commissary of Dr. Henry Compton, the bishop of London. In 1691 the General Assembly sent Blair to England as its representative to secure a charter and endowment for the College of William and Mary. His mission a success, Blair was appointed as the first president of the college (Earl G. Swem, "James Blair," *DAB*) .

where free navigation terminated, possessed many beauties and advantages, while it had no other fixed character than that of being suitable for the reception of tobacco to be inspected. Thither the general business of the Commonwealth, legislative, executive, and judicial, were adjourned by law, to the impoverishment of many industrious and respectable families in Williamsburg, who had been for years raising a home for their declining years in small portions of land within its limits.[35] This was, however, a casualty which conveys no censure on the legislature. It has had one good effect. It has stimulated the youth to wing their way in new fields of enterprise rather than to waste their lives in snatching the contingencies which might attend the favor of those who frequented a metropolis enjoying no advantages from commerce or manufactures.

With the tacit assent of Europe to American charters, Virginia has always asserted the nullity of purchases made from the native Indians within her limits by individuals not authorized by the crown. At this session an express law was passed for the abolition of them, not as being then original, but to give more publicity to an old law which from the early difficulties of diffusing information by printing was little known and to a principle which, if it had never been formerly announced, was a plain right of charter.[36]

Some incidents had given birth to suspicions that the confidential intelligence communicated to Congress had been abused by members engaged in trade. An oath was therefore enjoined by law upon every delegate from Virginia, present or future, to abstain from all mercantile connection.[37] If an antidote had been desirable at all, a better one would have been not to elect a known merchant and to displace one who should become so after election. But merchants of real knowledge, experience, and integrity could not be expected to renounce the means of livelihood for a seat in Congress, and it is notorious that such as these were among the great authors of revolutionary success, for the accomplishment of which, military supplies must

35. See Hening, *Statutes*, X, 85–89. For a discussion of Williamsburg, see Carl Bridenbaugh, *Seat of Empire: The Political Role of Eighteenth Century Williamsburg* (Charlottesville, Va., 1963).

36. "An Act for declaring and asserting the rights of this Commonwealth, concerning purchasing lands from Indian natives," Hening, *Statutes*, X, 97–98. This act was designated to establish Virginia's "exclusive right of preemption from the Indians of all lands within the limits of its own chartered territory."

37. See *ibid.*, p. 113.

come to us through channels and by circuits and stratagems unknown to unpracticed men. The proceedings of the secret committee appointed by Congress for these ends are a history of unexampled utility.[38]

The law of citizenship was liberal toward every oppressed nation of the world,[39] and besides, the legislature never hesitated, on petition, to receive, *flagrante bello,* into citizenship the subjects of Great Britain who were really inimical to British tyranny over America. The confiscated estates of several of them were restored.

For the seal of the Commonwealth, the following device was ordained: Virtus, the genius of the Commonwealth, dressed like an Amazon, resting on a spear with one hand, and holding a sword in the other, and treading on *tyranny,* represented by a man prostrate, a crown fallen from his head, a broken chair in his left hand, and a scourge in his right. In the exergon the word "Virginia" over the head of Virtus, and underneath, the words "Sic semper tyrannis." On the reverse side, a group: Libertas, with her wand and pileus; on one side of her, Ceres, with the cornucopia in one hand and an ear of wheat in the other; on the other side Aeternitas, too with the globe and phoenix. In the exergon these words: "Deus nobis hoc otia fecit." [40]

We have seen that the erection of the province of North Carolina curtailed the chartered limits of Virginia, and that [in] the early part of the last century (beginning with the year 1700) Joshua Fry and Peter Jefferson, as commissioners of Virginia, and other commissioners of North Carolina ran a dividing line from the Atlantic Ocean in the latitude of 36° 30′ north in the supposed direction of due west. The Assembly resolved to continue that line, if it should be formed on that latitude, due west to Tennessee River. Thomas Walker, the commissioner from Virginia, and Richard Henderson, the commissioner from North Carolina, commenced the work but differed so widely on principles and execution that they diverged at every step and left a tract of country in the shape of a wedge to be a ground of contention which was not removed for many years afterwards.[41]

38. This reference is to Robert Morris and his work in behalf of Continental finances.
39. See *ibid.,* pp. 129–30.
40. See *ibid.,* pp. 131–32.
41. Peter Jefferson (d. 1757), the father of Thomas Jefferson, was one of the original settlers of Albemarle County. As a planter of some reputation he served as a colonel in the militia, county surveyor, and member of the House of Burgesses. In 1749 Jefferson and Joshua Fry extended William Byrd II's dividing line between Virginia and North Carolina from Peter's Creek ninety miles to Steep Rock Creek, now known as the Laurel Fork of the Holston, in Washington County (Morton, *Colonial Virginia,* II, 554; Malone, *Jefferson the Virginian,* pp. 9–33). When in 1750 the Board of Trade directed the Vir-

Virginia had so habitually copied from English institutions, even upon the topic of ease to scrupulous consciences, that until this session affirmations were not universally substituted in the place of oaths. The apprehensions entertained for an Established Church inspired on this occasion, when too late, a vigilance and alertness not commensurate with reason and right; and thus the solemnity of an oath had not hitherto seemed to be ensured by any form not connected with the touch of the cover of the printed evangelists.

Under the sequestration law of 1777, large sums of paper money were paid into the treasury in satisfaction of debts due to British subjects. But the stamina of that currency had at this date been exhausted to such a degree that the Assembly, contemplating the possibility of compensation either to the creditor or payer, repealed the right of making such payments.[42]

Congress were now approaching the ultimation of all projects on paper money, when they passed the resolutions of March 18, 1780.[43] The legislature being called upon to act in conformity with them, George Mason and Richard Henry Lee advocated them, as being the only expedient remaining for the restoration of public credit. Patrick Henry poured forth all his eloquence in opposition but proposed nothing in their place. He disseminated, however, the jealousy which has since been denominated antifederal and stated some precise objections to the plan, as being incompetent upon its own principles. Had it been finally lost, after having been promulged as the only mean of safety and as being founded on the ruins of the former currencies,

ginia authorities to have a map made of the inhabited part of Virginia, Joshua Fry and Peter Jefferson were engaged to do the work, which was published in London in 1751 (see *The Fry and Jefferson Map of Virginia and Maryland:* Facsimiles of the 1754 and 1794 printings. Introduction by Dumas Malone [Charlottesville, 1966]). Dr. Thomas Walker was the agent and leading member of the Loyal Company of Virginia, a land company which had received a large grant from the Virginia Council on July 12, 1749. He headed the commission which extended the Virginia-Carolina boundary line from where Fry and Jefferson had left off (Morton, *Colonial Virginia,* II, 575–76; see also Archibald Henderson, *Dr. Thomas Walker and the Loyal Company of Virginia* [reprinted from the *Proceedings of the American Antiquarian Society;* Worcester, Mass., April 1931]). No agreement was reached when the commissioners quarreled, and a strip of land was left as a source of irritation for some years (Hening, *Statutes,* X, 541–43).

42. See Hening, *Statutes,* X, 241–54.

43. This reference is to Congress's announced repudiation which set a ratio of forty Continental dollars to one in gold. Almost $200 million of debt were thus wiped out (Edmund C. Burnett, *The Continental Congress* [New York, 1941, repr. 1964], pp. 406–26, esp. pp. 426–27). On July 23, 1781, Randolph wrote that "paper money is viler than the rags, on which it is printed" (Burnett, ed., *Letters of Members of the Continental Congress* [Washington, D.C., 1921–36], VI, 151).

the finances of the United States would have been destitute of the little succor which the old paper money might still have afforded for a little time. Every day gained to the *existence* of paper money was a point gained in the war, for it was foreseen, though not avowed, that at the close of it, its *real*, not its nominal, value would be the standard of redemption. For a time this scheme of Congress was negatived.[44] Omnipotent as Henry was while present and asserting himself in the Assembly, he had one defect in his politics: he was apt to be contented with some *general* vote of success, but his genius did not lead him into detail. For a debate on great *general* principles, he was never surpassed here; but more laborious men, who seized occasions of modifying propositions which they had lost on a vote or of renewing them at more fortunate seasons, often accomplished their purpose after he had retired from the session. In this instance, the perseverance of Mason and Lee introduced in Henry's absence the same resolutions, and they were carried into a law.[45]

Until this session, the Church of England had retained by law the exclusive right of celebrating marriages; but law must always be weak when it confronts reason as well as passion and is supported chiefly by considerations drawn from a preference to a particular religious sect. Hence the right of celebration was extended to ministers of other denominations.[46]

Nor were the Assembly unmindful of their duty and gratitude to the officers of Virginia in the army. Provision was made by half pay of seven years for the widows and children of such of them as had died or should die in the service,[47] and half pay was granted for life to the officers who should continue in the service to the end of the war.

To Baron Steuben and others, liberal bounties were allowed in lands. Steuben had been trained in the armies of Prussia and was a complete master of their discipline. He had arrived very opportunely for the instruction of the American army. He instituted plans of reform, which invigorated our arms, and his talents were recommended not only by the most ample encomiums but also by immediate experience. Dis-

44. See Hening, *Statutes*, X, 241–54; Henry, *Patrick Henry*, II, 51–53.

45. The legislative session of May 1780 authorized £2,000,000 (Hening, *Statutes*, X, 279–86).

46. This law of Dec. 1780 provided that four dissenting ministers in each county be eligible to perform the marriage ceremony in the county in which they resided. Previously marriages could be celebrated only by Anglican clergymen (*ibid.*, p. 361; Lingley, *Transition*, p. 202).

47. See Hening, *Statutes*, X, 23, 24, 25, 27, 161.

satisfaction was afterwards entertained here at the losses of some military stores, which it was supposed his force would have enabled him to protect had he enjoyed the past activity of his youth, and he was threatened with a revocation of his grant; but the ebullition spent itself after cool reflection.[48]

It was conceived in the ardor of self-importance and the deficiency of political knowledge that Great Britain, whose subjects had been enriched by their trade with Virginia, would be alarmed into some relaxation of hostility or some favorable overture by a demonstration that she was in danger of losing the facility of proving book debts, which had enabled her to engross by long and extensive credits the whole of that trade. An act therefore was passed discouraging extensive credits and repealing the acts for prescribing the method of proving book debts. It limited the credit to be enforced in courts of law to six months from the delivery of the article sold and compelled them to take notice of the limitation whether it was pleaded or not. The real truth was, as to this intercourse, that the British merchants gained by the custom of the planters the preemption of their raw materials and commodities; and the imprudence of those planters often brought ruin upon themselves by their extravagance. But where they were discreet this connection was the foundation of loans of money, which were employed in the purchases of lands and slaves to the great improvement of their fortunes.

To foreign nations who should acknowledge our independence, a lure was thrown out of admitting consuls with the usual powers and with the privilege of being heard in our courts without waiting the ordinary dilatory routine.[49]

There is no state which has enacted more wholesome laws against gaming than Virginia or whose courts have been more punctual in their execution. The act to suppress excessive gaming will be an evidence of these assertions.[50] It cannot, however, be denied that the vice has not been extirpated; but being one which depends for correction on the

48. Friedrich Wilhelm Augustus von Steuben (1730–94) was a soldier of fortune who had joined Washington's army at Valley Forge. His claim that he had been a lieutenant general in the Prussian army and Frederick the Great's aide-de-camp was pure nonsense. In reality, his real name was Steube and he had never risen above the rank of captain. The general had a serious misunderstanding with the civilian authorities of Virginia over his methods of procuring local labor (Ward, *War of the Revolution*, II, 550–51; Malone, *Jefferson the Virginian*, pp. 342–43; for Steuben's land grant, see Hening, *Statutes*, X, 375).

49. See Hening, *Statutes*, X, 202–3.

50. See *ibid.*, pp. 205–7.

censorship which the people possess over morals, on religion, and on the force of example and character, we are refreshed by a hope of eradicating it from the practice being now chiefly in the hands of the most worthless part of society, who screen themselves from ignominy only by the ostentation and allurements of fashionable life.

In a second instance, besides that of independence, a sentiment which had been nurtured with the greatest care vanished on a sudden. We had clung to paper money with the affection due to an old servant, though impaired in strength.[51] Depreciation was lamented, but we could recount some of the most brilliant exploits of the Revolution achieved by armies which depended on paper money, and we were infatuated with a whimsical gratitude for it. But now those were wondered at as shortsighted philosophers who ever dreamed that it was to be redeemed dollar for dollar. Revolutions may not be always famous for the purest morality, and it may be that the deception favoring such a redemption was too long deliberately propagated. Notwithstanding the dearth of specie, the administration of justice was returned into its old channel, but a scale of depreciation was formed from January 1, 1777, until the extinction of paper money at this session. Opinions were contrariant as to the time when depreciation actually commenced, and the arguments for a somewhat later and even for a somewhat earlier origin are not destitute of probability. But equity in the settlement of contracts was adhered to; and no system could *a priori* promise more success than that which authorized the courts to depart from the scale when it would be unjust to obey it. The paper on every passage through the hands of its momentary masters was clipped of a portion of its value and furnished no great cause of complaint to any. But in bargains for the conveyance of real property, the judges softened the transactions by considerations of compromise. Still depreciation ruined many estates. It enabled some wicked guardians or executors to sink them into their own purses at a hundredth part of their value and debtors to extinguish their obligations with trifles of no import. Rules may seem innocent during the pressure of a crisis, but morality becomes deeply wounded when the legislature countenances a pollution of it.

Mr. Jefferson, in his *Notes on Virginia*, speaks with great bitterness against those members of the Assembly in the years 1776 and 1781 who

51. The session of May 1780 had authorized £2,000,000 in paper money, that of Oct. 1780 £6,000,000; March 1781 £10,000,000; May 1781 £20,000,000 (*ibid.*, pp. 279–86, 347–50, 399, 430–31).

espoused the creation of a dictator.[52] Coming from such authority, the invective infects the character of the legislature, notwithstanding he has restricted the charge to less than a majority and acknowledges the spotlessness of most of them. This would not have been here noticed, did it not militate against that genuine republicanism which has been boasted of in this work as the attribute of the people. The subject was never before them, except as an article of newspaper intelligence, and even then not in a form which called for their attention (from instructions). Against this unfettered monster, which deserved all the impassioned reprobation of Mr. Jefferson, their tone, it may be affirmed, would have been loud and tremendous. Let the error be traced to the panic which the novelty of positive war in 1776 produced, and in the year 1781 to the false applications of ancient history to a case wholly unlike. Let it be understood that the power which may have saved Rome would have made Virginia revolt.

The military transactions in Virginia during this year [1781] may be said to have silenced offensive war; and as they bear a strict connection with other movements in the southern states and were influenced by causes anterior in time, a wider range will be here taken than the author has hitherto allowed himself. He cannot in this place so much fear the intrusion of matter which though deeply interesting to himself as a Virginian may not be equally so to others.

52. *Notes on Virginia*, ed. Abernethy, pp. 120–24. On Dec. 21, 1776, the House of Delegates passed a resolution proclaiming that the present danger made it necessary that "the usual forms of government should be suspended during a limited time." The Senate struck out this passage and replaced it with a statement, accepted by the delegates, that "additional powers be given the Government and Council." There may have been more drastic private discussions, but Jefferson's comments may well have been exaggerated because of his resentment against Patrick Henry. As for 1781, there is nothing in the proceedings of the legislature to confirm Jefferson's charges. However, there was probably a good deal of informal talk about dictatorship (Malone, *Jefferson the Virginian*, pp. 305, 360–61).

Chapter IX   The Revolutionary War

 The decisive catastrophe in the surrender of Yorktown in Virginia [1] is referred by different tempers to different causes. To the skeptical philosopher it appears as the necessary effect of the general system and constitution of the world and its affairs. By the enthusiastic Christian, the hand of Providence is seen to lead to that event, by a special interposition. The historian, even while he feels it to be consistent with gratitude to heaven, is bound to investigate those circumstances which manifestly contributed to its accomplishment.

Of these the number is so great, and arose from points so widely distant in time and place, from such accidents, from such omissions, from such miscarriages in some of the seemingly best connected plans, from such blunders and misapprehensions, from such acute penetration and extensive views, that those who are incredulous of miracles must yet allow that a parallel example is not registered in the annals of human experience.

1. The labors, precautions, and vigilance of Washington had for many months secured the eastern states from danger; and the city of New York itself, the focus of the British force, was not beyond the reach of alarm. It had long been contemplated by the enemy to direct his activity against the southern states.

2. Almost all the military movements upon a large and influential scale had spread a gloom throughout the United States and flattered the enemy with the hope of general conquest. The siege of Savannah, which had not been raised, notwithstanding the attempt of the combined armies to raise it, and the surrender of Charleston, [as well as] the extermination of the remaining corps of opposition in the south under the command of Buford,[2] induced Clinton to consider the states of

1. The main British army commanded by Lord Cornwallis surrendered at Yorktown on Oct. 20, 1781.

2. Savannah, Ga., had fallen to the British on Dec. 29, 1778. On Oct. 9, 1779, a combined Franco-American force attacked the British entrenchments at Savannah, but they

South Carolina and Georgia as reannexed to the British dominions and to embark for New York, leaving about four thousand British troops under the command of Lord Cornwallis. He, too, from the defeat of Gates at Camden, believed the British arms to be invincible in the southern states.

3. It was little expected, until the return of the marquis de Lafayette from France, that he was incessantly occupied while there in soliciting from his monarch, and had finally obtained, a promise of a powerful land and naval armament for the campaign of 1780 in the United States. Sir Henry Clinton was compelled by the delay of the assembling of transports to postpone the attack of the French troops under the command of Rochambeau and thus lost the prospect of a brilliant *coup de main*. Embarrassments of every sort had obstructed the execution of a plan, which General Washington had embraced with ardor, for an enterprise against New York.[3]

4. Major Ferguson had fatally remained longer near the mountains in North Carolina than had been originally intended by Cornwallis and exposed himself to a defeat by the corps of militia, who had voluntarily assembled.[4] The intercepting of Ferguson's messenger to

---

were beaten back, and eleven days later the siege was abandoned (see Alexander A. Lawrence, *Storm over Savannah: The Story of Count d'Estaing and the Siege of the Town in 1779* [Athens, Ga., 1951]). Col. Abraham Buford (1749–1833) commanded a force of 350 Virginia Continentals and a small party of William Washington's horse. On May 29, 1780, he was overtaken by Tarleton's Tories and several hundred British regulars at the Waxhaws, a district near the South Carolina–North Carolina border. In the battle that followed the Americans were so completely defeated that Buford raised a white flag and ordered his men to ground their arms. But Tarleton would not restrain his troops, who fell upon the unarmed men with such ferocity that even wounded men were bayoneted (Ward, *War of the Revolution*, II, 705–6).

3. When Lafayette returned to France on leave in 1779 he was received with favor, and he won the admiration of the foreign minister Vergennes for presenting an accurate picture of affairs in America. Although Lafayette failed to get approval of the many schemes he advocated—such as hiring part of the Swedish navy for service in America and an invasion of England, Ireland, or Canada—he did lay the groundwork for sending a French expeditionary force to serve under Washington (Gottschalk, *Lafayette and the Close of the Revolution*, pp. 1–76). Clinton was restrained by the fear that a French fleet would appear off the American coast. Jean Baptiste Donatien de Vimeur, comte de Rochambeau (1725–1807), the commander of the French army in America, arrived in North America in May 1780 with some 5,500 troops (for a recent biography, see Arnold Whitridge, *Rochambeau* [New York, 1965]). In the summer of 1781 Washington undertook a campaign to drive the British from New York, but the strength of his adversary and the strategic difficulties were so great that he was forced to abandon his plans in favor of a southern campaign against Cornwallis.

4. The battle of Kings Mountain, S.C., Oct. 7, 1780 (see Don Higginbotham, *Daniel Morgan: Revolutionary Rifleman* [Chapel Hill, N.C., 1961], p. 111).

Cornwallis destroyed his expectation of being covered in a retreat by the latter, who was himself thus driven out of North Carolina. Clinton had resolved on a diversion in Virginia and for that purpose had detached about 3,000 men under General Leslie, with whom Cornwallis was to form a junction for operations in the south, but the defeat of Ferguson occasioned an order from Cornwallis to him to proceed to Wilmington in North Carolina.

5. Tarleton had been defeated by Morgan at the Cowpens early in January of this year 1781. The party which Tarleton had left in his rear with the baggage, immediately upon intelligence of the disaster, set fire to such of it as they could not remove and rejoined Cornwallis's main army. He was thus deprived of a fifth of his numbers and lost as far as respects infantry the most active part of his army. Had Morgan's corps been destroyed, Cornwallis would have pressed forward without a check through North Carolina into Virginia. As it was, he did move with great dispatch and was disabled from overtaking Morgan by the sudden rise of the Catawba River.[5]

6. Cornwallis had been victorious at Guilford, but at a great price.

We are now brought to the contemplation of Virginia in a more especial manner.

On January 4, the infamous General Arnold, who commanded a detachment of about 1,000 men from the army at New York, reached Westover on James River, distant about 140 miles from the capes, and twenty from the city of Richmond.

General Nelson was active in summoning the militia. But Arnold, as soon as he had landed, marched with the greater part of his army to Richmond. The efforts of the militia could not oppose his advance nor prevent Lieutenant Colonel Simcoe, of a British legion, from destroying many buildings, much private property, and many military stores, which had been deposited for safety at Westham, about five miles above it.[6] Arnold, proceeding through Smithfield and by Mackie's Mills, where he destroyed some stores, returned to Portsmouth. It must be

5. Gen. Daniel Morgan (1736–1802), a cousin of Daniel Boone, had served with Washington on Braddock's disastrous expedition. In 1775 he enlisted in the Virginia militia as a captain, and in 1777 he joined Washington's main army with a body of 500 sharpshooters he had recruited. Morgan's riflemen played a decisive role in winning the two battles of Saratoga. By the time Cornwallis was finally able to get his full forces across the river, Morgan and his men had departed (*ibid.,* pp. 55–77).

6. Arnold is, of course, infamous for his defection from the Continental army (see Van Doren, *Secret History of the Revolution,* pp. 143–390). Gen. Thomas Nelson succeeded Jefferson as governor of Virginia in 1781. John G. Simcoe (1752–1806) commanded Simcoe's Tory Queen's Rangers, a part of Arnold's force.

confessed that Arnold received less interruption than he ought among a people contending for liberty, but it is a well-known fact that the [lower country of Virginia, extending from the ocean to the falls of the rivers, is particularly unfavorable to the prompt assembling of militia. The white population is not numerous and is divided by large navigable rivers not to be passed, unless boats are previously prepared for the purpose, not then if the smallest vessel should oppose the attempt.] [7]

There were other forcible reasons which detained the militia at home. The helpless wives and children were at the mercy not only of the males among the slaves but of the very women, who could handle deadly weapons; and these could not have been left in safety in the absence of all authority of the masters and of union among neighbors. Indeed the militia were destitute of arms of every sort and upon so sudden an invasion had no opportunity of equipping themselves in an instant even in their imperfect manner, but they showed afterwards how highly they valued their great stake by exertions of bravery and constancy.

The aids from France conspired so directly to the successes of this year in Virginia that the mission of Lieutenant Colonel Laurens to Paris from Congress forms naturally a part of this history.[8] He was charged to procure from the French king a supply of money and a naval superiority in the American seas.

In the year 1777, we have already seen that upon the first propounding of the Articles of Confederation to the legislature of Virginia, they were eagerly, and from an affection to the union, adopted by her. She, as well as other states, has not fulfilled with punctuality in time, quantity, and sum all her obligations flowing from the league. But most sincere was she in her expectations of performing what she undertook; and that sincerity was the more meritorious as that instrument from its extensive delegations of power clashed with her strongest jealousies and might invade some of her choicest interests. In February 1781, the ratification was completed by all the states, some of which

---

7. Quoted from Marshall, *Washington*, IV, 388. The passages in this chapter from Marshall are indicated with special brackets.

8. John Laurens (1755–82), the son of Henry Laurens, a prominent South Carolina merchant and president of the Continental Congress, entered the Continental service at the age of twenty-two and became an aide to Washington. He served notably in a number of battles and by age twenty-three rose to the rank of lieutenant colonel. Laurens did secure four ships loaded with money and military supplies from the French government. Three arrived safely.

had been reluctant, until others, possessing large vacant territories, should consent to consider them as the common stock of the United America, wrested from the British king by the united prowess of her arms. The demand was not without an appearance of plausibility as to Virginia, for according to the colonial relation between that state and her sovereign, in him as lord paramount were vested all vacant lands, and under his grant alone could they be acquired. But a keen pursuit of interest obscured the true aspect of the Virginian title.

Frivolous as charters may appear in a dialectic or a strictly prudential school they are established on a conventional law of the European world and have been confirmed by solemn decisions in the forum of the United States. Their seeming original defect could raise a question only upon some principle of Indian occupancy or from some conflict from the occupancy of other nations, but as between the king and Virginia there could be none. The first adventurers migrated and the colony was settled on his faith that he as the supreme lord and trustee would hold the lands within the chartered limits for their use. He was conquered, but a sister state could not be spoiled of rights of which he was the mere fiduciary for her. It was suspected by Virginia that the great land companies had contrived to infuse some discontents with her title to her just domains, hoping to operate upon Congress, in case they should be ceded to the United States, with specious purchases from the aborigines, which Virginia had always exploded. It is a decisive evidence of the truly federal temper of Virginia that she renounced the difficulty by her liberality.

The instrument of a federal government contained in it the radical absurdity of depending for its full operation upon the harmony and fidelity of thirteen separate sovereignties without a particle of power in the general council to coerce a delinquent state. Upon the fund of the enthusiasm which animated all at the beginning of the Revolution and from the danger and dreaded consequences of subjugation, the war had hitherto been supported; and it cannot be said that the Confederation would, if consummated, have produced any other effect among the states themselves than to rivet by a solemn compact the principle of honor by which each state was obliged to the others, by their declarations intended to inspire mutual confidence at the first assumption of arms. But impotent as it must always have been in many of the great desiderata of war, it furnished at least a standard for ascertaining the universally admitted duties of each, of stamping with irrevocable certainty the fiat of independence, and of assuring to foreign nations that its unfinished state was not the effect of any disunion by which those nations might be injured. Perhaps it would not be too great a refinement to add that the habit of looking to this act as the central impulse of the union preserved the temper for a calm and accurate revision and improvement of it at a future day.

The naval superiority by which the enemy had been enabled to block up in the harbor of Newport the French fleet from its first arrival on the American coast was now destroyed for a time by a storm on the east end of Long Island.[9] The first glimpse of this advantage kindled the promptitude of Washington to seize the opportunity of detaching twelve hundred men from the lines of New England and New Jersey, under the command of Lafayette, for the head of the Chesapeake, where they were to embark for Virginia under the convoy of a French frigate, which Admiral Destouches was expected to supply.[10] [Letters were also addressed to the Baron Steuben and to Governor Jefferson, requesting the most immediate preparations to be made for the purpose of giving every aid to the expedition which the state could furnish and especially desiring them to dispatch the most experienced pilots to the fleet, the arrival of which might be daily expected. He immediately communicated this measure to the count de Rochambeau and to M. Destouches, to whom he also states his conviction that no serious advantage could be expected from detaching to the Chesapeake a few ships unaided by land troops. There were, he said, a variety of positions to be taken by Arnold, one of which was Portsmouth, his present station, where his ships might be so protected by his batteries on the shore as to defy a mere naval attack, and where he would certainly be able to maintain himself until the losses sustained in the late storm should be repaired and the superiority at sea recovered, when he would unquestionably be relieved.

[There was, therefore, no prospect of effecting anything considerable with such a force, unless the ships detached should have the good

9. The French fleet appeared off Rhode Island in the summer of 1778 to assist an American assault on Newport. When the British fleet commanded by Admiral Lord Howe appeared, the French commander, Charles Hector Theodat, comte d'Estaing (1729), set sail only to be followed by the British. As they were about to engage in battle a great gale blew up, scattering and damaging both fleets (Mackesy, *War for America*, pp. 218–20).

10. Adm. Charles-René-Dominique Gochet, chevalier Destouches (d. 1780), sailed from Newport with three frigates carrying the promised 1,200 troops, but British Adm. Marriott Arbuthnot (1711–94), with an almost equal force, overtook the French at the entrance of the Chesapeake. In the battle that followed, Destouches was worsted and forced to return to Newport, leaving Lafayette's small army with little support.

fortune to fall in with him unexpectedly, in the very moment when embarked to proceed from one place to another. To ensure the success of the expedition, he recommended that the whole fleet should be employed on it and that a detachment of one thousand men should be embarked for the same service. Although Arnold's fortifications could not be considerable, yet they might be sufficient to resist, until he could be relieved, all the efforts which an inferior regular force, however aided by militia, might make against them; but if the Continental troops under the marquis should be joined by one thousand French infantry, with a proper train of artillery, his ruin must be certain and immediate.[11]

⌈These representations of the commander in chief did not prevail. The original plan had already been put in execution. A sixty-four–gun ship with two frigates under M. de Tilly had sailed for the Chesapeake; and as the *America* had now returned and the *Bedford* had been remasted, the French admiral did not deem it prudent to put to sea with the residue of the fleet.

⌈As had been foreseen by General Washington, M. de Tilly found Arnold in a situation not to be assailed with any prospect of success.[12] After showing himself therefore in the bay and making an ineffectual attempt to enter Elizabeth River, he returned to Newport. At the capes he fell in with and captured the *Romulus*, a fifty-gun frigate coming from Charleston to the Chesapeake.

⌈Both the count de Rochambeau, and the chevalier Destouches were well disposed to execute the plans suggested by General Washington. When, therefore, M. de Tilly, with his squadron strengthened by the *Romulus*, rejoined the fleet at Newport, those officers determined on a second expedition to the Chesapeake, with the whole fleet and eleven hundred men.

⌈General Washington, therefore, repeated his orders to the marquis de Lafayette to continue his march to the southward and hastened to Newport, that in a personal conference with the commanders of the land and naval forces of France, he might facilitate the execution of an enterprise from which even yet he entertained sanguine hopes. He

11. John C. Fitzpatrick, ed., *The Writings of George Washington* (Washington, D.C., 1937), XXI, 229–32.

12. Le Bandeur de Tilly was sent in command of the 64-gun ship *Eveille* and two frigates to destroy Arnold's vessels and leave him without naval support. But Arnold wisely withdrew his ships up the Elizabeth River to Portsmouth, a place where Tilly's larger vessels were unable to follow.

supposed that ships judiciously stationed within the Chesapeake might defend its entrance against a superior naval force and therefore deemed it essential to the success of the expedition to use the utmost dispatch in order to preoccupy the bay.

⌈Early on March 6 he reached Newport and went instantly on board the French admiral, where he was met by the count de Rochambeau. It was there determined that a detachment from the army, then in perfect readiness, should be embarked under the count de Viomeril [13] and that the fleet should put to sea as soon as possible. The wind was favorable to the French and adverse to the British, who lay in Gardiner's Bay. Yet the fleet did not sail until the evening of the eighth. It appears from a letter of M. Destouches that this delay was in some measure attributable to a disaster which befell one of his frigates in getting out of port, and there is reason to suppose that it may be ascribed to a want of supplies. Whatever may have occasioned it, the effect most probably was that Arnold escaped a fate well merited by his treason.

⌈Two days after Destouches had sailed, he was followed by Arbuthnot, who overtook him on the sixteenth off the capes of Virginia. After some maneuvering, a partial engagement ensued, which commenced a few minutes after two in the afternoon and continued about an hour, when the fleets were separated.

⌈The next day, the French admiral called a council of war, in which it was declared unadvisable to renew the action; and he returned to Newport.

⌈In this engagement, the hostile fleets were nearly equal to each other, the English having a small superiority in the number of guns, which the French counterbalanced by men. Each party claimed the advantage, but the substantial benefits of victory were unquestionably obtained by the English. They entirely defeated an enterprise from which they had much to fear.

⌈It was, however, a cause of triumph to the allies that a naval action had been fought in which the French, without a superiority of force, had maintained an equality of fortune; and the chevalier Destouches received on the occasion the congratulations of the commander in chief and the thanks of Congress.

⌈Lafayette had embarked his detachment at the Head of Elk and

---

13. Charles Joseph Hyacinthe de Houx, vicomte de Viomeril, was the brother of baron de Viomeril, who commanded the French army in America after Rochambeau's departure.

had proceeded with it to Annapolis in Maryland, where it waited for a frigate from the French squadron to convoy it to Virginia.

⌈The rencontre of the fleets and the consequent return of Destouches to Newport having rendered the object of the expedition unattainable, Lafayette reembarked his detachment for the Head of Elk, at which place he received orders to join the southern army.⌉ [14]

Flushed with the intelligence that the action between the British and French fleets on March 16 off the capes of Virginia had rendered the transportation of a reinforcement to Arnold at Portsmouth perfectly safe, two thousand troops under the command of General Phillips were detached from New York.[15] The immense superiority which their arrival must give to the enemy over any military force which Virginia could assemble reversed the destination of Lafayette, to whom the defense of this state was now happily committed.

⌈The troops under his command had been taken chiefly from the eastern regiments and had imbibed strong prejudices against a southern climate. The service on which they were detached was not expected to be of long duration, and they were consequently unprepared for a campaign in a department where no relief to the most pressing wants could be procured.

⌈From these causes desertions became so frequent as to threaten the dissolution of the corps.

⌈This unpromising state of things was completely changed by a happy expedient adopted by Lafayette. Appealing to the generous and honorable principles of his soldiers, principles on which the feelings of his own bosom taught him to rely, he proclaimed in orders that he was about to enter on an enterprise of great danger and difficulty, in which he persuaded himself that his soldiers would not abandon him.

⌈If, however, any individual of the detachment was unwilling to accompany him, he was invited to apply for a permit to return to his regiment, which should most assuredly be granted.

⌈This measure had the desired effect. The disgrace of applying to be excused from a service full of hazard was too great to be encountered, and a total stop was immediately put to desertion. To keep up the good disposition of the moment, this ardent young nobleman, who was as unmindful of fortune as he was ambitious of fame, borrowed from the merchants of Baltimore on his private credit a sum of money

14. Marshall, *Washington*, IV, 419–23.
15. Maj. Gen. William Phillips (1713?–81) was sent by Clinton to Portsmouth with 2,600 men to join Arnold and supersede him as commander.

sufficient to purchase shoes, linen, spirits, and other articles of immediate necessity for the detachment.

⌐Having made these preparations for the campaign, he marched with the utmost celerity to the defense of Virginia. That state was in great need of assistance. The enemy had penetrated deep into its bosom and was practicing on its inhabitants those excesses which will ever be experienced by a country unable to repel invasion.

⌐On his arrival, General Phillips took command of all the British troops in Virginia; and after employing some time in completing the fortifications of Portsmouth, he commenced his offensive operations.

⌐About 2,500 men were embarked on board the smallest vessels of his fleet, and proceeding up James River, landed at various places in the neighborhood of Williamsburg. Different detachments spread themselves over the lower port of that neck of land which lies between York and James rivers; and after destroying, without opposition, a shipyard belonging to the state, with some armed vessels and public stores, the troops reembarked and proceeded toward City Point, where they landed. The next day they marched against Petersburg, where immense quantities of tobacco and other stores were deposited.

⌐Baron Steuben, the commanding officer in Virginia, was not in a situation to check their progress. The regular force of that state had marched to the aid of General Greene, and the whole number of militia at that time in the field did not much exceed two thousand men. With these, if even collected at one point, no serious resistance could be made; and the certain consequences of risking an action would be the loss of arms and the still greater discouragement of the country.

⌐Yet he was unwilling to abandon so important a place as Petersburg without the semblance of fighting; and therefore the troops in that quarter, amounting to about one thousand men, were posted a mile below the town with orders to skirmish with the enemy. The disposition made by the baron is said to have been well calculated for the object contemplated; and the British troops, without having been able to bring him to a close engagement, were two or three hours employed in driving him across the Appomattox, the bridge over which being taken up as soon as the militia had passed it, a further pursuit became impracticable.[16]

⌐This skirmish having terminated with scarcely any loss on either side, the baron retreated toward Richmond, and Phillips took quiet

16. The American force of about 1,000 militia was commanded by Gen. Peter Muhlenberg (1746–1807), a prominent Pennsylvania German.

possession of Petersburg, where, without further molestation, he destroyed a considerable quantity of tobacco and all the vessels lying in the river.

[This service being accomplished, Arnold was detached to Osborne's, a small village on the south side of James River, fifteen miles below the metropolis, while Phillips marched to Chesterfield Courthouse, which had been the place of rendezvous for the new levies of Virginia, where he destroyed the barracks, with a few public stores that had not been removed.

[At Warwick, nearly midway between Osborne's and Richmond, a respectable naval force consisting of small armed vessels had been collected with the intention of cooperating with the French fleet against Portsmouth, and a few militia were stationed on the northern bank of the river to assist in defending the fleet. On being summoned to surrender, the commodore answered that he was determined to defend himself to the last extremity. Two six- and two three-pounders were immediately brought down to the bank, where it was nearly on a level with the water, and within one hundred yards of the nearest armed ship of the American flotilla.

[After firing a few shot the vessels were scuttled and set on fire, and their crews escaped to the opposite shore and dispersed with the militia.

[A junction was formed in the neighborhood of Warwick, between Phillips and Arnold, who marched without interruption to Manchester, a small town on the southern bank of James River, immediately opposite to Richmond, where, as was the general practice, the warehouses were set on fire and all the tobacco consumed.

[On the preceding evening, the marquis de Lafayette, who had made a forced march from Baltimore, fortunately arrived with his detachment at Richmond; and that place, in which a great proportion of the military stores of the state were then collected, was saved for the present from a visit which was certainly designed.

[The regular troops detached under the marquis were joined by about two thousand militia and sixty dragoons. Not thinking it advisable to attempt the passage of the river in the face of so considerable an army, General Phillips marched back to Bermuda Hundred, a point of land in the confluence of the James and Appomattox, destroying in his way property to an immense amount. At that place he embarked his troops and fell down as far as Hog Island, which was reached by the van of his fleet May 5.

[Detaching small parties to watch the motions of the enemy, the marquis fixed his headquarters on the north of Chickahominy, about eighteen miles from Richmond, where he remained until a letter from Lord Cornwallis called Phillips again up James River.

[When that nobleman determined on marching from Wilmington into Virginia, at the head of less than two thousand men, he signified his wish that the British troops in that state, who had been placed under his command, should take their station at Petersburg.

[On May 7, Phillips received this letter and immediately prepared to comply with the request which it contained. As soon as the fleet moved up the river, Lafayette returned to the defense of Richmond. Having, on his arrival, received intelligence that Cornwallis was marching northward, and finding Phillips landed at Brandon on the south side of the river, he was persuaded that a junction of the two armies was intended and hastened to take possession of Petersburg before Phillips could reach that place. In this, however, he was anticipated. The march of that general was so rapid, and he entered Petersburg so unexpectedly, that he surprised and seized a party of officers, some of whom had been sent forward to collect boats for the use of the America army.

[Being thus disappointed in the design of taking a position which might have enabled him in some degree to retard the junction of Lord Cornwallis with General Phillips and having found on reconnoitering the British army that every part of it was unassailable by the force under his command, he recrossed James River, and encamping a few miles below Richmond, used his utmost exertions to remove the military stores to a place of greater security.

[In this position his army was permitted to repose itself but a few days. Lord Cornwallis had moved from Wilmington about the last of April, and he reached Petersburg in less than a month without having encountered any serious opposition.

[On his arrival, he took command of the whole army, which, by the death of General Phillips on May 13, had devolved on General Arnold.

[Finding himself at the head of a force which nothing in Virginia could resist, this active officer instantly determined on a vigorous plan of offensive operations. His immediate object was to bring the marquis to an action, which must certainly terminate in the defeat of that officer.

[For this purpose, he put his troops in motion without delay, and crossing James River at Westover, where he was joined by a reenforcement which had lately arrived from New York, he attempted by turn-

ing the left flank of the American army to get into its rear. Lafayette
was in no condition to risk an engagement. The native ardor of his
temper and the reluctance with which he exposed himself to the charge
of giving up the country without even an attempt to save it by an action
required all the vigilance of his judgment to restrain him from haz-
arding more than his present situation would justify. On his part, the
immediate objects to be effected were the security of the public stores,
the preservation of his small army for future service, and a junction with
the Pennsylvania line, which was on its march to the southward under
the command of General Wayne.[17]

[The most valuable stores having now been removed from Richmond, that post was no longer important, and the marquis abandoned
it as Lord Cornwallis crossed James River. He retired toward the upper country, inclining his route to the north in order to favor the contemplated junction with Wayne.

[The number of fine horses which were found in the stables of
private gentlemen gave to the British general an efficient cavalry and
enabled him to mount so many of his infantry as to move large detachments with unusual rapidity. Possessing these advantages, he was so
confident of overtaking and of destroying the army of the marquis as
to say exultingly in a letter which was afterwards intercepted, "the boy
cannot escape me." His sanguine hopes, however, were disappointed.
Lafayette, who was joined by several troops of well-mounted volunteer
cavalry from Virginia and Maryland, moved with so much celerity and
caution as to convince Cornwallis of the impracticability of overtaking
him or of preventing his junction with Wayne.

[After having marched for some distance up the northern side of
the North Anna, his lordship relinquished the pursuit and turned his
attention to objects of less magnitude which were supposed to be more
attainable.

[Military stores, indispensable to the prosecution of the southern
war, had been collected in various parts of the upper country, and
among others at the Point of Fork, a point of land made by the confluence of the Rivanna and Fluvanna, the two branches of James River.

[This post was protected by between five and six hundred new levies,
who had marched to the borders of North Carolina under Baron

17. Lafayette's strategy was to avoid battle and keep his force intact. Gen. Anthony
Wayne (1745–96), one of the most dramatic figures of the war, was popularly known as
"mad Anthony Wayne" (see Hugh F. Rankin, "Anthony Wayne: Military Romanticist," in
Billias, ed., *Washington's Generals*, pp. 260–90).

Steuben for the purpose of joining General Greene but had returned on finding that Lord Cornwallis was about to enter Virginia.

⌈This detachment had halted at the Point of Fork, where the militia on the south side of James River had been directed to join them. Against this place Colonel Simcoe was detached with five hundred men.

⌈At the same time, an expedition was also planned against Charlottesville, where the General Assembly had convened and was employed in digesting schemes for the further prosecution of the war. This last expedition was entrusted to Colonel Tarleton; and the detachment employed on it, consisting of two hundred and fifty men, was composed entirely of cavalry and mounted infantry.

⌈So rapid were the movements of Tarleton that a mere accident prevented his entering the town before any notice of his approach was given. A private gentleman, on a very fleet horse, who suspected his object and was acquainted with a nearer route than the great road, hastened to Charlottesville with the interesting intelligence and entered the town about two hours before the British cavalry. Nearly all the members of the legislature made their escape and reassembled at Staunton, on the western side of the Blue Ridge. Only seven of them fell into the hands of Tarleton. After destroying the stores at Charlottesville, he proceeded down the Rivanna to the Point of Fork.

⌈The detachment commanded by Simcoe, being composed chiefly of infantry, could not move with equal celerity. That able officer, however, conducted his march with so much secrecy and address that Steuben seems to have been either totally unapprised of his approach or to have had no accurate information of his numbers.

⌈Intelligence of the expedition to Charlottesville had reached him, and he had prudently employed himself in removing his stores from the Point of Fork to the south side of the Fluvanna.

⌈The river, having been raised by the fall of rain, was unfordable, and the boats were all secured on its southern bank. Yet Steuben, suspecting the party under Simcoe to be the van of the British army, withdrew precipitately in the night and marched near thirty miles from the Point of Fork, leaving behind him such stores as could not be removed. These were destroyed the next morning by a small detachment who crossed the river in a few canoes.⌉ [18]

At this session of the Assembly, the usual antidote for public distress was resorted to. Two persons were named with acrimony as delinquent, Baron Steuben, for not having succeeded in protecting the stores in

18. Marshall, *Washington*, IV, 423–34.

the vicinity of the Point of Fork, and Thomas Jefferson, the governor at the time of Arnold's invasion, as not having made some exertions which he might have made for the defense of the country. It was even hinted in the course of some debate that the grant, which had been made to Steuben, of lands, by an act of Assembly, ought to be rescinded. What was the opinion of the commander in chief upon his conduct does not appear, nor is it known that any court of inquiry ever sat upon it. But his bravery had been too well tried to be doubted; and his fidelity was spotless, although his flight might require explanation. Colonel George Nicholas and Mr. Patrick Henry were those who charged Mr. Jefferson. They aimed to express themselves with delicacy toward him, without weakening the ground on which they supposed that their suspicions would be found ultimately to stand. But probably without design, they wounded by their measured endeavor to avoid the infliction of a wound. Colonel Nicholas moved, however, for an inquiry into the conduct of the governor at the succeeding session. The motion was carried with the concurrence of his friends and his foes; of the former, to afford him an opportunity for exculpation; of the latter, who conceived him to be ruined. He appeared at that session as a delegate from Albemarle and at the appointed day called for some accusation. Neither of those gentlemen having pledged themselves to become prosecutors, they did not feel it to be a personal duty of either to appear as such. But Mr. Jefferson did not affect to be ignorant of the general imputation which had been circulated, but was destitute of any precise shape; and in an address to the house, which amounted to a challenge of impeachment, he reviewed his administration so as to draw forth votes of eulogium, which by some men unambitious of true fame would have been deemed cheaply purchased by past calumnies. He ought to have been satisfied, because they were the undivided voice of his country, which had been prejudiced against him.[19]

Nelson, who as a brigadier in the militia had been actively employed, was unanimously elected successor to Mr. Jefferson, whose second year

19. On June 12, 1781, the House of Delegates passed a resolution to investigate the conduct of the chief executive during the past twelve months. By the time the legislature was finally ready to act on the resolution, Cornwallis had surrendered at Yorktown, and the matter seemed superfluous. Finally, it was resolved "that the sincere thanks of the General Assembly be given to our former Governor," praising him for the conduct of his administration and proclaiming "the high opinion which they entertain of Mr. Jefferson's ability, rectitude and integrity, as Chief Magistrate; and mean by thus publicly avowing their opinion to obviate and remove all unmerited censure" (Hening, *Statutes*, X, 568–69; for a discussion of this controversy, see Malone, *Jefferson the Virginian*, pp. 361–66).

of office had expired and who declined to be nominated for the third.

⌐To secure his junction with Wayne and to keep open his communication toward the north, Lafayette found it necessary to cross the Rapidan. The waters of this river were raised by the heavy rains which fell about that time so as to render its passage extremely difficult to the enemy.

⌐These movements of the two armies had thrown Cornwallis completely between Lafayette and the military stores which had been transported from Richmond up James River and deposited at different places, but principally at Albemarle Old Courthouse, high up the Fluvanna, on the south side of that river.

⌐To avail himself of this position, Lord Cornwallis turned to the south, and recrossing the Pamunky, directed his march up James River toward Albemarle Old Courthouse. The marquis had now effected a junction with the Pennsylvania line, consisting of eight hundred men. Emboldened by this reenforcement, he recrossed the Rapidan and advanced with so much celerity toward the British army that he encamped within a few miles of them when they were yet upwards of a day's march from their point of destination.

⌐Lord Cornwallis still possessed a decided superiority; and as he was confident that the object of the American general must necessarily be to protect the magazines on the Fluvanna, he encamped at Elk Island and advanced his light troops to a position commanding the road by which it was supposed that the Americans must necessarily pass. From this disposition of his force, he promised himself the advantage of obliging his enemy either to risk a general action or to expose his left flank to ruin.

⌐Lafayette, however, discovered and opened in the night a road which was nearer but had long been disused; and the next morning, when the British general expected to seize his prey, he had the mortification to perceive that the American army had crossed the Rivanna and taken a strong position behind Mechunck Creek. This position, which in a great measure commanded the route leading from the camp of his lordship to Albemarle Old Courthouse, could not be attacked but with disadvantage. At this place too, a strong reenforcement of mountain militia was received.

⌐Apprehending the force opposed to him to be greater than it was in reality, Lord Cornwallis abandoned the objects which he had pursued and retired first to Richmond and afterwards to Williamsburg. It is not improbable that on perceiving the difficulties to be encountered near the mountains, where even a victory might be attended with no decisive consequences, he chose to transfer the war to the lower country, the face of which was more favorable to his views.

⌈The marquis followed with cautious circumspection, taking care to keep the command of the upper country and to avoid a general engagement. On June 18, while in the neighborhood of Richmond, he was reenforced by Baron Steuben, with four or five hundred new levies. His army was now increased to 4,000 men, of whom 2,000 were regulars, but only 1,500 of them were disciplined troops. That of Lord Cornwallis was probably rather more numerous, was composed entirely of veterans, and was furnished with a powerful and well-mounted cavalry, who had spread terror as well as desolation through the country and had greatly intimidated the militia.

⌈As the British army retreated to Williamsburg, Lafayette, who sought a partial, though he avoided a general, engagement, kept his main body at the distance of about twenty miles, while his light parties pressed on their rear, which was covered by a strong corps commanded by Colonel Simcoe.

⌈That officer was overtaken by Colonel Butler about six miles from Williamsburg, and a sharp action ensued attended with loss on both sides.[20] The Americans claimed the advantage; but they were obliged to retire by the approach of the whole British army, which moved out to protect their rear. After this skirmish the marquis encamped about twenty miles above Williamsburg, in a secure position near James River, interposing the Chickahominy between him and the enemy.

⌈In the bold and rapid course taken by Lord Cornwallis through the lower and central parts of Virginia, much private, as well as public, property was destroyed. The tobacco especially was everywhere committed to the flames, and the resources of the state were considerably diminished; but no solid advantage was obtained from which a reasonable expectation might be indulged that any considerable progress had been made in accomplishing the great object of the war. Although from various causes, especially from a want of arms and from that general repugnance to the service which a harassed, unpaid militia must be expected to manifest, less resistance was encountered than the strength and population of the state had rendered probable; yet no disposition was openly manifested, except in a remote quarter, to join the royal standard or to withdraw from the contest. The marquis

20. Col. Richard Butler (1743–91) commanded one of the Pennsylvania regiments that had joined Lafayette's forces in June 1781.

complained of "much slowness, and much carelessness in the country."
"But the dispositions of the people," he said, "were good, and they
required only to be awakened." This he thought would be best effected
by the presence of General Washington, an event for which he expressed the most anxious solicitude.

⌈The governor also, with most of the members of Congress as well
as many other respectable citizens, urged the commander in chief to
the defense of his native state.²¹

⌈But Washington, contemplating America as his country and the
general safety as his object, deemed it of the utmost importance to
remain on the Hudson, for the purpose of digesting and conducting
a grand plan of combined operations then meditated against New York.
By executing this plan, he counted more certainly on relieving the
southern states than by any other system of conduct it was then in his
power to adopt.

⌈An express carrying letters which were designed to communicate to
Congress the result of his consultations on this subject with the commanders of the land and naval forces of France was intercepted in the
Jerseys; and when brought before Sir Henry Clinton, his letters disclosed the views of the American general against the seat of the British
power in the United States. This interesting discovery seems to have
alarmed Sir Henry for the safety of New York and to have determined
him to require the return of a part of the troops in Virginia. Supposing
himself too weak, after complying with this requisition, to remain at
Williamsburg, Lord Cornwallis took the resolution of passing James
River and retiring to Portsmouth.²²

⌈In pursuance of this resolution, he marched from Williamsburg
and encamped in such a manner as to cover a ford into the island of
Jamestown; and on the same evening, the Queen's Rangers crossed
over into the island, and the two succeeding days were employed in
passing over the baggage.

⌈The morning after the evacuation of Williamsburg, Lafayette
changed his position, and crossing the Chickahominy, pushed his best

21. Jefferson to Washington, May 28, 1781, *Official Letters of the Governors of the
State of Virginia* (Richmond, 1926–29), II, 524–25.

22. Clinton, who was in command of all the king's forces in America, never quite gave
Cornwallis a free hand, nor did he give explicit orders. On July 8, Cornwallis received
orders to send 3,000 troops to Philadelphia, on July 12 to dispatch them immediately to
New York, then on July 20 not to send them at all but to occupy Old Point Comfort and,
if possible, Yorktown as well (see William B. Willcox, ed., *The American Rebellion: Sir
Henry Clinton's Narrative of His Campaigns, 1775-1782, with an Appendix of Original
Documents* [New Haven, 1954]).

troops within nine miles of the British camp, with the intention of attempting their rear when the main body should have passed into Jamestown.

[Suspecting this design, Lord Cornwallis encamped the greater part of his army on the mainland, as compactly as possible, and displayed a few troops on the island in such a manner as in appearance to magnify their numbers. All the intelligence received by Lafayette concurred in the representation that the greater part of the British army had passed over into the island of Jamestown in the night. Believing this to be the fact, he detached some riflemen and militia to harass their outposts, while he advanced at the head of the Continental troops in order to cut off the rear should the intelligence he had received be well founded.

[Every appearance was calculated to countenance the opinion which had been formed. The British light parties were all drawn in, and the pickets, which lay close to the encampment, were forced by the riflemen without much resistance. Lafayette, however, who arrived a little before sunset, determined to reconnoiter the camp and judge of its strength from his own observation.

[It was in a great degree concealed by woods; but from a tongue of land stretching into the river at no great distance, he soon perceived the British force to be much more considerable than had been apprehended and hastened to call off his men. On his return he found Wayne closely engaged.

[A piece of artillery had been left but weakly defended, which Wayne determined to seize, and Major Galvan was advanced for that purpose. Scarcely was the attempt made, when he discovered the whole army arranged in order of battle, moving out against him. A retreat was now impossible, and the boldest had become the safest measure. Under this impression, he advanced rapidly, and with his small detachment not exceeding eight hundred men, made a gallant charge on the British line. A warm action ensued which was kept up with great spirit for several minutes, when Lafayette, who had now come up, perceiving Wayne to be outflanked both on the right and left, ordered him to retreat and form in a line with the light infantry, who were then drawn up about half a mile in his rear, after which the whole American force saved itself behind a morass.

[Fortunately for Lafayette, Lord Cornwallis did not improve the advantage which he had gained.[23]

---

23. Cornwallis delayed because he wanted to wait until he could be sure the rest of Lafayette's army was at hand to offer a prize worth taking.

[Suspecting this to be a stratagem of the American general to draw him into an ambuscade, a suspicion equally favored by the hardiness of the measure and the time of the attack, Lord Cornwallis, who still supposed the opposing army to be much stronger than it was in reality, would admit of no pursuit and in the course of the night crossed over into the island, whence he soon afterwards proceeded to Portsmouth.

[In the American accounts of this action, the militia are not mentioned, nor is there any statement of their loss. The British represent a detachment of them to have been brought into the engagement but to have been broken and driven off the field at its commencement. It appears from the returns that 118 of the Continental troops, among whom were ten officers, were killed, wounded, or taken, and two pieces of artillery were left on the field, the horses attached to them being killed. The British loss was less considerable. It is stated, in both killed and wounded, at five officers and about seventy privates.

[All active operations were now for a time suspended, and the harassed army of Lafayette was permitted to repose itself.

[Although no brilliant service was achieved by this young nobleman, the campaign in Virginia enhanced his military reputation and raised him in the general esteem. That with so decided an inferiority of effective force and especially of cavalry, he had been able to keep the field in an open country and to preserve a great proportion of his military stores, as well as his army, was believed to furnish unequivocal evidence of the prudence and vigor of his conduct.] [24]

Whether ambition or some nobler motive brought Lafayette to America it is not necessary to ask before we assign to him that portion of applause which he deserved as the commander of the military force in Virginia. He is at this day venerated by every planter who had an interview with him, or by their descendants to whom he has been transmitted by their forefathers. His military praise may be well conceived, though not rightly appreciated by unmilitary men. The materials of our army, which he had to manage, were not to be governed with the discipline of Europe nor to be contemned with the hauteur of nobility. But he had learned from Washington how to conciliate friends among militia and to place in the registers of public safety, necessity, and justice every act which savored of severity. The trifling circumstance of the fondness with which fathers baptized their children with the name of Fayette and with which several positions which he took have been mentioned, since his depression, as the poor marquis's camp, or field, are utterances from the heart of the benevolence of his

24. Marshall, *Washington*, IV, 434–44.

character. Deference to the civil authority and tenderness for civil rights were his characteristic qualities. His merit as a soldier is appreciated by these important facts, that he saved his army, imperfect as it was in the part composed of militia, from the superiority of Cornwallis in numbers, in equipments, in naval cooperation, in the experience of service, and in the impetuosity of attack.

[To digest a system adapted to contingent events, conferences had been held with the count de Rochambeau, in consequence of which orders were transmitted to that officer, directing him to be in readiness to march to the North River as large a portion of the French troops as could be spared from the protection of the fleet. Their place, when they should actually move, was to be supplied with militia. These orders were given in the beginning of April, not with the intention of putting the troops immediately in motion, but of having everything in readiness when a movement should become proper, and in the meantime, of preventing further detachments to the south, by impressing on Sir Henry Clinton some fears for New York.

[Early in May, the count de Barras,[25] who had been appointed to the command of the French fleet stationed on the American coast, arrived in Boston accompanied by the viscount de Rochambeau and brought the long-expected information from the cabinet of Versailles.[26] An interview between General Washington and the commander of the French forces was immediately held at Wethersfield, for the purpose of digesting their plan for future operations as definitively as their present knowledge of circumstances would admit.

[Before the arrival of Colonel Laurens in Europe, Dr. Franklin had received the instructions of Congress and had commenced the negotiation to which they related. His applications did not meet with a very favorable reception. M. de Vergennes [27] complained that the demands of Congress were excessive and indicated an opinion that they wished to throw too much of the burden of the war on their ally. He said that the exertions and expense with which France supported the war in different parts of the world fully employed her means, and that her public credit had its limits, to surpass which would be fatal to it. But to give the United States a signal proof of his friendship, His Majesty

25. Admiral Jacque-Melchior Saint-Laurent, comte de Barras, (d. 1800) who had succeeded Destouches in command, sailed from Newport with eight ships of the line.
26. Barras brought word that a large fleet was to be dispatched to American waters.
27. Charles Gravier, comte de Vergennes (1717–87), the French foreign minister, who had supported the American cause from the beginning as a means for gaining revenge against the British, was the chief architect of the Franco-American alliance.

would grant them a donation of six millions of livres tournois, a part to be invested in arms and clothing for the army according to a list to be furnished by Dr. Franklin and the residue to be paid to the drafts of General Washington. It was impossible, he said, for His Majesty to favor the negotiation in the kingdom of the loan which was required because it would prejudice those which he had occasion himself to make for the support of the war.

⌈No part of the communication was more interesting to the United States than that which respected the naval armament designed to act in the American seas. According to the arrangements made on this subject, twenty ships of the line, under the command of the count de Grasse,[28] were destined for the West Indies, twelve of which were to proceed to the continent of America and might be expected to arrive in the month of July.

⌈Some movement of the British fleet having been made which required the presence of the count de Barras at Newport, he was unable to attend the conference at Wethersfield, and the plan of operations was settled by the two generals. It was determined to unite the troops of France to those of America on the Hudson and to commence the most vigorous operations against New York. The regular army at that station was estimated at only 4,500 men, and though it was understood that Sir Henry Clinton would be able to reenforce it with five or six thousand militia, it was believed that the place could not be maintained without recalling a considerable part of the troops from the southward and consequently enfeebling their operations in that quarter. Should this happen, it was resolved to strike a blow wherever success should be most probable.

⌈The resolution for vigorous offensive operations against New York being taken, the generals separated for the purpose of superintending the preparations for its execution.

⌈The prospect of expelling the enemy from New York roused the northern states from that apathy into which they appeared to have been sinking, and vigorous measures were immediately taken to fill their regiments. Yet those measures were far from being entirely success-

---

28. François Joseph Paul, comte de Grasse (1722–88), a member of one of France's oldest aristocratic families and considered one of the handsomest men of the period, played a decisive role in the Yorktown campaign. The arrival of his ships from the West Indies and the damage he inflicted on the British on Sept. 10, 1781, enabled the rest of the French under Barras to slip into the Chesapeake. As a result, the British fleet was forced to abandon Virginia and Cornwallis was trapped by sea as well as on land (Mackesy, *War for America*, pp. 413–32).

ful. When, in the month of June, the army moved out of winter quarters, and encamped at Peekskill, 6,510 rank and file were wanted to complete the regiments under the immediate command of General Washington. The total of every description, including the garrison at West Point and those on command in Virginia and elsewhere, amounted to 7,854 men. Of these, 4,541 were fit for action and might be brought into the field. In this estimate, however, was not comprehended a detachment from the line of New York under the command of General Clinton,[29] which had garrisoned the posts on the northern frontier of that state and had not yet joined the grand army.

[Such was the American force with which the campaign of 1781 was opened. It fell so far short of that on which the calculations had been made when the plan of operations was concerted at Wethersfield as to excite serious doubts respecting the propriety of adhering to that plan. For this deficiency of men on the part of the states, some compensation was made by the arrival of a reenforcement of 1,500 men to the army of Rochambeau under convoy of a fifty-gun frigate.

[To supply even this army regularly with provisions required exertions much greater than had ever been made since the system of requisition had been substituted for that of purchasing. The hope of terminating the war in a great measure produced these exertions. The legislatures of the New England states, from which country flesh, spirits, and salt were to be drawn, took up the subject in earnest and passed resolutions for the necessary supplies. In order to secure the cooperation of all, a convention of delegates from those states assembled at Providence and agreed upon the quotas to be furnished by them, respectively, each month throughout the campaign. But until these resolutions could be executed, the embarrassments of the army continued; and, for some time after the troops had taken the field, there was reason to apprehend either that the great objects of the campaign must be relinquished for want of provisions or that coercive means must still be used.

[New England not furnishing flour, this important article was to be drawn from New York, New Jersey, and Pennsylvania. The two first-mentioned states, having been for a long time the theater of war and the system of impressment having fallen heavily on them, were much exhausted, and the applications to Pennsylvania did not promise to be very successful. On the subject of a supply of flour, therefore, serious

29. Gen. James Clinton (1733–1812), brother of George Clinton, the governor of New York, had commanded a division on the New York frontier.

fears existed. These were in a considerable degree removed by the activity and exertions of an individual.

[The management of the finances, a duty at all times intricate and difficult but peculiarly so in the United States at a period when without energy in government funds were to be created and a ruined credit restored, had been lately committed to Mr. Robert Morris, a delegate to Congress from the state of Pennsylvania.[30] This gentleman, who had been very active in establishing the bank in Philadelphia, united considerable political talents with a degree of mercantile enterprise, information, and credit seldom equaled in any country. He had accepted this arduous appointment on the condition of being allowed the year 1781 to make his arrangements, during which time the department should be conducted by those already employed and with the resources which government could command. But the critical state of public affairs and the pressing wants of the army obliged him to change his original resolution and to enter immediately on the duties of his office. The occasion required that he should bring his private credit in aid of the public resources and pledge himself personally and extensively for articles of the most absolute necessity which could not be otherwise obtained. Condemning the system of violence and of legal fraud which had too long been practiced as being calculated to defeat its own object, he sought the gradual restoration of confidence by the only means which could restore it—a punctual and faithful compliance with the engagements he should make. Herculean as was this task in the existing derangement of the American finances, he entered upon it with courage, and if not completely successful, certainly did more than could have been supposed practicable with the means

30. Robert Morris (1734–1806), "financier of the Revolution," had emigrated to Pennsylvania at age 13 from Liverpool, Eng. In 1754 he became a partner in a Philadelphia counting house, and for the next 39 years the firm of Willing, Morris and Company and its successors under other names held the leading position in colonial trade. On Feb. 20, 1781, Morris was appointed superintendent of public finance, a unique office established to salvage what appeared to be a total loss. By employing a variety of expedients and daring maneuvers Morris was able to finance the decisive Yorktown campaign. He borrowed $20,000 from the French and a similar sum from his fellow businessmen in Philadelphia. Morris received nothing from the states until after Cornwallis's surrender. On Nov. 4, 1780, Congress had passed a measure adopting a mixed system of specific supplies and monetary contributions with the supplies to be delivered by certain designated dates over the period from Jan. 1 to July 15, the balances of money to be paid quarterly, beginning May 1, 1781. The fact is that in Pennsylvania from 1778 to 1781 less than half the taxes assessed were collected (Miller, *Triumph of Freedom*, pp. 458, 583–84; Burnett, *Continental Congress*, pp. 473–74; for Morris, see Clarence L. Ver Stegg, *Robert Morris: Revolutionary Financier* [Philadelphia, 1954]).

placed in his hands. To him, in no inconsiderable degree, is to to be attributed that the very active and decisive operations of the campaign of 1781 were not impeded, perhaps entirely defeated, by a total failure of the means for transporting military stores and feeding the army.

[On determining to undertake the management of the American finances, he laid before Congress the plan of a national bank, the capital of which was to consist of $400,000, to be made up by individual subscription. It was to be incorporated by government and to be subject to the inspection of the superintendent of the finances, who was at all times to have access to the books. Their notes were to be receivable as specie from the respective states into the treasury of the United States. This beneficial and necessary institution received the full approbation of Congress, and the subscribers were, on the last day of the present year, incorporated by an ordinance made for that purpose.

[This measure was of great importance to the future operations of the army, as it enabled the superintendent of the finances to use by anticipation the funds of the nation, a power of infinite value when prudently and judiciously exercised. But a contract entered into by him with the state of Pennsylvania was of more immediate utility.

[It will be recollected that the army was principally to rely on that state for a supply of flour, and that there was reason to apprehend a continuance of the most distressing disappointments in this essential article. After having relieved the wants of the moment by his private credit, Mr. Morris proposed to take on himself the task of complying with all the specific requisitions made by Congress on Pennsylvania for the present year, on receiving as a reimbursement the taxes imposed by a law just enacted. This proposition being accepted, the contract was made; and in consequence of it, supplies which the government found itself incapable of furnishing were raised by an individual.

[As the French troops approached the North River, intelligence was received that a large detachment from New York had made an incursion into Jersey, under appearances which indicated an intention not immediately to return. This being thought a favorable moment for gaining the posts on the north end of York Island, a plan was formed for seizing them by a *coup de main*; and the night of July 2 was fixed on for its execution. As the possession of these posts would greatly promote the ulterior views of the allies, General Washington had fixed a time for the enterprise, by which it was supposed that the count de Rochambeau might join the American army at Kingsbridge and thus secure the ground which might be gained. An aide-de-camp was therefore dispatched to meet that officer with letters explaining the enterprise contemplated and requesting him to hasten his march and to file off from Ridgebury to Bedford, so as to meet the commander in chief at the time and place appointed.

[With the proposed attack on the works on the north end of York Island was to be combined an attempt to cut off some light troops stationed on the outside of Kingsbridge at Morrisania, under the command of Colonel De Lancey. This part of the plan was to be executed by the duke de Lauzun, to whose legion were to be added Sheldon's Dragoons and a small body of Continental troops dispersed on the lines under the command of General Waterbury.[31]

[As the most exact cooperation of the two armies could not ensure success unless the enemy should be completely surprised, it became necessary, in addition to the usual precautions, to assign some cause for the movement about to be made. The orders, therefore, which were issued on June 30, announced the expectation of forming a junction with the French army in two days and the desire of the commander in chief that the American line should be, on that occasion, as full and as respectable as their numbers would permit. The afterorders gave notice that the French army would not come to that ground, and as the general was desirous of showing all the respect in his power to those generous allies who were hastening with the zeal of friends and the ardor of soldiers to share the fatigues and dangers of the campaign, he proposed to receive them at some other more convenient place and for this purpose would march the whole line of the American army at three in the morning.[32]

---

31. The skirmish at Morrisania on Jan. 22, 1781, was a victory for the Americans in which barracks and quantities of stores belonging to the British army were destroyed. Lt. Col. James De Lancey was in command of the Tory battalion in Westchester County stationed at Morrisania. After the defeat of Jan. 22 De Lancey was able to regroup his scattered forces and make life uncomfortable for the retreating Americans. Armand-Louis Gontaut Biron, duc de Lauzun (1747–93), commanded a proprietary corps raised by him for colonial service under the authority of the minister of marine, a part of the French forces that came to America in 1780 under General Rochambeau. After having served in the Estates General of 1789 and as a diplomat for the Republic he was condemned on the charge of having participated in a conspiracy against the Republic and guillotined. Sheldon's Dragoons was the Second Connecticut Dragoons, commanded by Col. Elisha Sheldon. Brig. Gen. David Waterbury, Jr., arrived after a hot and fatiguing forced march only to find the intended surprise of De Lancey impossible. He gave support to Lincoln, and Washington hastened down from Valentine's Hill. The British took to their boats and escaped (Ward, *War of the Revolution*, II, 880–81).

32. See Fitzpatrick, ed., *Writings of Washington*, XXII, 286–88.

⌈General Lincoln,[33] who commanded the detachment destined to attack the works, embarked on the night of July 1 at Teller's Point in
boats with muffled oars and fell down the river undiscovered to Dobbs
Ferry, where he concealed his men and his boats. Upon reconnoitering
in person the post to be attacked, he perceived that the detachment
had returned from Jersey and that the British were encamped on that
part of the island in much greater force than had been expected. In
addition to this circumstance, a ship of war had taken a station which
rendered it difficult if not impossible for the American boats to make
the landing place without being perceived. On observing these unexpected obstacles, General Lincoln relinquished the design of attacking the works and prepared to execute the eventual orders which had
been given him.

⌈These were to favor the execution of the enterprise entrusted to
the duke de Lauzun, if the more important part of the plan should
appear to be impracticable; and for this purpose, he was directed, after
landing above Spuyten Duyvil Creek, to march to the high grounds in
front of Kingsbridge and there to conceal his detachment until the
attack on De Lancey's corps should commence. He was then to take
such a position as would enable him to oppose any reenforcements
from the island, which might attempt to pass the bridge and turn
the flank of Lauzun. He was also to place himself in such a manner
as to intercept the corps of refugees if it should attempt a retreat into
the island. The legion of Lauzun was unable to reach the point of
action by the hour agreed on for the attack. Meanwhile, the return of
day betrayed Lincoln, and a sharp skirmish ensued between him and a
corps of light troops sent out to engage him, who retired into the island
on the approach of the army under General Washington.

⌈As the commander in chief had counted on the exertions of the
whole British force to wrest from him those strong posts on the island
which he flattered himself with being able to seize by surprise and had
determined to risk a general action to maintain the possession of them,
every arrangement had been made to bring to his aid not only the
troops of France but all the American strength which could thus
suddenly be collected. The Jersey line, therefore, received orders to
reach the North River, opposite to Kingsbridge; and the governor of
New York had been requested to take secret measures to draw out the
militia, on certain signals being given, which were preconcerted be-

---

33. Maj. Gen. Benjamin Lincoln of Massachusetts commanded the troops around
Charleston. In 1780 he was forced to surrender the city and was taken prisoner.

tween them. The arrangements for making these signals in the event
of success being taken with the officer who commanded at West Point,
the Continental army commenced its march from Peekskill at three in
the morning of July 2 and reached Valentine's Hill the next day about
sunrise. As soon as the engagement with General Lincoln commenced,
the army was again put in motion, and on its approach, the British detachment retreated into the island.

[Both parts of the plan having thus failed, and the French army not
having yet come up, the troops were permitted to remain on their arms
until the afternoon, and the day was employed in reconnoitering the
posts of the enemy. In the evening the army retired to Valentine's
Hill, and the next day to Dobbs Ferry, at which place the count de
Rochambeau arrived on July 6. The thanks of the commander in chief
were given in general orders to that officer for the unremitting zeal
with which he had proceeded to form the so-long-wished-for junction
with the American army; and he was requested to convey to the officers
and soldiers under his command the grateful sense which was entertained by the general of the cheerfulness with which they had performed
so long and laborious a march, at so hot a season. He sought not only by
his own attentions but by encouraging the same dispositions in the
American officers to obviate all those jealousies and misunderstandings
which frequently exist among troops of different nations serving in
the same army.

[Every nerve was now strained to be in complete readiness for the
grand enterprise projected against New York. But as the execution of
any plan which could be formed depended on events which had not
yet taken place and were necessarily uncertain, the commander in chief
directed his attention to other objects to be pursued if that which was
most desirable should prove unattainable.[34] Should circumstances take
a shape so unpropitious to his hopes as to render the siege of New
York unadvisable, his views were turned to Virginia, and after the
destruction of the enemy in that state, to the Carolinas, and to Georgia.
Should a naval superiority be acquired, some valuable results might
certainly be obtained from it, unless Sir Henry Clinton should previously reassemble all his forces in New York or Lord Cornwallis should
retire through North Carolina to Charleston. To prevent a measure so
much to be dreaded as the first, General Washington was desirous

34. The truth is that Washington and the French commanders agreed that Clinton,
with 14,000 troops and a strong defensive position, could not be defeated. The wonder
is that the enterprise was ever seriously undertaken.

that the count de Barras, whose fleet was understood to have been rendered superior to that of the English by the departure of the *Royal Oak* for Halifax, should immediately take possession of the Chesapeake. The French admiral, however, was unwilling to engage in an expedition which he deemed so full of hazard, and the general forbore to press it.

[Early in August, the apprehensions of the commander in chief that he should be unable to accomplish his favorite object began to influence his conduct. His army received no considerable addition to its strength, and no certain assurances were given him that his requisitions for men would be complied with. Letters from the marquis de Lafayette announced that a large portion of the British and German troops in Virginia were embarked and that their destination was believed to be New York. These circumstances induced him to turn his attention more seriously than heretofore to the southward and to prepare for giving his efforts that direction. As it was of the utmost importance to conceal from Sir Henry Clinton this eventual change of plan, his arrangements were made secretly, and in the meantime, there was no relaxation of the preparations for acting against New York. A reenforcement from Europe of near three thousand men being received by Sir Henry Clinton, he was induced thereby to countermand his orders requiring Lord Cornwallis to detach to his aid a part of the army in Virginia and to direct that nobleman to take some strong position on the Chesapeake from which he might conveniently execute the plans meditated against the states lying on that bay so soon as the storm which now threatened the British power should blow over. In a few days after the arrival of this reenforcement from Europe, the count de Barras communicated to General Washington the interesting information that de Grasse was to have sailed from Cap-Français for the Chesapeake on August 3 with a squadron of from twenty-five to twenty-nine sail of the line, having on board 3,200 soldiers, and that he had made engagements with the officers commanding the land and naval forces of Spain in the West Indies to return to those seas by the middle of October.[35] It was now necessary to determine absolutely on the object against which the arms of the combined forces should be directed.

[The shortness of the time appropriated by de Grasse for his continuance on the American coast, the apparent disinclination of the naval officers to attempt to force a passage into the harbor of New York,

35. See Jared Sparks, ed., *The Writings of George Washington* (Boston, 1858), VIII, 522–23.

and the backwardness of the states in complying with the requisitions which had been made on them for men decided in favor of southern operations; and the views of the commander in chief were entirely directed toward the waters of the Chesapeake. This change of plan, which had before been suggested to Lafayette as probable, was now communicated to that nobleman as certain; and he was requested to make such a disposition of his army as should be best calculated to prevent Lord Cornwallis from saving himself by a sudden march to Charleston.

[In pursuance of the engagements entered into by the minister of His Most Christian Majesty, the count de Grasse had sailed from Brest early in March with a squadron of twenty-five sail of the line, five of which were designed for the East, and twenty for the West Indies.[36] Admiral Rodney, who commanded the naval forces of Great Britain in the West Indies, seems to have been absorbed in securing the immense plunder acquired by the capture of Saint Eustatius from the Dutch;[37] and de Grasse, after an indecisive engagement in the channel of Saint Lucia with Sir Samuel Hood,[38] who had been detached to intercept him, formed a junction with the ships of his sovereign already on that station and was rendered thereby greatly superior to Rodney.[39] After some operations, in the course of which Tobago was taken by the French, de Grasse sailed with a large convoy from Cap-Français, which he conducted out of danger, and then directed his course with twenty-eight sail of the line and several frigates to the Chesapeake, where he arrived late in August. At Cape Henry, he found an officer dispatched from Lafayette with full intelligence of

36. De Grasse, with 24 ships of the line and six frigates, arrived outside Hampton Roads, Va., on August 30, 1781.

37. Adm. George Brydges Rodney (1719–92), descended from an old military family, had been governor and commander in chief of Newfoundland. During the Seven Years War he won distinction by capturing Martinique, St. Lucia, Grenada, and St. Vincent in the West Indies. On Feb. 3, 1781, Rodney captured the Dutch possession of St. Eustatius. Under the rules of eighteenth-century warfare he stood to make a personal fortune, but he overlooked the fact that much of the captured merchandise belonged to English merchants. Confiscating everything, he sold a good deal at auction and sent much of it back to England. However, Rodney's dreams of wealth were shattered when the French Admiral Lamotte-Piquet intercepted and captured a large portion of his convoy and subsequent lawsuits took most of the remaining booty (Mark Mayo Boatner, III, *Encyclopedia of the American Revolution* [New York, 1966], pp. 942–44).

38. Sir Samuel Hood (1724–1816) had been sent to the West Indies in 1780 as Rodney's second in command. He played an important part in the defeat of de Grasse off Saint's Passage in April 1782.

39. The French fleet in American waters, commanded by Admiral de Barras, consisted of eight ships of the line.

the situation of the armies in Virginia. Lord Cornwallis, who had received notice that a French fleet was to be expected on the coast, had collected his whole force at Yorktown and Gloucester Point, where he was fortifying himself assiduously; and the marquis had taken a position on James River for the purpose of opposing any attempt which the British army might make to escape into South Carolina. In consequence of this information, four ships of the line and several frigates were detached for the purposes of blocking up the mouth of York River and of conveying the land forces brought from the West Indies under the command of the marquis de Saint-Simon [40] up the James to form a junction with Lafayette. In the meantime, the fleet lay at anchor just within the capes. On August 25, the count de Barras sailed from Newport for the Chesapeake.

[Rodney was apprised of the destination of de Grasse but seems not to have suspected that he would sail with his whole fleet for the American continent. The convoy which had departed from Cap-Français was so valuable that the English admiral appears to have been persuaded that a large part of the French fleet would continue to protect it until it should be safe in port. Supposing, therefore, that a part of his squadron would be sufficient to maintain an equality of naval force in the American seas, he detached Sir Samuel Hood to the continent with only fourteen sail of the line. That officer made land to the southward of the capes of Virginia a few days before de Grasse entered the Chesapeake, and not seeing any ships belonging to either nation, proceeded without delay to the capes of the Delaware, and thence to Sandy Hook, which he reached on August 28.

[Admiral Graves,[41] who had succeeded Arbuthnot in the command of the fleet on the American station, lay with seven sail of the line in the harbor of New York, when Hood appeared off the Hook. Two of his ships had been considerably damaged in a late cruise near Boston and were then under repair, so that he had only five which were fit for service. On the same day that Hood appeared and gave information which rendered it probable that de Grasse, if not at that time on the

40. Gen. Claude Anne, marquis de Saint-Simon Montblern, a distant relative of the famous social philosopher, was commander of those French troops transported to Yorktown by Admiral de Grasse.

41. Adm. Thomas Graves (1725?–1802) was sent in 1780 with six ships of the line to join Admiral Arbuthnot. When the crisis of the Yorktown campaign arrived, he tried to reach Cornwallis, fought a losing battle off Chesapeake Capes, and returned to New York to refit. He headed back toward the Chesapeake with twenty-five ships of the line, but the day he sailed from New York, Cornwallis surrendered.

coast, might be expected daily, intelligence was also received that de Barras had sailed from Newport. Without waiting for the ships under repair, those fit for sea were ordered out of the harbor; and Graves, who, as the senior officer, took command of the whole fleet consisting of nineteen sail of the line, sailed immediately in quest of the French. Not suspecting the actual strength of de Grasse, he hoped to fall in with the one or the other of their squadrons and to fight it separately.

[Early in the morning of September 5, the French fleet, consisting of twenty-four ships of the line, was discovered lying at anchor just within the Chesapeake, extending across its entrance from Cape Henry to the middle ground. No previous information of the approach of Graves had been received, nor had the British admiral obtained any accounts either of the strength or arrival of his adversary. Orders were immediately given by de Grasse for the ships to slip their cables, and leaving their anchorage ground, severally to form the line as they could come up, without regard to their particular or specified stations. The French fleet stretched out to sea, and Graves formed the line of the battle ahead. As the two fleets came nearly parallel to each other, the British admiral made the signal for his whole fleet to wear, by which maneuver it was put on the same tack with his adversary, so that his rear became his van. About four in the afternoon the action commenced between the headmost ships, and continued until sunset. Several ships were much damaged, but neither admiral could claim the victory.[42] For five successive days the hostile fleets continued in view of each other, repairing the damages which had been sustained and endeavoring by a course of maneuvers to gain some advantage which might lead to decisive consequences. As the French generally maintained the windward, it was in the power of de Grasse to have brought on a close action; but the capture of the British army in Virginia was an object of too much importance to be put in hazard by an engagement which might have lost the command of the Chesapeake, and he, therefore, determined to regain his former station within the capes. On returning to his anchorage ground he found the count de Barras with the squadron from Newport and fourteen transports laden with heavy artillery and military stores proper for carrying on a siege. That admiral, when he sailed from Rhode Island, had taken a very wide circuit for the pur-

42. The stronger French fleet did fare better than the English though the outcome was inconclusive. Despite the advantage in their windward position Graves handled his fleet rather confusedly, and the heavier metal of the French so greatly damaged five British ships that the English were in no condition to renew the action (Ward, *War of the Revolution*, II, 885) .

pose of avoiding the enemy and had fortunately entered the bay during the absence of de Grasse. On approaching the capes, the British admiral found the entrance of the Chesapeake defended by a force with which he was entirely unable to contend and therefore bore away for New York, in order to repair his ships and form a junction with such re-enforcements as might be expected soon to arrive on the American station.

[Having determined to direct the immediate active operations of the allied arms against Lord Cornwallis, General Washington prepared to execute the plan which he had formed. The defense of the posts on the Hudson was committed to General Heath,[43] who was also directed to protect the adjacent country, so far as was compatible with the still more important object of his attention, and for these purposes the two regiments of infantry from New Hampshire, ten from Massachussetts, five from Connecticut, Sheldon's Legion, the third regiment of artillery, together with the corps of invalids and the state troops, with the militia called into actual service, were placed under his command. General Washington resolved to lead the southern expedition in person. All the troops of Rochambeau and a strong detachment from the Continental army, consisting of the light infantry under Scammell, four light companies from New York and Connecticut, the regiment of Rhode Island, Hazen's Regiment, two regiments of New York, the residue of the Jersey line, and Lamb's Artillery, amounting in the whole to upwards of two thousand men, were destined for this service.[44] On August 19, Hazen's Regiment and the line of Jersey were directed to pass the Hudson at Dobbs Ferry and take a position between Springfield and Chatham, where they were to cover some bakehouses to be instantly constructed in the vicinity of those places for the purpose of more certainly veiling the real designs of the American chief and of

43. William Heath (1737–1814) of Massachusetts was a farmer, militiaman, and politician before the Revolution. Washington was quick to recognize Heath's limitations and during the New York and New Jersey campaigns posted him at places where no major threat was expected.

44. Col. Alexander Scammel (1747–81) of Massachusetts, a major of the New Hampshire militia, had served during the siege of Boston and in Canada. In the Yorktown campaign he commanded 400 troops. Moses Hazen (1733–1803) of Massachusetts and Canada, a lieutenant in a ranger company, had fought at Crown Point (1750), Louisburg (1758), and Quebec (1759). Having become engaged in many successful commercial enterprises, he was a wealthy man when the Revolutionary War began. On Jan. 22, 1776, Congress commissioned him colonel of the Second Canadian Regiment. This unit, known as "Congress's Own" and "Hazen's Own," was recruited from Albany and composed of Canadians, including refugees. John Lamb (1735–1800) of New York, a colonel of artillery, led his regiment south as part of Knox's brigade for the Yorktown campaign.

exciting fears for Staten Island. On the same day the whole army was put in motion, and on the twentieth and twenty-first, the American troops crossed the Hudson at Kings Ferry. The circuit made by the French was rather more extensive, and they did not complete the passage of the river until the twenty-fifth of the month.

⌈As it was desirable to conceal as long as possible the real object of the present movement, the march of the army was continued until August 31 in such a direction as to keep up the fears which had been excited for New York, and a considerable degree of address was used by the preparations made in the American camp and by the declarations of the general and other officers to countenance the opinion that the real design of Washington was either to make himself master of Staten Island or to take a position about Sandy Hook, which would favor any attempt that might be made by the French fleet to force a passage over the bar into the harbor of New York. The intelligence contained in the letters which had been intercepted by Sir Henry Clinton favored this deception; and even after it became necessary for the combined army to leave the route leading down the Hudson and to march directly for the Delaware, the British general is stated to have retained the strong impression which he had received respecting the danger of New York and not to have suspected the real object of his adversary, until he had actually passed the last-mentioned river and was at too great a distance for his march to be molested.

⌈It being too late to obstruct the progress of the allied army toward Virginia, Sir Henry Clinton, probably with the hope of recalling General Washington, immediately resolved to act offensively in the north. An expedition was planned against New London in Connecticut, the command of which was entrusted to General Arnold. A strong detachment was embarked on board a fleet of transports, which passed through the sound and landed on both sides of the harbor, about three miles from the town.

⌈New London is a seaport town on the west side of the New Thames, in which were collected naval and other stores to a considerable amount. For its defense a fort, called Fort Trumbull, and a redoubt had been constructed somewhat below it on the same side of the river; and opposite to it, on Groton Hill, was Fort Griswold, a strong square fortification, but not sufficiently garrisoned.

⌈General Arnold, who commanded in person the troops which landed on the western side of the harbor, immediately advanced against Fort Trumbull, the redoubt, and New London. These posts.

being totally untenable, were evacuated on his approach, and he took possession of them with inconsiderable loss. To prevent the escape of the shipping up the river, Lieutenant Colonel Eyre, who commanded the division which landed on the Groton side of the harbor, consisting of two British regiments, a battalion of New Jersey volunteers, and a detachment of jägers and artillery, had been ordered to storm Fort Griswold, which had been represented to Arnold as too incomplete to make any serious resistance. This fort was defended by Colonel Ledyard, with a garrison of about one hundred and sixty men, part of whom had just evacuated the works on the New London side of the river. Being of some strength, and the approach to it difficult, the garrison resolved to defend it and rejected the summons to surrender. The British marched up to the assault on three sides, and overcoming with persevering valor the difficulties which a steep ascent and a continued fire opposed to them, at length made a lodgment on the ditch and fraised work and entered the embrasures with charged bayonets. A further defense being hopeless, the action ceased on the part of the Americans, and Colonel Ledyard delivered his sword to the commanding officer of the assailants. Irritated by the obstinate resistance which had been experienced and the loss which had been sustained, the British officer on whom the command had devolved tarnished the glory which victory gave him by the inhuman use he made of it. Instead of respecting with the generous spirit of a soldier the gallantry which he had encountered and subdued, he indulged the vindictive feelings which had been aroused by the slaughter of his troops and revenged them on men who no longer resisted. In the account given of this affair to General Washington by Governor Trumbull, he says that "the sword presented by Colonel Ledyard was immediately plunged into his bosom, and the carnage was kept up until the greater part of the garrison was killed or wounded." [45] In this fierce assault, Colonel Eyre was killed and Major Montgomery, the second in command, also fell as he entered the American works. The total loss of the assailants, in killed and wounded, was not much less than two hundred men.

[The town of New London, and the stores contained in it, were

45. Jonathan Trumbull (1710–85) had by 1766 become deputy governor and chief justice of Connecticut. On the death of Governor Pitkin in Oct. 1769 the Assembly named Trumbull to succeed him, and he held the office until his voluntary retirement in 1784. When the Revolutionary War began, Trumbull was the only colonial governor on the Patriot side. His main contribution to the war effort was in organizing the supply of food, clothing, and munitions for Washington's army, Connecticut being the main source among the colonies (see Glenn Weaver, *Jonathan Trumbull: Connecticut's Merchant Magistrate* [Hartford, 1956]).

consumed by fire. To escape the odium which invariably attends the useless and wanton destruction of private property, this fire was attributed to accident; but all the American accounts unite in declaring it to have been intentional. It is a fact which seems to manifest the respect entertained by this detachment for the militia of Connecticut that their retreat was so early as to leave the barracks at Fort Griswold standing and a magazine of powder at that place untouched.

⌜The march of General Washington was not arrested by this incursion into Connecticut. He pressed forward with the utmost possible celerity and at Chester received the important intelligence of the arrival of Admiral count de Grasse in the Chesapeake. Having made the necessary arrangements for the transportation of his army and directed those for whom transports could not be furnished at the Head of Elk to march on to Baltimore, he proceeded in person to Virginia, attended by the count de Rochambeau and the chevalier de Chastellux,[46] and on September 14 reached Williamsburg.

⌜As it was of the utmost importance to arrange a plan of cooperation with the French admiral, who had just returned from his engagement with Graves to his former ground within the capes, the commander in chief, accompanied by Rochambeau, Chastellux, Knox, and Duportail,[47] repaired to the fleet and went on board the *Ville de Paris,* where everything was adjusted in conformity with his wishes, except that de Grasse, who declared his utter inability to remain on the American coast longer than November 1, declined as too hazardous a proposition which was made to him to station some of his ships in the river above Yorktown, for the purpose of aiding the approaches in that quarter.

⌜While the close investment of the British army was only delayed

46. François-Jean de Beauvoir, marquis de Chastellux (1734–88) was a major general in Rochambeau's expeditionary force. His fame in America rests primarily with the publication of his *Travels in North America in the Years 1780, 1781 and 1782* (1786; trans. and ed. by Howard C. Rice, Jr., Chapel Hill, N.C., 1963).

47. Gen. Henry Knox (1750–1806) was in 1775 only a beefy young man with a maimed hand earning a good living as a proprietor of The London Book-Store. He served as a volunteer during the battle of Bunker Hill and the Boston siege. From the beginning Washington was so favorably impressed by Knox that he appointed the 25-year-old military amateur colonel of the Continental Regiment of Artillery, eventually raising him to chief of Continental artillery. Knox's most extraordinary exploit was the successful movement of cannon captured at Fort Ticonderoga to be used at Boston as siege artillery (see North Callahan, *Henry Knox: General Washington's General* [New York, 1958]). Louis Le Begue de Presle Duportail (1743–1802), the son of a nobleman, was one of four officers chosen by the French court in response to Franklin's request for trained military engineers. On July 22, 1777, Congress gave him seniority over all engineers previously appointed, and on Nov. 17 he was promoted to general and chief of engineers.

until the arrival of the troops from the north should render the contemplated operations perfectly secure, serious apprehensions were excited that the brilliant results confidently anticipated from the decided superiority of the land and naval forces of the allies would be put in the most imminent hazard.

[Information was received that a reenforcement of six ships of the line under Admiral Digby had reached New York.[48] Deeming it certain that the British fleet would be induced by this addition to its strength to attempt everything for the relief of Lord Cornwallis, de Grasse expected to be attacked by a force not much inferior to his own. Thinking his present station unfavorable for a naval combat, he designed to change it and communicated to General Washington his intention to leave a few frigates to block up the mouths of James and York rivers and to put to sea with his fleet in quest of the enemy. If they should not have left the harbor of New York, he purposed to block them up in that place and supposed that his operations in that quarter would be of more service to the common cause than his remaining in the bay, an idle spectator of the siege of York. The commander in chief was very much alarmed at this communication. It was obvious, and indeed the fact had been stated by the admiral, that should he put to sea, the winds and a variety of accidents might prevent his return to the Chesapeake. During his absence, a temporary naval superiority might be acquired by the enemy in those waters, and the army of Lord Cornwallis might, with the loss of his artillery and a few men, be placed in perfect security. This was exposing to the caprice of fortune an event of infinite importance, which was now reduced to almost certain calculation and which could be endangered only by relinquishing the station at present occupied by the fleet. The admiral was therefore entreated to preserve that station, or if it should be essential to take the open sea, to cruise within view of the capes so as to be able to reenter them at pleasure, and in the meantime to intercept any enemy endeavoring to make the bay. Fortunately, the wishes of the general prevailed; and the admiral, having resolved to erect a battery on Point Comfort for the purpose of commanding the entrance into the Chesapeake, consented to relinquish those plans of active

48. Adm. Robert Digby (1732–1814) had served with distinction in the Seven Years War and was from 1779 to 1781 second in command of the Channel Fleet and in the expeditions of Admiral Rodney and Admiral Darby to relieve Gilbralter. In August 1781, he was sent to America as commander-in-chief to succeed Graves, but since he arrived just as the latter was about to sail for the Chesapeake he courteously deferred his assumption of command.

enterprise which his thirst of military glory had originally suggested and to maintain a station deemed by the American general so conducive to the interests of the allies.⌝ [49]

⌐What a long chain of events thus led to fix Cornwallis in Yorktown! What a multitude of links, a chasm in a very few of which might, perhaps, have averted this contingency!

⌐At length, the last division of the troops arrived in James River, at the landing near Williamsburg, where they were disembarked; and the preparations for advancing against the enemy were soon completed. York is a small village on the south side of the river which bears that name, where the long peninsula between the York and the James is only eight miles wide. In this broad and bold river a ship of the line may ride in safety. Its southern banks are high, and some batteries facing the water had been constructed on them by a small corps of artillery belonging to the state of Virginia formerly stationed at this place. On the opposite shore is Gloucester Point, a piece of land projecting deep into the river and narrowing it at that place so that it does not exceed one mile. Both these posts were occupied by Lord Cornwallis, who had been assiduous in fortifying them. The communication between them was commanded by his batteries and by some ships of war which lay under his guns.

The main body of his army was encamped on the open grounds about Yorktown, within a range of outer redoubts and fieldworks calculated to command the peninsula and impede the approach of the assailants; and Colonel Tarleton, with a small detachment consisting of six or seven hundred men, held the post at Gloucester Point.

⌐The legion of Lauzun and a brigade of militia under General Weedon, the whole commanded by the French General de Choisy, were directed to watch and restrain the enemy on the side of Gloucester; [50] and the grand combined army moved down on the south side of the river, by different routes, toward Yorktown. About noon, the heads of the columns reached the ground assigned to them respectively, and after driving in the pickets and some cavalry, encamped for the

49. Marshall, *Washington*, IV, 452–80.

50. George Weedon (*ca.* 1730–93), a Fredericksburg, Va., innkeeper and prewar acquaintance of Washington, had helped organize military resistance to British raids in Virginia. During the Yorktown campaign he commanded the militia investing Gloucester. The marquis de Choisy, a recent arrival in America, had an excellent reputation in the French army as the hero of the siege of Cracow. Under his command the Virginia militia and the Lauzun Legion, reinforced with 800 marines from the fleet, moved down toward Gloucester Point to halt English foraging parties and force the enemy into fixed positions (Whitridge, *Rochambeau*, p. 217).

evening. The next day was principally employed in reconnoitering the situation and works of the garrison and in digesting the plans of approach, after which the right wing, consisting of Americans, extended farther to the right and occupied the ground east of Beaverdam Creek, while the left wing, consisting of the French, were stationed on the west side of that creek. In the course of the night, Lord Cornwallis withdrew within his inner lines; and the next day, the works he had evacuated were possessed by the besieging army, which now completely and closely invested the town on that side.

[No attack on Gloucester Point being intended, the arrangements in that quarter were only calculated to keep up a rigorous blockade, and the force allotted to this service consisted of rather more than two thousand men. On approaching the lines a sharp skirmish took place which terminated unfavorably for the British, after which they remained under cover of their works, and the blockade sustained no further interruption.

[Until October 6, the besieging army was incessantly employed in disembarking their heavy artillery and military stores and drawing them from the landing place on James River to camp, a distance of six miles. This work being at length accomplished, the first parallel was commenced in the night of October 6, within six hundred yards of the British lines, with so much silence that the operation appears to have been unperceived until the return of daylight disclosed it to the garrison. By that time, the trenches were in such forwardness as to cover the men. The loss on this occasion was consequently inconsiderable. In killed and wounded it amounted only to one officer and twenty men, and was principally sustained by the corps of the marquis de Saint-Simon on the left. By the evening of the ninth several batteries and redoubts were completed and cannon mounted in them. A heavy fire was immediately commenced on the besieged, the effect of which was soon perceived. Many of their guns were dismounted and silenced, and their works were in different places demolished. The next day, new batteries were opened, and the fire became so heavy that the besieged withdrew their cannon from their embrasures and scarcely returned a shot. The shells and red-hot balls from the American batteries reached the ships in the harbor, and in the evening set fire to the *Charon,* of forty-four guns, and to three large transports, which were entirely consumed. Reciprocal esteem and a spirit of emulation between the French and Americans being cultivated with great care by the commander in chief, the siege was carried on with unexampled rapidity.

On the night of the eleventh, the second parallel was opened within three hundred yards of the British lines. This advance was made so secretly, and so much sooner than had been expected, that no suspicion of the measure seems to have been entertained by the besieged until daylight discovered the working parties to their pickets, by which time the trenches had progressed so far as in a great degree to cover the men employed in them. The three succeeding days were devoted to the completion of the second parallel and of the batteries constructed in it, during which the fire of the garrison, who with indefatigable labor had opened several new embrasures, became more destructive than at any previous time. The men in the trenches were particularly annoyed by two redoubts advanced three hundred yards in front of the British works, which flanked the second parallel of the besiegers. It was necessary to possess these redoubts, and preparations were made to carry them both by storm. To avail himself of the spirit of emulation existing between the troops of the two nations and to avoid furnishing matter to excite the jealousy of either, the attack of the one was committed to the Americans and of the other to the French. The marquis de Lafayette commanded the American detachment, composed of the light infantry, which was intended to act against the redoubt on the extreme left of the British works on the river bank; and the baron de Viomeril [51] led the grenadiers and chasseurs of his country against that which, being further toward the British right, approached rather nearer the French lines. Toward the close of day, the two detachments marched with equal firmness to the assault. Emulous of glory both for themselves and their country, every exertion was made by each. Colonel Hamilton, who throughout this campaign had commanded a battalion of light infantry, led the advanced corps of the Americans, consisting of his own and of Colonel Gimat's battalions; [52] and Colonel Laurens, another aide of

51. Antoine Charles de Houx, baron de Viomeril (d. 1792), Rochambeau's second in command, led the advanced guard of the French army at Yorktown. When Rochambeau went home Viomeril took command, and although he was a hot-tempered man who did not get along with the Americans as well as Rochambeau or Chastellux, there was no question about his ability. "As soon as the Revolution broke out in France he became an unquestioning supporter of the royal family, and he fell mortally wounded in their defense during the attack on the Tuilleries, August 10, 1792" (*ibid.*, p. 79).

52. Alexander Hamilton (1757–1804) had volunteered for military service in 1755. He rose quickly, was promoted to lieutenant colonel at age twenty, and in March 1777 became secretary and aide-de-camp to General Washington. His desire for a field command was finally realized by an expansion of the light infantry corps, and on July 31, 1781, Hamilton took command of a battalion in Moses Hazan's brigade of Lafayette's division (see Broadus Mitchell, *Alexander Hamilton: Youth to Maturity, 1755–1788* [New York, 1957]). Jean-Joseph Sourbader de Gimat (b. 1743 or 1747), son of a French officer, went

the commander in chief, turned the redoubt at the head of eighty men in order to take the garrison in reverse and intercept their retreat. The troops rushed to the charge without firing a single gun; and so great was their ardor that they did not give the sappers time to remove the abatis and palisades. Passing over them, they assaulted the works with irresistible impetuosity on all sides at once and entered them with such rapidity that their loss was inconsiderable. This redoubt was defended by Major Campbell, with some inferior officers, and forty-five privates.[53] The major, a captain, an ensign, and seventeen privates were made prisoners, eight privates were killed while the Americans were entering the works, and a few escaped. The redoubt attacked by the French was defended by a greater number of men, and the resistance being greater, was not overcome so quickly or with so little loss. Of one hundred and twenty men commanded by a lieutenant colonel who were originally in this work, eighteen were killed, and forty-two, among whom were a captain and two subaltern officers, were made prisoners. In killed and wounded the assailants lost near one hundred men. The commander in chief was highly gratified with the active courage displayed in this assault. Speaking of it in his diary he says, "The bravery exhibited by the attacking troops was emulous and praiseworthy. Few cases have exhibited greater proofs of intrepidity, coolness, and firmness than were shown on this occasion." [54] The orders of the succeeding day, congratulating the army on the capture of these important works, expressed a high sense of the judicious dispositions and gallant conduct of both the baron de Viomeril and the marquis de Lafayette and requested them to convey to every officer and man engaged in the enterprise the acknowledgments of the commander in chief for the spirit and rapidity with which they advanced to the attack and for the admirable firmness with which they supported themselves under the fire of the enemy without returning a shot. "The general reflects," conclude the orders, "with the highest degree of pleasure on the confidence which the troops of the two nations must here after have in each other. Assured of mutual support he is convinced there is

---

to America with Lafayette and was commissioned a major in the Continental army. He served as Lafayette's aide-de-camp, and in 1781 Washington appointed him commander of the light infantry regiment just being formed.

53. Major Campbell had worked hard as superintendent of Indian affairs in Canada to enlist the Indians under the British standard in 1755. At Yorktown, he commanded about 70 men.

54. See John C. Fitzpatrick, ed., *The Diaries of George Washington* (Boston, 1925), II, 266–67.

no danger which they will not cheerfully encounter . . . no difficulty which they will not bravely overcome." [55]

⌈On the same night that these two redoubts were taken, they were included in the second parallel; and in the course of the next day, some howitzers were placed in them, which by five in the afternoon were opened on the besieged.

⌈The situation of Lord Cornwallis was now becoming desperate. His works in every quarter were sinking under the fire of the besiegers. The batteries already playing on him had silenced nearly all his guns, and the second parallel was about to open, which in a few hours must infallibly render the town altogether untenable. To suspend for a short time a catastrophe which appeared almost inevitable, he resolved on attempting to retard the completion of the second parallel by a vigorous sortie against two batteries which appeared to be in the greatest forwardness and which were guarded by French troops. The party making this sortie consisted of three hundred and fifty men commanded by Lieutenant Colonel Abercromby.[56] It was formed into two detachments, which about four in the morning attacked the two batteries with great impetuosity and carried both with inconsiderable loss; but the guards from the trenches immediately advancing on them, they retreated without being able to effect anything important, and the few pieces which they had hastily spiked were soon rendered fit for service.

⌈About four in the afternoon, the besiegers opened several batteries in their second parallel, and it was apparent that in the course of the ensuing day the whole line of batteries in that parallel, in which was mounting an immense artillery, would be ready to play on the town. The works of the besieged were in no condition to sustain so tremendous a fire. They were everywhere in ruins. Their batteries were so overpowered that in the whole front which was attacked they could not show a single gun, and their shells were nearly expended. In this extremity Lord Cornwallis formed the bold design of endeavoring to escape by land with the greater part of his army.

⌈He determined to leave his sick and baggage behind, and crossing over in the night with his effectives to the Gloucester shore, to attack de Choisy. After cutting to pieces or dispersing the troops under that

55. See Fitzpatrick, *Writings of Washington*, XXIII, 223.
56. Sir Robert Abercromby (1740–1827) had served with distinction in both the Seven Years and Revolutionary wars. He went on to distinguish himself in nine years of fighting in India, becoming a major general in 1790, and succeeding Lord Cornwallis as commander in chief in 1793.

officer, he intended to mount his infantry on the horses belonging to that detachment and on others to be seized on the road and by a rapid march to gain the fords of the great rivers, and forcing his way through Maryland, Pennsylvania, and Jersey, to form a junction with the army in New York.

[Scarcely a possibility existed that this desperate attempt could be crowned with success; but the actual situation of the British general had become so absolutely hopeless that it could scarcely be changed for the worse.

[Boats prepared under other pretexts were held in readiness to receive the troops at ten in the evening in order to convey them over the river. The arrangements were made with the utmost secrecy, and the first embarkation had arrived at the point unperceived, and part of the troops were landed, when a sudden and violent storm of wind and rain interrupted the further execution of this hazardous plan and drove the boats down the river. It was not until the appearance of daylight that the storm ceased, so that the boats could return. They were sent to bring back the soldiers, who without much loss were relanded on the southern shore in the course of the forenoon.

[In the morning of the seventeenth several new batteries were opened in the second parallel, which poured in a weight of fire no longer to be resisted. Neither the works nor any part of the town afforded security to the garrison; and in the opinion of Lord Cornwallis, as well as of his engineers, the place was no longer tenable. About ten in the forenoon his lordship beat a parley and proposed a cessation of hostilities for twenty-four hours, that commissioners might meet at Moore's house, which was just in the rear of the first parallel, to settle terms for the surrender of the posts of York and Gloucester. To this letter the American general immediately returned an answer declaring his "ardent desire to spare the further effusion of blood and his readiness to listen to such terms as were admissible"; but as in the present crisis he could not consent to lose a moment in fruitless negotiations, he desired that "previous to the meeting of the commissioners, the proposals of his lordship might be transmitted in writing, for which purpose a suspension of hostilities for two hours should be granted." [57] The general propositions stated by Lord Cornwallis as forming the basis of the negotiation to be entered into, though not all of them admissible, being such as led to the opinion that no great difficulty would occur in adjusting the terms of the capitulation, the suspension of hostilities

57. See Fitzpatrick, *Writings of Washington*, XXIII, 236–37.

was prolonged for the night. In the meantime, to avoid the delay of useless discussion, the commander in chief drew up and proposed such articles as he would be willing to grant.[58] These were transmitted to Lord Cornwallis, who was at the same time informed that if he approved them, commissioners might immediately be appointed to digest them into form. In consequence of this message the viscount de Noailles and Lieutenant Colonel Laurens were met on the eighteenth by Colonel Dundas and Major Ross; [59] but being unable to adjust definitively the terms of the capitulation, only a rough draft of them could be prepared, which was to be submitted to the consideration of the British general. Determined not to expose himself to those accidents which time might produce, General Washington could not permit any suspense on the part of Lord Cornwallis. He therefore immediately directed the rough articles which had been prepared by the commissioners to be fairly transcribed and sent them to his lordship early the next morning, with a letter expressing his expectation that they would be signed by eleven and that the garrison would march out by two in the afternoon. Finding all attempts to obtain better terms unavailing, Lord Cornwallis submitted to a necessity no longer to be avoided and surrendered the posts of Yorktown and Gloucester Point with the garrisons which had defended them and the shipping in the harbor with their seamen to the land and naval officers of America and France.

[The army with the artillery, arms, and accouterments, military chest, and public stores of every denomination were surrendered to General Washington; the ships and seamen to the count de Grasse. The total amount of the prisoners, excluding seamen, rather exceeded 7,000 men, of whom 5,963 were rank and file. Of this number 4,017 are stated to have been fit for duty. The loss sustained by the garrison during the siege, in killed, wounded, prisoners, and missing, amounted to 552 men, including six officers.[60] The soldiers, accompanied by a due pro-

58. For the terms of surrender, see *ibid.,* pp. 237–38.

59. Louis Marie Antoine, vicomte de Noailles (1756–1804), Lafayette's brother-in-law, was a senior officer on Rochambeau's staff. After returning to France, influenced no doubt by his observation of society in the New World, Noailles gave an impetus to the French Revolution by proposing in the National Assembly the abolition of feudal rights. Later he served as a general in the Revolutionary armies and was killed in battle with the British in West Indian waters (Whitridge, *Rochambeau,* p. 78). Thomas Dundas (1750–94), the son of a member of Parliament, had served in the West Indies and was transferred to America in 1779, taking part in Arnold's raids in Virginia and the Yorktown campaign. Maj. Alexander Ross was an aide to Lord Cornwallis.

60. The number of British prisoners surrendered at Yorktown was 8,081. English casualties were around 6,000. The Continental army at Yorktown totaled 7,980 plus 3,153 militia for a grand total of 11,133. The French forces, including navy personnel aboard

portion of officers, were to remain in Virginia, Maryland, and Pennsylvania. The officers not required for this service were permitted to go on parole to Europe or to any maritime port occupied by the English in America. Lord Cornwallis earnestly endeavored to obtain permission for his European troops to return to their respective countries, under the single restriction of not serving against France or America; but this indulgence was peremptorily refused. His effort to introduce an article for the security of those Americans who had joined the British army was not more successful. The subject was declared to belong to the civil authority, and the article was rejected. Its object, however, was granted without the appearance of conceding it. Lord Cornwallis was permitted to send the *Bonetta* sloop of war unsearched, with dispatches to Sir Henry Clinton; and on board this vessel were embarked the Americans who were most obnoxious to their countrymen.

[There are some circumstances which would indicate that in this transaction the commander in chief held in recollection the capitulation of Charleston. The garrison was obliged to march out of the town with colors cased and drums beating either a British or German march, and General Lincoln was appointed to receive them on their going through the ceremony of grounding their arms.

[The allied army to which that of Lord Cornwallis surrendered may be estimated at 16,000 men. The French were stated by the count de Rochambeau at 7,000. The Continental troops amounted to about 5,500, and the militia to about 3,500. In the course of the siege, their loss in killed and wounded was about 300. It is full evidence of the vigor and skill with which the operations of the besiegers were conducted that the treaty was opened on the eleventh, and the capitulation signed on the thirteenth day after the ground was first broken before the works. The whole army merited a high degree of approbation, but from the nature of the service, the artillerists and engineers were enabled particularly to distinguish themselves. Generals Duportail and Knox were each promoted to the rank of major general, and Colonel Govion and Captain Rochefontaine of the corps of engineers were each advanced a grade by brevet.[61] In addition to the officers belonging

---

ships directly supporting the siege, excluding 15,000 on other ships, totaled 8,800. Therefore, the combined Allied forces added up to 19,993. Combined Franco-American casualties were around 378.

61. Colonel "Govion" was probably Col. Jean Baptiste Bouvion (1747–92), one of the four engineers sent to America at the request of Congress (the others were Duportail, La Radiere, and de Laumoy).

to those department, Generals Lincoln, de Lafayette, and Steuben were particularly mentioned by the commander in chief in the orders issued the day after the capitulation; and terms of peculiar warmth were applied to Governor Nelson, who continued in the field during the whole siege at the head of the militia of Virginia and also exerted himself in a particular manner to furnish the army with all those supplies which the country afforded. The highest acknowledgments were made to the count de Rochambeau, and several other French officers were named with distinction. So many disasters had attended the former efforts of the United States to avail themselves of the succors occasionally afforded by France that an opinion not very favorable to the alliance appears to have gained some ground in the country and to have insinuated itself into the army. The commander in chief seized this occasion to discountenance a course of thinking from which he had always feared pernicious consequences; and he displayed the great value of the aids lately received in language highly flattering to the sovereign, as well as to the land and naval forces of France.[62]

[Sir Henry Clinton was well informed of the danger which threatened the army in Virginia and could not be insensible to the influence which its fate would have on the war. He determined therefore to hazard everything for its preservation, and having embarked about seven thousand of his best troops, sailed for the Chesapeake under convoy of a fleet augmented to twenty-five sail of the line. This armament, which did not leave the Hook until the day that the capitulation was signed at Yorktown, appeared off the capes of Virginia on October 24. Unquestionable intelligence being there received that Lord Cornwallis had surrendered, no sufficient motive remained for attacking an enemy so superior in point of force as was the count de Grasse, and the British general returned to New York.

[The exultation manifested throughout the United States at the capture of this formidable army was equal to the terror it had inspired. At all times disposed to draw flattering conclusions from any favorable event, the Americans now, with more reason than heretofore, yielded to the suggestions of this sanguine temper and confidently indulged the hope that the termination of their toils and privations was fast approaching. In Congress the intelligence was received with a joy proportioned to the magnitude of the event; and the sense entertained by that body of this brilliant achievement was manifested in various resolutions returning the thanks of the United States to the commander

---

62. Fitzpatrick, *Writings of Washington*, XXIII, 244–47.

in chief, to the count de Rochambeau, to the count de Grasse, to the officers of the allied army generally, and to the corps of artillery and engineers in particular. In addition to these testimonials of a grateful nation, it was resolved that a marble column should be erected at York-town in Virginia with emblems of the alliance between the United States and His Most Christian Majesty and inscribed with a succinct narrative of the surrender of earl Cornwallis to His Excellency General Washington, commander in chief of the combined forces of America and France; to His Excellency the count de Rochambeau, commanding the auxiliary troops of His Most Christian Majesty in America; and to His Excellency count de Grasse, commander in chief of the naval army of France in the Chesapeake. Two stands of colors taken in York-town were presented to General Washington; two pieces of field ordi-nance to the count de Rochambeau; and application was made to His Most Christian Majesty to permit the admiral to accept a testimonial of their approbation similar to that presented to the count de Rocham-beau. Congress determined to go in solemn procession to the Dutch Lutheran Church to return thanks to Almighty God for crowning the allied arms with success by the surrender of the whole British army under Lord Cornwallis and also issued a proclamation appointing December 13 as a day of general thanksgiving and prayer, on account of this signal interposition of Divine Providence.[63]

[It was not by Congress only that the public joy for this great event and the public approbation of the conduct of General Washington were displayed. The most flattering and affectionate addresses of con-gratulation were presented from every part of the union; and state governments, city authorities, and learned institutions vied with each other in the testimonials they gave of the high sense they entertained of his important services and of their attachment to his person and character.] [64]

63. It was Randolph himself who made the motion for these resolutions (Worthington C. Ford *et al.*, eds., *Journals of the Continental Congress* [Washington, D.C., 1912], XXI, 1071–72, 1107).
64. Marshall, *Washington*, IV, 480–98.

 Slavery had been riveted in Virginia by disabilities of emancipation, except with the approbation of the executive for notorious services. The Society of Quakers, which had never ceased to ply the Assembly with the bill of rights and the topics arising from human nature, succeeded in a law permitting the owners to emancipate slaves under certain limitations.[1] Full of their late triumph over the British at Yorktown, the Assembly seemed to think that the political sky was so clear from all dangers that they did not anticipate, and therefore did not guard against, the evils which this indulgence to one of the best feelings of the human heart may from the conversion of black into free population, from the want of due precautions, occasionally produce.

Members of Congress had been eligible to the General Assembly, and many of them had availed themselves of the reputation which the supposition of their being versed in the interest of the Union had given them to obtain seats in the state legislature, assume a degree of importance, and forward by the influence of Virginia in Congress their own ideas. This perhaps would not have been so much objected to, had it not been feared that these delegates with double powers would

---

1. "An act to authorize the manumission of slaves" was enacted in May 1782. Although the law relaxed the legal blocks against manumission, it still maintained certain restrictions. It provided that the local court decide whether the slave in question be "of sound mind and body, not be above the age of forty-five, or being males under the age of twenty-one, or females under the age of eighteen years" unless they "shall be supported and maintained by, the person so liberating them, or by his or her estate" (Hening, *Statutes*, XI, 39–40). Many planters took advantage of the opportunity, and within two years the free Negro population doubled. It seemed to many that slavery was on the way to gradual extinction in Virginia. But even though the committee on revisal of Virginia's laws had in 1777 laid plans for gradual abolition, these grand hopes came to nothing, and a Methodist and Baptist petition in 1785 calling for abolition encountered resentful opposition. Before long manumission was again discouraged by law (Boyd, *Papers of Jefferson*, II, 470–73; Alden, *South in the Revolution*, p. 335; and Winthrop D. Jordan, *White over Black: American Attitudes toward the Negro, 1550–1812* [Chapel Hill, N.C., 1968], pp. 346–47).

have aimed at vesting in Congress larger authority than that for which
state jealousy was yet ripe. Indeed their journeys from Congress to the
state legislatures commonly issue[d] in the generation of some faction,
for at that time Congress was an assemblage of different diplomatic
corps rather than a national senate.

Taxes imposed in coin had never been known in the rudest state of
Virginia, tobacco being always a species of currency which was a substitute for the precious metals. But paper money and the circumstances
of the country had banished coin into the most secret recesses, so as to
leave too little of it for a circulating medium. Grain and other commodities were therefore receivable by the collector. The people had
the credit of paying large sums in value into the public treasury, when
from waste, fraud, spoilation, and other dimunitions the defalcations
which they underwent before their arrival thither demonstrated the
unfitness of specific articles to be chosen as the sinews of war.[2]

Kentucky mounted a step nearer to an independent sovereignty by
obtaining a district court beyond the control of any Virginian jurisdiction except the Court of Appeals.[3] This is the strongest example
in the history of a government keeping equal pace with a portion of
the people inclined to dismember it and even seconding their wishes
sincerely and zealously.

To what a tissue of feebleness and contradiction the old Confederation was reduced, was exemplified by the application to the Assembly
to grant to Congress a power to be without which was a phenomenon
indeed. Below high-water mark, Congress might confiscate hostile
property; but they could not oppose

---

2. A law covering taxation in kind was passed as early as 1779 (Hening, *Statutes*, IX,
369, X, 66, 79, 233, 241, 338, 490, 501; for the years after 1781, see Nevins, *American
States*, p. 498; Hening, *Statutes*, XI, 289, 290, 540).
3. See Hening, *Statutes*, XI, 85–90.

Index

Index